BROADWAY BABIES SAY GOODNIGHT

Broadway Babies Say Goodnight

Musicals Then and Now

MARK STEYN

faber and faber

LONDON · BOSTON

First published in 1997
by Faber and Faber Limited
3 Queen Square, London, WC1N 3AU

Typeset by RefineCatch Limited, Bungay, Suffolk
Printed in England by Clays Ltd, St Ives plc.

A CIP record for this book
is available from the British Library

ISBN 0–571–16202–9

2 4 6 8 10 9 7 5 3

Contents

CONTENTS

Overture

The Fix

William Wheatley, the manager of Niblo's Garden, has a problem. His huge barn of a theatre (at Broadway and Prince Street) has an expensive commitment to *The Black Crook*, a Faustian melodrama by Charles M. Barras. Unfortunately, the script is preposterous – but Wheatley is lumbered with it.

And then, almost as if on song cue, a solution hoves into view. A Parisian ballet troupe has been stranded in New York since its theatre burnt down. Wheatley engineers an implausible marriage between a rotten play and 100 underdressed coryphées, and, to the delight of all except the usual outraged clergymen, turns in a smash. And, incidentally, winds up inventing the American musical.

The Black Crook opened in September 1866, became the longest-running theatre production in New York to date – the first to run over a year – and passed into legend as the first Broadway musical, though mainly for reasons of sentiment and convenience. Granted, it did introduce several key ingredients of the genre: lavish scenic effects, conjuring the enchanted grottoes underneath the Harz Mountains of Germany; bare-limbed dancing girls, pretending to be water sprites; and, of course, a disgruntled author claiming that his work had been brutally violated. Wheatley shut him up with $1,500 and the travesty proved so financially rewarding that, after deciding that this new form of entertainment was beneath his station, Barras retired to Cos Cob, Connecticut, where he got run over by a train and ended up beneath his station. But not before he left his mark on history. Nobody remembers anything about *The Black Crook*: it's unrevivable, its songs are duds and Charles M. Barras' script may well be the origin of the phrase, 'This script is so bad it's M Barrassing.' And, on top of that, the popular story of its creation – the shoehorning of dancing girls into a straight play – is most probably bunk.

But what matters about *The Black Crook* is not the show but its mythic status: it gave Broadway its attitude; it inaugurated the tradition of the musical as, in Oscar Levant's phrase, 'a series of catastrophes ending in a floor show'; it made a drama out of a crisis. For over a century, those who thrived on the Main Stem revelled in their artlessness. For Broadway veterans, writing a play in your study and opening it as written is for sissies. You earn your spurs by what you can come up with at three in the morning in a New Haven hotel room after the choreographer's been sacked and your star is demanding a new song. George Abbott, the greatest of Broadway play doctors and the most reliable of directors, prided himself on being able to get a show on-stage with half a script and a few songs. At the first rehearsal of *High Button Shoes* (1947), he had just eighteen pages of script and, addressing the company, made the rest up as he went along. Nothing counts until it's proved before an audience. Or, as Abbott put it, articulating his guiding principle and Broadway's first rule: forget Art; does it *work*? It doesn't always: *High Button Shoes* was a hit, but *The Girl in Pink Tights* (1954), a musical about the making of *The Black Crook*, wasn't.

Does it *work*? Such a practical measurement . . .

*

February 1989, and at the Mark Hellinger Theatre, where long ago *The Girl in Pink Tights* danced and sang, nothing seems to work, no matter how hard the opening number strains to be loved:

> You know I'll dance and I'll sing
> I'll do anything
> Just to get my name in lights!

Laurence Olivier and Vivien Leigh played on this stage in *Romeo and Juliet*, Rex Harrison and Julie Andrews in *My Fair Lady*, Ann Miller and Mickey Rooney in *Sugar Babies*; and Rice and Lloyd Webber made their New York débuts here with *Jesus Christ Superstar*. Today, the Mark Hellinger is presenting *Legs Diamond*, music by Peter Allen, lyrics by Peter Allen, starring Peter Allen as the famous gangster.

Up on stage, Allen wiggles and grinds his way through a performance that makes Liberace look a paragon of understatement. Panned by all reviewers bar Jacques Le Sourd of the Gannet group, *Legs*, since its opening, has been resorting to a dreadful, unconvincing bravado. To avoid tempting fate, the show's one memorable line, 'Only a critic can kill me', has been amended to '*Even* a critic can't kill me'. But who needs critics when so many others are prepared to wield the knife? A mere month after opening, *Legs*' landlord and co-producer James Nederlander has announced that, from 'whatever date *Legs Diamond* closes', he will be leasing this landmark theatre, this most bookable of houses, to an evangelical ministry. Here at last is a long run to rival the good old days of *Fair Lady*: for the next five years, the Mark Hellinger will be the home of Pastor David Wilkerson and the Times Square Church.

Up and down Broadway, what remains of the 'theatre community' is casting its eyes heavenward. 'I'm going to my synagogue tonight and pray that *Legs* has a long run,' announces Harvey Sabinson of the League of American Theatres and Producers. He concedes it's something of a long shot, dependent as it is on God being a Peter Allen fan.

How did everything go so wrong when they did everything so right? They took no chances, they spent years and years in workshops and development. And as a final confirmation of the show's unstoppability, that reliable barometer of celebrity status, the Stage Deli, unveiled the latest addition to its menu – the Peter Allen Sandwich; off for ever, consigned to the doggy bag of history, went the Mike Tyson Sandwich.

And then the show began six weeks of previews, and the six weeks turned into two months – *two months* – of previews! In Jerome Kern's day you could break even in that time, then take the show on the road and really clean up. But Broadway's *schadenfreude* set started talking, and the word was that the Peter Allen Sandwich would have made a better job of writing the show than Peter Allen. In that two months, what little was right with the show was gradually unfixed, every attempt to staunch the blood caused another haemorrhage elsewhere, and each week brought new and increasingly desperate manoeuvres: 'The role of Eddie Diamond, which was being played by Robert Stillman, has been written out.' There were rumours even of Peter Allen's dismissal, which would have been the first time a star's been fired from a show he's also written. So precarious are the *dramatis personae* that current billboards have the players' names displayed on individual stickers which can be easily removed. It is, though, an unusually mild winter, and a freak January heat wave has warmed the glue so that now, when you pass the Mark Hellinger, the cast's labels dangle perilously from the poster by ever more elongated membranes of adhesive. Even before previews, the choreographer had been sacked, after a short illness. The producers were convinced Michael Shawn had Aids; he said it was sinusitis. He's suing, and, if the show runs as long as the law suit looks set to, the producers will be very lucky. Replaced by Alan Johnson, Shawn has only just secured another job – a Japanese tour of *My Fair Lady*.

Well, it's *Legs Diamond*, so all this carnage and bloodshed backstage is surely appropriate to a show about a cold-hearted killer. And so it would be if Allen's character bore any relation to the real Legs of the Prohibition era. But audience research (the enemy of art) indicated that the customers would find a musical about a murdering hoodlum a bit of a bummer. So Legs was transmuted into yet another victim of hard times, forced into crime by an uncaring society. And by the time five librettists, from Anne Elder to Harvey Fierstein, had filleted each other's efforts, you needed a road-map to follow the book. Meanwhile, James Nederlander, owner-operator of the world's biggest theatre chain, was cheerfully confiding that the book – the story, the characters, the structure – didn't matter anyhow; once Allen began strutting his stuff, they'd be home and dry. Nederlander is a businessman, and he apparently thinks it's good business to sink $11 million into a nightclub act, even when the nightclub act isn't singing his pop hits – 'Arthur's Theme', 'I Go To Rio' – but a dull collection of non-dramatic songs, some of which he wrote originally for Bob Fosse's *Big Deal* (which never used them) and one of which he's called, with breathtaking arrogance, 'Say It Isn't So', inviting wholly unfavourable comparisons with the Irving Berlin ballad of the same name:

> Say that ev'rything is still alright
> That's all I want to know
> And what they're saying
> Say It Isn't So.

From out of the past, Berlin's song echoes like a forlorn plea from the producers. But, a few hours after Harvey Sabinson's supplications at his synagogue, what they're saying *is* so: *Legs* posts its closing notices and prepares to surrender its home to the Times Square Church.

Pastor Wilkerson doesn't usually talk to the media, but my contact at the church, Wally, has managed to arrange an interview. 'We're praying for *you*, Mark!' adds Wally.

'We don't mind where we preach,' says the Pastor. 'Christ spoke in open fields. But, frankly, with so many theatres dark, our money's as good as anybody's. And we've made a pledge to Mr Nederlander that we'll return the theatre to him in better shape than we received it.'

With a Nederlander house, that's not difficult. And it was the shabbiness of the Hellinger that most appealed to me when, at an impressionable age, I first went backstage. 'This is a theatre, y'understand?' explained the doorkeeper, as I tramped up two flights of dingy stairs, past the slime-encrusted, roach-infested toilet, to emerge into the composer Jule Styne's office, a suite of converted dressing rooms lined with posters, awards and pictures of Frank and Barbra. Styne, a short, dapper man with cigar and dark glasses, was swearing and yelling. When he yelled, he waved his arms around and you noticed that he wore a gold bracelet. On the inside, the inscription read: 'To Jule, who knew me when – Frankie' – a present from Sinatra, delivered by Cartier's the morning after the singer's first ever solo concert. This was showbiz – just like you see it in the movies.

'We're letting Mr Styne stay rent-free,' says Pastor Wilkerson, with the graciousness of one who knows it's a buyer's market and he's the only guy in sight. 'We want to help the theatre, we're bringing in staff who'll care for it, and it's going to cost us half a million above the million-dollar annual rent. Without us, what would happen? We were offered the Biltmore, but it's been dark for a year and it's now in total ruins. Street people have broken in, taken the seats and wrecked everything.'

I'm impressed. The Pastor's knowledge of Broadway houses is as comprehensive as any producer's. In January 1988, a few weeks after founding the Times Square Church, he moved into the Nederlander, nominally a Broadway theatre but located three blocks too south on a seedy cross-street far enough removed from the glamour of Shubert Alley to make its fate of any concern. Those who now wonder why Jimmy Nederlander didn't simply unload another of his less bookable houses, like the Lunt–Fontanne, are missing the point.

'We were offered six theatres,' the Pastor says, 'but this was the only one that had the seats – over 1,600. And that's what we need. We're at full capacity at the Nederlander with people sitting in the aisles and others being turned away. We've become one of the largest evangelical churches in the city, so we need as big a theatre as we can get.' He wanted the Gershwin, but there's a clause in the lease preventing its use as anything but a theatre. Otherwise, Pastor Wilkerson had the pick of the litter: he turned around the Nederlander; his coffers are groaning; he can call the shots.

Back in London, they say Cameron Mackintosh was considering the Hellinger for the Broadway production of *Miss Saigon*. But that's at least a year away and, with no other shows in sight and with $3 million of his own blown on *Legs Diamond*, Nederlander was made an offer he couldn't refuse.

A sad parable of Broadway's terminal decline? Actually, it's not entirely unprecedented. In the 1850s, the great evangelist Finney played to capacity crowds at the Chatham Street Theatre. But then the spiritual revival fizzled out and the showbiz shysters regained control. This time, Pastor

Wilkerson believes the revival's here to stay, and he's planning to expand. 'My son is planning to do the same in downtown London,' he says. 'We're good for the community. That's why we call our show *Revival on Broadway*.'

And, for its first service, the Hellinger stage will retain a vestige of its legit past in the shape of Jeff Fenholt, who created the title role of *Jesus Christ Superstar* back in 1971. 'Jeff has now been converted to Christ,' the Pastor reveals, 'and on March 12th he'll be on that stage singing live. We wouldn't be here if we didn't believe we had the hottest show on Broadway.'

*

Christmas 1993: Jule Styne, last of the Broadway giants, composer of *Gentlemen Prefer Blondes* and *Funny Girl*, is enthusing about his new musical. His first Broadway show was *High Button Shoes*; now, the footwear has come full circle, with *The Red Shoes*. Michael Shawn is dead of Aids, and Peter Allen, too; the Mark Hellinger is still a church and Styne, a few weeks shy of his 88th birthday, no longer has his office there. But otherwise he and his passion for Broadway are undimmed. When he's excited, his mercurial brain races ahead faster than his mouth can cope with, so that he's wont to leave out every third word or so – 'Stynese', his long-time lyricists Betty Comden and Adolph Green call it – and Styne is excited now. But, with the missing words filled in, his thought is this: 'The theatre is the closest form of collaboration there is,' he tells me and, musing on Bosnia and the Middle East, adds, 'The world should be more like the theatre.'

Really? In the preceding weeks Styne and his producer on *Red Shoes* have fired so many of his closest collaborators that the Broadway smart-asses have rechristened the show *The Pink Slips* (a pink slip's the American equivalent of Britain's P45). The director's been sacked, her successor has come and gone, a new lyricist has been brought in and most of the principals have been replaced, including leading man Roger Rees ('Nice fellow,' says Styne, generously). Saddam Hussein's regime may need lessons in brotherly love, but not from a Jule Styne musical.

The day after we spoke, *The Red Shoes* opened. The day after that, the reviews appeared. The day after *that*, the show closed, having cost $8 million and ten years of Styne's life. With *Jelly's Last Jam* playing up the road, the wags nicknamed it, prophetically, *Jule's Last Jam*. It was to prove his final obsession: he died the following autumn, having outlived the Broadway he loved. We should fall on our knees and thank God that, for all its travails, the world is *not* like the theatre. *The Black Crook* and *The Red Shoes* played by the same rules. Somewhere along the way, the odds increased.

Act One

i

The Op'nin'

'To me, there's nothing like the overture ending and the curtain going up,' says Arthur Laurents, librettist of *Gypsy* and *West Side Story*. 'I think that's the most exciting moment in the theatre. And I wish we still had curtains.'

Here's the opening of *The Pajama Game* (1954):

'This is a very serious drama. It's kind of a problem play. It's about Capital and Labour. I wouldn't bother to make such a point of all this except later on if you happen to see a lot of naked women being chased through the woods, I don't want you to get the wrong impression. This play is full of *symbolism*.'

Wham! And cue title song.

In a few lines, George Abbott has distilled the show's spirit: this is a musical comedy about a strike at the Sleep-Tite Pajama Factory in Cedar Rapids, Iowa. If you don't care for it, fine, leave now; but at least, 40 minutes into Act One, you can't complain you've been misled. What's wrong with most musicals can usually be traced to something in the first ten minutes. This can also be true of plays: with a comedy, the most important decision you make is when and what your first laugh is. But with a musical there are other considerations: in the first ten minutes, you have to communicate the tone of the piece, its atmosphere, its concerns, the musical style, and the staging vocabulary – are we in for dream ballets or buck'n'wings or naturalistic movement?

Every truly great show has a great op'nin':

Kiss Me, Kate (1948) has 'Another Op'nin', Another Show' – and immediately we're backstage.

Porgy and Bess (1935) has that languorous lullaby 'Summertime' – not much to do with storyline or *dramatis personae*, but immediately it transports us to Catfish Row in Charleston. By the time the chorus joins in the harmony, the song has infused the community with a spiritual dimension and become its anthem. Because this is a 'folk opera', Catfish Row is in its way a character in the drama, perhaps the most important character, and the authors use this song as the community's *leitmotif*.

13

Guys and Dolls (1950) has the trio of horse-gamblers arguing about the best bet of the day: 'I got the horse right here!' – or, to give the song its proper title, 'Fugue For Tinhorns'. Here's a truly inspired piece of musicalization: three guys with a different opinion on the same subject, noisily insistent that each one knows which horse to bet; and what better way to express this in song than in a sort of Broadway fugue? It underlines Damon Runyon's heightened, stylized vernacular with a musical formality – entirely appropriate because, despite the breezy brashness, despite the Broadway low life, the world we're about to enter has as elaborate a protocol as any European court.

My Fair Lady (1956) has a longish (for a musical) dialogue scene, to let you know this show is about words and language, and then goes into 'Why Can't The English Learn To Speak?' – and there's the theme of the drama in a nutshell.

West Side Story (1957), conversely, begins with no words but a musical 'Prologue' to accompany the Sharks and Jets dancing – or miming, or moving – their increasing hostility. At the end of this sequence, the Shark leader cuts the ear of a Jet, and a police whistle is heard. This sets the scene for the drama which follows, as well as the music: the composer establishes all the pitches and polarities which bind the *West Side* numbers together right from the very first chord, a major–minor triad. Obviously, you're not sitting eighth row centre figuring all that out, but by the end of the Prologue you know at least that what follows will be spiky, finger-snappy, urban – and tragic. Just as importantly, you also know that this story will be told as much through movement as anything else; the *West Side* opening indicates the score's symphonic and choreographic ambitions.

Gypsy (1959) begins with Uncle Jocko's Kiddie Show in Seattle: the stage is filled with grotesque moppets in tacky, home-made costumes. Suddenly, from the back of the auditorium, a rasping voice shouts, 'Sing out, Louise!' and barging her way down the aisle comes the ultimate stage mother, Mama Rose. This is an inspired opening: effectively, the principal character hijacks her own show and disrupts the opening number. If you object that it doesn't seem very *musical*, relax: the score's already home and dry. Most Broadway overtures are arbitrary medleys of choruses of the big songs cobbled together by the orchestrators. Jule Styne overtures aren't: he supervised them himself and he attached great importance to them. For *Gypsy*, when it came to the blaring strip-joint bump'n'grind E-flat shrieks, he instructed the second trumpet to blow the roof off. The audience applauded wildly. By the end of the overture, they were already on the show's side.

Sweeney Todd (1979) establishes itself on the very first word of the very first line:

Attend the tale of Sweeney Todd . . .

Attend. A less scrupulous dramatist would have written 'This is . . .' or 'Here comes . . .' The prosody fits, they get you into the meat of the number. But, by choosing this word, the author is already conjuring time and place – nineteenth-century London. This is a fine example of musical theatre's best qualities: compression, economy, making the most of every aspect of the production so that even this one tiny insignificant word is working in the service of the play. For what it's worth, it's a modal tune. So what? Only one theatregoer in 100,000 sits up and goes, 'Ah-ha! A modal tune!' But modal tunes are common in old English ballads, and chances are most of the other 99,999 recognize that what they're hearing sounds as if it's a dark legend, risen up out of a grimy, smoke-shrouded past. Within a few bars, *Sweeney Todd* is on its way. It's as different as you could imagine from *The Pajama Game*, but it operates to the same principles. It's a way of answering the most important question on any musical: 'What is this show about?'

It isn't just the audience who wants to know. Jerome Robbins, co-director of *Pajama Game* and superstager of *West Side*, always bugs his authors with this question because it's even more critical for them. A good musical is such a freak coalescence of different elements – book, lyrics, music, orchestrations, choreography, design – that, if the creative team doesn't have an agreed answer to that question, chances are they're unlikely to be able to persuade an audience. The best answer Robbins ever received to his nagging poser comes in the opening number of *Fiddler on the Roof* (1964).

What is this show about?

Tradition!

Fiddler is based on a handful of Sholom Aleichem stories about a dairyman in a Ukrainian *shtetl*, stories which appeared separately between 1895 and 1914. Aleichem's Tevye is not concerned with tradition. When he hears that his daughter has pledged herself to the penniless tailor's son, he's not bothered about the tradition of arranged marriages being broken, only that he's been left out of it. As a theme, tradition is the invention of the stage version, cooked up by librettist Joseph Stein, musicalized by composer Jerry Bock and lyricist Sheldon Harnick, and magnificently staged by Robbins to bind the short stories together into a coherent whole. It doesn't have a clever lyric; it goes:

> Tradition!
> Tradition!
> Tradition!

It's set up explicitly in Tevye's opening speech, which is less a song cue than a formal announcement:

> We stay because Anatevka is our home. And how do we keep our balance? That I can tell you in a word – tradition!

And at the end of the number, in case you've still missed the point, Tevye puts a tag on it:

> Without our traditions, our life would be as shaky as . . .

(*The original violin theme is recapitulated.*)

> . . . as a fiddler on the roof!

This is what's at stake in the drama. Don't say you weren't warned.

*

Even if a musical gets its first ten minutes right, things can still go wrong. But, if it gets the opening wrong, it's highly unlikely to recover. The audience's expectations have been sent in the wrong direction and, as they begin to realize that those expectations won't be fulfilled, they'll be left feeling pretty short-changed.

Two examples from similar shows: *Crazy for You* (1991) is the 'new' Gershwin musical; *High Society* (1987) was a 'new' Cole Porter musical. In both cases the adaptors had been given free range to roam through their respective composers' catalogues and choose what songs they needed. *Crazy for You* opens backstage at the Zangler Theatre, New York, where Bobby, desperate to break into showbusiness, performs an impromptu audition for the great impresario Bella Zangler. This is not a 'book number' – that's to say, the music is not an expression of character or plot point arising from the dialogue, the defining convention of musical theatre. Instead, more prosaically, it's a real number, a 'prop number':

Bobby is backstage and doing the song for Zangler. So it's sparely orches-
trated – little more than a rehearsal piano and some support; it's one
chorus; and its tap-break ends with Bobby stamping on Zangler's foot.
This is grim reality: Bobby is expelled from the theatre. Outside, he makes
a decision, and sings 'I Can't Be Bothered Now' – the second song, but the
real opening number: the first 'book number' in the show. There is an
automobile onstage (it's the 1930s) and, as Bobby opens the door, one
showgirl, pretty in pink, steps out, then another, and another, and more
and more, far more than could fit in any motor car; finally, Bobby raises
the hood of the vehicle and the last chorine emerges. The audience leans
back, reassured and content: Susan Stroman's fizzy, inventive choreography has told them that what's about to follow is romantic fantasy. More
to the point, it's true to the character of the song, and the choice of song is
true to Bobby's character and the engine of the drama:

> My bonds and shares
> May fall downstairs
> Who cares? Who cares?
> I'm dancing and
> I Can't Be Bothered Now . . .

This lyric captures the philosophy of Ira Gershwin's entire oeuvre – which
is important: the show is a celebration of Gershwin. But it's also an exact
expression of Bobby's feelings and the reason why he heads to Dead Rock,
Arkansas. So the number does everything it should: it defines the principal's motivation; it kick-starts the plot; and it communicates the spirit of
the score and the staging. Audiences don't reason it out like that; we just
eat it up. But that's why.

   High Society, a West End adaptation of Philip Barry's *Philadelphia
Story* (1939), was an almost identical project. Where *Crazy for You* was
derived from the Gershwins' *Girl Crazy* (1930) but drew on other songs as
needed, *High Society* started with Cole Porter's score for the 1956 film
and augmented it as necessary. The plot concerns the arrival of a journalist and photographer from *Spy* magazine to cover a society wedding, and
the complications that ensue. Librettist/director Richard Eyre decided
that, although the rest of the show takes place in Philadelphia, he would
open with a prologue set in the *Spy* editorial offices, back in New York, as
the reporters are given their assignment. Sounds fair enough. So Eyre
trawled the Porter catalogue for a song that was apropos and came across
'How Do You Spell Ambassador?', originally written for a chorus of
stupid, lazy reporters:

'How do you spell "Moscow", men?'
'Too tough, by far . . .'
'How do you spell "administration", then?'
'Just put FDR.'

You can see Eyre's reasoning: he opens the show with a scene set in a newspaper office; here is a song set in a newspaper office. But what's the song about? It's about how thick and careless hacks are. This isn't the theme of *High Society*, so, on those grounds alone, it would be irrelevant. But, actually, it's worse than irrelevant: the journalist and photographer (Frank Sinatra and Celeste Holm in the 1956 film) are the most sympathetic characters in the piece – the one a noble but frustrated would-be novelist, the other a wisecracking but vulnerable lady snapper; they're our point of view on the caperings of society folk. By giving them this song as the first expression of their character Eyre is destabilizing the axis of the drama. So this song is actively misleading about all that follows. And, apart from anything else, whatever the superficial aptness of its lyric content, it's musically undistinguished. As a result, audiences at the Victoria Palace sat restless and confused through the first half of Act One.

Eyre is no fool. He's the director of the Royal National Theatre, and few men have as sharp an understanding of non-musical drama. But, in this instance, he'd approached the show with a plodding literalism. He didn't understand that, in a musical, the first number has to be more than just the number which comes first.

Some weeks after the first night Eyre realized what was happening and decided to change the song. He reverted to the opening number as used in the film, 'High Society Calypso'. But this was never anything more than just a bit of fluff for Louis Armstrong and his band, though they did it with great charm. Eyre didn't have Satch, nor could he use the lyric:

Just dig that scenery floatin' by
We're now approachin' Newport, Rhode I.

The movie was set in Newport, Rhode Island; Eyre's version restored the original setting, Philadelphia. So that couplet had to go. Then:

I wanna play for my former pal
He runs the local jazz festival.

In the movie, he *did* run the Newport festival; but not in Eyre's version. So goodbye, verse two. Unable to fit Porter's lyric, Eyre was obliged to call in Richard Stilgoe to rewrite the song. So he winds up with a Cole Porter show which doesn't open with a Cole Porter song. This was less disruptively misleading than 'How Do You Spell Ambassador?', but still unsatisfying.

What should he have done? Well, the show limped along for three-quarters of an hour or so until the two hacks, surveying the wedding presents, sing 'Who Wants To Be A Millionaire?': at last, a song that *lands*. Why not open with this? In the offices of *Spy* magazine, the reporters are contemplating their next assignment, which both of them despise. 'Who Wants To Be A Millionaire?' would have been not merely a correct expression of their own sentiments, but it's what the show's about, too: 'the privileged classes enjoying their privileges' and the journalists' reaction to it. You could have coasted on the goodwill it engenders for a good 30 minutes. Eyre, unlike the creators of *Crazy for You*, misunderstood the form. So *Crazy for You* plays on, while *High Society* is a forgotten flop. Those first ten minutes did for it.

*

Conventional Broadway wisdom says you should always write the first song last, because by then you know what the show's about – and, besides, the original curtain-raiser always gets junked and replaced. *Annie*'s did, so did *Guys and Dolls*'. Almost alone among Broadway authors, Kander and Ebb make a point of doing the first song first. 'The reasons you give for writing it last,' says Fred Ebb, 'are exactly the reasons why we do it first – to *define* the show before you begin writing it. It's like a court of law: first you get up and say I'm going to prove to you this man is guilty, and then you proceed to do so. But you state your case up front.'

So Kander and Ebb always do the opening number first – and that may be why, alone among the major Broadway writers of the past 30 years, they've never had a major disastrous humiliating floperoo. Come smash hit or modest success, their shows open with numbers that set the tone, the atmosphere, the time and place brilliantly. *Chicago* (1975) had 'All That Jazz', but even *The Rink* (1984) had 'Coloured Lights', as Angel, ugly-duckling flower-child, prepares to return home after seven years and recalls long-ago nights at the roller rink:

> Noisy boys long and lean
> Giggles of girls in the mezzanine . . .

A peach of an image, wistful and nostalgic, but a delusion. When she gets back, there are no coloured lights, no giggles or girls, only a derelict, rotting ruin.

'With *Cabaret*, we were trying to find the piece, to write our way into it,' John Kander remembers. 'The first thing we wrote was "Willkommen" and the very first thing that ever happened was that little vamp.' Kander is routinely hailed as the champ of the vamps, those little musical figures that, when they work, really kick-start a song – the 'dum-dum-*da*-de-dum' at the front of 'New York, New York' is his surefire killer. 'When you find something you like, *it* tells *you* about the direction you want to go in.'

The *Cabaret* opener has embedded itself in our cultural vocabulary. For the film *Blazing Saddles*, Mel Brooks wrote Madeline Kahn, who was playing a Teuton saloon chantoosie in the *Destry*/Dietrich manner, a dressing-room scene where she greeted every knock on the door with the trilingual spoken instruction, 'Willkommen, Bienvenue, Welcome': he knew we'd get the joke. At first glance, it seems for *Cabaret* the most obvious and old-fashioned opening you could come up with: 'Welcome to the show.' But Joel Grey is seducing us, slyly beckoning us into the club as a retreat from the troubles of the world – whereas what happens in the cabaret is, in fact, a comment and a mirror on what's going on in the wider world. It's a frequent complaint that the 'concept' musical undervalues the score, but Kander and Ebb at least have managed to give the production concept a musical character too, just as their predecessors did for character and location. In *Cabaret*, the cabaret is the main character, and it's set up perfectly. In *Chicago*, Bob Fosse staged a 1920s murder trial as a vaudeville, so Kander and Ebb's opener is an invitation to hit the town and enjoy 'All That Jazz' – in both senses: the music and the vaudeville, but also all the flim-flam and huckstering and razzle-dazzle of the legal process. In *Chicago*, the 'jazz' is the character.

We have Rodgers and Hammerstein to thank for making these principles stick, in one blockbuster hit after another. If R&H seem conventional today, it's because they invented the conventions – especially the most important one: let the story dictate the tone. To those who scoff at the R&H format, there's a simple retort: *what* format? These boys start their first show – *Oklahoma!* (1943) – with a woman alone on-stage churning butter. In the distance, we hear a solo voice:

> Oh, What a Beautiful Mornin'
> Oh, what a beautiful day . . .

It seems as simple as a folk-song, but no anonymous, demotic farm-hand's singalong would have Curly sing '*mor*-nin'' on D natural and then, in the equivalent spot two lines on, '*fee*-lin'' on D sharp. You need a professional composer for that: they signal Curly's intensity of feeling about the land he belongs to. This is more than mere pastiche can ever achieve: Rodgers and Hammerstein have taken a folk form and imbued it with deep, rare passion.

But for their next trick, *Carousel* (1945), there's no butter churner, no solo from the wings. Instead, they dump the overture and lay out all the exposition and the principal characters in a pantomime. A pantomime in waltz time, too. More than that, a pantomime in waltz time that manages to be utterly naturalistic. And then, and then . . . we're into dialogue and underscoring, effortlessly, unobtrusively matched – and matched to the mill machinery, too – and then the two girls' colloquial rhythmic chatter flowers into song – 'You're A Queer One, Julie Jordan' and 'When I Marry Mister Snow' – and then Billy Bigelow, the carnival barker, appears and he and Julie speculate on what might happen 'If I Loved You'. This is an entire courtship in song: by the end of it, we know that Billy and Julie love each other, will always love each other, and that this love will bring great pain to them.

Mozart may have better music, Shakespeare better words, but only in the American musical play do we see the constituent elements fusing to create a unified, indissoluble identity. There are no rules: you can start with dialogue or song or dance or all three, but it must be the appropriate conveyance for the themes of the play. We've known all this since the opening night which opened it all up: 27 December 1927. Accustomed only to racy musical comedy or florid operetta, the first-night audience at the Ziegfeld gave an audible gasp as the curtain rose on the most startling of any Broadway chorus to date – sweating black stevedores loading cotton and singing:

> *Niggers* all work on the Mississippi
> *Niggers* all work while the white folks play . . .

From that first shocking word, confronting midtown Manhattan with aspects of their society they preferred not to think about, Jerome Kern and Oscar Hammerstein II presented their audience with something new: drama in music, with neither element constrained by the other. It is the ultimate opening number, because it is the opening number for all that follows.

ii

The Show

It's the oldest question of all: what came first – the words or the music? And the correct answer is: what came first was the First Flying Velocipede. There are many ways of examining the evolution of musical theatre, but the easiest and most instructive is water capacity. Here then is a rough history of the modern stage measured in gallons:

Ebb and Flow of Water in Musical Theatre

1874 – *The Deluge*   Splashy Old Testament spectacle; Noah business like show business, etc.

1899 – *An Arabian Girl and Forty Thieves*   Highlight of show: torrential cascade of water in moonlit glen soaks star performer (a donkey).

1909 – *A Trip to Japan*   First show with twin waterfalls, both bathed in 'prismatic lights'.

1915 – *Ziegfeld Follies of 1915*   Opening scene set underwater, plus 'Gates of Elysium' flanked by spouting elephants.

1927 – *Show Boat*   Bone dry: 'Ol' Man River' represented by a mere song and some painted cloths.

1935 – Rodgers and Hart's *Jumbo*   First show to co-star Jimmy Durante plus elephant with loaded trunk.

1949 – *South Pacific*   Mary Martin washes man right out of hair; first musical with new all-in-one shampoo'n'showtoon; now you can just wash'n'crow.

1952 – *Wish You Were Here*   First musical with swimming pool on-stage; critics found it shallow.

1974 – Burt Shevelove/Stephen Sondheim adaptation of *The Frogs*   First musical to be staged in a swimming pool, at Yale; critics found it too deep.

1984 – Tommy Steele's *Singin' in the Rain*   Sodden.

Even at a casual glance, a rough rule of thumb can be discerned: the success and durability of a musical are in inverse proportion to the amount of water in it. *South Pacific* has a teensy aquatic effect, but it's subordinate to song and story, whereas Tommy Steele gingerly tippy-toeing through a controlled downpour in rubber pumps works against the carefree joyousness of the number and the dramatic moment: rain stops play, literally. Significantly, the most enduring entry on the list has not a drop yet, 67 years after the original production, was back on Broadway. Unlike *A Trip to Japan*, *Show Boat* is spectacular merely in its score and subject. In Edna Ferber's original novel the narrative rolls across the decades, bound together only by the *Cotton Blossom* boat and the Mississippi River. But how do you convey that on-stage? Forget the prismatic lights and Gates of Elysium; Jerome Kern managed it better: his banjo-plunk theme for the boat – '*Cot-ton-Blos-som*', – is simply inverted to represent the Mississippi, 'Ol'-Man-Riv-er'. With four notes, he ties together the contrasting faces of the story: the gaiety of river life and the darker, unchanging elemental qualities of the river itself. The lessons of Kern and Hammerstein's Broadway epic course through the history of the musical, but those four notes in particular symbolize the concise discreet ingenuity of the genre at its best.

A Trip to Japan, though, is more typical – torrential cascade being a lot easier than four neat notes. One moment from *Winnie*, a West End flop in 1988, makes the point – its re-creation of the wartime bombing of the Café de Paris: suddenly, a crowded dance-floor is blown to pieces; the contrast between the carnage and the gaiety of only a moment before should be truly shocking. So why, before the dust had settled and while the bodies were still strewn about the stage, did the audience burst into wild applause and cheering? Because they had just witnessed a spectacular scenic effect and, it seems, their appreciation of the technology overrode any involvement with the drama. It was an unsettling reminder of the tense see-saw between any play and its staging: the more extravagantly you illustrate the event, the more likely it is that the event will be overlooked completely.

To many, that imbalance sums up our own time. 'Who wants to come out of a show whistling the lightbulbs?' Jule Styne demanded to know after seeing *Starlight Express* (1984). The answer seems to be quite a few. Critics may derive most satisfaction from those dramas with minimal staging – 'raw', as they like to say – but audiences feel differently. If you're paying £30 a ticket, you get pretty impatient to see where the money's gone and, when a big-budget item makes its entrance, it requires enormous self-restraint not to express your gratitude. Sometimes, it doesn't even have to be very expensive, just a little something the audience couldn't get except by going to see that particular show (as useful a definition of live theatre as anything else): Jim Dale or Michael Crawford successfully walking the highwire in the Act One finale to *Barnum* (1980); or, conversely, Stacy Keach, who took over the role on tour and wasn't a tightrope walker, falling off every night. We expect a musical to have song and dance, but what else can they do? Trevor Nunn's revival of *The Baker's Wife* (1989) became the first show in which a baker sang and simultaneously kneaded his dough live on stage. On the other hand, maybe they needed more dough; considering its rapid closure, *The Baker's Wife* would have done better with a hologram of a giant croissant. Theatregoers get harder to please each season.

This is the very stuff of theatre – and musical theatre especially. You can just about read a play on the page: that's how schools teach Shakespeare – though, as it seems to put kids off the Bard for life, maybe that's no recommendation. But try reading the script of a musical:

> Oh, What a Beautiful Mornin'
> Oh, what a beautiful day
> I've got a beautiful feelin'
> Ev'rything's going my way.

Big deal. How'd you ever know it was the best opening number in the world? Until you see it. Musical theatre takes place in three dimensions. You're always looking at something – and, because of the way the senses work, you register what you're seeing before you register what you're hearing. Stephen Sondheim learned an important lesson on *West Side Story* when he handed in his lyric for 'Maria'. 'Now what happens here?' asked Jerome Robbins.

'Well, you know, he is standing outside her house,' said Sondheim, 'and, you know, he senses that she's going to appear on the balcony.'

'Yeah, but what's he doing?'

'Oh, he's standing there and singing a song.'

'What is he doing?'

'Well, he sings, "Maria, Maria, I just met a girl named Maria and suddenly that name will never be the same to me."'

'And then what happens?'

'Then he sings . . .'

'You mean he just stands looking at the audience?'

'Well, yes.'

'Okay,' said Robbins, '*you* stage it.'

In other words, even as you write the book and score, you should know in your mind what the stage picture will be: it's not a song cycle, it's not a cast album, it's part of a three-dimensional drama happening now. Since then, whenever he writes a number, Sondheim stages it within an inch of his life: 'All right, now when he starts to sing the song he's sitting down in a chair. Now around the second quatrain he gets up and crosses to the fireplace and throws her note in the fireplace. Then he sings the third quatrain directly to the audience, then he goes back and shoots himself and sings the fourth quatrain.' The choreographer and director may use nothing of those directions, but at least they know the number's been written as a number to be staged, to be seen.

This is the theatre's trump card, and we mock it at our peril. Whatever happened, we moan, to tunes you could whistle? But even in the good old days, people wanted more than just whistleable tunes. Indeed, long before Styne, Rodgers, Kern or anybody else had produced any tunes worth whistling, Broadway was famous for its staging gimmicks. In this respect, the turning-point was a long-forgotten show of 1869. That year, the Kiralfy Brothers, a troupe of Hungarian dancers, made their Broadway début with a whirling csardas in *Hiccory Diccory Dock*. They noticed, however, that, for all the skill and effort required in their dance, it was the First Flying Velocipede that was getting all the attention, and reached the conclusion that the big bucks lay in producing lavish spectacles of their own.

Over the next 20 years, they pioneered theatrical conventions we now take for granted, most notably the ritual postponements of opening night due to technological hitches – a tradition inaugurated in 1879 when the Kiralfys delayed the opening of *Enchantment* because the set for the Land of the Ephemerals had run amok. Virtually any designer could conjure the Land of the Ephemerals nowadays, but none would bother: audiences flocked to *Enchantment* only because it was new. That's the problem with stage technology: like Oedipus, its ambition sows the seeds of its own destruction.

In those days, though, theatrical endeavours gave little thought to posterity. It was an age of novelty where Donato the celebrated one-legged dancer earned far more than any bipedal rivals. The Kiralfys had a particular contempt for writers, often refusing to give them any billing. After all, they got there first: the plot was a pretext, the songs you found where you could; what counted was visual distraction.

Again, a broad sweep of the post-Kiralfy era might be helpful:

Special Effects in Musical Theatre

1873 – *Azreal* or *The Magic Charm*   Starring Lulu the Eighth Wonder of the World in his Wonderous Flight Through Space; most sophisticated use of trampoline to date.

1888 – *Evangeline*   First musical to use electric light, requiring personal supervision of Thomas Edison.

1898 – *A Trip to Mars*   First musical to use flying midgets' heads with wings on.

1908 – *Piff! Paff!! Pouf!!!*   First musical to use chorus girls with luminous skipping ropes.

1919 – *The Capitol Revue*   Featuring 50 girls with electric lights on their shoes introducing George Gershwin and Irving Caesar's 'Swanee'; shoes boffo, no one notices song.

1928 – *Rain or Shine*   Decline of technology, return to naturalism, with first musical to feature banjo-playing leopard.

1953 – *Peter Pan*   Mary Martin simultaneously sings and flies.

1965 – Lionel Bart's *Blitz!*   First musical to self-destruct.

1986 – Dave Clark's *Time*   First musical to star giant Fabergé egg containing hologram of Laurence Olivier's head with one nostril in wrong place.

1989 – *Miss Saigon*   First musical to erect statue of Ho Chi Minh in front of paying Americans.

As the survey indicates, eventually writers of distinction did emerge, but only to find themselves working to a producer's gimmick. When they protested that the priorities were the wrong way round, that they'd prefer to write for flesh and blood performers rather than mechanical effects, producers would nod sympathetically and then hire Jocko the juggling crow, the star of *Get Together* (1921) and *Better Times* (1922). Broadway's most sought-after crow, he worked only with the best, heading a cast which included juggling bulldogs, dancing elephants, ice skaters, 100 bathing beauties and the great Russian ballet choreographer Fokine. But, to the show's writers, Jocko was a deadbeat: what's the point of composing exquisite arioso ballads of love and despair if they're going to give them to a crow?

In the same category came the Shubert brothers' *Artists and Models*, the first Broadway revues to feature naked women. To comply with local by-laws, the nudes were obliged not to move, so instead, they were draped in cloths connected to strings which the supporting cast handed out to the tired businessmen in the audience. When the strings were pulled, the girls were revealed in all their splendour. To accompany this scene there was a song called 'Pull My String' – written by J. Fred Coots, composer of 'You Go To My Head' and 'Santa Claus Is Coming To Town' and by no means the most distinguished man to find himself penning nude revues. For example, the same year he wrote *The Student Prince* (1924), Sigmund Romberg, the *maître d'* of goulash operettas, found himself supplying a score for *Artists and Models*.

'Pull My String' isn't a very good song; if they'd asked Harold Arlen and Ted Koehler, *Artists and Models* might have ended up with 'I've Got The World On A String', which is a much better number and would have suited the situation just as well. We shouldn't forget that it's the context of a song which impresses it on the audience. On *The Pajama Game*, director–author George Abbott suggested to the songwriters that it might be a neat idea to have a song dictated by the company superintendent into a dictaphone. Adler and Ross came up with 'Hey There', which Abbott cued with his usual efficiency:

> SID: (*picking up mouthpiece*) Memo: Time-keeper. Be sure all girls fill out time cards properly and . . . (*shuts it off and then back on again*) Memo to Sid Sorokin . . . (*sings*)
>
> > Hey There!
> > You with the stars in your eyes
> > Love never made a fool of you . . .

After the first chorus, the dictaphone plays back Sid's memo, and he joins in, in a kind of automated auto-duet:

> DICTAPHONE: Hey There!
> You with the stars in your eyes . . .
> SID: Who me?
> DICTAPHONE: Love never made a fool of you . . .
> SID: Not until now.

Such gimmicks are eaten up by audiences because they're consistent with the subject and style of the piece, and they land the song. That's different from a luminous camisole.

To take two contrasting peaks in musical theatre, *Hip-Hip-Hooray* (1915) enticed the crowds into the Hippodrome by offering them the opportunity to see the cast 'ski down the mountainside and leap a seemingly impassable chasm'; *The Sound of Music* (1959), also set in the mountains, made do with painted cloths. *Hip-Hip-Hooray* did well, but *Sound of Music* did better. In fact, after *Hip-Hip-Hooray* it was all downhill for mountain glens and impassable chasms. Audiences acquired a taste for music and lyrics for which no amount of special effects could compensate. It took another half-century for innovative writing in musicals to splutter to a halt and power to pass once more to the directors and designers. Sean Kenny's sets for *Blitz!* sounded a warning shot. By the mid-eighties, most musicals needed all the help they could get. For a brief but terrible period – through *Mutiny*, *Starlight Express*, *Ziegfeld* – we were back to the days of the Kiralfys. It seemed so simple: the theatre was torn up to get the set in, the producer arranged the catering for the first-night party, sent out invitations to Bonnie Langford and Christopher Biggins and, with all the important business done, they then looked for someone to write the book and score.

At its best, however, a stage effect transcends mere novelty and renders the drama more potent than it could ever be otherwise. It's hard now to appreciate the sensation caused by the arrival in New York in 1863 of the latest theatrical illusion, the Pepper's Ghost. Every play instantly jumped on to the hearse and transformed itself into a spectral melodrama, prompting one Broadway columnist to offer his own spoof listings:

> Wallack's Theatre: *Ghost*
> New Bowery: *Ghost*
> Old Bowery: *Ghost*
> Bryant's Minstrels: *Colored Ghost*

None of these ghost shows has survived, but that's not the point. At the time, America was in the midst of a civil war and, for the first time, the young republic had to come to terms with a mortality rate it had never contemplated, as the best and brightest of its youth were wiped out. Today, the Pepper's Ghost effect – an actor's reflection cast on to a sheet of glass between stage and audience – would be laughable, but, preoccupied with mortality and the afterlife, theatregoers found the luminous figures parading on-stage oddly reassuring. No effect has ever been more effective.

The Music

There are three writing assignments on a musical: the music, the lyrics and the book (that's the story and dialogue). Most people would place them in that order of importance and difficulty, too:

1 music
2 lyrics
3 book

After all, there are plenty of playwrights and screenwriters around, so writing dialogue can't be that hard. Writing words that rhyme sounds a little more specialized. But, either way, you're dealing in language, which all of us use every day of our lives. Music, though, is either a God-given gift or, anyway, requires years of study at a conservatory.

But here's a curious fact. For most of musical theatre history, there have been far more good composers than good lyricists. And far more good lyricists than good book-writers. There must be more to writing sung words than meets the eye (or ear). And even more to writing spoken words for musicals – still a despised activity, even though 'book trouble' kills more musicals than anything else. Seventy-five years ago, we had great songs, but hadn't figured out a way to connect 'em up. A century ago we had great tunes but nothing to put on top of them except doggerel. To skim history via three landmark hits: *The Merry Widow* (1905) sells on Franz Lehár's lilting melodies; *Anything Goes* (1934) has Cole Porter's songs – music and lyrics; while *South Pacific* (1949) has the lot, memorable numbers sung by real people, embedded in a coherent plot – music, lyrics and book.

In the theatre, opera is the purest musical form. Which is to say that the music comes first, and you make allowances for everything else. Nothing wrong with that. If the music's good enough, you're happy to make allowances. Just as in 1920s musical comedy, if the *songs* are good enough, you're happy to make allowances. But, to compare the last popular opera composer with his heir in English-language theatre, no one ever talks about 'a Richard Rodgers musical'; it's always 'Rodgers and Hart' or 'Rodgers and Hammerstein'; whereas no one refers to *Tosca* as 'that terrific opera by Puccini, Giacosa and Illica', except possibly the Giacosa and Illica families. Those guys' job is to create conditions which enable the composer to shine and then keep out of the way.

Music is abstract, and, therefore, general. And opera, in which music dominates, is so general that today most directors keep the raw musical emotions – love, power, betrayal – and relocate the piece in Fascist Italy or a tube tunnel or whichever other environment tickles their fancy. The operas which resist this treatment are those which most approach the condition of a musical, like *Carmen*, or which have a narrative stong enough to compete with the tunes, like *Madam Butterfly* – which is in any case based on a solid hit by one of the first Broadway showmen, David Belasco, who wrote straight plays but ones which tended to have the size of musicals. But, for the most part, a music-dominated form inevitably tends towards abstract generalities, denied the plot anchors and lyrical images which make those generalities real and specific. Obviously, operas have words, because otherwise the singers would just be 'la-la-la'-ing (and there's enough of that in opera as it is). But the words have no relationship to the music. Or, to put it the other way round, the music takes no *account* of the words:

LA donna è mobile . . .

The worst Tin Pan Alley hack wouldn't give that much weight to the definite article because he'd know it was the most insignificant word in the line. This isn't particularly to denigrate opera, but merely to note the difference. Stravinsky admired Gilbert and Sullivan but recognized that Sullivan's willingness to accommodate himself to Gilbert's words was not for him.

Twenty years ago, the above remarks would have been strictly of historical interest. Back then, 'musical' meant 'Broadway musical', and the progression was clear: it was a straightforward family tree from Jerome Kern to Stephen Sondheim via Kern's partner and Sondheim's mentor Oscar Hammerstein and various collateral branches. But since then, deliberately or otherwise, the clock has been turned back. If you take the dominant figure in musicals now, he seems to have far more in common with musical theatre pre-Broadway: luxuriant tunes, emotional generalities, operetta certainties. Today, you could argue that Broadway's three-quarters of a century was a blip, a freak, an agreeable detour which the central thruway of musical theatre development bypasses entirely. As an alternative to the Kern–Sondheim view of history, how about this? Operetta – from the Golden Age (Strauss) to the Silver Age (Lehár) to the Rhinestone Cowboy (Lloyd Webber).

*

Musical theatre has had many addresses but none more distinguished than the Theater an der Wien in Vienna. This was where, in 1791, *The Magic Flute* was premièred, and then, in 1874, *Die Fledermaus* – the theatre's first hit operetta, written by Johann Strauss II, Hofbalmusikdirektor to Emperor Franz Joseph. From Strauss to Millöcker to Lehár, this theatre alone introduced and exported *The Gypsy Baron*, *The Beggar Student*, *The Merry Widow*, *The Count of Luxembourg*, *The Countess of Maritza*, *The Count of This*, *The Countess That*, *The Merry Baron of the Other* – more minor nobility than you'd find in the Almanach de Gotha. Welcome to Mitteleuropa, where it's always springtime in your heart and lilacs bloom in your ventricles, where every widow is merry and every hussar gay, where two hearts can beat in three-quarter time for between five-sixths and seven-eighths of the day – *nein*? And where every simple peasant girl holds out the possibility of being the Margravine of Reuss-Schleiz-Greiz in disguise, and every cheery barrow boy is mayhap the Count Tassilo Endrody-Wirttenburg.

But it happens even in the noblest families: the heirs can't match the standards of their forebears, can't afford the upkeep on the old place. And then what happens? The most frightful *arrivistes* move in. That's Mitteleuropa today: just another stop on the tour for British musicals. Since 1983 they've packed Vienna's most historic houses: *Cats* at the Ronacher, *Les Miz* at the Raimund, *Phantom* at the Theater an der Wien. Lloyd Webber *is* the heir to Mozart – at least from a real estate point of view.

After sitting through *Cats* in German at the Ronacher, I repaired for a stiff drink to the Ambassador Hotel's Lehár Restaurant, its plush red walls adorned with giant autographed manuscripts of the old boy's many operettas. Outside, it's hard to avoid the merciless gaze of those *Cats* eyes and *Phantom* masks, lurking round every corner like the Third Man. But, in here, we retreat into old Vienna, and a fragrant echo of Lehár's muted strings dances 'The Merry Widow Waltz' across the floor.

Well, let's not get carried away. Lloyd Webber is not *that* alien a usurper of the tradition of Lehár.

'It's very clear,' says Michael Kunze, who writes the German libretti for the Brit hits, 'that Andrew Lloyd Webber is going back to the old European opera tradition, and this tradition belongs very much to Vienna. Suddenly, we discover that the European tradition of operetta and opera is not dead at all. It comes out in a new form and conquers the world. I'm not surprised about that because the formula is not just the invention of one genius, but it was developed by a very high culture over hundreds of years. And it still works.'

'I don't really think that I connect particularly with the operetta tradition,' says Andrew Lloyd Webber. 'I don't really know very much about it and I haven't ever had a desperate urge to hear *The Vagabond King* or *Prince* or whatever he is, because I think that my interest starts with the musicals where the subject matter starts to get quite interesting or challenging.'

Is *Cats* interesting? Is *Starlight Express* challenging? When I suggested to the dean of Austrian musicologists, Herr Doktor Marcel Prawy, that Lloyd Webber and the operetta crowd might have something in common, he dismissed it as nonsense. Operetta is like *Dallas*, he said. Viennese audiences wanted to live in a fancy pad like the Princess of Trebizond, the Flirting Princess, the Slim Princess, the Duchess of Dantzic, the Baron Golosh . . . and J. R. Ewing. Who, said Doktor Prawy, wants to be hideously disfigured and live in a sewer?

Ah, but we're not talking content, but form and priorities. 'I have conducted many operettas at the Vienna Volksoper,' says Caspar Richter, 'and then in 1988 I began conducting musicals – in the last few years, mainly Andrew Lloyd Webber. I believe he is the Lehár of today, however funny that sounds. His orchestration, heavily based on strings, isn't far from the Viennese tradition.' Both men have a common hero: Lehár was called 'the Puccini of operetta'. And *Phantom* has made operetta hip, after half a century of being outflanked by musical comedy and the musical play. Before the First World War, *The Merry Widow* was one of the few shows to approach internationally the scale of today's Lloyd Webber mega-smashes: at one point there were over one hundred productions around the world. And, just as today we ask how British is the British musical, how Viennese is this most Viennese of operettas?

For historical tidiness, *The Merry Widow*, opening in 1905 six years after Johann Strauss II's death, is usually hailed as ushering in Vienna's Silver Age – a term intended to distinguish the exclusively romantic second generation from the comic convolutions of nineteenth-century operetta. Here's another theory we can push out on the dance-floor and see if it'll waltz: the history of musical theatre, in whatever form, across the centuries, is one of major gag-amputation, of total jokectomy, of having colonic irrigation devices stuck up your farce. From Mozart to Puccini, Offenbach to Lehár, Porter to Lloyd Webber: jokes, satire, wit are flushed out until all that remains is earnest, portentous, four-square romance. These works are fantastically successful . . . and then the form dies: opera did, and operetta . . . and musicals?

The only flaw in this theory is *The Merry Widow* itself, which is still pretty funny – not in the style of the Golden Age, with its ghastly comic grafts, but with a smart, contemporary knowingness. Its world-view is a million miles from *Zigeunerliebe* (1910) or *The Land of Smiles* (1929). Far from *inaugurating* the Silver Age, it's almost a premature satire of the later Lehár and his contemporaries.

Take the widow's fictitious Balkan homeland. Operetta has always loved escapism, but in this show it's the escapism they're trying to escape from: anybody who's anybody has skipped the bankrupt one-horse kingdom and is whooping it up in Paris, Hanna to find a husband, Count Danilo to pursue more transitory relationships. That's why in all the versions Maxim's and the Parisian scenes stay, but their beloved native land goes through what, even by the standards of Central and Eastern Europe, seems an excessive number of name changes: originally, Hanna and Danilo were citizens of Pontevedro (Vienna production, 1905), then Marsovia (London, 1907), Monteblanco (silent film, 1925), Marshovia (film remake, 1934) . . . It's a pretext, whose irrelevance is nicely caught by Ernst Lubitsch in the opening of MGM's second and best adaptation: a diligent geographer, peering through a huge magnifying glass, tries in vain to locate Marshovia on a map of Europe. Adrian Ross, lyricist for the first British production, knows the score too, giving Danilo a splendid mock-formal opening which is immediately undercut:

> My fatherland, it is for thee
> I ought to work from one to three
> Though as there isn't much to do
> I only come at half-past two . . .

What counts is the chorus:

> I go off to Maxim's
> Where fun and frolic beams . . .

A world away from those Ruritanian romances beached on the wilder shores of Mitteleuropa, the *Widow* revived Viennese fortunes in Paris,

London and New York, selling on a combination of traditional operetta musicality and the morality and cynicism of turn-of-the-century musical comedy. Lehár never pulled it off again, bècause everybody told him the tunes were terrif. Yes, they were, but *Merry Widow* also had, for a supposedly Silver Age operetta, a very contemporary sensibility. That's why so much product was sold off the back of it: *Merry Widow* gowns and gloves and broad-brimmed hats and corsets and trains and cocktails and cigarettes – a spin-off unsurpassed until the Brit hits of the eighties. 'It was the first musical that had merchandising,' says Lloyd Webber. 'Cameron Mackintosh has learned everything he knows from it.'

Inch by inch, the *Widow* and the *Phantom* reach across the decades to touch hands: they're both big on music, merchandising and money – Lehár was a multimillionaire within two years of the première, and wound up richer than any other Viennese composer ever. Like the Brit hits, *The Merry Widow* has a strong sense of location. But, like Lloyd Webber's, Lehár's music seems to defy the best efforts of lyrics: in both *Phantom* and *Widow* the words hang on for a while before being swept off while the tune whirls along on a rollercoaster ride up to top C. The lyricists of such diverse confections as 'The Abode of Madame La Mode', 'Yes, Sir! That's My Baby' and 'The Lady Is A Tramp' have all had a stab at *The Merry Widow*, without ever quite hitting the target. According to Alan Jay Lerner, 'the music predominated so overwhelmingly that there was no room or musical accommodation for lyrical humour or the well-turned rhyme'. Lerner was particularly scathing about lines like 'Come where the leafy bower lies': 'Not a lyric for a tenor with bridge work.'

That's not entirely fair. Adrian Ross was no Gilbert, but he was a wag and steered clear of the flowery archaisms beloved by journeymen librettists. As to the music overwhelming – the hallmark of operetta – while Lehár may not have got rhythm, he did have tempo, and his score offers more scope than the unrelieved lushness of later Silver works. That's why the *ideas* of the 'up' numbers – 'Maxim's', 'Girls, Girls, Girls' – have never been substantially altered. Even though the words fly by, impossible to catch, Lehár's music is always in tune with the moment: unlike generalized operatic arias, this music is as specific as you can get. And, once in a while, a lyricist manages to cling on long enough to match Lehár note for note. Lorenz Hart had great fun in the 1934 film, in an extraordinary scene on the packed floor at Maxim's where Maurice Chevalier and a gaggle of grisettes are engaged in a ferocious jogging exercise straight out of the Royal Canadian Air Force manual:

When there's wine and there's women and song
It is wrong not to do something wrong
When you do something wrong, you must do something right
And . . .
    (*Chevalier rolls his eyes and leers at the girls*)
. . . I'm doing all right tonight.

But the power of the score is in the romance, most particularly in the shimmering eroticism of Valencienne and Camille's Act Two duet (Lehár's equivalent of *Tristan*'s *Liebestod*) and that famous waltz. By the end of the nineteenth century, there were two kinds of waltzes: the Viennese, which hesitated, and the French, which didn't, and was therefore despised by the Viennese as just a 3/4-time tune. 'The Blue Danube''s par for the course:

    Da-da-da-ker-*plunk*! [Hesitation] Da-dum da-dum . . .

That's Viennese. Yet *The Merry Widow*'s is no more or less than a French waltz. It doesn't, formally, hesitate. Instead, it starts tentatively, with a cautious, hummed chorus; then, almost reluctantly, Danilo and the widow begin to waltz; and, gradually, decorous, restrained formal move-ment blossoms into a giddily confident, sweeping lyricism. You're sur-prised that Lehár and his librettists, Victor Léon and Leo Stein, don't make more of it: by the end of the number, you want Hanna and Danilo to have made love in dance. Perhaps they didn't know what they'd stumbled upon, but certainly the public got the message. Where previously show dance had meant marches, drills, ballets, big chorus set-pieces, the Silver Age operetta introduced dancing not by the dancers but by the characters in the drama – though neither Lehár, Kalman nor anyone else ever ac-complished it to such dizzying effect as here. With this one waltz, Lehár overturned the notion of dance as an expression of community – the martial formations of both courtly and country dancing – and endowed it with a far more alluring image, establishing a line that led through Vernon and Irene Castle (America's pre-eminent dance team in the run-up to the Great War) to Astaire and Rogers and beyond; with a single melody, Lehár changed dance from a group social activity to the most potent stage metaphor for intense, intimate romance.

   Lloyd Webber is a big fan of the tune, as he once told me. 'It's so simple . . .

          Da-da-dee-da
          Da-da-dee-da
          Da da da . . .

And then what's so clever is that he just does it again . . .

> Da-da-dee-da
> Da-da-dee-da
> Da da da . . .

And then he varies it ever so slightly . . .

> Da-da-dee-da-da-da
> Da-da-dee-dee-da . . .

'You're doing an awful lot of da-dee-da-ing,' I said.

'Well, I don't think I really know any of the words,' said Lloyd Webber. 'What are they?'

From somewhere at the back of my mind, I pulled out the middle section of the lyric:

> Ev'ry touch of fingers
> Tells me you are mine . . .

'Well, if that's what the words are like,' Lloyd Webber said, 'I'm glad I don't know them.'

Ev'ry touch of *fingers*? Ugh! Strange how no lyricist has ever managed to articulate the irresistible, heady perfume of the tune. Adrian Ross opts for:

> Though I say not
> What I may not
> Let you know . . .

Treading water. Christopher Hassall, for Sadler's Wells, offers:

> Strings are playing
> Hear them saying
> 'Love me true' . . .

But it's an external image, and the power of Lehár's music is not that it's being sawed by an orchestra but that it seems to have been conjured from within by the emotional moment. Even Lorenz Hart, who gave us 'My Funny Valentine' and 'It Never Entered My Mind', is unable to rise above:

> Now or never
> And forever
> I love you . . .

Waltzes are deceptively tricky for lyric-writers. The logic of the tune demands lots of rhymes, yet the feminine rhymes ('say not'/'may not', 'playing'/'saying', 'never'/'forever') usually wind up sounding obtrusive and the sentiments pat. Lehár's music is actually conveying rather complex emotions: two people, in love long ago, realistic and resigned, rediscovering their faith in romance and then, falteringly, surrendering to it; it's not a hesitation waltz, but a waltz that seduces you *from* hesitation. It's a spare melody, a distillation of the essence of melody: key of G, minim, crotchet, minim, crotchet, D, G, A, B ... Hanna's answering section is notey, fluttery, a heart beating faster, on the brink of giving in. The whole sequence is a melody which trembles with restraint and is, technically, well within the reach of English lyrics.

Why then does it resist words? The traditional emotional trajectory of the American musical can be seen in any Astaire–Rogers picture: they talk; and then, when they reach an emotional point beyond speech, they sing; and then, when they reach an emotional point beyond song, they dance. In this scene in *The Merry Widow*, Lehár makes that journey by music alone. This isn't an operatic generality: it's specific, it arises from *those* characters in *that* situation, and it develops those characters and advances that situation. In popular musical theatre, it was without precedent – a fine piece of music, but the finest piece of dramatically effective music. Most of us will be lucky to find a relationship which merits such a rhapsody, but aspiration is an important part of pop potency. When American audiences saw Hanna and Danilo, suddenly the point of social dancing became plain. At the time, one-steps and two-steps were the rage; waltzes were seen as 'old-fashioned'. Most Viennese waltzes, most operetta waltzes are. Cole Porter summed it up in the verse to his three-quarter time parody 'Wunderbar':

> Gazing down on the Jungfrau
> From our secret chalet for two ...

You can't gaze down on the Jungfrau: it's the highest mountain in its range. But Porter has got the measure of operetta waltz-time romance: his lovers' heads are literally in the clouds; this is the oom-pah-pah bombast of the Viennese school. Lehár's, though, is not an old-fashioned waltz, not a Strauss waltz, a 'prop' waltz played by orchestras in ballroom scenes for genteel community dancing; Lehár's waltz is personal and adult, in a human, naturalistic, colloquial range.

Viennese operetta died with Archduke Franz Ferdinand in Sarajevo. In America, *The Merry Widow* had sparked a succession of Viennese imports and local imitations: at the New Amsterdam Theatre, it was followed by *The Pink Lady* (1911), with 'The Pink Lady Waltz', and

Sweethearts (1913), with the beautiful Princess Sylvia of Zilania. But, in August 1914, as the European powers went to war, Jerome Kern's 'They Didn't Believe Me' was heard for the first time; in December, the New Amsterdam, instead of operetta, unveiled 'The First All-Syncopated Musical', Irving Berlin's *Watch Your Step*. The new world needed new forms, forms which would combine music with words with drama in ways the Viennese had never foreseen. Opera and operetta were absolute monarchies ruled by composers; the American Republic would make a musical theatre of checks and balances, of collective congressional will, of composers and lyricists and librettists and stagers. So *The Merry Widow* is the last waltz, a final fling for the *ancien régime*; and yet, even as Lehár sums up the operetta tradition and triumphantly vindicates the absolute power of the composer, he also anticipates what lies ahead: 'The Merry Widow Waltz' is the first waltz of the twentieth century, the first modern waltz.

*

The history of American song is the triumph of 4/4 over 3/4. 'Fly Me To The Moon' was written by Bart Howard in 1954 as a waltz. Have you ever heard it played that way in the last 30 years? We think of Quincy Jones's arrangement for Sinatra and the Basie band, as heard over the opening titles of the movie *Wall Street*, as the commuter trains and ferries and buses and subways feed the workers into the city: 'Fly Me To The Moon' in 4/4, the all-American time signature, what Nelson Riddle called 'the tempo of the heartbeat'. Aside from in revivals of *Anything Goes*, who now sings Cole Porter's waltz-teetering triplets . . . ?

> I get no *kick from cham*pagne . . .

Everyone follows Sinatra:

> I get no *kick* . . .
>   *(bang!)*
>   . . . from champagne . . .

A minim and two crotchets with a real kick: Porter should have written it that way. At some recording session or other, Sinatra was asked by an arranger if he could sing in a particular key: '*Sing* in it?' he said. 'I can't even *walk* in that key.' 4/4 is a time signature you can walk in, chopping up the syllables evenly:

> Stick-with-me-ba-by-I'm-the-fel-ler-you-came-in-with . . .

That's Frank doing *Guys and Dolls*. 4/4 is a democratic time signature, for guys, for dolls, for show ballads and surging big-town swing and 'Hound Dog' and 'Jailhouse Rock'.

At the time of *The Merry Widow*, an American score like Victor Herbert's *Babes in Toyland* had 2/4 and more 2/4 and 6/8 and 12/8 and everything except 4/4. The composer who established 4/4 as Broadway's home colours – more ubiquitous than 3/4 time ever was in Vienna – was Jerome Kern. Herbert was Irish born, which is one thing, but German trained, which is quite another: he never shook off his European operetta roots. Kern began his writing career in London in 1903, was as Anglophile as you can get, married an English girl and remained to the end a big fan of Leslie Stuart, the *Florodora* man. Richard Rodgers described Kern as having one foot in the Old World, one in the New – but that still put him one foot ahead of Herbert. He first appeared on Broadway when E. E. Rice asked him to do some interpolations for his production of *Mr Wix of Wickham* (1904). Rice had pioneered American 'farce-comedy', the prototype of Broadway musical comedy. Shows like *Evangeline* (1874) and *Adonis* (1884) had great gals and great gags but indifferent music – for *Adonis*, Rice had taken the tunes from wherever he could get 'em; for *Evangeline*, he'd written them himself. In boosting Kern's career, he was to remedy the fledgling American musical's one great weakness.

You couldn't tell that from *Mr Wix of Wickham* or any of the other London imports for which Kern was called upon to supply a few extra tunes. For ten years, he was imitative, of British Gaiety musicals and the European school. And then in a forgotten flop called *The Laughing Husband* comes a spirited song, with, amazingly, some raggy syncopation, and, even more surprisingly, what would soon become a favourite Tin Pan Alley trick – of putting in a little parenthetic phrase ('Incident'lly' or whatever) over the filler notes between the middle section and the main theme . . .

> You're Here And I'm Here
> So what do we care?
> You won't be lonely if only
> The music is there
> That little dip you do is great!
> Oh, how I wish you'd hesitate
> > (A little longer . . .)

They printed it in 2/4 time on the sheet, but it's a 4/4 song. And, suddenly, Kern *is* here.

The Girl from Utah is the first Broadway opening since the outbreak of war in August 1914: it's another silly London import, something about a girl from Utah on the run from a bigamous Mormon. But, because of the war, the producer, Charles Frohman, wants to reduce the comedy, and asks Kern to write a love ballad. He obliges with what may well be the single most influential song in the history of the American musical:

> And when I told them
> How wonderful you are
> They Didn't Believe Me
> They Didn't Believe Me . . .

For a popular theatre song, it's structurally all over the place, with an early middle section and then a modified main theme with a solitary triplet dropped on it. Yet the whole is effortless, and tender and warm and fully resolved. The triplet, by the way, comes on:

> And when I tell them
> And I'm *certainly* goin' to tell them . . .

Except, if you look at the sheet music, the lyric by Herbert Reynolds (the pseudonym for a ho-hum Englishman, M. E. Rourke) reads. . .

> And I *cert'nly am* goin' to tell them . . .

Is he nuts? That's impossible to sing on three little notes. Almost immediately, singers began singing 'certainly' on that triplet. There would be lessons for lyricists in this new democratic age: songs would have narrower ranges, and demand the contours of conversational speech.

The war changed everything. Kern's patron, Charles Frohman, took the *Lusitania* to England to go scouting for more terrible London shows to bring over, and was sunk by a German sub – bad news for Frohman, but, as events transpired, liberating for Kern. He had to stay in New York, and, in so doing, altered the course of the American musical.

And, meanwhile, a boy called Richard Rodgers hears Kern for the first time and realizes it's 'the beginning of a new form of musical theatre in this country. Somehow I knew it and wanted desperately to be a part of it.' And a young man called George Gershwin goes to his Aunt Kate's wedding and hears 'You're Here And I'm Here' and 'They Didn't Believe Me' and decides to quit being a Tin Pan Alley song-plugger at Remick's. 'I wanted to be closer to production music,' he said later, 'the kind Jerome Kern was writing.'

And an older man called Cole Porter goes off to war and pens his own version of Kern:

> And when they ask us
> How dangerous it was
> We never will tell them
> We never will tell them
> How we fought in some café
> With wild women night and day
> 'Twas the wonderf'lest war you ever knew . . .

In the sixties, in London's East End, Joan Littlewood put this parody into *Oh, What a Lovely War!*, though she didn't know it had such a distinguished author.

By the time Porter returned, the Broadway musical had Americanized itself. And 4/4 had won out over waltzes. Despite that one foot in the Old World, Kern seemed indifferent to 3/4 time. I can't think of a Kern standard that isn't 4/4: 'Look For The Silver Lining', 'Make Believe', 'Ol' Man River', 'Can't Help Lovin' That Man', 'Why Was I Born?', 'She Didn't Say Yes', 'I've Told Ev'ry Little Star', 'The Song Is You', 'I Won't Dance', 'Yesterdays', 'Smoke Gets In Your Eyes', 'A Fine Romance', 'The Way You Look Tonight', 'All The Things You Are', 'I'm Old Fashioned', 'Dearly Beloved', through to his final song in 1945, for a *Show Boat* revival, 'Nobody Else But Me' . . . : the great American, idiomatic songbook flowing from 'They Didn't Believe Me'.

*

Back in Vienna, Einzi Stolz steps across to her late husband's piano. Robert Stolz was the composer of 'Two Hearts In Three-Quarter Time' – a song title which is every Silver Age operetta plot in capsule form; he was in at the dawn of the Silver Age – he conducted the première of *The Merry Widow* in 1905. And today Einzi, a very merry widow, keeps her apartment in Robert Stolz-Platz as a shrine to his memory. From the clutter of memorabilia on top of the piano she picks up 'the famous baton of the Waltz King': Johann Strauss II had presented it to Franz Lehár, who in turn had presented it to Robert Stolz. 'Today,' Einzi tells me, 'I don't know to whom I could give it. And so I have to keep it for a while.'

And yet, and yet . . . even after Kern and 'They Didn't Believe Me', from out of the past, the waltz taunts us:

Remember the night
The night you said
You loved me
Remember?

Maybe, with 'The Merry Widow Waltz', the baton passed from the Viennese to the moderns, to the New World. New York had de-Viennesed musical theatre; they could do the same for the waltz, taking up the challenge of Lehár and stripping down the overblown Viennesey excesses for a vernacular age. Kern steered clear, but America's greatest musical dramatist and America's greatest songwriter both returned to waltz again and again. Hal David, lyricist of 'I Say A Little Prayer For You', 'Raindrops Keep Falling On My Head' and 'Twenty-four Hours From Tulsa', as well as Broadway's *Promises, Promises*, remembers hearing for the first time Liza Minnelli and Michael Feinstein's medley of Irving Berlin's 'Always', 'Remember' and 'What'll I Do'. 'At a very difficult time of my life,' he says, 'that recording meant so much more to me than anything else around. In three minutes, a song can touch a chord and, ever after, define certain moments for you – more than books, plays or any of the supposedly more difficult forms. At first I preferred the more sophisticated songs with unusual rhyme schemes, like "Let's Face The Music And Dance". But, like most songwriters, I eventually come back to those Berlin waltzes of the mid-twenties: they're the quintessential popular songs.'

The quintessential popular songs: waltzes. And what about the quintessential theatre songs? America's Waltz King is, no question, Richard Rodgers. He grew up hearing his parents sing and play selections from *The Merry Widow*, *Mlle Modiste*, *The Chocolate Soldier*; the first show he was taken to see was at the New Amsterdam, *Little Nemo* (1908), by Harry B. Smith and New York's most famous waltz peddler of the day, Victor Herbert. As a teenager, Rodgers met up with a jazzy, jangly, jittery lyricist, Lorenz Hart, but he never forgot those childhood waltzes. You can hear him experimenting with the form in 'Do You Love Me?', a forgotten song from *The Garrick Gaieties* (1925), then with 'Lover', and, from *Jumbo*, 'The Most Beautiful Girl In The World'. This is 1935, the heyday of the 32-bar popular song in AABA – main theme, repeated, middle eight, back to the original theme. 'The Most Beautiful Girl' is a rich, full waltz with a wide range – we're an octave up as we hit the middle – and its form is main theme, modified, release, back to the modified theme and then an eight-bar tag; it's 72 bars in all – and yet it sounds utterly American.

And then came 'Falling In Love With Love' and 'Wait Till You See Her' and waltz after waltz after waltz . . .

In *Oklahoma!*, 'Oh, What A Beautiful Mornin'', confident and muscular, and 'Out Of My Dreams', dreamily flowing;
and the *Carousel* waltz, the mechanical rinky-dink hurdy-gurdy jingle of the fairground transformed into art;
and, in *State Fair*, 'It's A Grand Night For Singing', a rousing back-porch charmer;
and, in *South Pacific*, 'This Nearly Was Mine', grand and stately, and then Hammerstein's contemptuous denunciation of the white man's bigotry, set to that whitest of white musical forms:

> You've got to be taught
> To be afraid
> Of people whose eyes
> Are oddly made
> And people whose skin
> Is a diff'rent shade
> You've Got To Be Carefully Taught . . .

and, in *The King and I*, 'Hello, Young Lovers', wistful and unaffected;
and, in *The Sound of Music*, 'My Favourite Things' and 'Edelweiss';
and the one that sums it up, the title song of *Do I Hear a Waltz?*:

> Do you hear a waltz?
> Oh, my dear, don't you hear a waltz?
> Such lovely Blue Danubey
> Music, how can you be
> Still?

Except that all the above, most of them routinely marked '*tempo di valse*', are not Blue Danubey at all, but unmistakably modern and unmistakably Rodgers.

And, on top of all that, when it came to his own big dance moment, the Rodgers equivalent of 'The Merry Widow Waltz', what did he write? Not a waltz but a polka. The most romantic – the sexiest – polka ever written: 'Shall We Dance?' from *The King and I*.

Richard Rodgers died on 30 December 1979. He wrote his last waltz for *I Remember Mama*, which opened on Broadway eight months earlier.

And, if only because of Martin Charnin's lyric, he seems, 54 years after *The Garrick Gaieties*, to be taking his leave:

> Time . . .
> Time . . .
> Time, how it flies
> When did it happen?
> Where were we looking?
> What were we list'ning to?

We were list'ning to Rodgers waltzes, quintessential American theatre songs, part of the endless, effortless medley that links Lehár and the music of Rodgers' childhood with his lyricist on *Do I Hear a Waltz?*, Stephen Sondheim. Who'd have thought the waltz would survive the American century? It made it, because Rodgers personalized and humanized it, for cowboys and sailors and mill workers. That last song from *I Remember Mama* has an apt marking: 'Moderate Waltz'.

iv

The Lyrics

What's the difference between this . . .

> Say you'll share with me one love, one lifetime
> Say the words and I will follow you

. . . and this?

> While soft winds sigh
> It is then we forget that the world
> Has a snare or a care
> Life's a dream then!
> Love's supreme then!

Answer: not much. The former is from *Phantom of the Opera*. 'I think the lyric is very flabby. No one knows a word of it, even though a lot of people like the song,' Herbert Kretzmer, lyricist of *Les Misérables*, once told me. Go into the Gents at Her Majesty's Theatre and listen to the guys at the *pissoirs*: 'Say you'll da-da da-da da da da-da . . .' It's a hit tune that has words only because it has to. Once again, if you step back from recent history, from the Kern–Sondheim tradition, the modern British musical seems to connect directly with Kern's predecessors. We think of 'Andrew Lloyd Webber's *Phantom of the Opera*' in the same way we used to think of 'Victor Herbert's *Mlle Modiste*' – which is where the second lyric came from. *Mlle Modiste* was the smash Broadway opening of Christmas Day 1905, the one about the Parisian hat-shop girl who wants to be a singer. Henry Blossom's lyrics are florid, declamatory, typical of an era when Broadway and much of American wannabe-high culture took its cue from Germany, and the words, even though created in English, sound like translations.

Not that the originals are tricky to decipher. Even the most rudimentary acquaintance with the language will suffice for the limited vocabulary of German song: *Liebe, Leiden, Ewig, Tod*. Which boils down to: love means suffering forever and then you die. This was the condition to which

America's earliest writers, mostly émigrés or students from Central Europe, believed musical romance should aspire. If not physically painful and constitutionally debilitating, it should at the very minimum be ardent and ponderous. It took Broadway many years to emerge from the long *Dämmerung* of the Teuton school and stake out its own distinctive position on the subject:

> As Columbus announced when he knew he was bounced
> 'It was swell, Isabelle, swell'

... with which fatalistic shrug, Cole Porter kicks in the chorus of 'Just One Of Those Things'.

Lyric-writing at its best is a miniature art, an exercise in compression. You can plough through all the Foreign Office assurances to the people of Hong Kong after the Chinese takeover or you can grab a Cole Porter couplet which says it all in a thousandth of the space:

> If they ever put a bullet in your brain
> I'll complain.

How did lyricists learn to say it in such a short space? Because they only had those few notes to say it *to*.

*

'We all come from Gilbert,' Johnny Mercer used to say. He is, indeed, the father of all lyricists, but, strictly speaking, W. S. Gilbert himself is no lyricist. It comes back to the old question again: which comes first? In the Savoy operas, the words always came first and, on the one occasion when Gilbert made an exception and allowed Arthur Sullivan free rein with the music, the crusty old librettist dismissed the result as 'mere doggerel, but words written to an existing tune are nearly sure to be that.'

Au contraire. 'When the lyric's written first,' says Tim Rice, 'it comes out "Di-dum-di-dum-di-dum-di-dum/Di-dum-di-dum-di-dum-di-dum", which is very boring for a composer.' This is the tumty-tumty trap: in other words, doggerel. Gilbert's is the best kind of doggerel: he's witty, acerbic and rhymes inventively, but his entire *oeuvre* is tumty-tumty. And that makes him a versifier not a lyricist:

> Here's a first-rate opportunity
> To get married with impunity
> And indulge in the felicity

Of unbounded domesticity
You shall quickly be parsonified
Conjugally matrimonified
By a doctor of divinity
Who resides in this vicinity . . .

This looks good on paper. In fact, it looks so good on paper, you wonder what's to be gained by adding a tune. It's sung by pirates, of Penzance, to a bevy of maidens they've come upon. Clearly, pirates, of Penzance or any other municipality, do not talk like this: the polysyllabic rhyming is an end in itself. So, as with 'Modern Major-General', Sullivan's music makes a virtue of a crippling disadvantage and turns the number into a piece of virtuoso exhibitionism, a song about straining for flamboyant rhymes. It's to Sullivan's credit that he sets these light verses with verve and invention, but he can never obscure the fact that light verse is what it is: a fixed, formal, measured metrical pattern. This is how almost all the earliest lyricists worked:

If a pair of blue eyes have deceived you
And a pair of red lips said you nay
Don't appeal to champagne
All its bubbles are vain
You will only feel worse the next day
Just forget fortune's snub
And drop in at the club
Where you know all the good fellows are
There the tonic you're after
Is gossip and laughter
You light up a long dark cigar . . .

Thus Harry B. Smith, borrowing from Kipling, in '(A Woman Is Only A Woman But) A Good Cigar Is A Smoke' from *Miss Dolly Dollars*, a Broadway hit in 1905. You can usually tell when the words are written first, because, even when the tumty-tumtiness isn't as overpowering as in the above example, it's clear that the words and music have no particular relationship to each other. Smith's lyric could just as easily have been a droll bit of verse published in *Punch* and, no matter how efficiently Victor Herbert has set it, that's what it sounds like: a setting.

Smith, to Reginald De Koven's music, wrote the first successful American book musical, *Robin Hood*, premièred in 1891 and regularly revived for the next half-century. Afterwards he helped Victor Herbert to his first hit operetta, *The Fortune Teller* (1898), and then supplied a string of serviceable fillers with titles like *The Singing Girl* (1899), *The Casino Girl* (1900) and *The Office Boy* (1903). He wrote some 300 shows and lyrics for 6,000 songs. As a writer, he could occasionally be waggish, and was always competent, but he didn't speak American:

> Thro' the forest wild and free
> Sounds our Magyar melody
> Ever dancing none can be
> Half so merry as are we . . .

It sounds like he's parodying the goulash school, but that's unlikely. Smith shared with them the view that there was a special, high-flown language for theatre song entirely separate from vernacular American. The first lasting hit song from an American musical is 'Oh, Promise Me' – music by Reginald De Koven, lyric by *Daily Telegraph* drama critic Clement Scott – which was included in *Robin Hood*. You don't hear it too much these days. Indeed, for me the shock value of the 1980 film *SOB* consisted not in Julie Andrews revealing her breasts but revealing her knowledge of this song: quite out of the blue, she sings it at the funeral scene. Still, it had a good run and, until fairly recently, was virtually *de rigueur* at American weddings. 'Oh, Promise Me' became a sort of standard, but one reserved for a formal ceremonial occasion – a subtle reminder, even in its ubiquity, that theatre songs were not democratic, not everyday.

Did anyone worry about this at the time? Not on Broadway. But a few blocks away, in Tin Pan Alley, the rhymes they were a-changin'. The first generation of commercial pop writers wrote in verse-and-chorus form, long, *long* songs stretching from stanza to stanza with only the most perfunctory refrain. The titles give you the gist: 'Mother Was A Lady', 'Take Back Your Gold', 'She Is More To Be Pitied Than Censured'. These songs were the equivalent of today's TV movie of the week and, as with Lorena Bobbitt, Tonya Harding, Amy Fisher, the Menendez brothers and all those other cautionary tales proudly labelled 'Based on a true story', their subject matter was drawn from the newspaper columns. In the 1890s, as much as the 1990s, artists were as impotent as John Wayne Bobbitt after his emasculation to counter the public preference for real-life freak shows over professionally crafted drama: then as now, we simply liked stories. The prototype pop hit, Charles K. Harris' 'After The Ball' (1892), was 'based on a true story', as was his grisly ballad of an orphan girl asking the telephone operator to be put through to her dead mother, 'Hello, Central, Give Me Heaven'. My personal favourite is Gussie L. Davis' pop hit of 1898 about an overnight train full of railway passengers irritated by a sobbing infant and demanding to know of her young father where the mother is, only to be told that she's in a mahogany casket 'In The Baggage Coach Ahead'.

Story songs are rarely distinguished as songs: if you've got five, seven, twelve verses to a ballad but the same music each time, the tune is unlikely to connect with the words except in the most minimally functional way. Almost all turn-of-the-century blockbusters have the simplest of tonal structures, usually in a major key, with three basic chords; their favourite harmonic trick is a succession of chromatic chords before the final cadence; the piano parts are as basic as possible, with cumbersome octave doubling for the right hand.

But the effect is always the same: these are lilting, capering waltzes – no matter that their verses spin gloomy gaslight tales of death and despair. Even as their subject matter proclaims its modernity (railroads and telephones) the music underneath belies it. *A Trip to Chinatown* (1891), a forerunner of *Hello, Dolly!* and the biggest Broadway hit of its day, produced one of these waltzes, 'The Bowery':

> The Bow'ry!
> The Bow'ry!
> They say such things
> And they do strange things
> On the Bow'ry . . .

The words hint at naughtiness; the tune's about as naughty as serving tea without a doily. Half a century later, Cole Porter revived what he called 'Bowery waltz tempo' for *Kiss Me, Kate*:

> Brush Up Your Shakespeare
> Start quoting him now
> Brush Up Your Shakespeare
> And the women you will wow . . .

To have a couple of gangsters who mugged up on Shakespeare in the prison library singing a genteel turn-of-the-century waltz is a cute comic mismatch, but no more so than the mismatch of music and lyrics in the original 'Bowery waltzes'.

But even in the 1890s, there are signs that the new century will not be like its predecessor:

Hello! Ma Baby
Hello! ma honey
Hello! ma ragtime gal
Send me a kiss by wire
Baby, my heart's on fire!

A telephone song, a 'coon song', a ragtime song – and suddenly lyrics about the latest novelty find an echo in a musical novelty. By 1900, there were some 150 telephone songs, but Ida Emerson and Joe Howard's is striking because of the union of music and words: the text seems an expression of the identity of the tune; it makes explicit what's implicit in the notes – a definition of songwriting. The Tin Pan Alley songs were tabloid stories in waltz time; the operetta numbers were lush tunes with waffle. Why does 'Hello! Ma Baby' seem more satisfying as a *song*? Again, we're back to the old question: which comes first? Rags and cakewalks were written music first, and the trick the lyricist then had to perform was to express that music in words. Lyricists, it seems, are far more sensitive to the character of a tune than composers are to the character of a lyric. 'When a composer sets a lyric,' says Stephen Schwartz, composer/lyricist of *Godspell* (1971) but a man who's also written words for Leonard Bernstein (*Mass*) and Charles Strouse (*Rags*), 'there's a tendency for ac*cents* to wind up on the wrong syl*lab*bles.' And there's nothing a good lyricist hates more. Frank Loesser once wrote a Latin American parody:

Upon the island from
Which we come
There is a natio*nal* chara*cter*istic which is very strong
That is we put *the* ac*cent* upon *the* wrong syl*lab*ble
And we si-i-i-i-ing
A tropi*cal* song . . .

On Broadway, the unity of words and music we take for granted in Loesser was first found in George M. Cohan: 'I'm a Yankee Doodle Dandy!', 'Give My Regards To Broadway!' – big fat words that bounced off bright, clean notes at the dawn of the century and have remained in our collective memory ever since. Presented with a new lyric, Sigmund Romberg used to take it, run it through once and then inform his collaborators: 'It fits.' At first Oscar Hammerstein and Irving Caesar and Rommie's other lyricists took this as a great insult, but, gradually, they came to understand that he meant it sat snugly and cleanly on the notes – the minimum entry qualification for a good lyric.

Cohan was a competent songwriter – a novelty on Broadway in the century's first decade – but, his flag-wavers aside, he compares badly with those who came after. The first American theatre lyricist who still holds up today was, as it happens, an Englishman. Here's another view of musical theatre evolution: that, just as the dominant genre of the day is running out of steam – operetta in the 1910s, the musical play in the 1970s – some fellow from across the Atlantic comes along and reinvents the form. Andrew Lloyd Webber isn't the first British subject to remake the American musical in his own image: P. G. Wodehouse did it 60 years earlier. (These two men briefly shared the stage in 1975: *Jeeves* was Lloyd Webber's only book musical, and his only flop.)

That's right: P. G. Wodehouse, novelist and lyricist. And, whereas his novels are praised mostly as a triumph of artifice, for their glorious unreality, his stage work was revolutionary for precisely the opposite reason: he brought naturalism to a field where it was hitherto unknown.

His ally was Jerome Kern, and the partnership was struck at the Princess Theatre on 23 December 1915, the first night of *Very Good Eddie*. No comma in the title as it wasn't a compliment but an assessment of Eddie's character, and not a flattering one: an 'eddie' is vaudevillian slang for a ventriloquist's dummy, so a 'very good eddie' is a pliant dummy. In this plot, Eddie the dummy was one half of one of two honeymoon couples preparing to board a Hudson River dayliner. We mock it today, but the book by Guy Bolton (also British born) was functional, contemporary and concerned ordinary, believable characters, and the music was by the Americanized, semi-syncopated Kern. Only the lyrics – supplied by diverse hands – disappointed. P. G. Wodehouse attended the opening night in his capacity as *Vanity Fair* dramatic critic, and, when one of the authors muttered something about how 'it looks like a good house', it was misheard as 'it looks like Wodehouse', and Plum was brought over to be introduced: if you buy that story, you should be writing musical comedy plots. Anyway, Wodehouse signed on as the third member of the team, and the first Princess musical proper opened in February 1917: *Oh, Boy!*, book by Bolton, music by Kern, lyrics by Wodehouse. In a humble introductory verse he stakes out his turf:

> I've always liked the sort of song
> You hear so much today
> Called 'When it's something-or-other time
> In some place far away'
> Oh, tulip time in Holland

A pleasant time must be
While some are strong
For apple blossom time in Norman*dee*
But there's another time and place
That makes a hit with me . . .

And, so saying, Wodehouse brings musical theatre home, to a walk-up rental in Brooklyn:

When it's Nesting Time In Flatbush
We will take a little flat
With 'Welcome' on the mat
Where there's room to swing a cat . . .

Not a baron, not a countess in sight. And then, to a perky tune, the principal comedienne lists the individual attractions of various beaux but complains:

But I'm pining
Till there comes in my direction
One combining
Ev'ry masculine perfection
Who'll be Eddie
And Joe and Dick and Sam
And Freddie
And Neddie
And Teddie
Rolled In One.

This is very fine writing: the rhymes fall on the words which ought to be emphasized (not always true in Gilbert) and they're unusual – 'pining'/'combining' – but, when sung, seem natural and appropriate.

After *Oh, Boy!* came *Leave It to Jane* and *Oh, Lady! Lady!!* and a flop called *Sitting Pretty* with a peach of a score, and by then every tyro lyricist wanted to be like Wodehouse. These songs from the Great War to the mid-twenties capture musical comedy in transition: we're not quite there, but we're on our way to the Gershwins, Rodgers and Hart, Cole Porter . . . Operetta and musical comedy are not really forms, but locations – like, in movies, the western. There are many different kinds of westerns, but only up to a point. You can't make a western set on Park Avenue or the Riviera. Likewise with operetta: it's always something-or-other time in some place far away. Bolton, Wodehouse and Kern gave the American musical a location of its own: the Meadowsides Country Club on Long Island (*Oh, Boy!*), Atwater College for the Thanksgiving Day football game (*Leave It to Jane*) and (for *Oh, Lady! Lady!!*) Greenwich Village, where . . .

> They learn to eat spaghetti
> Which is hard enough, as *you* know
> They leave off socks
> And wear Greek smocks
> And study Guido Bruno . . .

Had Wodehouse died in 1918, he would have been remembered not as a British novelist but as the first great lyricist of the American musical. To the delight of audiences accustomed to tweeting twaddle, he proved you could make music in romances that aspire no higher than the seventh floor on Flatbush Avenue. If boy-meets-girl now seems a Broadway cliché, it still beats boy-Count-disguised-as-goatherd-meets-girl-Princess-disguised-as-scullery-maid. It's clear too that, in working with Kern and the other showbiz Jews at the Princess Theatre, Wodehouse absorbed Broadway's indifference to the refinements of class. In his autobiographical *Performing Flea*, he writes to Bill Townend about H. G. Wells: 'The first time I met him, we had barely finished the initial pip-pippings when he said, apropos of nothing, "My father was a professional cricketer." If there's a good answer to that, you tell me.' And that's that: a joky reminiscence . . . in the British edition. You have to turn to the American edition, *Author! Author!*, to get the full version and discover the real point: 'What a weird country England is,' Wodehouse continues, 'with its class distinctions and that ingrained snobbery you can't seem to escape from. I suppose I notice it more because I've spent so much time in America. Can you imagine an American who had achieved the position Wells has, worrying because he started out in life on the wrong side of the tracks? But nothing will ever make Wells forget that his father was a professional cricketer and his mother the housekeeper at Uppark.'

To certain critics, the subject matter of Wodehouse's novels implies some sort of endorsement of the class system, which is rather like deducing from *Macbeth* that Shakespeare liked palling around with regicidal maniacs. The stage work offers quite a different picture and raises an interesting question: in what sense is Wodehouse a *British* writer? He lived in America on and off from before the First World War and permanently from the Second; he never visited Britain after 1939 for fear of prosecution for his wartime broadcasts, and official forgiveness did not come until

1975 when six weeks before he died Her Majesty, cutting it exceedingly fine, knighted him: by then, he had been a US citizen for 30 years.

He was also closer in spirit to the rough and tumble of the Broadway theatre than he was to literary London. When pressed upon the construction of his novels, he always mumbled something about them being 'like a musical comedy without music' – which, to the Eng Lit boys, sounds like a frightful underestimation but, to Wodehouse, who blazed the trail of coherent, integrated, democratic theatre lyrics, was a source of great pride. The Blandings Wodehouse is earls and manservants; the Broadway Wodehouse is a home in the suburbs where the neighbours don't play the gramophone each night till after three. This *soi-disant* Englishman invented that quintessentially American form, musical comedy.

Musicals are fantasies, a 'Dancing Time', as Wodehouse put it, '. . . when the stars are shimmying up in the sky'. But the Princess shows were down-to-earth fantasies, for all of us. Wodehouse wrote songs for shop girls who hear the siren songs of the cabarets:

> Take me where you hear all those saxophones moaning
> Where can those ukuleles be?

And for the morning after when they'd show up late at the midtown department stores:

> Why pick on some poor little thing
> Who's been out all night tangoing?

And for frustrated young men who despair of ever finding anyone to march down the aisle:

> For all the punch that march of Mendelssohn's has
> He might as well have written nothing but jazz . . .

And for unexpected romantic encounters in summer showers:

> What bad luck! It's
> Coming down in buckets . . .

And for dreams of domestic bliss out on Long Island:

> Let's Build A Little Bungalow In Quogue . . .

And for railroad commuters and the little woman back in the 'burbs:

> Down at the gate
> I shall listen and wait

> Oh, how excited I'll be
> And how I'll cheer it
> Each night when I hear it
> Bringing you back to me.

And, as today's passengers will tell you, Wodehouse nailed the Long Island Rail Road pretty accurately:

> It's quite a humble train, you know
> And some folks grumble that it's slow
> It stops to ponder now and then
> The air inside needs oxygen . . .

He Americanized the history lesson:

> I wish that I had lived there
> Beside the pyramid
> For a girl today don't get the scope
> That Cleopatterer did . . .

And, what so appealed to Ira Gershwin in particular, Wodehouse's literate drollness: pull a Tin Pan Alley formula and just tweak it ever so slightly. Here's a dotty Wodehousian take on the 'Pack Up Your Troubles In Your Old Kit-Bag' school of chin-up song:

> Crying never yet got anybody anywhere
> So just stick out your chin
> And shove all your worries in a great big box
> And sit on the lid and grin!

Wodehouse's British admirers seem to look on all this as an aberration, disregarding the inconvenient fact that for two decades he was at the centre of the Broadway maelstrom and that to the end he continued to write lyrics. One of his most distinguished biographers, Frances Donaldson, is particularly sniffy about his bunking off from the serious business of novel-writing: 'Without the music they were written for,' she writes, 'Wodehouse's lyrics seem dexterous and neat but totally uninteresting.' This seems pretty harsh on the man who produced the most audacious couplet of the 1919 season, when his oriental heroine rhymed 'Los Angeles' with 'man jealous'.

But why study them without the tune? Surely Lady Donaldson, otherwise very thorough, could have invested the odd tenner in, say, the 1959 revival album of *Leave It to Jane* (one of the longest-running

Off-Broadway hits ever)? Besides, her principal criticism is actually Wodehouse's greatest virtue. As we've seen, anybody can write light verse that looks good on the page but leaves the composer hemmed in by formal scansion. Not Kern and Wodehouse:

> He can't play golf or tennis or polo
> Or sing a solo
> Or row
> He isn't half as handsome
> As dozens
> Of men that
> I know . . .

That verse is in the '94 revival of *Show Boat* and in the cabaret acts of discriminating *chanteuses* in New York and London – eight decades after its composition. As Wodehouse used to say, it would never have occurred to him to write a verse in that pattern, if it hadn't been for the accents of Kern's tune, usually barked down the telephone at three in the morning and jotted down by Wodehouse in the form of a 'dummy lyric'. A dummy lyric is a sort of *aide-mémoire* of meaningless words which helps the writer remember the stresses of the music: 'It Ain't Necessarily So' is a dummy lyric which Ira Gershwin liked so much that he decided to keep. Famously interrupting a pre-party nap Irving Caesar was taking, Vincent Youmans played a new tune and demanded a dummy lyric there and then. Caesar improvised:

> Picture you
> Upon my knee
> Just Tea For Two
> And two for tea
> Just me for you
> and you for me
> Alone . . .

'That's lousy,' said Caesar. 'But I'll write a proper lyric later.' He never did. Seventy years later, does he still think it's lousy? 'Nah,' says Caesar. 'Now I think it's great.' These are words that respond to the tune, in shapes the operetta set could never have imagined. Here's Rodgers and Hart:

> We'll have Manhattan
> The Bronx and Staten
> Island, too

> It's lovely going through
> The zoo . . .

By inverting the G&S process, Wodehouse's collaborator Jerome Kern was freed from the restrictions of word-setting and Plum himself was able to forge a new kind of lyric writing. None of this cuts much ice with Lady Donaldson: 'Musical comedy was an ephemeral and unimportant art,' she writes. 'If the reputations of Wodehouse, Bolton and Kern rested on their work for the theatre, only Kern's name would survive.'

Well, you could cite innumerable dissenters, but let Alan Jay Lerner stand for them all: 'As Kern had become the first modern composer in the musical theatre, Wodehouse was the forerunner of Lorenz Hart, Ira Gershwin and all who toiled thereafter in the lyrical vineyards. He brought charm, literacy and rhyming ingenuity to the theatre.'

No show ever failed because of its lyrics, but Wodehouse's standards are still worth pursuing. The great musicals are those which achieve a true coalescence of their constituent parts – book, music, lyrics, dance, design – but, even then, most of those elements are concerned with big gestures: the book bounces you along from A to B with a savage narrative shorthand, the music deals with emotional extremes. Such *detail* as exists in a musical is usually found in the lyrics. In his first draft of 'Bill', Wodehouse wrote:

> A motor car he cannot steer
> And it seems clear
> Whenever he dances
> His partner takes chances . . .

'Now that,' Ira Gershwin would say enviously, '*that's* a lyric': an immaculately compressed character sketch, rendered rueful by the notes on which it sits. It's detail: it's what stops the best musicals being just up-and-down emotional rollercoaster rides for cardboard cut-outs. You can pinpoint the difference between Wodehouse and the operatic excesses of his predecessors to a moment in 'Bill' as it's heard today in *Show Boat*:

> I love him
> Because he's – I don't know
> Because he's just
> My Bill.

Using 'I don't know' to cover Kern's awkward little triplet is a brilliant stroke: an operetta man would have said . . .

> I love him
> More than the stars above

. . . or some such, but Wodehouse understood that a naturalistic conversational shrug would be far more effective and touching. The song finds poetry in inarticulacy.

*

To list Wodehouse's admirers is to understand: the Gershwins, Rodgers and Hart and Hammerstein, Howard Dietz, Alan Jay Lerner, Sheldon Harnick . . . Not long before W. S. Gilbert's death, the young P. G. Wodehouse found himself attending a dinner at the great man's house. As a symbolic moment – the passing of the torch – the meeting is not wholly satisfactory. Wodehouse was in such a funk that he blew one of Gilbert's jokes and was thereafter incapable of speech. But that, in itself, has a sort of symbolism: Wodehousian diffidence makes a better song model than Gilbertian patter. Plum's songs are funny, but funny in character, rather than drawing attention to the lyricist. He gave ordinary folks a plausible singing voice on the American stage. Gilbert and his dated Major-General retain their allure, but they're the soft option: if in doubt, throw in a triple rhyme. 'Writing music takes more talent,' Johnny Mercer used to say, 'but writing lyrics takes more courage.' On the other hand, as Mercer put it in song:

> Fools Rush In
> Where wise men never go
> But wise men never fall in love
> So how are they to know?

By lyric-writing courage, I like to think Mercer had in mind Dorothy Fields – as far as I'm concerned, the greatest woman writer of the twentieth century, though unlikely ever to be anthologized by Virago with an introduction by Victoria Glendinning. Miss Fields could be an exhibitionist rhymester like Hart and Porter, but she could also write:

> I'm In The Mood For Love
> Simply because you're near me
> Funny, but when you're near me
> I'm In The Mood For Love . . .

It'll look like nothing in the *Collected Lyrics* but, set to Jimmy McHugh's tune, it's bewitching. It fulfils the highest objective of lyric-writing: it says

58

those notes; it takes the vague emotional mood of the music and makes it specific. And, unlike all that verse-and-chorus patter stuff, she says it all in one chorus. Try writing a second stanza to 'I'm In The Mood For Love' or Irving Berlin's 'Always' or any of those deceptively slight masterpieces: you can't; it's all been said in eight couplets. Miss Fields does it again in 'Sunny Side Of The Street':

> Grab your coat and get your hat
> Leave your worries on the doorstep
> Just direct your feet
> To the Sunny Side Of The Street
> Can't you hear that pitter-pat?
> Oh, that happy tune is your step
> Life can be so sweet
> On The Sunny Side Of The Street
> I used to walk in the shade
> With my blues on parade
> Now I'm not afraid
> This rover
> Crossed over . . .

Compare and contrast with Gilbert and Harry B. Smith. Miss Fields and Jimmy McHugh wrote the song for *Lew Leslie's International Revue* in 1930. Twenty years earlier it would never have occurred to Smith or any other theatre lyricist to rhyme across the quatrains: 'hat'/'doorstep'/ 'pitter-pat'/'your step'. Or to structure a middle eight so that a three-rhyme ('shade'/'parade'/'afraid') is followed by two meaty short-stopped phrases. You only write that way if you're writing to a tune, and, if you do it as well as Dorothy Fields did here, it blasts across the footlights and chisels itself into the national consciousness. It seems simple, but that first line is seven of the most memorable monosyllables ever written. There was a cartoon in *The Spectator* a few years ago showing one of those glass cases you see in office vestibules and above it a sign: 'In case of fire, grab your coat and get your hat, leave your worries on the doorstep . . .'

Dorothy Fields wrote with Jimmy McHugh (very vaudevillian) and Fritz Kreisler (very Viennese). For sassy, brassy, jazzy guys like Cy Coleman (*Sweet Charity*), she could write . . .

> The minute you walked in the joint
> I could see you were a man of distinction
> A real Big Spender

. . . whereas, for Jerome Kern, she offered . . .

> Someday when I'm awf'lly low
> When the world is cold
> I will feel a glow
> Just thinking of you
> And The Way You Look Tonight.

It takes a highly refined craftsmanship to understand how wistful that potentially perilous word 'awf'lly' will sound when it sits upon that pair of notes.

*

There's an old story of Mrs Kern and Mrs Hammerstein being at some social function, at which the hostess introduced Mrs Kern by saying: 'Her husband wrote "Ol' Man River".' Mrs Hammerstein corrected this misapprehension politely but firmly: 'It was *my* husband who wrote "Ol' Man River". Mrs Kern's husband wrote "Da-da-da-da".'

'You can't listen to an orchestra playing "Ol' Man River" without hearing Hammerstein's lyric and understanding what it's about,' says Herbert Kretzmer. 'It's a question of finding what Johnny Mercer called the sound of the music. You're trying to capture something as elusive as a sound which suggests a word from which, eventually, a complete lyric emerges.'

Mercer had a special knack for evocative images which were also aurally seductive – 'my huckleberry friend' in 'Moon River' – but that perfect union of words and music comes only when a lyricist is given a melody first. No composer tinkers with a 32-bar tune the way lyricists fiddle with the words. 'Alan Lerner,' says Charles Strouse, composer of *Annie*, 'was convinced that somewhere in the lexicon there was the right word for every situation. Let's say, "Man asks difficult question about songwriting." He'd say, "Somewhere there's a word just right for that." I'd say, "There's no such word", we'd finish the song and I'd move on to something else. Then he'd call up three weeks later and he'd have been ill for days trying to find that word, but that one word would make the song.'

Lerner was particularly proud of turning 'pavement' into one of the most joyous words in the language:

> I have often walked down this street before
> But the pavement always stayed beneath my feet before . . .

'The first requirement of a good lyric,' said Lerner, 'is good music.' P. G. Wodehouse would have agreed. With Kern, he comes close to what you'd think was a mutually exclusive combination: art songs for regular folks. For *Miss 1917* they wrote an oddly affecting ballad assembled from Tin Pan Alley clichés:

> It's a land of flowers
> And April showers
> With sunshine in between
> With roses blowing
> And rivers flowing
> 'Mid rushes growing green
> Where no-one hurries
> And no-one worries
> And life runs calm and slow
> And I wish some day
> I could find my way
> To The Land Where The Good Songs Go.

Kern and Wodehouse found the Land Where The Good Songs Go: Broadway musical comedy. The tradition they initiated is a long overdue vindication of the *Encyclopaedia Britannica*, whose definition of song Ira Gershwin liked to quote. This scholarly entry did not have the Broadway musical in mind, but it's Broadway that exemplifies it: 'Song is the joint art of words and music, two arts under emotional pressure coalescing into a third.'

Wodehouse's legacy is recognized officially in the Tony Awards each year. In opera, the score means the music. But at the Tonys the 'Best Score' award goes to the composer and lyricist; a score is music *and* words. And when it works, it works so well that to start disentangling the tune and the lyrics is to realize how firmly wedded they are.

'Which comes first? That's all baloney,' says Irving Caesar. 'Baloney! George Gershwin and I wrote "Swanee" in five minutes. Five minutes, I tell you! Now, when everything's happening that fast, who knows who does what to whom when?'

The Book

There's a story of a *Sound of Music* production meeting where someone nervously wondered whether the show wasn't just a teensy bit controversial. 'You mean,' asked Richard Rodgers, 'it might upset people who like Nazis?' That's Rodgers and Hammerstein for you: family entertainment, safe, undemanding, a sure thing for unadventurous touring managements in America, the sort of candy-coated schlock the British would have nothing but without government subsidy of the arts. Inaugurated by *Oklahoma!*, the Rodgers and Hammerstein partnership celebrated its 50th anniversary in 1993 as indestructible as ever – but then their entire catalogue seems to have been designed for elderly couples to celebrate anniversaries. Look at these guys in their every snapshot: sober neckties, white pocket handkerchiefs, grey-suited, greyer-haired provincial Rotarians flanking Mary Martin or Gertrude Lawrence as if they're presenting a Sales Clerk of the Month award. You'll have to do better than that if you want to be interviewed on a BBC arts show or be hailed in the fashionable prints as part of the *Zeitgeist*.

Oh, well. As they say on Broadway, nobody likes it but the public (the West End public too: in recent years *South Pacific*, *The King and I*, *The Sound of Music* and *Carousel* have all returned). But, even on Broadway, showfolk don't *love* Rodgers and Hammerstein the way they love Rodgers and his first writing partner. Rodgers and Hart is sassy, cynical, metropolitan: 'We'll have Manhattan', and to hell with the world that lies beyond, 'Way Out West On West End Avenue'. Rodgers and Hammerstein is either *way* out west or down east in Maine fishing villages peopled by all those dumb clucks whose favourite things include whiskers on kittens, bright copper kettles and two on the aisle for a junky *Sound of Music* tour starring someone who used to be in a sitcom. No wiseacre has to expend much effort demolishing Rodgers and Hammerstein; it's all in the play: *Oklahoma!*? 'The corn is as high as an elephant's eye'; *South Pacific*? 'Corny as Kansas in August'.

Yet even to hurl the songs back scornfully is to acknowledge their potency. What other dramatists have planted their lines so solidly in our lives? Oscar Hammerstein II *invented* the clichés of 'I'm In Love With A Wonderful Guy' – 'high as a flag on the Fourth of July' – and it's not his fault he did it so well that clichés is what they've become.

This is Hammerstein's revolution: he changed the question. 'What comes first – the music or the lyrics?' says Betty Comden. 'What comes first is the *book* – the character, the situation. You have a situation where a character is in a town and he's lonely, so you write "Lonely Town".'

She's citing her own fine ballad from *On the Town* (1944), a work heavily influenced by the previous season's *Oklahoma!* 'There was a phrase that was around at that time,' her director George Abbott told me, ' "the integrated musical". And they lived by it.'

It was Hammerstein who integrated the musical. Before him it was a careless rapture. In the 1910s Guy Bolton made some sort of sense of the plot and, for a librettist, earned a unique celebrity. As one anonymous critic wrote in *The New York Times*:

> This is the trio of musical fame
> Bolton and Wodehouse and Kern
> Better than anyone else you can name
> Bolton and Wodehouse and Kern . . .

What other librettist who didn't also write lyrics (like Hammerstein and later Lerner) took precedence over his partners? Herbert Fields didn't: we don't think of *A Connecticut Yankee* as being by Fields and Hart and Rodgers. Nor *West Side Story* as by Laurents and Sondheim and Bernstein. But Bolton deserves his credit. As Dorothy Parker wrote of *Oh, Lady! Lady!!*: 'Bolton and Wodehouse and Kern are my favourite indoor sport. I like the way they go about a musical comedy. I like the way that action slides casually into songs.'

Up to a point. Plots and numbers and characters were still interchangeable, and that's how audiences liked it. Essentially, there's one joke: wherever you are, Long Island or Texas or Zululand, you look at it through the jaundiced shades of Shubert Alley. The eponymous hero of *A Connecticut Yankee* finds himself in King Arthur's court surrounded by jousting knights and biddable ladies, and goes partying at Morgan Le Fay's castle, where a band is playing bad jazz.

'They are really finished musicians,' says Morgan Le Fay.

'They will be if they don't quit that,' says the Connecticut smartass. He has them dragged off and hanged. 'Gosh. That's a system that should never have been abolished.'

It's a good joke, but it's unambitious. Herb Fields has Mark Twain for source material and Rodgers and Hart for the songs, but you never feel he belongs in the same class. The gag illustrates the limits of twenties musical comedy: whatever was up for adaptation, it didn't musicalize the property so much as simply absorb it within the needs of a musical comedy. Kafka's *Metamorphosis* isn't dissimilar in premise to Mark Twain's *Connecticut Yankee*: instead of waking up in Arthurian Camelot, the guy wakes up and discovers he's a dung-beetle. Herb Fields was a professional: if you'd said to him 'Make a musical of *Metamorphosis*', he would have, but you can bet he'd have changed the dung-beetle to Otto the Wonder Poodle; he'd have made it . . . like a musical. 30 years later, Lerner and Loewe set to work in the same territory: T. H. White's *The Once and Future King*. But, instead of taking the source material and shoehorning it into the formula of musical comedy, they tried to convey its character in music. That's an important difference: as we've seen, early musicals were, like operetta, a location; it was Hammerstein who, in expanding their horizons, made them a form.

A Connecticut Yankee opened in November 1927. That season, the most crowded in Broadway history, saw the first nights of 264 new plays and musicals. On 26 December alone, there were 11 openings, and to cover them New York editors were forced to co-opt boxing and football reporters as drama critics – not, as Alan Jay Lerner liked to gloat, that anyone noticed the difference.

As for those 11 premières, Rudolf Friml's *The White Eagle* is typical: the Earl of Kerhill's brother is on the lam, holed up in the west disguised as a cowhand and romancing an Injun girl called Silverwing. Talented men wrote these shows (Vincent Youmans, the Gershwins) but they accepted implicitly the low ambitions of the genre, and were concerned mainly that you notice their contributions: this was, as Oscar Levant said, the classical period of popular music. So today 'The Best Things In Life Are Free' and ''S Wonderful' remain high-earning standards, while the shows from which they came – *Good News* and *Funny Face* – languish unrevived and unrevivable: the Golden Age of Theatre Song left us lotsa song but very little theatre.

The following night, 27 December, there were only two openings, a Philip Barry play and a musical by Jerome Kern and Oscar Hammerstein II – *Show Boat*. 'There's no explanation for *Show Boat*,' says James Hammerstein, Oscar's son. 'It came from nowhere in an era when silly musicals with silly books with silly Mitteleuropean comedians were the rule. You wrote the book around what your best songs were and hoped it would make sense. Not only did Jerry and my dad not do that, but they tried to embed the songs into the characters and the story.' It was the truthfulness of Edna Ferber's novel which attracted Kern and Hammerstein to the material. Operetta offered its sophisticated audience unfamiliar non-metropolitan locales – Arabian deserts, Balkan kingdoms – but almost always ended up trivializing and demeaning their inhabitants. At least musical comedy, preoccupied with country club idlers and bootleggers and purpose gals, was reasonably honest in its depiction of them. Hammerstein, a prototype showbiz liberal, wondered whether you could apply that honesty to less fashionable groups.

It's difficult to appreciate how lowly he was regarded before *Show Boat*. Journeyman librettist to Romberg and Friml, Hammerstein had never got to grips with the Jazz Age; he wasn't a droll rhymester like Gershwin and Hart, and, when he tried to pep it up, the results were embarrassing:

> Come On And Pet Me
> Why don't you pet me?
> Why don't you get me
> To let you pet me . . . ?
>
> I'd like to bask in
> Your fond caressin'
> You do the askin'
> I'll do the yessin' . . .

Vincent Youmans showed what he thought of that lyric by recycling the tune, with new words by Irving Caesar, as 'Sometimes I'm Happy'.

It was Hammerstein's misfortune to seek logic in frivolity. 'Dad was always puzzled by "Darktown Strutters' Ball",' says James. ' "I'll be down to get you in a taxi, honey", all that urgency, and then it's *tomorrow* night. He could never figure that out. He lived a lot of lyrics through.' He was especially puzzled by all those dance crazes – 'The Tickle-Toe', 'The Varsity Drag' – that promise to teach you the steps but never do. Years later, catching that month's hit on the radio, he was nonplussed by:

> Do the Hucklebuck
> Do the Hucklebuck
> If you don't know how to do it
> Then you're out of luck . . .

A man who looks for dramatic logic in 'The Darktown Strutters' Ball' is bound to find twenties musical comedy difficult. But, making the best of it, in 1925 Hammerstein, with Kern and Otto Harbach, sat down to write

Sunny. 'Charles Dillingham, the producer, had signed Cliff Edwards, who sang songs and played the ukulele and was known as Ukelele Ike,' he recalled. 'His contract required that he do his specialty between ten o'clock and ten fifteen! So we had to construct our story in such a way that Ukelele Ike could come out and perform during that time and still not interfere with the continuity. In addition to Marilyn Miller, the star, there was Jack Donahue, the famous dancing comedian, and there was Clifton Webb and Mary Hay, who were a leading dance team of the time, Joseph Cawthorn, a star comedian, Esther Howard, another, Paul Frawley, the leading juvenile. In addition to the orchestra in the pit we had also to take care of George Olsen's Dance Band on stage.'

Wow! Harbach and Hammerstein's plot – about a circus bareback rider in England who stows away on an ocean liner because she loves an American called Tom but then has to marry another American called Jim in order to disembark in New York – was, under the circumstances, a work of genius. It was also a huge hit and even produced a driving song in which Hammerstein proved he could rhyme with the best of 'em:

> Who
> Stole my heart away?
> Who
> Makes me dream all day?
> *Dreams* I *know* can *never* come *true*
> *Seems* as *though* I'll *ever* be *blue*!

How's that for a rhyme scheme?

But, with *Show Boat*, Hammerstein made himself something more important than a rhymester: the first dramatist of the American musical. When the songs started, the story didn't stop, but forged on, illuminating and enlarging. On that first night, the miscegenation scene had more impact, but 'Ol' Man River' is technically the more impressive: the suffering and resignation and bitterness of an entire race compressed into 24 taut lines, and so naturally that most people think it's a genuine Negro spiritual, as opposed to a showtune cooked up in 1927 by two guys who needed something for a spot in the First Act. Similarly, his very last song, 'Edelweiss', is invariably taken for a real Austrian folk-tune (to the extent that, at a state banquet at the White House, the orchestra played it for the Austrian President on the assumption that it was the national anthem). Hammerstein's is an unobtrusive craft, an artless art. Imagine the same number written by Lorenz Hart, full of contrived musical-comedy triple rhymes about giving your special *Fräulein* some edelweiss . . . so you can put your arms around her and *cradle* vice. With Hart, as with Cole Porter, you hear the lyricist, not the character.

Hammerstein's composer, Jerome Kern, had a higher reputation. But, even though he'd inaugurated a distinctively American school of musical comedy, these shows were still no more or less than a collection of songs which could, relatively painlessly, be interchanged with those in other works. *Show Boat* is the first true Broadway *score*. 'Jerry had *leitmotifs* that wove in and out,' says James Hammerstein, 'almost imperceptibly but terribly emotionally. When you hear the underscoring, you can tell what the scene's about. Jerry was a dramatist in music, and that's different from a songwriter.'

It's easy to make too much of *leitmotifs* and underscoring. 'Cut the kindergarten stuff,' George Abbott liked to tell composers who tried to explain the construction of their scores. But *Show Boat* isn't kindergarten stuff. In it Kern and Hammerstein managed an adroit union of the two schools of American musical: the sweep of operetta with the intimacy of musical comedy, the musicality of an operetta score with the naturalism of musical comedy lyric-writing. And, as the years unfold from the 1880s to 1927 and the fragrant ballads yield to raucous rags and jazz, *Show Boat* – the only Broadway epic – comes to represent the hurly-burly of America in its most rapid period of expansion, a period which saw the drift from rural roots towards the cities and the dilution of local folk art by a national culture disseminated by commercial interests. The river alone is immune: he jes' keeps rollin' along.

Show Boat defies all of Hammerstein's own rules: take a short story, preferably one that takes place within a few days. 'When I'm doing a musical,' says *Sunset Boulevard*'s Don Black, 'I always like a story with a clock on it' – that's to say, confined within a clearly delineated time frame. The classic example is *On the Town*, which is over and out within 24 hours, opening at dawn, wrapping up the following dawn. With Edna Ferber's novel, Hammerstein had half a century, and he organized it superbly: Act One, setting up the romance between Cap'n Andy's daughter Magnolia and the riverboat gambler Gaylord Ravenal, covers just a couple of weeks; Act Two is a cavalcade across the decades. This is good, clean theatrical layout. And, in Kern, Hammerstein found a composer who could tie it together: *Show Boat* has a slave chorale, a banjo tune, a coon song, a torch ballad – but it all sounds like Kern.

Like much of Ferber's work, the story has strong women and weak men. Kern and Hammerstein build this into the structure of the show, as the relationship between the principals, Gay and Noley, prompts distorting echoes, either comic (Cap'n Andy and his wife), tragic (Steve and Julie) or cross-racial (Joe and Queenie, the Negro couple).

The root song comes early in Act One when Magnolia meets Gay on the levee at Natchez. It's a gorgeous, pure, unforced melody.

> Only Make Believe
> I love you
> Only Make Believe
> That you love me . . .

The show boat is a boat of shows, of actors, so the two are play-acting, as if they're lovers in an old melodrama. Alas for them, though they profess it 'Make Believe', the sincerity of their feelings is all too plain. Kern gives it an operetta sensibility, including a notey, fluttering answering section for Magnolia just like Hanna's in *The Merry Widow* and, very unusually for this composer, in waltz time. In the verse, Hammerstein even provides a few operetta trills:

> The game o-of just supposi-ing
> Is the sweete-est game I kno-ow
> O-our dreams are mo-ore ro-omantic
> Than the world we see . . .

Broadway lyricists are not melisma men. They like songs to follow the cadences of speech, a note per syllable and long notes for important syllables. This is a good rule: in Sinatra's almost 60-year recording career, he's given melismas the bum's rush, won't go near 'em, thinks they're cheap and phoney. Today, in pop songs, with Barry White and Mariah Carey and a zillion others, we're awash in melismas: is 'love' a more emotional word for being stretched out to 'lu-u-u-u-u-u-urve'? This is fake soulfulness. In this as in many other respects, the rock era has returned us to operetta posturing. So, in letting real speech lapse here, in permitting insignificant monosyllables to twitter across two notes, the song signals that it's unreal – that the-eir dreams *are* mo-ore ro-omantic than the world, and that, if they follow them, there will be a price to pay. Here's something really radical: operetta with consequences. In Act Two, Gay gambles his money away, loses his home, abandons his child, leaves his wife to make a living in nightclubs . . . Kern and Hammerstein have taken the passion of operetta and anchored it in truth.

After the song, Noley and her friend Julie, the *Cotton Blossom*'s leading lady, are in the ship's black quarters with Queenie. They sing a coon song, 'Can't Help Lovin' That Man' – and, because Julie and Queenie are teaching it to Noley, you think it's just one of those 'prop songs' musicals have to fill out the time – a song presented not as a character's soliloquy, but just as a song, like 'Vilja' in *The Merry Widow*. As sung by Queenie to Jo across the kitchen table, it seems the stereotypical 'shif'less coon' routine for the umpteenth time, but Hammerstein makes it subtly real: Julie can't help lovin' Steve, Nola can't help lovin' Gay, and the sisterly singalong of Act One is transformed in Act Two into a shared recognition of fate.

The sheriff boards, and accuses Julie of having Negro blood, which means, in Mississippi, her marriage to a white man is against the law. But, alerted in advance, Steve has sucked some blood from her finger in full view of everybody else: he tells the sheriff he has 'more than a drop' of Nigra blood in him. The men are all for big dramatic gestures, but they can't stay the course. By Act Two, Steve has gone and Julie is a blousy lush who can only be cranked into life to sit atop the piano and sing 'Bill'. Another prop song, another song sung as a song, and yet Hammerstein again makes it real: she's singing about Bill, who's wonderful, but we all know it's really about Steve, who isn't. This is a Hammerstein lesson he doesn't often get credit for: the hoariest old convention can be freshened, stood on its head, made to *work*.

And then there's 'Ol' Man River', through whom the play is spectacularly, dramatically enlarged:

> Don't look up an' don't look down
> You don't dast make de white boss frown
> Bend yo' knees an' bow yo' head
> An' pull dat rope until yo're dead . . .

Show Boat doesn't claim to be 'about' racial injustice, but it shows how a popular musical can paint individual stories on a larger social canvas. *Miss Saigon*, to take one current example, is in direct descent from Kern and Hammerstein's trail-blazer. It courses through Broadway history, still current and, for those who want to hear, still giving lessons.

Oh, sure, you can say bits are creaky and melodramatic, but have you ever looked at the early Eugene O'Neill? How many American plays – straight or musical – from *before* 1927 are performed today? *Show Boat* is the most important work in American musical theatre: it sums up what's gone before and points the way ahead. And Hammerstein is the most important single figure, for similar reasons: he worked with Romberg and Kern, and he trained Stephen Sondheim.

*

Two weeks after *Show Boat*, it was business as usual with *Rosalie* – half a score by Romberg and Wodehouse, half a score by the Gershwins, half a plot based on Lindbergh's solo flight to Paris, half a plot inspired by Queen Marie of Romania's visit to America, glued together by Bill McGuire and Guy Bolton into a musical about the mythical kingdom of Romanza and produced on Broadway by Flo Ziegfeld for no other reason than that Rosalie was his mother's name. But why chide Wodehouse and the Gershwins and the rest when Hammerstein himself went straight back to operetta hokum? Nine months after *Show Boat*, he was reunited with Romberg for *The New Moon*. It is 1788, and, in the French colony of New Orleans, a nobleman wanted for murder is attempting to find ten stout-hearted men who will fight for the right to liberty. Hang on, though: wasn't New Orleans a *Spanish* colony in 1788? Who cares? It was as if *Show Boat* had never happened. Hammerstein had set new standards for musical theatre and then spent the next 16 years conspicuously failing to live up to them.

Book-writing in the twenties had been a specialist's activity: you get Fred Thompson or Guy Bolton or Herbert Fields. These men were consistent and reliable, but only within the narrow demands of a musical comedy book. Rodgers and Hart and Fields were a triumvirate, through *Dearest Enemy*, *The Girl Friend*, *Peggy-Ann*, *A Connecticut Yankee*, *Present Arms*, *Chee-Chee* . . . But, with the exception of *Annie, Get Your Gun*, Fields never changed: his last book was for *Redhead* in 1959, with Gwen Verdon and Bob Fosse, but it could have easily been his first. His more distinguished partners had great ambitions, but it's all comparative. *I Married an Angel* (1938) was set in Budapest, but Rodgers and Hart wanted to write a number about Radio City Music Hall.

'Why?' asked Joshua Logan, directing his first musical.

'We can't expect an audience to stay in Budapest all night,' said Hart.

'How do we explain it?' asked Logan.

'You don't,' said Rodgers. 'The less you explain, the happier the audiences are.'

Next, Hart decided he wanted the backdrop to be Dalíesque surrealism. Logan queried what Dalí had to do with Radio City.

'Nothing,' said Hart. 'But what's that got to do with it?'

Even their more disciplined shows are disfigured by this approach: 'Zip!', a song for a stripper with intellectual pretensions (*à la* Gypsy Rose Lee), may or may not be a good idea, but it certainly has nothing to do with *Pal Joey* and brings the play juddering to a halt. It doesn't advance the plot, it doesn't reveal character; it's a prop song whose dated topicality now rusts up that section of the show – notwithstanding its boldness as, in George Abbott's phrase, 'the first musical with a hero who was a villain'.

It was Hammerstein's work on musical plays and Abbott's work on musical comedies that made book-writing an activity beyond hack work. In their wake, distinguished figures from Ogden Nash to Truman Capote have written books for musicals, but most have been glad to return to the comparatively sane worlds of novels, plays, TV and motion pictures. It's a world where experience doesn't seem to count, where every show is your first outing. In the years following *Show Boat*, Hammerstein bumped his way through *The Gang's All Here*, *Free for All*, and *East Wind* (set in Indo-China 60 years before *Miss Saigon*); and *May Wine* (a Viennese psychiatrist loves the penniless Baroness von Schlewitz, who, unfortunately, prefers Baron Adelhorst); and *Gentlemen Unafraid*, *Very Warm for May*, *Sunny River* – just as Alan Jay Lerner wrote the book for *My Fair Lady* and then (in descending order of competence) those for *Camelot*, *Coco* and *Carmelina*. And these are the guys who are *good* at musicals. When, at last, he returned to form, and had smash notices to prove it, Hammerstein took an ad in *Variety* listing his long line of spectacular flops: 'I've done it before and I can do it again!'

After *Show Boat*, musical theatre reverted to happy inanities, with occasional hints of something more ambitious: *Of Thee I Sing*, *Porgy and Bess*, *Pal Joey*, *Lady in the Dark* . . . But, because everyone had gone back to their bad old ways, Hammerstein – like Flight Lieutenant Jerry Rawlings in Ghana or Colonel Sitiveni Rabuka in Fiji – was forced to stage his revolution a second time – or, if you like, having already served as John the Baptist, was forced also to play Jesus.

'*Oklahoma!* changed everything,' says Mark Bramble, librettist of *42nd Street* and *Barnum*. 'Oscar Hammerstein created a new kind of structure for a musical libretto which integrated all the elements – dialogue, lyrics, music, dance.' *Show Boat* was too epic, too special to impart lessons. But *Oklahoma!* is *Show Boat* discipline applied to basic boy-meets-girl: drama out of cliché. It's a story about who'll take whom to a picnic, set in Oklahoma Territory on the edge of statehood. As with *Show Boat*, it came from nowhere – famously dismissed by Mike Todd out-of-town as 'no gags, no gals, no chance'. Actually, there *were* gags – Ado

Annie and her peddler are pretty funny – and gals, too – Jud Fry's dirty postcards rise lasciviously to life in the dream ballet. But these were gags and gals tied to the plot, and Todd couldn't see the point of that. The big hit in '43 was supposed to be *Something for the Boys*; gags, gals, Cole Porter songs, Ethel Merman belting, and, as there has to be a story, how about three guys from back east inheriting property in Texas? We can make all the usual Broadway jokes about hicks out west ('where seldom is heard an intelligent word' – Lorenz Hart) and, for local colour, Cole can write a song for the burghers of San Antonio about famous Texans:

> Say, in a sweater
> Who looks better
> Than Missus Sheridan's Ann?

You're looking at the San Antonians, but you're hearing Porter's penthouse smarts.

Oklahoma! is set one state north of Cole Porter's Texas, but it's another world.

It seems obvious now, but it wasn't then: let the story dictate the tone, let the characters find their own singing voice: – 'I'm Just A Girl Who Cain't Say No' for freewheeling, unaffected Ado Annie; for respectable Laurey, 'People Will Say We're In Love', a song about not being in love that tells the audience she is. Those who scoff at R&H predictability ought to look more closely. These boys make the extended dream ballet *de rigueur* on Broadway ('Laurey Makes Up Her Mind') and then, in *South Pacific*, they dispense with the choreographer altogether, staging 'Nothin' Like A Dame' so that the horny, frustrated sailors just stomp about like horny, frustrated sailors. Predictable? Before Hammerstein the term 'musical' referred to the content as well as the form: regardless of story, it meant gags and gals and tap-dancing; 'Broadway' was a point of view, a sensibility. After Hammerstein, content dictated form, and Broadway was only a venue.

Even the despised happy endings are, in fact, hopeful endings: the King (of Siam) is dead, long live the King. 'I see plays and read books that emphasize the seamy side of life, and the frenetic side and the tragic side,' said Hammerstein, 'and I don't deny the existence of the tragic and the frenetic. But I say that somebody has to keep saying that that isn't all that there is to life . . . We're very likely to get thrown off our balance if we have such a preponderance of artists expressing the "wasteland" philosophy.' Rodgers and Hammerstein's America, with its sense of building community through commitment and justice, is art as aspiration: this is what we'd like it to be. And that's part of the problem. *Oklahoma!*, *Carousel*, *South Pacific* . . . These shows are radical, revolutionary, trail-blazing, yet they're not flawed masterpieces like Weill (*Street Scene*) or Bernstein (*Candide*) or Sondheim (pretty well everything). They're just regular masterpieces that stack up a ton of money. And how can anything that popular be that good? The receipts of *The Sound of Music* alone have obliterated everything else – like Jud Fry, the hired hand with the dirty pictures fuelling his sexual frustration, fantasizing about Laurey in his 'Lonely Room':

> Her long, yeller hair
> Falls across my face
> Just like the rain in a storm . . .

This isn't folksy gingham-check sentimentality, but a flesh-creeping glimpse of the darker realities of rural existence, culminating in a tense, taut, nasty subversion of that most innocent of rustic traditions – the auction of the girls' picnic hampers to the boys. This is boy-meets-girl for real. Rodgers and Hammerstein are Broadway's revolutionaries – even though, in defiance of Scott Fitzgerald's dictum that there are no second acts in American lives, they weren't angry young men but painstaking middle-aged men.

Larry Hart, who turned down *Oklahoma!* because he thought it was dull, understood. Alan Jay Lerner once told me of being with Hart and Fritz Loewe during a wartime blackout. Loewe switched on a radio: it was playing something from *Oklahoma!* and Hart's cigar puffed furiously in the dark. Loewe tuned to another station, and another: all were playing *Oklahoma!* and Hart's cigar puffed brighter and brighter. Eventually, they found a station playing some other tune, and Hart's cigar subsided. When the lights came on, Hart continued the conversation as though nothing had happened, but Lerner described it to me as a man confronting his own obsolescence. Rodgers and Hart were kids doing the show in a barn; with Hammerstein, the musical grew up.

The Jews

In *Gypsy*, Mama Rose finally gets a chance to audition her kids for Mr Goldstone, the chief booker on the Orpheum vaudeville circuit. As Rose sees it:

> There are good stones and bad stones
> And kerbstones and Gladstones
> And touchstones and such stones as them
> There are big stones and small stones
> And rhinestones and gallstones
> But Goldstone is a gem!

The image of the American showbusiness Jew seems indestructible, a favourite stereotype in a thousand comedy sketches, plays and movies. Behind the scenes, alas, he appears to have had his day: Hollywood's head honchos are the unflamboyant Japanese; the most influential multimedia mogul is a born-again Christian from Australia; a Welshman, of all things, became president of CBS television. Only Broadway has kept the faith – as the most casual round-up of my near namesakes will illustrate. To paraphrase Rose:

> There are Bernsteins and Blitzsteins
> And flop Steins and hit Steins
> And Hammersteins with Mama Steins and Pops
> There are Feinsteins and Fiersteins
> And Bornsteins and mere Steins
> And Jule Styne is tops!

Bern- is Leonard, composer of *West Side Story*; Blitz- is Marc, composer but best known as lyricist of the English-language *Threepenny Opera*; Hammer- is various Oscars and Williams with the odd Arthur and James; Fein- is Michael, Ira Gershwin's archivist turned Broadway cabaret darling; Fier- is Harvey, librettist of *La Cage aux Folles*; Born- is Saul, Irving Berlin's publishing partner; and Jule Styne is the composer of *Gypsy* and a personal favourite of mine. The 'mere' Steins? They include Joseph, co-writer of *Fiddler on the Roof*; Gertrude, playwright and occasional lyricist; and Leon, librettist of *The Merry Widow* and a reminder that musical theatre Jews predate Broadway.

How does a nation express itself? In Habsburg Austria, it was operetta and waltz time. But, if empire and operetta were two hearts beating as one, who was plucking the strings? Kálmán was Jewish, so was Grünbaum; even the Strausses came from a Jewish family. After the *Anschluss* the Nazis decided to Aryanize show business. *White Horse Inn* was unacceptable because of its Jewish authors, so Fred Raimund was signed to write *Season in Salzburg*: it had all the yodelling and other hokum of *White Horse Inn*, but no Jews. It was never anything other than a poor substitute.

Adolf Hitler took a personal interest in these matters. As a young man, he had returned again and again to sit in the gallery during the long run of *The Merry Widow*, and his love for the work never diminished, despite the fact that both librettists were Jewish, as was the composer's wife. Lehár was Hitler's favourite musician and thus untouchable, but his collaborators weren't so lucky. His librettist Fritz Löhner-Beda died in a concentration camp in 1942, the same year his *Land of Smiles* was produced with Lehár conducting. To the end, he expected his partner to intercede and save him. But Lehár either couldn't help, or wouldn't help. Recalling the awards the old man had accepted from the Nazis, Alan Jay Lerner said: 'To this day, when I am transported by the music of Franz Lehár, my glass of champagne is rimmed with aloes' – a fine operetta image. Whatever the truth, after Lehár's death there was no more champagne. In removing Jews from the theatre, the Nazis ended up throwing the bathwater out with the babies. Result: end of operetta; death of Austria's musical voice. Those crowds of happy Austrians cheering Hitler into Vienna were hailing the death of their own culture.

At the turn of the century, Vienna and New York were not dissimilar: two teeming cities, both high-density human experiments in multiculturalism. We know about the pogroms that drove the Jews from Eastern Europe to America – if only because we've seen *Fiddler on the Roof*. But less easy to explain is how so many of those Jewish immigrants jostling together on New York's Lower East Side made the journey uptown to Broadway. One man's progress became the American dream incarnate: as George M. Cohan introduced him at the Friars Club, 'a Jew boy that has named himself after an English actor and a German city' – Irving Berlin.

'Irving's seven years older than me,' says Irving Caesar, lyricist of

'Swanee' and 'Tea For Two', 'but we both grew up on the Lower East Side, like a lot of songwriters – Kalmar and Ruby, the Gershwins. Our parents arrived from Europe at Ellis Island and they just settled in the ghetto – those were the days before immigrants started moving north or out to Brooklyn. I've never known why so many songwriters came from the East Side, but I will say this. The Jewish immigrants always liked to rhyme. You'd call out to one, "Izzy", and he'd say, "I'm not busy." Most of us learned from the little Jewish patter songs of those days. Irving started as a singing waiter – he worked at Nigger Mike's in Chinatown.' Nigger Mike was a swarthy Russian Jew, whose café was underneath a whorehouse run by Chinatown Gertie. Nigger Mike? Chinatown Gertie? In those days, at least in that part of the city, everyone was a minority. The titles of Berlin's early songs, novelty numbers about whichever ethnic group was in fashion, tell their own story: 'Marie From Sunny Italy', 'Oh, How That German Could Love'. He wrote minstrel songs, too – 'I Want To Be In Dixie' was introduced by a Jewish vaudevillian in blackface. Minstrelsy as a metaphor: for many Jews, blackface was a code, one race's pain speaking in the form of another. There were double acts like 'The Hebrew and the Coon': the Hebrew was the genuine article; the coon was Al Jolson. Uniquely excluded from the Ellis Island myths, America's blacks do not, understandably, subscribe to the view that cultural appropriation is the sincerest form of flattery.

But, on Broadway, the Jews prospered. By the 1860s, 'Hebrew citizens' were assiduous theatregoers, as they are to this day; and, as they also remain, Jews were becoming prominent backstage, too: Ford's Theatre, to name one example, was run by the Jewish H. B. Phillips until the assassination of Lincoln forced its closure. Later came Belasco and the Shuberts and the Hammersteins. You have to search pretty hard for comments as sour as that of John Corbin, a *New York Times* critic, who complained in 1933 that 'for years now, Jewish playwrights have repeatedly attempted the thing Edmund Burke declared impossible: the indictment of the American people entire.' In fact, Broadway's Jews gave the American people their voice. As we've seen, where his predecessors like Reginald De Koven and Victor Herbert still deferred to the lush grandiloquence of European art song, it was Jerome Kern who, cautiously, accidentally even, Americanized the theatre song. He and Oscar Hammerstein were at one time planning a musicalization of Donn Byrne's *Messer Marco Polo*. 'Here is a story laid in China about an Italian and told by an Irishman,' said Hammerstein. 'What kind of music are you going to write?'

Kern replied: 'It'll be good Jewish music.'

By then, good Jewish music was good American music. The pioneer Alleymen had been Jewish: Charles K. Harris, Edward Marks, Monroe Rosenfeld. And before that there was Henry Russell, an English Jew who lived in America and wrote, among others, 'Woodman, Spare That Tree' and 'A Life On The Ocean Wave'. But it was Kern, Berlin, Gershwin, Rodgers, Arlen and all who followed who established the brassy/modest, raucous/tender vernacular of Broadway song. Cole Porter, the token Wasp, took longer to hit the big time. Moneyed and Protestant, he felt he would never be able to write genuinely popular songs, until one day he told Rodgers that he'd stumbled on the formula. 'What is it?' asked Rodgers.

'Simplicity itself,' said Porter. 'I'll write Jewish tunes.'

And so, in a way, he did. Except for Arthur Schwartz ('Dancing In The Dark') and some of Sigmund Romberg ('Softly As In A Morning Sunrise'), Porter was the only Broadway composer to write in the minor key – brooding chromatic sinuous melodies that warmed and deepened his nonchalant lyrics. That's the magic ingredient many other exhibitionist rhymesters miss, and which kept him in business from 1929 to the late fifties. As Rodgers noted, 'It is surely one of the ironies of the musical theatre that, despite the abundance of Jewish composers, the one who has written the most enduring "Jewish" music should be an Episcopalian millionaire who was born on a farm in Peru, Indiana.'

At which point perhaps we should consider what we mean by 'Jewish' music. The first talking picture, *The Jazz Singer*, is about a cantor's son (and in what other country could that have happened in 1927?) who becomes a successful 'jazz' singer. It's an old plot: the guy who embraces popular entertainment and thereby turns his back on his own culture. But maybe popular entertainment *is* his own culture. The definitive work in this field is by A. Z. Idelsohn who, in a survey of Jewish folk-song from Eastern Europe (which is where most New York songwriters, or their parents, came from) observes that 88 per cent of this traditional music uses 'the minor scale or at least has minor character' – hence, Cole Porter's Jewish tunes. We can look elsewhere for 'Jewishness' in America's music, too: in the 'blue notes' of Gershwin's showtunes and, most famously, his *Rhapsody*, an almost organic soundtrack of the city, as Woody Allen recognized in his film *Manhattan*. A 'blue note' is the third, fifth or seventh degree of the scale, with its pitch tweaked slightly to give it a bluesy, jazzy tinge. The minor third can be a 'blue note' but, in its broader sense, it's also characteristic of Jewish folk-song. It's an interval you find all over the score of *Porgy and Bess*, in 'My Man's Gone Now', 'It Ain't Necessarily

So' and several other songs: yes, the score sounds bluesy and southern and Catfish Row on a lazy summer day, but, if you set it in Eastern Europe, you'd realize also how Jewish it sounds. ''S Wonderful' is a minor third tune, and apparently lifted from 'Noah's Teive', a song in Abraham Goldfaden's Second Avenue Yiddisher operetta *Akeidas Izchok* (1908): instead of ''S Wonderful, 's marvellous', they sang '*Kum zu mir in Teive arein*' (Come to me in the ark). 'Funny Face' is built on minor thirds, little triple see-saws beginning with G and B flat:

> I love
> Your fun-
> -ny face.

The harmony makes it less obviously Jewish. However, I can't resist quoting Idelsohn's stupendous (ten-volume) *Thesaurus of Hebrew-Oriental Melodies*: 'The Jewish folk has never attempted to add harmonic combinations to its music. The song remains for single voice. In all likelihood because of his Oriental origin, the Jew prefers melody. To him, music means melody, means a *succession* rather than a *combination* of tones.'

It's a provocative theory: as far as American song is concerned, you can find plenty of harmonic invention in Kern and (perhaps more surprisingly) Berlin. But at heart Idelsohn is right: Christianity has produced great choral music; the Jews prefer the solo cantor. Kern believed that the true test of a song was that, if you tapped it out on the piano with one finger, it still sounded good: 'Long Ago And Far Away' passes, as does 'They Didn't Believe Me' and 'The Way You Look Tonight'. I'm not sure how many of the classical gang you could say that of. But it does get to the crux of the difference between Broadway and the standard song, on the one hand, and rock'n'classics, on the other.

Berlin, it's worth remembering, played the piano terribly in one key only (F sharp), never actually *wrote* a note but dictated his tunes to an amanuensis and anyway only became a composer because he misunder-stood a publisher's assignment: asked to supply a lyric, he assumed he had to write the melody as well. Yet, a few days after his death in 1989, at a get-together of British and American songsmiths, I heard Berlin hailed as one of the greatest composers of the century by both Morton Gould, highly trained writer of symphonies and concertos, and Phil Collins, the well-known rock star. Whatever you think of their respective fields, both men have mastered them totally: the conservatory-trained composer calls it orchestration, the rock'n'roller record production, but both believe their job is to colour a finished sound portrait from which any transcription or cover version is a deviation. Surely, by comparison the untrained tune-dictator is no composer at all.

'Some composers think in terms of the piano, but I pay little attention to it,' Victor Herbert once said. 'I consider all the resources of orchestra and voice given me to work with. If I did not work out my own orchestrations, it would be as if a painter conceived the idea of a picture and then had someone else paint it.' But, after Herbert, that's precisely what happened: the only self-orchestrating composer on Broadway in the last 75 years has been Kurt Weill. Otherwise by operatic standards, Broadway 'composers' have had a very light load, assisted by a platoon of orchestrators, vocal arrangers and dance arrangers. Some writers, like Jule Styne and Stephen Sondheim, work very closely with their orchestrators; some supply three-stave voice-and-piano copies; others just lead sheets (melody line plus chord indications) with some sort of vague instruction ('In the style of Tchaikowsky,' the orchestrator Max Rabinowitz was once told); some fellows tap out the tunes on toy xylophones; others whistle – Irving Caesar whistled an extraordinary long-lined melody to 'If I Forget You' and was so taken by its success that he then whistle-composed an entire cantata, which was rather less successful. But all recognize that on Broadway the composer is the guy who comes up with the tunes. You can be taught to notate and score, but no conservatory in the world can tell you how to create memorable melodies. Victor Herbert once tried to get Berlin to take composition lessons, on the grounds that, if he wanted to develop his talents, he'd need some formal training. Berlin stuck it for two days before he wised up. 'That sonofabitch,' he said. 'Instead of doing this, I could be writing songs.'

Was it coincidence that the arrival of the Jews in Tin Pan Alley and on Broadway also saw the birth of the 'standard' song? Or did some deep, instinctive understanding of their inheritance lead them to create works which pared composition to the essence? Idelsohn's description of Jewish folk music is virtually a definition of the 'standard': a song for single voice, built on melody – a melody so muscular that it shrugs off the pop fashions of the day and endures for decades. Bronski Beat's version of 'It Ain't Necessarily So' is nothing like *Porgy and Bess*, and U2's 'Night And Day' is a world away from Fred Astaire in *The Gay Divorce*. There are a million other examples: Broadway songs which have their keys abandoned, harmonies muddied, signatures changed and phrases extended (pop versions of 'Maria' from *West Side Story* usually stretch, much to Leonard Bernstein's irritation, the opening section from seven bars to eight), and yet survive, apparently indestructible. A standard is not an art song: nobody does Schubert as a bossa nova. But the principles underlying traditional Jewish music seem to have been inherited by their Broadway descendants.

We think we can hear these elements in the songs of the city, in the plaintive moans and blue notes. But the supposedly urban Jews gave the mountains and prairies *their* soundtrack, too. Even today, northern New England, where I happen to live, is a vast swathe of Baptists and Congregationalists, among whom even an Episcopalian seems exotic. Yet who would deny the authenticity of Hammerstein's poetry for *Carousel*, whether lyrical and capering ('That Was A Real Nice Clambake') or dark and brooding:

> You can't hear a sound – not the turn of a leaf
> Nor the fall of a wave hittin' the sand
> The tide's creepin' up on the beach like a thief
> Afraid to get caught stealin' the land . . .

Strictly speaking, Rodgers and Hammerstein's *Oklahoma!* may be no more truthful than Gershwin and Caesar's 'Swanee', written when neither man had been further south than Canal Street, but R&H is so affecting, we *wish* it were true. I saw it at first-hand in Oklahoma City in April 1995.

'You're here for the bomb, right?' said the guy at the gas station.

Actually, no. Unlike every other out-of-towner, I'm not there for the bomb. I'm in Oklahoma for the pre-Broadway try-out of a new musical. But that's as good a reason as any – let's face it, the only thing anyone knows about Oklahoma is that it's a musical:

> Ooooooooooooklahoma
> Where the wind comes sweeping down the plain . . .

The wind was unusually still on the Oklahoma plain that week. No bright golden haze on the medder, just rain, which washed out Saturday's '89er Day parades. But on Monday the temperatures started to climb – up into the sixties, pushing seventy, still no wind – and downtown, two or three blocks away, we could all smell the decomposing bodies. The bomb that shattered the Alfred P. Murrah Federal Building also shattered Oklahoma's self-image – an image created, in large part, by a musical.

Anyone who thinks Rodgers and Hammerstein present an impossibly sugar-coated view of human nature should have been sitting in the lobby of my inn two days after the blast when an obviously distraught woman came in and hugged the plump, mumsy innkeeper. She was a paediatrician and she'd seen three of her patients from the Federal Building crèche die that morning: for an Oklahoman doctor, that's a lot of dead kids. 'I need to be somewhere where I feel safe, Phyllis,' she said. Phyllis went and put on some coffee – '89er blend.

As even the most casually briefed network anchor could have told you that week, '89ers are the pioneers of the first Oklahoma Territory land-rush, the inspiration for R&H:

> We know we belong to the land
> And the land we belong to is grand!

To Phyllis, the '89ers are virtually arrivistes: her great-great-great-grandfather was trading (and consorting) with the Chickasaw Indians in the 1850s. Like everyone else, she was surprised to hear, as the media insisted in the immediate aftermath of the bomb, that Oklahoma is a hotbed of Islamic Fundamendalist groups. But even Rodgers and Hammerstein understood that there was more to the state than farmers and cowmen: Ado Annie, the girl who cain't say no, is much taken by a pedlar called Ali Hakim.

I wouldn't have given much for his chances in the two days after the blast. Every rangy, leathery, stump-toothed good ol' boy at every sports bar volunteered the line: 'Those fellers better hope the cops find 'em before we do.' But, as it turned out, the feller the good ol' boys were so keen to exercise natural justice on was a good ol' boy himself who also believed, to devastating effect, in natural justice. As for the Islamic Fundamendal-ists, it seems that in Oklahoma most of the Muslims are black and most of the Arabs are Christian.

'I feel terr'ble,' said Lori, a waitress at Hooters and near-namesake of *Oklahoma!*'s heroine. 'I feel like I jes' wanna 'pologize to anyone of Muslim or Islam descent or whatever they are. I swore if an Islam person were to come in here, I weren't gonna serve him.'

I was amazed: even the Oklahoma bombing was operating to a Hammerstein plot. For what could be more quintessentially Hammer-steinian than that we should learn not to rush to judgment on the basis of a man's skin colour?

Oklahoma! is a romanticized Oklahoma. Let's be frank: the place is a nondescript urban sprawl in the middle of a dreary plain. But my memory of those few days is very clear: Oklahomans were distraught that their image had been taken away from them – that, thanks to a couple of crazies with a ton of explosive fertilizer, their state's name now brought to mind not the surrey with the fringe on top but the lunatic fringe with the slurry on tap. As much as they might quibble with a detail here or there, they wouldn't dissent from Rodgers and Hammerstein's view of them: two big-town showbiz Jews (though Hammerstein was raised as a Christian) who knew nothing of their state and their lives had either managed to capture something of their essence or had invented such a seductive alternative that, in its darkest hour, Oklahoma was determined to measure up to it. This is a state where the licence plates offer the same ringing affirmation as R&H's title song: 'Oklahoma OK!' And, in the week after the bomb, more than anything else, everyone was at pains to prove that Oklahoma was still OK – still worthy of Rodgers and Hammerstein.

*

Observational or aspirational, the most potent musical Americana is Jewish. Irving Berlin understood. He knew about anti-Semitism: his marriage to Ellin Mackay resulted in her expulsion from the Social Register. 'Irving Berlin,' said the editor, 'has no place in society' – an unconscious echo of Jerome Kern's response when asked to assess Berlin's place in American music: 'Irving Berlin has no *place* in American music. He *is* American music.' Today, the seasons turn to Berlin anthems, to 'Easter Parade' and 'God Bless America' and 'White Christmas'. As a child in New York, Berlin would skip across the street from his orthodox Jewish home to his neighbours, the O'Haras, to play under the Christmas tree and eat the non-kosher food. They had white Christmases in Temun, Siberia, where he was born, but it's not about the weather: a white Russian Christmas wouldn't be the same.

This is America's songwriter: not a Tin Pan Alley tunesmith, not a Hollywood vehicle man, not an upscale Broadway dramatist – but all those and more; if 'How Deep Is The Ocean?' has become the property of tremulous Rainbow Room chanteuses, well, according to that grizzled old leftie Pete Seeger, 'Blue Skies' is a true American folk-song. Yet, precisely because of its universal appeal, the Berlin *oeuvre* seems to have floated free of its creator: in becoming America's soundtrack, it ceased to be his. In the long twilight of his life, with loyal retainers holding the world at bay, even the known facts took on mythic status, all the clichés of Ellis Island and the Lower East Side rolled into one all-purpose never-to-be-made Hollywood biotuner: little Izzy Baline from Siberia who saw the Cossacks raze his village; the singing waiter who turned his hand to novelty songs; the Tin Pan Alley Jew boy who set his heart on a society bride . . . His life became as emblematic as his catalogue. And, because these are the songs everyone got married to, went to war to, it's always assumed that's how they were written, by an Alley opportunist with an eye to the main chance. We forget how much of himself is in those hits.

'Blue Skies' was composed for his first child, Mary Ellin, at her birth. For his son, there was 'My Little Feller', actually written for Al Jolson's second talkie but coinciding with the arrival of Irving Junior in December 1928:

> Sweet as can be
> Climbing on my knee
> Wait'll you see
> My Little Feller . . .

But Jolson threw the song out in favour of 'Sonny Boy' and Irving Junior died three weeks later on Christmas Day. Does that cast the sentiments of 'White Christmas' in a different light? The song is no jingle; it has a dark chromatic phrase, a daring melodic line, and a plangent, wistful quality: it is, in more ways than one, a Jewish Christmas song. Afterwards, every 24 December, while the rest of America was listening to 'White Christmas', the Berlins would explain to their daughters that they had some last-minute preparations to take care of, leave the house and, as the sisters found out many years later, lay flowers on the grave of the baby brother they never knew they had. When the girls grew up and left home, Irving Berlin, a symbol of the American Christmas, gave up celebrating it: 'We both hated Christmas,' Mrs Berlin said later. 'We only did it for you children.'

Was Berlin ever bitter? Did he curse his uncanny ability to articulate perfectly the sentiments of his compatriots, even as fate deprived him of the possibility of sharing them? A pioneer of the inclusive secular American Christmas, Berlin ended his life as an agnostic. About America he had few doubts, and in his songs he expressed his feelings simply and honestly. Only he, alone among the greats, could have written without embarrassment:

> God Bless America
> Land that I love . . .

Not everyone felt as grateful. His wife's 18-year-old sister moved in with a Nazi diplomat and proudly showed the composer her charm bracelet and its diamond swastika. Throughout his life, fate seemed deter-mined to test to the limit Berlin's faith in both his adopted land and in the simple certainties of popular song. One of his early numbers was 'I'll See You In C-U-B-A'. In Cuba, on their honeymoon in 1912, his first wife contracted typhoid fever and died, leaving Berlin to pour out his feelings in his most personal ballad to date, 'When I Lost You'. His second courtship – the cantor's son and the society girl – was played out to those sensuous twenties waltzes, from their first meeting ('What'll I Do?') through an enforced separation ('All Alone').

Clarence Mackay hires round-the-clock detectives to catch this unsuitable upstart in bed with some chorine or in an opium den; he throws a party for the Prince of Wales and tells the guards to make sure Berlin doesn't get in. But, in one sense, Berlin has already penetrated the sacred precincts: the Prince asks Ellin Mackay to dance; they waltz dazzlingly . . . but what's the orchestra playing?

> What'll I do
> When you
> Are far away
> And I am blue . . .

It's a nice image, both romantic and personal but also capturing something of the subversive, democratic quality of popular music. Poor old Clarence Mackay: he never stood a chance. After their elopement, he disinherited his daughter, and Berlin gave her the royalties of his latest song as a wedding present:

> I'll be loving you
> Always . . .

At the time the biggest hit on Broadway was an execrable play by Anne Nichols about a Jewish boy and a Catholic girl. It was much mocked but it looked as if it would run for ever; as Rodgers and Hart wrote:

> Our future babies
> We'll take to *Abie's*
> *Irish Rose*
> Let's hope they'll live to see
> It close . . .

It's easy to laugh. But just because the corn is high doesn't mean it isn't true: the romance of Irving and Ellin Berlin is *Abie's Irish Rose* with a bigger budget and a fabulous score. And you could only play it in America: nobody staged *Abie's Irish Rose* in Europe.

*

The Habsburg experiment in melting-pot culture ended in failure. We forget that in a society of many races and religions, of many private traditions, a common public culture is even more important. That's what Berlin gave to his adopted homeland. Perhaps the Yankees took the sleigh rides and winter wonderlands for granted. You had to have grown up on the Lower East Side, with deeply ingrained folk memories of other crueller landscapes, to see (like Mitchell Parish) that:

> It's a happy feeling nothing in the world can buy
> As they pass around the coffee and the pumpkin pie . . .

Whether American audiences know or care about the Jewish contribution to their culture is a moot point. But it's fitting that the show that marked the end of the Golden Age should have been specifically Jewish, almost a piece of collective autobiography, a farewell to the world those Lower East Siders left behind: *Fiddler on the Roof*. Even after its success on Broadway, the creators were advised that it was 'too Jewish' for London, for Europe, for anywhere except New York and its Jewish theatre parties. They were wrong every time. During the Tokyo run, a fan of the show came up to the librettist Joseph Stein and marvelled that the show could ever have worked in America because 'it is so Japanese'. Yes, it is. It's about Jews in the far-away dim and distant Russian Empire, but it's also about tradition and change – and that's Japanese, and Dutch, and Australian. On Broadway, the Jews universalized their culture.

But musicals are such an artless art that the better you do your job, the less credit you get. I wouldn't mention this except in the light of *Corinna Corinna*, a 1994 movie about cross-racial romance in the fifties: Ray Liotta is a nice Jewish boy, Whoopi Goldberg his coloured nanny – sort of *Guess Who's Cooking the Dinner?* The final image is of the non-approving Yiddisher momma being dragged reluctantly into a spiritual. It's a familiar assumption that hip black music liberates uptight honkies and hymies: Ray and Whoopi are brought together by their shared pleasure in Louis Armstrong growling 'You Go To My Head'. Okay, Satchmo sings it fine, but who *wrote* the damn thing? The great American song literature is mostly by Jews, but they're not Jewish songs; they're songs for everyone.

I'm not saying the best black records are by Jewish songwriters. Or, if I am, let's open it up a bit: the best Nazi song is also by Jewish songwriters. As with 'Ol' Man River', when *Cabaret* called for an ostensibly innocent pastoral hymn to German nationalism, the boys turned in such a plausible *doppelgänger* that it was immediately denounced as a grossly offensive

Nazi anthem. 'The accusations against "Tomorrow Belongs To Me" made me very angry,' says Fred Ebb. ' "I knew that song as a child," one man had the audacity to tell me. A rabbinical person wrote to me saying he had absolute proof it was a Nazi song.' It wasn't: it was written in the mid-sixties for a Broadway musical. But today it's the only Nazi song we all know: on election night 1987, when British TV's satirical puppet show *Spitting Image* decided to draw some crass parallels between Mrs Thatcher and another strong leader, they opted to show the Tories singing not the *Horst Wessel* song but 'Tomorrow Belongs To Me' – secure in the knowledge that we'd all get the joke.

In *Cabaret*, we first hear the song sung by the waiters at the Kit Kat Klub as they clear the tables at the end of the day: it's beguilingly innocent. Only at the end do we see the swastikas, only later do we hear the martial tempo rise inexorably from within that bucolic ballad. 'What's really awful,' says John Kander, 'is when it's taken for what it *doesn't* mean. I can remember a Jewish boys' camp calling us excitedly for permission to use the song in their camp show. I thought to myself, I don't think they quite get this.'

As Mel Brooks' *Springtime for Hitler* recognized, musical theatre and Nazism have certain qualities in common: Hitler's Germany is a bad musical – crudely manipulative, robotically choreographed, reducing individual characters to one faceless chorus performing in unison. Still, you'd have thought the subject beyond the vocabulary of the form – until *Cabaret* gave it a go. 'If You Could See Her Through My Eyes,' sings Joel Grey as he dances with a tutu-ed gorilla. But it's the final line, hissed by the leering Emcee to the audience, that tells you what the number's really about:

> If You Could See Her Through My Eyes . . .
> She wouldn't look Jewish at all.

During *Cabaret*'s try-out in Boston, a rabbi wrote to the authors saying that the ghosts of six million Jews were begging them not to use that last line. More pressingly, real live theatre parties were considering cancelling their bookings. 'It was the first show where we had a crack at success – not just John and me, but Hal Prince, too – and we were all more frightened than we might be today,' says Fred Ebb. 'But they were threatening to close us down before we opened, taking ads out accusing us of anti-Semitism. So, because of the pressure, I changed the punchline to what I thought was a very weak line. I'd thought our intention was very clear, but even in the movie, when Bob Fosse shot the song, if you notice, "She wouldn't look Jewish at all" is said with absolutely no accompaniment; Joel just whispers the line. And that's so, if Bobby had any trouble from people, he could substitute the line without getting the musicans back in. He was still afraid.'

By the 1987 Broadway revival, Prince, Kander and Ebb could afford the courage of their convictions. It's a moment of pure musical theatre: the Emcee sings the final line; we laugh, and then catch ourselves in the huge mirrors hanging over the stage; the laugh dies instantly, as we realize what we're laughing at, and the song shrivels to a shamed, stinging silence and some awkward applause. It happens so quickly. But, in only a moment, with seductive ease, we have journeyed from fun to mockery to bigotry. 'I'm very proud of that reaction,' says Ebb, 'and it's exactly what the mirror concept means in *Cabaret* – that we're all capable of this.' Music, lyrics, plot point, choreography, design and involuntary audience participation have fused to create an effective theatrical shorthand. Through song and staging, a point has been made which would require pages of straight-play dialogue: *musical* theatre.

*

Times change, and these days Broadway exists on a drip-feed from London. Cameron Mackintosh isn't Jewish, but his writers on *Les Miz* and *Miss Saigon*, Boublil and Schonberg, are. 'Claude-Michel Schonberg,' he says, 'is Hungarian-Jewish. His music is squarely in the tradition of Romberg and Friml, those Central European composers who founded the American musical.' Andrew Lloyd Webber isn't Jewish, but his lyricist on *Aspects of Love* and *Sunset Boulevard* is. Don Black wears his Jewishness lightly. Once, when discussing lyrics with him and Tim Rice, I asked whether either used a rhyming dictionary.

'Of course,' said Rice. 'Otherwise, if you need a rhyme for "bog", you have to sit there thinking "cog", "dog", "fog" . . . With a dictionary . . .'

'You can go straight to "synagogue",' said Black.

The Cues

Well, let's try again: what comes first – the words or the music? 'The idea comes first,' says Fred Ebb. 'Something that starts you off – a title or a line or a situation or . . . well, for example, while working on *Cabaret*, I had this dream one night. I dreamt I was on the set of *Hello, Dolly!* and suddenly Joel Grey came on dancing with a gorilla in a tutu.'

'That's great,' Hal Prince, their director, told him. 'You've got to get it in the show.' So Kander and Ebb wrote 'If You Could See Her Through My Eyes' to devastating effect. 'I don't mean you to go through the process in a doped-up haze,' says John Kander, 'but you have to trust your unconscious.' The gorilla dream gave the authors a fresh take on the show's themes of prejudice and bigotry.

The idea comes first. *Cabaret*, a protean concept musical, is a score brimming with strong song ideas: in the theatre, as a rule, the best song is only as good as its place in the drama, and what it has to say *about* that place in the drama. Similar principles apply crudely in opera: the music obviously has to be appropriate to the general emotion. But the American musical improved on these generalities. Operatic arias have no titles, using the first titles of the text merely as a matter of convenience – 'La donna è mobile,' 'E lucevan le stelle'; they're texts set to music, no more or less. By those rules, the Gershwins' 'Someone To Watch Over Me' would be known as 'There's a somebody I'm longing to see'; 'How Long Has This Been Going On?' as 'I could cry salty tears'; 'But Not For Me' as 'They're writing songs of love'. But, as Ira Gershwin liked to say:

> A title
> Is vital
> Once *you've* it
> Prove it.

A title is what gives the lyric its thrust; it gives you something to resolve:

> Nice Work If You Can Get It
> And if you get it
> Won't you tell me how?

To recite the titles of the American song catalogue is to celebrate the American language: 'The Best Things In Life Are Free', 'Thou Swell', 'Button Up Your Overcoat', 'I Can't Give You Anything But Love, Baby', 'Makin' Whoopee', ''S Wonderful', 'You're The Cream In My Coffee', 'Sunny Disposish', 'I Found A Million Dollar Baby In A Five And Ten Cent Store', 'Life Is Just A Bowl Of Cherries', 'I've Got A Crush On You, Sweetie Pie', 'Brother, Can You Spare A Dime?', 'It Never Entered My Mind', 'I Got Rhythm', 'It's Only A Paper Moon', 'Of Thee I Sing, Baby', 'Smoke Gets In Your Eyes', 'I Didn't Know What Time It Was', 'Let's Call The Whole Thing Off', 'Just One Of Those Things', 'They All Laughed', 'I Could Write A Book' . . .

Each of those titles is the result of the writer's search for a fresh approach to a particular situation. For the dance hostesses, bored out of their skulls in *Sweet Charity* (1966), Cy Coleman and Dorothy Fields could have written 'What A Boring Job'; instead, they chose 'Hey, Big Spender': a half-hearted come-on from girls too jaded to do more than go through the motions of their sales pitch. It's more interesting dramatically, and it's also more memorable.

*

'Give me a laundry list and I'll set it to music,' Rossini used to boast. He never got round to it, but Gershwin, Porter and Hart did: long laundry lists of reasons why 'I Can't Get Started' and 'You're The Top' and 'The Lady Is A Tramp'. In their heyday, they were, like most funny songs, an opportunity for lyrical exhibitionism. It may be Morgan Le Fay singing, but it's Lorenz Hart you hear:

> Sir Paul was frail – he looked a wreck to me
> At night he was a horse's neck to me
> So I performed an appendectomy
> To Keep My Love Alive . . .

No matter that far more of Hart's writing skills were compressed into a couplet like . . .

> Falling In Love With Love
> Is falling for make-believe . . .

'To Keep My Love Alive' was written for the 1943 revival of *Connecticut Yankee*. By then, Rodgers had moved on to Hammerstein and opened *Oklahoma!*, and there's a strong sense that, in reviving *Connecticut Yankee*, he was doing a favour to his old partner – to keep *him* alive. It didn't work: 'To Keep My Love Alive' was the last song Lorenz Hart wrote; he died on 22 November 1943. Hart and Hammerstein were the same age, but Hammerstein was the future; Hart's virtuoso farewell performance, with its triple rhymes and anachronisms and polysyllables, was already a throwback, a reminder of an era when songwriters were judged by the flamboyance of their comic songs.

> I'll be your nincompoop
> Just be my *in*come poop

... Yip Harburg once wrote. 'Just what,' enquired Dorothy Parker, 'is an income poop?' Harburg stormed out of the room. Rhyme had become a reason unto itself.

But look at Harburg's *Wizard of Oz* songs:

> I could show my prowess
> Be a lion not a mow-ess
> If I Only Had Da Nerve ...

The rhyming is still unusual and whimsical, but, more importantly, it's in the voice of the Cowardly Lion. When, in the late eighties, the Royal Shakespeare Company blew in, swept up *The Wizard of Oz* like a giant twister and left the show a battered windswept wasteland, the one thing the production couldn't harm was the score: we love these numbers because they're so in tune with the characters delivering them.

It's often been remarked how Rodgers' music changed with *Oklahoma!* The first half of his career was summed up by Cole Porter in 'Well, Did You Evah!':

> It's smooth!
> It's smart!
> It's Rodgers!
> It's Hart!

And they were: smooth, smart, swingin', cynical, a swellegant, elegant party. Nobody ever said that of Rodgers and Hammerstein: overnight, the *music* turns yearning, sincere, open-hearted, four-square, folksy. To all intents and purposes, it might as well be a different composer. Rodgers would never again be as effortlessly breezy and bittersweet as:

The furtive sigh
The blackened eye
The words 'I love you till the day I die'
The self-deception that believes the lie
I Wish I Were In Love Again . . .

But, granted he ever wrote a tune like that again, who – in the Rodgers and Hammerstein gallery – would you assign it to? Laurey in *Oklahoma!*? Mister Snow in *Carousel*? Ensign Nellie Forbush in *South Pacific*? The King of Siam? Sister Maria? Ah, but there's the real question: how do you solve a problem like Maria? or Anna and the King, Nellie and Emile, Julie Jordan and Billy Bigelow? Rodgers reinvented himself: not a songwriter, but a playwright; not 'is this a good tune?' but instead 'what should we be singing about here, and how should we sing it?'

*

The new philosophy declares itself in Rodgers and Hammerstein's very first number. Whenever I hear a supposedly 'new' song droning on about stars above or blue skies, I think of Hammerstein's inspired and arresting image: 'The corn is as high as an elephant's eye.' Of course, Curly, a cowboy, has never seen an elephant, but he's heard about them and he's seen pictures and it's exactly the comparison he'd use. The image is fresh and precise – and Hammerstein wrote it that way only because he thought himself into Curly's character and was looking at it from his point of view. Nobody writes a show score sequentially, but all the great ones play that way: they have an inevitability about them, and you can no more monkey with the song order than you can play Act IV of *Hamlet* before Act II (actually, Shakespeare and the two-act book musical are very similar in construction). When so-called serious music critics discuss Kurt Weill's Broadway work, they often say, 'Ah-ha! Look at this piece of music, which he cut from the show. It was obviously too harmonically complex for Broadway at the time. He was selling out to commercialism.' Phooey! He cut it because, whatever its purely *musical* merits, it was *dramatically* wrong: it wasn't what you ought to be singing about at that point in the show. Anyone can compose tunes into a vacuum, but to compose tunes into a drama . . . that's a much rarer gift. Don't take my word for it: Stephen Sondheim, for one, prefers Weill's Broadway work to the Brechtian stuff.

Eric Bentley, drama critic and Brecht translator, comes at it from the other end – the words. 'When drama takes on the abstract character of pure music or pure dance it ceases to be drama; when, as a compromise, it tries to combine the abstract with the concrete it is invariably the drama, the words, that suffer,' he writes in *The Playwright as Thinker* (1946 – great title, by the way), and goes on to discuss *Oklahoma!*: 'On the stage it is decked out in gay colour and from time to time enlivened by tricky dancing. But in all drama,' he declares, 'colour and dancing are only embellishments; in this case, they are the embellishment of a scarecrow.'

Oklahoma!, as Bentley sees it, is 'by' Hammerstein. But it's not. The drama is not, as he says, the words. It's the words and the music and the tricky dancing: the lot, combined. As Bentley sees it, Hammerstein wrote a drama – a play – which was then tricked out with songs. He obviously hasn't given it more than a cursory glance. The musical play is not a play with music. If you take the songs out of *Oklahoma!* or *Carousel* or *The King and I* or *West Side Story, Gypsy, Fiddler on the Roof*, what's left won't stand up on its own: most of the drama's gone; the play is *in* the music.

Here's Rodgers and Hammerstein next, on *Carousel*. Instead of the usual comic sub-plot, we have Carrie Pipperidge, dreaming of domestic bliss with solid citizen Mister Snow. The song has become so familiar we forget how unusual it is to make memorable singing material out of contentment, tranquillity, routine:

> When the children are asleep
> We'll sit and dream
> The things that every other
> Dad and mother dream . . .

And why does it hold the stage? Because, although the lyric is about routine, it's not a routine melody. Instead of the four-bar phrases of his *Pal Joey* days, Rodgers tugs and tweaks here, squeezes and extends:

> When the children are asleep
> And lights are low
> If I still love you
> The way
> I love you
> Today
> You'll pardon my saying
> I told you so!

The phrase begins as its predecessor does, and then goes into the briefest of sub-phrases, with rests after the two 'love yous' and a gorgeous octave leap on 'saying'. You don't notice the musical structure, because Hammerstein's lyric glides smoothly over it. This is mundane reflective domesticity but the music makes it magical and exciting. And Rodgers is artful enough to construct his tune so that its welling emotional force can be resolved only as a duet. Subliminally, he has told us that the sentiments are true, that the love between Carrie and Mister Snow is real and will endure. It's a necessary dramatic counterpoint to the central relationship of Julie Jordan and Billy Bigelow, and it's terrific show-writing: it enlarges the supporting characters, it sheds light on the main situation and it's a fine song idea that lands with an audience. These Broadway boys can hold their own with the heavy cats, but you don't think of it in *musical* terms, because it suits the drama so well. 'Suit' is a good way of looking at it: the sung moments in a musical are like a three-piece suit – book, lyrics, music. They all have to fit together, and what you notice is the whole. When I walk along Savile Row, I want people to say, 'What a snappy suit!'; if they say, 'What an unusual pair of trousers!', something's wrong.

The most common misconception is that the book-writer is responsible only for the dialogue scenes – for connecting up the bits between the songs – whereas, since R&H, he's been the guy who *enables* the numbers, framing the entire drama from which the songs spring. 'Song and dance obviously exist on a level of heightened reality, and the book should have that quality, too,' says librettist Mark Bramble. 'Inevitably, in a musical the major dramatic moments will be told in music, so the librettist has to provide a sound structure and smooth the transition between the songs. I try to build each scene towards the music. In *Barnum*, for example, I reached the end of the scene and wrote: "Now would be a good place for a song called 'The Colours Of My Life' and this is what it should be about." The songwriters went off, wrote the number as instructed and made it the highlight of the score.

'The way I always work is I do an outline,' says Arthur Laurents, 'in some cases indicating song titles, but certainly indicating where the musical material is. I've worked principally with Steve Sondheim as a lyricist and we work very closely togther. So he then feels free to what he calls "raid" the dialogue.' In *West Side Story*, when it was decided that Tony needed an 'I am' song early in the show, Bernstein and Sondheim wrote 'Something's Coming' with much of the lyric and many of the images – 'whistling down the river' – 'raided' from Laurents' dialogue.

'The high moments in a musical are given to the composer and lyricist,' Joseph Stein, librettist of *Fiddler on the Roof*, concedes, 'but that's the nature of the game. So what you get satisfaction from is the finished product, not the individual elements. Very often, I'll write a scene and part of that scene will change and become a lyric. In *Fiddler*, "Do You Love Me?" was originally just dialogue and it surprised and delighted me when Jerry Bock and Sheldon Harnick said, "We can musicalize that." If you listen to the song, it's still dialogue – "Do you love me?" "Do I what?" "Do you love me?" "Do I love you?" – but, when they musicalized it, they made it special.'

To have your own well-crafted scenes pilfered by your collaborators requires a self-effacement which doesn't come easily to most writers. But still, maybe what makes it special musically is that it has a solid dramatic bedrock.

'We had a song in *Barnum* called "A Woman Is", sung by Mrs Barnum, Susan B. Anthony and all these others,' remembers Mark Bramble. 'It was my favourite. Cy Coleman wrote a wonderful melody; it had wit, humour, style – and it was awful. We brought the story to a complete halt, so we could go into this big production number. The audience knew it, and they were right. I always sit in the middle of the stalls, and you can feel whether the audience is with you or not. If they're not, then whatever it is has to go, even though it may be your favourite song or favourite scene.' Bramble leans in close for his next line, the big article of faith. 'You should always remember,' he says, 'the audience never lies.'

Hmm. Sounds to me like slick showbiz craftsmanship rather than inspired creative artistry. Ibsen never said 'The audience never lies'; he was in his study, alone with his muse. 'Oh,' chides Bramble, 'he was only alone with his muse because he couldn't get Cy Coleman.' And, despite the laugh, he means it. Bramble is no frustrated playwright: he always wanted to be a musical theatre librettist. 'And anyway,' he retorts, 'I think structure is an art.'

So now you can't just sing a song, even a song with a distinctive hook. The improvements in structure wrought by Hammerstein and others demanded more of the number: now, you have to sing a song with a distinctive hook that also illuminates character or plot point. Where does that leave every songwriter's bread and butter, the love song? *Mack and Mabel* (1974), the story of Mack Sennett and Mabel Normand in pre-talkie Hollywood, is an easy show on an easy theme, but Jerry Herman's approach to the love songs is consummately professional. For Mabel, broken-hearted, he wrote torchy:

Time Heals Ev'rything –
Tuesday, Thursday
Time Heals Ev'rything –
April, August . . .
So make the moments fly –
Autumn, winter
I'll forget you by
Next year, some year . . .

This is familiar territory, but Herman's structure – his singer trying to fight off the graduated uncertainty – makes it fresh, and injects it with an emotional punch beyond the capabilities of most writers. 'In ballads, you should never say it dead-on,' he says. 'You never say . . .

My lover has gone and I'm depressed

. . . you find an odd corner of the situation and you focus on it from that angle. In *Mack and Mabel*, the situation is: he's not right for her. But I had to come up with a way of saying it that's purely Mack Sennett, that's the way he would say it. And when I found . . .

I Won't Send Roses
Or hold the door
I won't remember
Which dress you wore

. . . I ran around the room like a little squirrel.'
    'I Won't Send Roses' is a love song in character. Dozens of male singers have picked up the number for albums and club acts, but it works because it works in the show. Mack Sennett is selfish, but he's honest enough to let Mabel know that she's in for an unsatisfying romance:

I Won't Send Roses
And roses suit you so.

This isn't anything to do with how good you are at writing music or lyrics, but depends on an inventiveness and instinct for what the singing material ought to be. Lerner and Loewe were sitting around talking about the song they'd need for Eliza's elocution lesson. Alan Jay Lerner suggested they use one of the exercises she'd been learning – 'In Hertford, Hereford and Hampshire, hurricanes hardly happen' or perhaps 'The rain in Spain stays mainly on the plain'. Fritz Loewe liked the latter: 'Good. I'll write a tango,' he said, and completed the tune within ten minutes. The combination of the words and music – humdrum repeat-after-me phrases set to exotic Spanish rhythms – makes it a novel and theatrical button for the scene.

Later in *My Fair Lady*, when Eliza has been successfully passed off as a duchess at the Embassy ball, she and Higgins and Colonel Pickering return home in joyous mood. Pickering offers congratulations:

> Tonight, old man, you did it!
> You did it! You did it!
> You said that you would do it
> And indeed you did!

The scene has the same zest and glee and infectiousness as 'The Rain In Spain'. Pickering and Higgins have triumphed – and the notey, jittery tune and monosyllables emphasize their excitement. And then we notice that the one person who isn't singing is Eliza: the one who *really* did it. The song continues, but, instead of seeming celebratory, it now underlines their selfishness and insensitivity. We realize Eliza isn't a lump of clay – a chaps' wager. This is the moment in the drama when Lerner and Loewe shift the play's point of view, and our sympathies, from Higgins to Eliza. And it all takes place during the song.

Structure *is* an art. In some ways, it's the *only* art. When Ethel Merman sang 'I Got Rhythm', we didn't worry about *why* she was singing it. Those were the days when the song cues came shrieking at you in neon: 'Oh, I'm sick of Latin,' says Flo in *Good News!* (1927), 'and all the other courses at this stupid college. Let 'em worry about their dusty old books. We'll make Tait famous for the Varsity Drag!' The bell-tone sounds to give Flo her key, and off go the students into one of those bogus dance crazes – 'Down on your heels, up on your toes' – which nods perfunctorily towards the context – 'Stay after school, learn how it goes' – but which is really its own justification. It's the cheapest sneer of the through-composed opera crowd: 'Oh, cue for a song – ha-ha!'

But to snigger at the way the shift of gears grinds is to miss the point: there is still a shift. To overextend the metaphor, through-sung music theatre is equivalent to motoring down a deserted interstate in an automatic set on cruise control. The book musical, to switch transportation metaphors, deploys horses for courses. It's the Astaire and Rogers trajectory again: when emotions reach a certain intensity, beyond speech, they're sung; when they go beyond that, they're danced (that old staple of 1940s musicals, the dream ballet). Smooth transitions are difficult to achieve, but it's a more honourable attempt at drama in music than, say, *Il*

Trovatore, where the score overrides all other considerations: when the drama demands that he should get going and rescue his mother before the pyre consumes her, Manrico instead hangs around to sing 'Di quella pira' – a convention we accept, but still pretty lazy. Like 'The Varsity Drag', 'Di quella pira' walks in on a pretext and has its way at the expense of all logic because it's a good number.

With Rodgers and Hammerstein, justification became its own justification. So, if you examine Molnar's *Liliom*, you find there's no chorus. But the R&H adaptation of the play introduces one. Not because a chorus is Broadway convention, you understand; that would never do. But because, as with so much of the R&H oeuvre, *Carousel* is about the importance of community – so the chorus becomes an expression of community values. Not in a signposted, didactic sort of way, but unobtrusively. 'This Was A Real Nice Clambake' seems like a capering chorus number, until we get to the main course – the arrival of the clams steamed under rockweed – and the song moves into a processional rhythm. It's about ritual and sacrament and a secular Yankee communion, and all this percolates through a bright, jolly up-number. Billy is about to break faith with his community and the anticipation of that runs through the clambake scene. The song reminds us of what Billy is turning his back on. It's the right song at the right point in the drama. You can still enjoy it in a mindless production number way, but, if you want to pick an intellectual fight with the song, it can more than hold its own.

Still, you can see why some folks miss Rodgers and Hart. Suddenly, it's such a serious business. Rodgers and Hart is basic him-and-her romance; Rodgers and Hammerstein is hymns and hearse: all those anthemic exhortations – 'You'll Never Walk Alone', 'Climb Ev'ry Mountain'; all those corpses: Hammerstein was killing off characters in musicals as long ago as *Rose-Marie* (1924) but he only hit his stride with Rodgers – Jud in *Oklahoma!*, Billy in *Carousel*, Lt Cable in *South Pacific*; and, of course, *The King and I*, where you get to play the King an' die. It wasn't just R&H. Here's *A Tree Grows in Brooklyn* (1951):

HILDY: He collapsed while he was working. They took him to Bellevue.
KATIE: I'll go.
HILDY: Katie . . . he died there.
KATIE: (*after a moment*) You lie, Hildy Moran! You lie! You always hated me because Johnny wanted me instead of you. All these years you've been trying to get back at me. And you found out Johnny's

been gone a few days. So you came here . . . (*Beginning to break down*) Women have to go through so much, you'd think they'd stick together instead of always being so mean to each other. (*Pleading without hope*) Say you lied, Hildy. Say you lied! I won't hold it against you. (*The quiet tears come.*)

HILDY: (*taking Katie in her arms*) Katie . . . Katie . . .

KATIE: (*clinging to her friend*) Oh, Hildy, what am I going to tell Francie?

This powerful scene was written by Betty Smith (author of the original novel) and George Abbott. George Abbott! The farce master. The same George Abbott who gave us *Boy Meets Girl* and *Three Men on a Horse* and *On Your Toes* and *The Boys from Syracuse* and *High Button Shoes* and *Where's Charley?* and *Call Me Madam* . . . The same George Abbott who, when I asked him whether the departing sailors and their girls' beautifully throwaway conversational ballad 'Oh, well, we'll catch up Some Other Time' at the end of *On The Town*, was placed deliberately to conjure wistfully the uncertainties of the war years, said:

'We didn't think about that. We thought: what's funny?'

What's funny? Mr Abbott would never have written that scene in *A Tree Grows in Brooklyn* if Rodgers and Hammerstein hadn't paved the way. When musicals evolved from entertainments to dramas, they were bound to get less funny, if only because the most dramatically rewarding material isn't a barrel of laughs.

'Those two made it harder for everybody else,' sighed Cole Porter. Nobody could have been less interested in fitting songs to book needs. Standing at the back of the theatre with lyricist-turned-book-writer Dorothy Fields, Porter once overheard an excited matinée lady squeal with delight to her friend: 'I don't know how these actors think of such clever things to say to each other!' Porter turned to Miss Fields and said, 'And you *want* to write book?'

In Porter's thirties musicals, the songs were, as they say, signed all over, from the polysyllabic rhymes to the Park Avenue name-dropping, but who knew or cared who wrote the book? After *Oklahoma!*, though, the detachment from story which Porter had affected was no longer acceptable. The laundry list, his trademark ever since 'Let's Do It (Let's Fall In Love)', became obsolete almost overnight.

When Bella Spewack, adapting *The Taming of the Shrew* with her husband Sam, insisted on Porter for the score, the producers got worried. Since his last collaboration with the Spewacks a decade earlier, the composer's career had hit the skids and few showfolk thought he could recover. The doubters included Porter himself, who was intimidated by the source. Bella, who considered *The Shrew* one of Shakespeare's biggest clinkers, advised him to forget the Bard and look on it as Yiddish theatre: the younger sister (Bianca) can't marry until the older one (Kate) does – a Jewish custom which had motored innumerable Yiddish hits on Second Avenue.

'I swore it could not be done,' said Porter – meaning that, in the age of the Rodgers and Hammerstein 'integrated' musical, he couldn't cut it any longer. The Spewacks were more relaxed. Asked to differentiate between the new school and its predecessor, they offered an expert analysis: 'You may remember that the old musical comedy consisted of a story, songs, dances, scenery, girls and boys. On the other hand, the New Art Form consists of a story, songs, dances, scenery, girls and boys.'

So they wrote Porter a scene. He read it, liked it and wrote back a song. And in that piecemeal way the show proceeded: after receiving 'Another Op'nin', Another Show', 'Too Darn Hot', 'Always True To You In My Fashion' and a dozen more, the Spewacks begged him to send no more songs; 'Brush Up Your Shakespeare' arrived the next day. He was helped by Bella's conception: *The Shrew* is the play-within-the-musical and events on-stage are mirrored in the backstage drama between the principal players, loosely based on the Lunts. Today, *Kiss Me, Kate* represents the American musical in transition: the story depends on too slick a shorthand, an episodic structure sustained by one-liners. Yet the Spewacks' book did something no other musical comedy had done before: it confined Porter to a single *milieu* and thereby gave the numbers a consistency of tone. The score is his masterpiece because it was, for the first time, a *score*. You could swap around the numbers from *Anything Goes* to *The Gay Divorce* via *Panama Hattie* and no one would notice or care, but 'I Hate Men', 'Were Thine That Special Face' and 'Brush Up Your Shakespeare' could belong to only one show.

Today, *Kiss Me, Kate* is Porter's only *show*; all the rest is songs.

Irving Berlin, Porter's only rival as composer-lyricist, looked set to fare even worse. Here is the ultimate songwriter. Yet, in 1946, he gave us an astounding score for *Annie, Get Your Gun* – produced by Rodgers and Hammerstein. As with Porter and the Spewacks, Dorothy and Herbert Fields gave Berlin an environment – Annie Oakley and the pioneer west – and it inspired him to 'Doin' What Comes Natur'lly', 'You Can't Get A Man With A Gun', 'Anything You Can Do', song after song after song . . . in character.

Musical comedy has never had the respect it deserves. As Lord Berners once observed, we like to measure art by size and weight. But, while Hammerstein was applying the logic of serious drama to the musical play, George Abbott was applying the equally stern logic of farce to musical comedy. Hal Prince, an Abbott protégé, goes so far as to lump *Oklahoma!* and Abbott's *On the Town* together as landmark ground-breaking shows. And, structurally, the latter show, by Bernstein, Comden and Green, takes itself just as seriously.

'Leonard was away on a conducting tour,' says Betty Comden, 'and we had this idea – about two characters who keep getting carried away. There's a song in a show we always liked, *Pal Joey*:

> If my heart gets in your hair
> You Mustn't Kick It Around
> If you're bored with this affair
> You Mustn't Kick It Around . . .

So, to the same tune, just to get us started, we wrote

> I try hard to stay controlled
> But I Get Carried Away
> Try to act aloof and cold
> But I Get Carried Away . . .

'Obviously,' says Adolph Green, 'we didn't mention the tune to Leonard when he returned, because he wouldn't have been able to get it out of his head. But he looked at the lyric and came up with something far more operatic, because he realized that these were two extravagant, larger-than-life characters.'

We forget the usefulness of comedy in underpinning character. After all, one of Broadway's most enduring shows is pure *character* comedy. For *Guys and Dolls*, Frank Loesser, another Abbott disciple, originally wrote a number about a stripper who catches cold. Then he thought again and, following his dictum that songs should comment on character rather than events, decided to make it psychosomatic and apply it to the chronically engaged Miss Adelaide:

> From a lack of community property and a feeling she's getting too old
> A person can develop a cold.

It arouses more sympathy from us than if Loesser had written a whining song about 'Oh, God, when's he gonna marry me?' At the same time, it's not self-advertising in the way Porter and Hart can be.

It's a good idea, which counts for more than any number of internal rhymes.

*

The greatest of all Broadway musicals is a musical comedy – or is it a musical play? Either way, *Gypsy* (1959) is pretty funny. It's dramatically indestructible, but musically appealing enough to have produced more cast recordings than any other show. You still dispute that 'greatest' tag? Let's agree on this then: that it's the most *Broadway* of Broadway musicals, fusing the two strains of American musical theatre, seizing the principles of the R&H musical play and setting them to the gorgeous, vulgar rhythms of musical comedy – the dramatic ambitions of the former, the sass of the latter. 'When they came to me,' says Arthur Laurents, 'I said it isn't any good. Who cares about this woman who was the striptease queen of America? And then I thought: make it about the mother. And then we have parents and children, and that's why it's eternal. That's viable any day. The idiom of the characters was kinda trashy gutter talk, and you needed kinda trashy gutter music. That's not to disparage Jule. He wrote very gutsy music, but in that idiom.'

'Too many writers write self-pity,' Jule Styne told me. 'Audiences hate that in characters. In *Gypsy*, when Rose is deserted by her daughter, she's broke, the act's washed up, we could have had her sing about how miserable she is. Instead, we turned the moment in on itself.'

Rose seems dazed. And then she turns to Louise, the other daughter, the mousy nondescript who sewed June's costumes, and says: look at her, look at the new star. Styne gives her a classic, exuberant, look-out-world showtune:

> You'll be swell!
> You'll be great!
> Gonna have the whole world on a plate!

But, in the context of the show, it's a woman driving off the map. At this point in the play, Styne and his lyricist Stephen Sondheim have to top Arthur Laurents' powerful dialogue – not for personal reasons, but because in a musical the music has to soar beyond what's gone before. Styne's tune starts at the top of the register and blasts off. It's a hell of a first-act finale, an epiphany: the moment when Rose ceases being merely an opportunist stage mother and through sheer will transports herself and her ambitions beyond reality. Can she really make Louise a star? Or is she crazy? The long-suffering Herbie and little Louise are mute and passive, and their silence is eloquent. This is Broadway's answer to the mad scene from *Lucia di Lammermoor*.

For all that, Styne was the first to acknowledge that not every song needs to be this firmly embedded: 'On *Annie, Get Your Gun*, Irving Berlin originally wrote "There's No Business Like Show Business" for the two guys,' he said. 'Then Dick Rodgers said, "That's so good you have to let Merman do it." But nobody could figure out how to work it in. After all, the guys are supposed to be teaching her about show business. Eventually, they had the two fellers sing it to her, and then Ethel Merman went . . .

> You mean . . . ?
> There's No Business Like Show Business

. . . and she did the second chorus. It was naïve, it was corny, but it worked and audiences went wild. We don't have that kind of fun moment any more because everyone's too hung on trying to be smart. But it proves what you can do if you've got the right songs. That's why Dick Rodgers called *Annie, Get Your Gun* the greatest show score ever written.'

'There's No Business . . . ' is what Hal Prince calls a 'Once-a-Year Day' number, after a memorable song in the first show he produced, *The Pajama Game*. A 'Once-a-Year Day' number strolls in, announces a good time and then proceeds to deliver it. But even this has to be consistent with the show, and, at the most basic level, if the song has no value for plot propulsion, we have to like the characters enough to let the play hang about while they sing it.

*

Aimost four decades on from *Gypsy*, the relationship between book, lyrics and music has reverted to the imbalance of opera. The need to find song points spurred compression, the essence of the lyricist's craft; freed from those confines, the lyricist of an opera or a sung-through musical sprawls helplessly over the whole evening. There's no pressure for the compact observation of Broadway lyrics:

> Take Back Your Mink
> To from whence it came

. . . which prepositional pile-up, from *Guys and Dolls*, tells you everything about the uneducated Miss Adelaide's desire to improve herself.

Nor does the music tie itself so specifically to character: you couldn't swap Nellie's tunes (homespun, freewheeling) with Emile's (formal, grandiloquent) in *South Pacific* or Higgins' with Eliza's in *My Fair Lady*, but, in *Phantom* and *Aspects*, everyone expresses themselves to the same musical themes. 'Yes, but you can make the same criticism of Verdi,' an eminent opera critic replied when I said as much to him. Exactly: a through-sung score is not subjected to the same scrutiny as individual songs in a book show, and lapses inevitably into generality – happy, sad, angry, carefree. But you rarely feel that the music is a deeply personal, unconscious revelation of character, as you do in *Oklahoma!* when Jud, after the peddler's tried to sell him some dirty postcards, sits down and lets all his pathetic frustration bubble over:

> Don't want nuthin' from no peddler's bag. Want real things! Whut am I doin' shet up here – like that feller says – a-crawlin' and a-festerin'? What am I doin' in this lousy smokehouse?
>
> > The floor creaks
> > The door squeaks . . .
> > And I sit by myself . . .
> > By myself in a Lonely Room.

*

A few years ago, Trevor Nunn, director of cue-free *Cats* and *Les Miz* and *Aspects of Love*, said to me: 'When we did *Chess* in America, with a new book, I was reminded of one of the major pleasures of the musical play – the moment when the music enters, when text becomes underscoring, then introduction, then song – when something that has been explored in one form then moves into another.'

The major pleasure of the musical play – and all but forgotten today.

The Take-home Tune

Despite its location in a modern skyscraper dripping with chrome and aluminium, to enter Irving Caesar's office is to step back in time – to Remick's, say, or Mills Music, *circa* 1925. The sheet music covers are quaintly dated, the faded photographs show singers and writers long dead, and each chair has its own spittoon. Littering the floor, stacked up against desk legs, are dozens of awards, mostly from ASCAP, the American copyright collection agency, and mostly for 'Tea For Two' as 'Most Performed Song of the Decade' – not in the twenties, when it was written, but in 1984, 1985, 1986, 1987 . . . 'They give it me every year,' sighs Caesar, heading for his hundredth birthday. 'I don't know what to do with 'em any more.'

Being the song's lyricist, Caesar will tell you the phenomenal success is due to his lyric – and it certainly has one of the most memorable of all titles. But jazzmen dig, for example, Vincent Youmans' abrupt key shift from A flat major to C; soft-shoe dancers love the rhythmic pattern; and its harmonic structure has prompted arrangements by musicians from Tommy Dorsey (who did it as a cha-cha-cha) to Shostakovich (who didn't). It's also heard in restaurants and elevators. Between them these various incarnations keep 'Tea For Two' earning far more money in the nineties than almost any other song. And how did it get to the elevators and eateries and arrangers? Answer: from a show, from the musical comedy that epitomizes the twenties, *No, No, Nanette*.

'Almost all the great standards that last are theatre songs: all your Kern, Gershwin, Cole Porter, Kurt Weill,' Jule Styne told me. 'I feel sorry for young writers today. I knew when I wrote a good showtune that I'd get maybe 15 records on it – Sinatra, Como, Doris Day, Tony Bennett, the Four Aces, the Four This, the Four That . . . And that can give you longevity.' Styne liked to describe himself as a musical dramatist, but he also enjoyed giving the country songs it loves to sing – like 'Let It Snow! Let It Snow! Let It Snow!' and 'The Christmas Waltz', music that seeps across the landscape every minute of December from radios and elevators and shopping malls and sidewalk Santas. He followed the course of the war as closely as any military strategist: first came the ballads for parted lovers, 'I Don't Want To Walk Without You' and 'I'll Walk Alone'. These aren't refined, exclusive theatre songs; they're for anyone: he liked to talk of an old newspaper photograph of the Allies marching through Europe, and, on an abandoned German tank, some waggish GI had scrawled, 'I'll Walk Cologne'.

'We tried to stay one step ahead of the generals,' Sammy Cahn explained to me. 'One day I looked at the maps and I said to Jule, "You know, I think this war might be turning", so we wrote "Victory Polka". A while later, I looked at the maps again and I said to Jule, "You know, I think this war might be coming to an end"' – so, for the returning boys, they wrote:

> Kiss me once, then kiss me twice
> Then kiss me once again
> It's Been A Long, Long Time . . .

Of Cole Porter, Jule Styne once said, 'It wasn't just a *chi-chi* theatre crowd who liked him. His songs could make a shop girl feel that she'd *been* to El Morocco or 21.' But you always knew where he was writing from: you were in the depths; he was on the 90th floor. Porter's attempts at wartime chin-up songs are embarrassing, reassuring the men overseas that

> Miss Garbo remains as the Hollywood Sphinx
> Monty Woolley's still bathing his beard in his drinks . . .

Did he honestly think that's what your average GI was up to his neck in muck and bullets for? Yet, although he seemed to write purely for his Park Avenue smart set, for years Porter was second only to Irving Berlin as America's highest-earning composer. He symbolizes the strange tension between the theatre and the Hit Parade: Porter was pure Broadway – he personifies the era – but his songs were pop smashes for Artie Shaw and the Andrews Sisters. Styne made the journey in reverse: a titan of the pop charts, he subsequently became the most prolific and successful Broadway composer of the post-war era. Tin Pan Alley and Broadway are not quite synonymous – though the rock set frequently assumes so – but, for much of the last century, they enjoyed a mutually beneficial free trade area.

*

What's the first hit song from a Broadway show? 'The Mulligan Guard' from *The Mulligan Guard Ball* (1879)? Hardly; it was a smallish success but it never travelled beyond its theatrical context. I'd plump for 'Oh, Promise Me' from *Robin Hood* (1891) – but, significantly, the song's lyric was not by Harry B. Smith, who wrote the rest of the show, but by Clement Scott. It's as if Broadway writers weren't up to hit songs; they had to be bought in. Later, the same season, *A Trip to Chinatown* became the first American musical to produce three hit songs: there was 'Reuben And Cynthia', now forgotten; 'The Bowery', which survived (just about) into our own time; but the third hit was the biggest of all, and, once again, it had to be interpolated from elsewhere.

At the age of 18, Charles K. Harris hung a shingle outside his door advertising 'Songs written to order' and inaugurated what we now call the music business. There'd been music before, but, with Harris, it's the *business* that impresses. His first effort, the prototype pop hit 'After The Ball', began earning him 25,000 bucks per week almost immediately and went on to sell five million copies of sheet music. This was 1892, remember, when 25,000 bucks was still 25,000 bucks, and, what's more, you didn't have to split it with accountants, managers, executive masseurs, coke dealers and any traumatised kid whose father has a smart lawyer. Aside from the cost of a musical secretary to whom he would hum his melodies (he couldn't *write* music), Harris had virtually no overheads.

They don't write 'em like they used to – thank God. 'After The Ball' is a ludicrous verse-and-chorus saga about a fellow who ends his days a lonely old bachelor because he saw his best girl waltzing with another man who, unbeknown to him, is her brother. But most pop music has always been drivel and, hard though American feminist deconstructionist cultural studies professors may find it to believe, one day a long way away in the future Madonna writhing around naked on top of a German shepherd while a gay black dance troupe cavorts in the background will seem silly, too.

The difference is that 'After The Ball' was a bigger hit than any of Madonna's songs have ever been. Without benefit of radio, television, a movie theme-song deal, an advertising jingle or an oral-anal-S&M sex book tie-in, Harris' song was familiar within a few months to 90 per cent of the American people. That's the one kind of penetration Madonna seems unlikely to experience. 'After The Ball's' sheer reach is a definition of popular culture: a work in the vernacular of the times that becomes a part of the times, a shared culture, a shorthand we all recognize. Thirty-five years after it was written, the song was still so well known that, when Kern and Hammerstein needed an old warhorse to conjure the 1890s for the New Year scene in *Show Boat*, it was pressed into service again: it's still there, pleasing the customers, in the '94 revival. Even today, if you want to make a movie set in small-town America, 1892, on a lazy day when the piano's seeping from the parlour out on to the porch, 'After The Ball' is still the perfect accompaniment.

Did Charles H. Hoyt, producer, co-director, librettist and co-lyricist of *A Trip to Chinatown*, sense any of this when he decided to interpolate 'After The Ball' into his show? For 25 years we'd had American musicals of one sort or another – burlesques and farce-comedies – but, although they had music in them, their pleasures weren't chiefly *musical*: they were hits because of their comedy acts or their leggy blondes or their special effects. When Hoyt paid Harris for 'After The Ball', subconsciously or not, he was conceding that the Broadway musical had so far failed in what ought to be its defining characteristic. So the first monster pop hit became additionally the first monster show hit and offered audiences an unbeatable combination: a hit song in a hit play.

*

You *can* have it all: Irving Berlin did. 'When I first came to New York, I went to see *Annie, Get Your Gun*,' remembers Sheldon Harnick, lyricist of *Fiorello!* and *She Loves Me*, 'there was a song in there that I'd heard on the radio back in Chicago, "They say That Falling In Love Is Wonderful". And I'd always thought, "Oh, what a pretty song." But, when I saw the show, I realized what Berlin had done when he wrote . . .

> I can't recall who said it
> I know I never read it.

Of course, Annie Oakley had never *read* it: in the show, she's illiterate. And I thought that was such good writing: it's a specific character lyric which means something in the show but it can also be understood out of context.'

Sheldon Harnick wasn't the only Broadway baby on the aisle at that show. 'I'm still the kid whose parents took him to *Annie, Get Your Gun*,' says Jerry Herman, 'and who was thrilled because he could pick out "They Say That Falling In Love Is Wonderful" on the piano afterwards.' One of Herman's earliest songs evokes Berlin's showbiz anthem from that score, and sums up his own philosophy: 'There's No Tune Like A Show Tune'.

An adoring fan of Berlin, he has a similar faith in solid musical comedy virtues: if you don't leave the theatre whistling the tunes, it's not for lack of effort on his part. His trademark is the splashy production number, with a Busby Berkeley appetite for repeat choruses and all the tricks in the book – spare orchestration, then the whole band; vocal solo, then full company; dance break, double time, slow it down, speed it up, and hammer it home in a high-stepping, slam-bang, triple-rhymed finale: in the words of *Mame*'s Dixie belles,

> We're baking pecan pies again!
> Tonight the chicken fries again!
> This time the South will rise again
> Mame!

And when he's really cooking, Herman dispenses with rhyme altogether:

> Dolly'll never go away!
> Dolly'll never go away!
> Dolly'll never go away
> Again!

I once discussed take-home tunes with Hal Prince. 'Put it this way,' he said. 'I was asked to direct *Hello, Dolly!* They played me this title song, and I said, "This is for a scene where a woman who doesn't go out visits a restaurant?" They never mentioned directing *Hello, Dolly!* to me again.' It's pointless to query as Prince did whether, in strict dramatic logic, Dolly's return to an old haunt merits ten minutes of cavorting waiters. This song walks in out of nowhere, but it wowed audiences every night for 2,844 performances on Broadway, and that's justification enough. Besides, even in the era of the integrated musical, it seems a wee bit perverse that Herman should be chastised, as he is, for writing hit songs.

'If we were to list all the hits that came from shows of the forties,' he says, 'we'd be here all day. I wish it was like that now. But, even though I'm pleased if people can hear my songs on the radio or dance to them in discos, I always serve the show first. No one was more surprised than me when Gloria Gaynor had a hit with "I Am What I Am" from *La Cage aux Folles*. I wrote it for a very specific dramatic moment, in which a homosexual man breaks down and demands acceptance for what he is. If you were sitting down to write a disco record for Gloria Gaynor, you'd never write that lyric about "opening up your closet". As a matter of fact, my publisher had asked me, in case anyone did want to record it, to change some of those lines, so I put in something about "blow my horn and sound my trumpet/My song – and if you don't like it, you can lump it". But I never heard anyone use that. Gloria Gaynor did it with the "closet" line, so did Sammy Davis. If people like a song, they'll go ahead and do it.'

The number Herman never thought would be commercial was 'Hello, Dolly!' 'It's easy to laugh now, but in the show the melody and orchestration are very 1890s. The first time I heard Louis Armstrong's record I was in shock. I couldn't believe he'd gotten that jazzy record out of my little period song. Or Bobby Darin's finger-snappy version of "Mame", which I conceived as a southern cakewalk with banjos plunking. Or when Eydie Gormé did that brilliant torchy rendition of "If He Walked Into My Life" – I wrote that for an aunt to sing about her nephew. I don't know if that's the mark of a good song, but it means it's a *versatile* song.'

It doesn't hurt at the box office either. At *Mame*, the audience applauded the hit songs during the overture.

Here are ten take-home tunes, Broadway songs that have a life beyond the show, from the thirties on. As an ex-disc jockey, I'd usually count down the Top 10 in reverse order. But, as showtunes that make the charts have got fewer and smaller, it seems more appropriate to reverse the reverse order.

A Broadway Hit Parade

1 *'My Funny Valentine' (1937, Richard Rodgers/Lorenz Hart)*
Babes in Arms had more hit songs than any other Rodgers and Hart score: 'Where Or When', 'I Wish I Were In Love Again', 'Johnny One Note', 'The Lady Is A Tramp', and this. 'My Funny Valentine' is a high-earning pop song, but it's also, unmistakably, a theatre song – as the best and most enduring popular songs often are. No Alley lyricist would rhyme 'Your looks are laughable/Unphotographable', and make a six-syllable word seem like the most natural thing in the world to find in a love song. And no Alley composer would climb an octave higher for the climax of the lyric: 'Stay, little Valentine, *stay*!' But 'My Funny Valentine' is also an early, elementary attempt at integration: the character being sung about was a guy called Val, short for Valentine. Of course, if you've got Sinatra's recording or Elvis Costello's, you're none the worse off for not knowing that. Lesson: if you're going to mention proper names, pick ones with a more general application (see also 'Everything's Coming Up Roses' below).

2 '*You'll Never Walk Alone*' *(1945, Richard Rodgers/Oscar Hammerstein II)*

Not every take-home tune has to head straight for the charts. It can be just as helpful and profitable to carve out a more specialized niche. 'You'll Never Walk Alone', a hymn-like high-school graduation song from *Carousel*, has become outside the show a song used at real high-school graduations and a real hymn, much requested at American funerals. In Britain, more bizarrely, it's become a football anthem, sung on the terraces by Liverpool fans every Saturday afternoon. When Richard Rodgers was informed of this, at first he was aghast, and then he wanted his lawyers to see if he could have it stopped. But how many other showtunes are sung by soccer fans? Others in this 'occasional' category include 'Seventy-Six Trombones', a song sung in *The Music Man* by a fake musician trying to defraud a small-town band that's become a great favourite with genuine small-town bands; and then there's 'Easter Parade' (from *As Thousands Cheer*) and 'We Need A Little Christmas' (from *Mame*). At the first night of *Sunset Boulevard* (1993), I mentioned to the lyricist Don Black that I'd been struck, during 'The Perfect Year', at how few New Year songs there were, compared with the Santa/Rudolph/Frosty Christmas log-jam. 'Yeah,' said Black. 'I think we may have found an opening there.' That New Year, Dina Carroll's soul version of the song was in the Top 5. Black and Lloyd Webber had tapped into one holiday Irving Berlin hadn't got a hammerlock on and look like they've sewn up New Years until well into the next century. Lesson: check out the small print in engagement diaries: is there a song for Groundhog Day? (See below.)

3 '*Almost Like Being In Love*' *(1947, Frederick Loewe/Alan Jay Lerner)*

The easiest way to integrate a song, Frank Loesser used to say, was to put all the show-specific stuff in the verse:

> As the mayor of this town
> I'd like to thank you for voting for me
> And that's why I say . . .

And then keep the chorus general:

> Tweedly-tweedly-dee
> It's a great day for me . . .

This song from *Brigadoon* is a classic example. Tommy, an American tourist who stumbles on a mist-shrouded time-trapped Scottish village, is much taken by Fiona, and sings:

> Maybe the sun
> Gave me the pow'r
> For I could swim Loch Lomond
> And be home in half an hour!

But that's just the verse. By the time we get to the chorus, Lerner knows enough to cut the local colour and write generally:

> What a day this has been!
> What a rare mood I'm in!
> Why, it's
> Almost Like Being In Love

It fits the rare mood of the drama, but also the more common mood of Top 40 love ballads. It was a hit for Sinatra, Mildred Bailey and Mary Martin, and 45 years later Nat 'King' Cole's swingin' recording was chosen to close the Bill Murray film hit *Groundhog Day*, not just because the song broadly suited the scenario but also as a sly joke: *Brigadoon* was about a village which appears out of the Scotch mist for one day every hundred years; *Groundhog Day* is about a man who keeps living the same one day over and over and over. Lesson: keep the plot information in the verse; who sings verses?

4 *'Mack The Knife' (1928, Kurt Weill/Bertolt Brecht; 1954, English lyric by Marc Blitzstein*
'The Sheik Of Araby', 'The One I Love Belongs To Somebody Else' . . . There are hundreds of songs which testify to the mesmeric quality of the sixth interval. But, even allowing for that, 'Mack The Knife' is an unlikely hit. The off-Broadway production of *The Threepenny Opera* brought the show and the song to America's attention; Louis Armstrong had a hit record with it; Bobby Darin had an even bigger one, one of the all-time best-selling singles. Nobody seemed to object to the penultimate verse, which, in breach of all the rules about take-home tunes, is a virtual recital of the *dramatis personae* – Jenny Diver, Polly Peachum, Lucy Brown, and so on. Darin's recording even mentions one of the actresses, Lotte Lenya – the composer's wife had become part of the show's legend. Sinatra got to it in the eighties and added a second list, of

singers who've already done the song – Satchmo, Ella, Darin. In his introduction, he usually says, 'This is by Weill and Blitzstein. Sheesh, sounds like a law firm' or some such, and you can tell he's never seen the show. When he gets to the line about Polly Peachum, he shrugs and gives a 'Who?' gesture. But he sure taps into Mackie: it's Sinatra the loan shark, coming to collect, and, in the final stretch, having exhausted Blitzstein's lyrics he snarls some improvisations of his own:

> When I tell you all about Mack the Knife, babe
> It's an offer, uh, you cannot refuse

. . . and . . .

> I'm gonna tell you what I think that you should do:
> You better lock your door
> And call the law!

Which goes to show there are exceptions to every rule. Lesson: if you're going to mention specifics, be *real* specific (see also 'Don't Cry for Me, Argentina').

5 *'On The Street Where You Live' (1956, Frederick Loewe/Alan Jay Lerner)*
Outside *My Fair Lady*, this is a conventional love song; inside, it's introduced by a joke verse from Eliza's fat-headed suitor Freddie Eynsford-Hill and is later reprised strictly for laughs. A year or so before he died, Lerner and I discussed this song at his home in Chelsea. These days, I suggested, most writers would write, 'Here We Are On Bramerton Street' (the street where he lived). 'That's not "integrated",' he said. 'That's just describing what we're looking at or what's happening. You have to use the set and the situation to find a song idea or lyric line.' Lesson: don't let the sense of place overpower you.

6 *'The Party's Over' (1956, Jule Styne/Betty Comden, Adolph Green)*
When *Wonderful Town* opened, Lerner mentioned to their mutual publisher, Max Dreyfus, that he thought Bernstein, Comden and Green would have a hit with their loping ballad . . .

> Why-oh-why-oh-why-oh
> Why did we ever leave Ohio?

'No,' said Dreyfus. 'The public knows they don't mean it.' Comden and Green are Broadway bluechips, droll and larky, but those qualities don't usually translate into the Hit Parade. 'They write with me like they write with nobody! Nobody!' Jule Styne told me with his customary under-statement. 'Sure, they can write funny and all that, but all their best pop lyrics they wrote with me!' It's hard to argue with Styne, and you can see why he wouldn't want affecting (and potentially high-earning) ballads thrown away with whimsical special-material lyrics. He and Comden and Green scored with 'The Party's Over', a beautiful accumulation of rueful images:

> They've burst your pretty balloon
> And taken the moon away . . .

In the show *Bells Are Ringing*, for Ella Peterson (Judy Holliday), the party *was* over: she'd just been to one; it *was* 'time to wind up the masquerade': she'd been pretending to be someone else at the party, and so on. Lesson: make the plot details into metaphor.

7 *'Everything's Coming Up Roses' (1959, Jule Styne/Stephen Sondheim)*
Presented with the song for the First Act finale in *Gypsy*, Jerome Robbins complained, 'I don't understand that title.' He was the only one who didn't. Sondheim had come up with an expression that means everything's gonna be great from now on, that sounds as if it's been in the language for years – and which he just invented off the top of his head. Since then, it *has* passed into the language. Lesson: now that all the proverbial expressions and colloquial phrases have been used as song titles, make up one of your own.

8 *'I Believe In You' (1961, Frank Loesser)*
Outside the show, this is an optimistically faithful love song; inside *How to Succeed in Business Without Really Trying*, it's sung by an ambitious egomaniacal young executive to himself, as he's admiring himself in the mirror of the men's room. Lesson: you don't need boy-meets-girl to write love songs.

9 *'People' (1964, Jule Styne/Bob Merrill)*
For 'Small World' in *Gypsy*, Sondheim wrote the lyric: 'Funny, I'm a woman with children . . . ' Styne protested, 'But that means no man can sing the song!' Under duress, Sondheim de-genderized the line for the commercial sheet music, Johnny Mathis recorded 'Small World' and had a hit, small not world. Five years later, with lyricist Bob Merrill, Styne took no chances. The take-home tune wasn't about anything as specific

as men and women or boys and girls but just . . . people, people who need people being the luckiest people in the world. It's the ultimate take-home tune: it applies to everything and everybody. Today, when Barbra Streisand sings it, she's prone, over the instrumental break, to toss in a homily about world peace and how all of us, in America, in Bosnia, in the Middle East, young, old, black, white, gay, straight, transsexual, could learn from the song. But, when she first sang the song as Fanny Brice in *Funny Girl*, it was about the opposite: the character was so concerned about her public, worldwide life that she'd neglected the personal, neglected to find that 'one very special person'. Popular art is always at its most persuasive when it illuminates a small situation and leaves us to figure out the big picture for ourselves. Big lesson: 'A poet should address the specific and if there be anything about him he will articulate the universal' – Goethe.

10   *'The Impossible Dream' (1965, Mitch Leigh/Joe Darion)*
In the late sixties, customers calling to book tickets used to ask for seats for *The Impossible Dream* or the 'Impossible Dream' musical. In truth, the show was called *Man of La Mancha*, adapted from Cervantes, and 'The Impossible Dream' was but one number in it. Were there any others? *La Mancha* is the classic one-song score; the writers never repeated the trick, yet the show ran nearly six years. Lesson: sometimes the right take-home tune is all you need.

The best song in the world won't save the show. As a cautionary tale, how about a quick, bracing stroll down Flop Alley? Here are five hit songs from certified bombs:

1   *'As Time Goes By' (1931, Herman Hupfeld)*
You won't remember the musical comedy *Everybody's Welcome* unless you were in it. Elisabeth Welch was, and, as she says, '*Everybody's Welcome*. But nobody came.' It took Bogey and Bergman and Dooley Wilson and Rick's Café to raise the song to a totem: it has itself become one of the fundamental things that apply as time goes by. I can't resist, though, pointing out a small flaw, all the more surprising from a composer–lyricist.

> You must remember this
> A kiss is still a kiss
> A sigh is just a sigh.

There's no musical difference between '*still* a kiss' and '*just* a sigh', even though the lyric is clearly drawing a distinction. That's why newspaper headline writers always misquote the song: 'A kiss is just a kiss'.

2 '*All The Things You Are*' (*1939, Jerome Kern/Oscar Hammerstein II*)
Very Warm for May opened very cold in November 1939 at the Alvin Theatre: it ran seven weeks, just another in Hammerstein's parade of flops in the years before *Oklahoma!* but, as events transpired, Kern's farewell to Broadway. It contains a ballad he thought would be too complex for the public ear. Certainly, it's tricky: the last note of the release . . .

The dearest things I know are what you *are*

. . . is a G sharp: we're in the key of E major. The first note of the next phrase . . .

Some day my happy arms will hold you . . .

is A flat, which is actually the same note (if you're plunking on the piano) as G sharp: it's marked differently because we're now in F minor. That's what's technically known as an enharmonic change, and it's very rare in popular song. Only Kern could make it sound that . . . inevitable. It was a hit for Tommy Dorsey and Artie Shaw, and, over the next few decades, whenever they polled composers and lyricists on what was America's songwriters' favourite song. 'All The Things You Are' came up Number One. It's hard to disagree.

3 '*Come Rain Or Come Shine*' (*1946, Harold Arlen/Johnny Mercer*)
'If Harold and I had stuck together,' Mercer used to say, 'I think we could have come up with a *My Fair Lady*.' I'm not sure. Arlen is the composers' composer and Mercer is the lyricists' lyricist, but in both cases their stage sense let them down. *St Louis Woman* has 'Come Rain Or Come Shine' and several other gems, but none of them contributes to the drama. This song is beautifully written: no cissified fancy-pants Broadway types would have let one syllable – 'shi-i-ine' – stretch lazily across a three-note blues slide. But, as with 'Stardust' and many other classic pop songs, it's hard to know what you'd do during the number to give it some dramatic propulsion on-stage.

4 '*Here's That Rainy Day*' (*1953, Jimmy Van Heusen/Johnny Burke*)
When Nat 'King' Cole, Sinatra and others rescued this harmonically

distinctive ballad, it certainly implied no endorsement of its dramatic context, as part of a musical about a seventeenth-century Spanish duke who invades the Belgian village of Flacksenburg. The musical was called *Carnival in Flanders*, which deserves some sort of Least Likely Hit Title award.

5 *'The Snooker Song' (1991, Mike Batt)*
The Hunting of the Snark was a musical version of Lewis Carroll. The snark was a mythical beast no one ever saw – and so, as it proved, was the audience. Mike Batt, who'd written 'The Wombling Song', 'Wombling Merry Christmas' and 'Let's Womble To The Party Tonight', was the composer, lyricist, librettist, orchestrator, designer, director and producer, and had quite a bit of his own money in the show, too. But, from the rubble, he managed to place 'The Snooker Song' ('I'm gonna be snookering you tonight') as the signature tune for comedian Jim Davidson's BBC TV snooker game show, *Big Break*. As Jerome Kern and Buddy DeSylva said, always look for the silver lining.

*

The week before *Miss Saigon* opened, I lunched with one of its authors, Richard Maltby, Jr. Aside from *Saigon*, Maltby also devised and directed the Fats Waller revue *Ain't Misbehavin'*, and, as we talked, I couldn't help noticing Waller's 'Honeysuckle Rose' drifting over the crowded restaurant, along with a swathe of other standards all the way back to 1914 and 'They Didn't Believe Me'. Would any eateries, I wondered, be playing Maltby's songs in 75 years' time?

'No,' he said. 'Those days are over. Audiences' ears have changed. In the thirties, people went to musicals to hear the hit songs. Now, if the orchestra slows down and the lights dim, your heart sinks and you think, "Oh, my God, I'm going to get that hit song that's going to interrupt the flow of the story I'm so excited about."'

Maltby's collaborator on *Miss Saigon* puts it more bluntly. Asked about take-home tunes, Alain Boublil says: 'With us, you take home the whole show.'

The Property

I remember Joseph Stein, in London in 1989, fingering the latest script for *The Baker's Wife*. 'This is maybe the tenth variation,' he estimated, 'but, oddly enough, the show is now fairly close to the first draft we had fifteen years ago.'

Which is how it goes in musicals, a sort of upside-down board game where the hardest thing to do is stay put at the original starting-point and avoid getting kicked round the course on treble sixes. This one began as an intimate character comedy, adapted from a Marcel Pagnol/Jean Giono film of the 1930s, about the arrival of a new baker and his young wife in a Provençal village. By the time David Merrick's production began its try-out in 1976, the show was already wildly cartwheeling away from the writers' intentions, and Stein and his composer Stephen Schwartz eventually insisted on closing it out of town. Thirteen years later, they'd worked their way back to what they had originally. 'There's just a word change here and there,' said Stein, 'but basically this is the final version. Thank God.'

'The librettist,' says Mark Bramble, 'is the first to get the blame if the show fails and, if it succeeds, he doesn't get a word of credit. Who knows who wrote the books of *Annie, Get Your Gun, South Pacific* and *Hello, Dolly!*?' Well, we know the first one: the aforementioned Herbert Fields with his sister Dorothy; then, respectively, Oscar Hammerstein and Josh Logan, and Michael Stewart. But you take Bramble's point: 'book trouble' has killed more shows than anything else, yet few people bother to examine why certain books work and others don't. Let's face it: who would you rather bone up on – Irving Berlin or Herb Fields?

As Alan Lerner liked to say, 'It's the book that decides whether a show will work; it's the score that decides whether a show will last.' Lerner preferred the term 'book' to the fancier 'libretto' ever since he heard a notorious Mrs Malaprop of New York explain that she'd been to the Met last night to see some opera by Verdi called *Libretto*. 'Book' is as good a word as any: it's the spine of the show. But most of the people who make musicals incline instinctively to spinelessness, and so putting a spine into a musical is like trying to insert backbone into a blancmange. Take *Irene* (1973), a fluffy vehicle for Debbie Reynolds, written by Hugh Wheeler and staged by John Gielgud – 'a strange choice for director of a musical,' muses Joseph Stein. On the road, it was a disaster – culminating in one performance when Miss Reynolds didn't go on and Gielgud took her place on stage, reading the script, while somebody else did the songs.

'When I was called in, I asked "What about Hugh?" They said, "He's gone." We're down as collaborators and I never met him till after the show opened. I had one brief meeting with Sir John, who was *thrilled* . . . ' Stein pauses. ' . . . to *leave*. He'd had it. He couldn't wait to get out. So I made a serviceable entertainment out of a shambles, as a professional favour.'

On such occasions, he prefers not to take credit, because it's not his baby. 'Are you *ashamed* of this show?' Debbie Reynolds demanded. 'I said, "Well, no. Not *really*." She said, "Then your name goes on it." She insisted.' Most of us would have joined Gielgud on the first train out, but Stein's Main Stem practicality paid off: *Irene* ran two years on Broadway.

But *Irene* was only a rewrite, a revival. The original production opened in 1919, became Broadway's longest-running musical ever and at one time had 17 companies on the road simultaneously. The librettist back then was James Montgomery. In his day, the book was already the least glamorous of the authorial tasks, but it took only half an afternoon to write. Today, it's still the least glamorous, but it takes the best years of your life.

'All I know,' reckons Tim Rice, 'is, if someone says, "Hey, what a great idea for a musical!", it usually isn't.' But, if you were pitching to investors, which group would be easiest to sell: *Mata Hari – the Musical, Breakfast at Tiffany's – the Musical, Gone With the Wind – the Musical*? or *Cats, Starlight Express, Les Misérables*? A hit is always a freak, but, if you want a guaranteed flop, pick a million-dollar property.

In *My Fair Lady*, Broadway sowed the seeds of its own destruction. *Pygmalion – the Musical*! Rodgers and Hammerstein tried, and said it couldn't be done. Bernstein, Comden and Green were called in. 'We saw the film,' says Betty Comden, 'and at the end we said, "Gee, it's such a great movie, why turn it into anything? It's too good. Leave it alone." That wasn't such a smart move.' But Lerner and Loewe found a way, and in so doing redeemed musical theatre for the sins of its fathers. The last Shavian musical, *The Chocolate Soldier* (1908), was such a crass distortion of *Arms and the Man* that Shaw insisted that all programmes and posters carry a public disclaimer by him. But, with *My Fair Lady*, which used whole chunks of the original play, it seemed as if Shaw's dialogue had been waiting all along just to facilitate those songs.

'*My Fair Lady* was the perfect musical play,' says André Previn, Lerner's composer on the later *Coco* (1967). 'But it was so perfect that afterwards, what else could you do? Afterwards, they had to try other things – dance musicals like *West Side Story*. But Alan's adaptation was the last word as far as that kind of musical was concerned.' In *Merrily We Roll Along* (1981), Stephen Sondheim has an idealistic young Broadway writer sing:

> I saw *My Fair Lady* . . .
> I sort of enjoyed it

. . . which deftly skewers Sondheim's own ambivalence about the show: he admired it as a professional work of adaptation, but he couldn't see the *need* for it.

Adaptation had become the art. This was the lesson of Rodgers and Hammerstein: you take a certain kind of story and turn it into a certain kind of musical play.

So *Green Grow the Lilacs* became *Oklahoma!*, and then *The Match-maker* became *Hello, Dolly!*, and then *The Man Who Came to Dinner* went down the drain as a very weak *Sherry!* The exclamation mark, the final stage in the adaptive process, was coming to be seen as a premature ejaculation: if the show gets that excited in the title, chances are it's pooped by Act One, Scene Two. Besides, the point of *Oklahoma!* is not the exclamation point! The point is that *Green Grow the Lilacs* was a forgotten, flop play. *My Fair Lady* is an exception, not the rule. As a rule, the best source material makes the worst source material.

Most musicals are adaptations of something – a book, a play, a movie. When, almost a decade after *My Fair Lady*, Alan Lerner wrote *On a Clear Day You Can See Forever*, he was offering Broadway that rare thing: an *original* musical. James Kirkwood, librettist of *A Chorus Line*, remembers coming out at intermission and realizing that, for the first time in ages, he didn't know how a musical was going to end.

'I didn't either,' said Lerner, years later. 'That was the trouble.' This is a collaborative form: composer, lyricist, librettist, producer, director, chore-ographer are embarking on a difficult journey. With an adaptation, they at least know the final destination and can concentrate their skills on figuring out how to get there.

So we have adaptations. And, because *My Fair Lady* and *West Side Story* were big smashes, would-be adaptors invariably turn first to the all-time greatest hits. Indeed, since the American musical theatre first hit its stride, certain futile properties recur every generation. History repeats itself, first as tragedy, then as farce, then as pop opera. Victor Herbert's *Cyrano de Bergerac* (1899) opened less than two years after Rostand's original play and only a season after the Broadway spoof, *Cyranose de Bric-à-Brac*. According to Herbert's biographer, audiences were divided 'as to whether they had seen a great play travestied or a mediocre burlesque ennobled'. Either way, they didn't like it. In the thirties, the Shubert brothers, who always had a nose for a hit, tried again, shuffling the title from *Cyrano de Bergerac* to *Roxanne* to *The White Plume* to *A Vagabond Hero*, and closing on the road every time. In the seventies, the composer Michael J. Lewis and the novelist Anthony Burgess wrote yet another version, but once again it expired on Broadway after the shortest of runs. In the nineties, in the wake of a successful Steve Martin movie version, a Dutch team tried its own adaptation in New York, with English lyrics by Sheldon (*Fiddler on the Roof*) Harnick. This was Harnick's second blow on the nose: with another composer, he'd written an operatic adaptation of the story. True to form, the Dutch *Cyrano* didn't linger long.

The reason, I think, is that the play itself is already so musical, there's nothing to be gained from adding an actual score.

But *My Fair Lady* and *West Side Story* cast long shadows into the sixties, seventies and beyond . . . Today more than ever, the obvious ideas – wretched film adaptations and big-name biotuners – are the only things anyone's prepared to sink money into. On the boulevard of broken dreams, here's six of the best that turned into six of the worst:

The Case of the Singing Detective

Leslie Bricusse's *Sherlock Holmes* (1989) was regarded as a total joke by most critics, but the book did represent a credible approach to musicalizing the trickiest of subjects: Moriarty is dead, and Holmes is bored with his retirement, when, suddenly, Moriary's daughter appears, vowing revenge. It's not a love affair, but Holmes does get an undeniable *frisson* out of a fascinating creature who combines all the deadly villainy of his mortal enemy with the form of a woman. It's an interesting reconciliation between Holmes and the needs of the musical.

Holmes had previously starred on Broadway in *Baker Street* (1965), whose librettist Jerome Coopersmith had wisely chosen to concentrate on the Irene Adler story, the one Holmes adventure with at least a suggestion of romance. 'At that time,' says Sheldon Harnick, 'we thought romance was necessary. But it's not specifically a love affair that a musical needs, just strong emotions.'

Harnick, a Holmes buff, and his composing partner Jerry Bock were called in when *Baker Street* ran into trouble on the road. Much of it sounded like Henry Higgins retreads: an educated Englishman talk-singing very densely packed lyrics. In the wake of *My Fair Lady* and then *Camelot*, it seemed there was only one way to treat British subjects. 'What I'm proudest of in *Baker Street*,' says Harnick, 'is a line of Moriarty's, when Holmes is trussed up and waiting for the bomb to go off and his enemy looks forward to a time "When the stately Holmes of England is no more".'

Cute. But Holmes belongs to a genre peculiarly resistant to musicalization. There's no successful Feydeau or Agatha Christie musical because, with both writers, character is subordinate to a rapidly evolving plot. It's just possible to imagine a Christie *dénouement* where Poirot addresses all 15 suspects and reveals whodunnit in music (almost inevitably a Henry Higgins-style talk-song in a Belgian accent). But an entire evening of sung plot leads would be awfully wearisome. Both farce and detective thrillers are plot-heavy genres.

'Richard Rodgers called me in on *Arsenic and Old Lace*,' says Harnick. 'We went through the book and couldn't figure out how to get any songs in.'

More recently, Charles Strouse grappled with Dashiell Hammett's *Thin Man* stories: '*If* it works, and I've had terrible problems with it, it's because Arthur Laurents has made the story extremely emotional. But even so, the mechanics of the mystery, the convoluted plot, can *musically* be very boring.' Strouse's fears were well-founded. When *Nick and Nora* opened on Broadway in 1992, it just didn't seem musical enough. The title switch, on the other hand, presumably intended to refocus the subject on to its glamorous husband and wife detective team, instead ended up reminding everybody how the two stage principals weren't in the same league as William Powell and Myrna Loy in the movie versions.

It's a Bird! It's a Plane! It's Musicalman!

'I believe in Superman,' insists Charles Strouse. 'When you see him on the printed page, you take it as real – the muscles and the suit and the Kryptonite.' But how do you transfer that to the stage without diminishing the magic? In *It's a Bird . . . It's a Plane . . . It's Superman!* (1966), Harold Prince's staging relied in part on a two-level box set to give the look of comic book panels, emphasized by lettered insets bearing such standard *Superman* scene-shifters as '*Meanwhile* . . . ' Prince also used puppetry and Peter Pan wire-flying, which some thought made the show too silly for words.

For many, the real stars of the show were the book and score. Superman was not mugged by camp, as happened to poor old Batman on TV, but he did have a certain guileless charm. When complimented, he would just say 'Yes' in a manly voice. The songs had a comic-book feel when required – 'Pow! Bam! Zonk!' – but, in 'Didja See That?' and others, also found a colloquial breeziness ideal for the citizens of Metropolis. Despite its brief run in New York, the show has earned a kind of afterlife in summer stock, where, without the benefits of big Broadway budgets, Superman flies around aided only by well-sprung off-stage trampolines.

'In hindsight,' says Strouse, 'we were ahead of our time. We thought it was clever, but people thought we were being "clever", that we were trying for a trendy cult show – whereas we wanted something for everyone.' But, if you've got a good idea, hang on to it. Just over a decade after *It's a Bird . . . It's a Plane . . . It's Superman!* crash-landed on Broadway, the librettists David Newman and Robert Benton co-wrote the screenplay for the hugely successful movie *Superman*.

To those who say *Superman* is inherently unsuitable for live theatre, Strouse retorts: 'A comic strip is an ideal basis for a musical comedy because they are similar forms of popular culture, both dealing in broad strokes, telling simple stories in as few words as possible.' But not until *Annie* (1977) did Strouse really prove the validity of that theory. And, if comics make such good shows, how about *Batman the Musical*? 'No,' groans Strouse. 'I spent so much time wrestling with Superman to find a singing style that was real for him, I just couldn't face that again.'

You Never Know What You'll Beget

At the Vivian Ellis Awards for young theatre writers, the producer Charles Vance summed up the Bible's merits with characteristically brute compression: 'It's a damn good book and there's no royalties.' The heyday of the biblical show was the late sixties, when Adam and Eve in *The Apple Tree* begat *Joseph, Jesus Christ Superstar* and others. The Stephen Schwartz/ John Caird Noah show *Children of God* (1991) was a late addition to the musical scriptures, but its quick sinking made a forlorn contrast with Schwartz's earlier Bible blockbuster *Godspell*. Christ Himself always had the strongest appeal to the hippy generation; the bearded heavies of the

Old Testament proved a tougher sell at the box office. *Hard Job Being God* ran six days and on the seventh rested for good; *Two by Two* lasted longer but for reasons other than the show.

'Other shows,' claims librettist Peter Stone, 'managed only because of their contemporary scores. Ours tried to do it with a traditional book and traditional score.' The composer, Richard Rodgers, did not seem an obvious choice for Noah, but Stone demurs. 'For television, he and I had done Shaw's *Androcles and the Lion*. And, after all, there was a lion involved in that, which he coped with.'

The problems started when Danny Kaye tore a ligament. Stone persuaded him not to withdraw, suggesting that, with a few rewrites, he could easily play the role from his wheelchair. The publicity was great: 'Danny Kaye Is Back In The Cast' – *cast*, geddit? Unfortunately, as the weeks went by, the adlibs increased and Kaye took to trying to mow down the rest of the company with his chair. Naturally, people began turning up just to see what the star would do next. Rodgers never forgave Kaye, while Stone has come to learn another lesson: 'It's very easy for the show to become a hostage to its star.'

To Be Or Not To Be

Howard Dietz wrapped up *Hamlet* in one couplet:

> A ghost and a prince meet
> And ev'ryone ends in mincemeat

Frank Loesser took a little longer:

> He bumped off his uncle
> Then he mickey-finned his mother
> And he drove his gal to suicide
> Stabbed her big brother
> 'Cause he didn't want nobody else but himself should live
> He was what you might call
> Unco-operative.

It was, however, not until the rock era that composers sought to extend this joke beyond three minutes. Shakespeare, after all, looks like a rock star. In the wake of *Do Your Own Thing* (1968), a musicalized *Twelfth Night*, and a rocked-up *Two Gentlemen of Verona* (1971), it was only a matter of time before Broadway launched a full-scale rock *Hamlet*.

The composer was a Canadian, Cliff Jones. 'Cliff's score was very basic but very singable,' says Gordon Lowry Harrell, music director of *Rockabye Hamlet* (1976). ' "The Rosencrantz and Guildenstern Boogie", for example, was really Elton John, but it had integrity, it was Cliff's way of telling the story.' Unfortunately, it didn't seem that way to the director Gower Champion, legendary superstager of *Hello, Dolly!* 'Gower started making things silly. He started the show in a different way.'

But, even without Champion muddying the battle-lines, the show was obviously going to be a test of strength. And, although Shakespeare himself might not have opted for numbers like 'Pass The Biscuits, Mama', when the great Elizabethan tragedy squared up head to head with rock'n'roll, it was rock'n'roll that ended up all crumpled and broken. Caught between rock and a hard play, even Meat Loaf got squashed. 'I adore Meat Loaf, who played the priest who performed the unction,' says Harrell, 'but he didn't have a chance. The way he was staged he wasn't Meat Loaf at all but Mr Meat Loaf The Actor. That's just not his strength.'

Rockabye Hamlet folded after a week. 'But, after experiences like that, where your intentions get perverted, can you blame writers for abandoning Broadway?' asks Harrell. 'The word around town from contemporary composers is: "I never want to write for the theatre again." '

A Bore Is Starred

These days, most musicals are biotuners – the life of a real person told in song. I don't know why. Most flops are biotuners, too – *Winnie* (as in Churchill), *King* (as in Martin Luther), *Leonardo* (as in Da Vinci) . . . But on and on they come. 'About six times a year,' says Herbert Kretzmer, 'I'm sent musicals about Anastasia which all open in a Russian café in Paris with waiters with flaming kebabs on swords.'

The only thing worse than a biotuner is a showbiz biotuner – all those trite price-of-fame singalongs about Elvis and Marilyn and Jolson. 'When you see the name Jolson, you expect to see the greatest talent we've ever had singing "Swanee",' says Irving Caesar, who, as it happens, wrote 'Swanee'. 'You don't want some fellow who just comes out and sings very nicely a song which sounds like a poor man's "Swanee".' Amazingly, though, every year or two, producers insist on doing just that. In *Jolson* (1978), instead of singing 'Mammy', a weedy Jolson wannabe came out and sang 'Give Me A Mammy Song'; in *Joley*, a year later, another ersatz Al appeared and, instead of 'Waitin' For The Robert E. Lee', we were treated to 'The Robert E. Lee Cakewalk': pale imitations of a giant personality singing pale imitations of the Tin Pan Alley formulae of 70 years ago.

Jolson, winner of Best Musical in the 1995 London theatre awards, would seem to be a resounding refutation of the Curse of the Jolson Biotuner. But this version was even more airbrushed than the 1945 film and depended mainly on the likeability of its leading man, the TV star Brian Conley. Without him, all you've got is an expensive but tacky karaoke evening.

Still, what else is left? At a time when we lack personality performers, it's easier to exhume those of the past: if you can't have a star above the title, at least you'll have one *in* it.

Jule Styne regularly turned down biotuner projects with a simple question: 'What's your First Act finale?' *Crosby the Musical*: he becomes a star, he has a lot of success, he becomes a bigger star, he has even more success; where's your story? The striking thing about Styne's *Gypsy* is that it's such an effective stage biography you don't even notice it's a stage biography: Mama Rose and all the rest become living, breathing characters in their own right.

The Doppelgang's All Here

The Prisoner of Zenda, Anthony Hope's thrilling adventure of a dashing Englishman's substitution for the King of Ruritania, was quickly transferred to the stage in 1895. Since then, it's been unsuccessfully musicalized at least thrice – first in 1924, by the young Richard Rodgers and Herbert Fields, while still at college; then in 1925, as *Princess Flavia*, which title tells you everything about the shift of emphasis Sigmund Romberg and Harry B. Smith made; then in 1963, with a score by Vernon Duke. Two lyricists later, Martin Charnin went out to join a troubled *Zenda* in California. 'With *Zenda*,' says Charnin, 'you have to maintain the robust truths: everyone swashbuckles and smashes glasses, and that's fine if you do it truthfully. It was when Rassendyll had to sing not as the King but as himself that the difficulties started.' As Rudolph Rassendyll observes, sometimes it's easier to pretend than to be real. We routinely apply the adjective 'Ruritanian' to operetta and its mythical kingdoms, without reflecting on why the ultimate mythical kingdom has never been successfully musicalized. Hope's story is romantic, but surprisingly real – and it's hard to make operetta real. *Zenda* folded out of town.

Today, Charnin regards the period in which he wrote the show as one of stricter rules. 'Rules have a natural lifespan and then they fall into disuse, but there are laws of gravity: the piper cub flies the same basic way as a 747; *Hair* has the same internal engine as *Oklahoma!* Today, anything can, in theory, make a musical, but it's an advantage if it has a larger-than-life quality. That's why I wouldn't want to write a musical about doctors or lawyers. Having said that, I know this time next season "The Attorneys' Tango" will probably be stopping the show.'

*

Where do musical writers come from? 'I was working in television on the Sid Caesar show,' says Joseph Stein, 'and I was asked by a producer, who was looking for another *Oklahoma!*, to do a show about Pennsylvania. So Will Glickman and I wrote a story about the Pennsylvania Dutch.' As a setting for a Broadway musical, Amish country is even less fertile than Oklahoma Territory, but *Plain and Fancy*, if not quite a checked-gingham blockbuster on the R&H scale, proved to be one of the surprise hits of the fifties. It also set the tone for his career. We think we know what we mean by 'a Jule Styne musical' or 'a Leonard Bernstein musical', but we don't often talk about 'an Arthur Laurents musical' – even though he gave both Styne and Bernstein their defining hits (*Gypsy* and *West Side Story*); we recognize a Rodgers and Hart song, but nobody goes around spotting snappy Herbert Fields dialogue – though the latter introduced the former throughout most of the 1920s. Librettists adapt such a diverse range of subject matter, it's not surprising that an individual voice fails to emerge. With Stein, the source material has been typically eclectic – Eugene O'Neill, Sean O'Casey, Sholom Aleichem – but the *oeuvre* does sort of cohere. 'The plays of mine I like best – starting with *Plain and Fancy*, then *Juno, Zorba, The Baker's Wife* – are basically about simple, elemental people in a very unsophisticated environment, centered round a larger-than-life figure. I don't write the kinds of things Doc Simon writes – about sophisticated people. I like it, but I can't write it.'

Stein's simple folk aren't *that* ordinary: *Take Me Along* had Jackie Gleason, *Zorba* Anthony Quinn. But he insists he's not in the business of star vehicles. 'When I write for the theatre, I am *not* writing for a star. The only time I ever did was for Sammy Davis in *Mr Wonderful*. Aside from that, I write my play and then it's cast, hopefully with someone who can play it. He may be Zero Mostel or Anthony Quinn. But Zero was not in my mind when I was writing *Fiddler*.' Still, the star, *de facto*, has the last word. As Tevye, Mostel took to throwing in bits of Yiddish and adlibbing, much as he'd done on *A Funny Thing Happened on the Way to the Forum*. 'On *A Funny Thing*,' says Stein, 'he got away with it because it was that kind of show; on *Fiddler*, he got away with it because Zero could get away

with anything. He was an enormous talent but – how shall I put it? – not
the most disciplined. I once went backstage after a show where he'd been
cutting up a little and he said, "Listen, when I'm on stage, it's between me
and the audience. Everybody else has gotta get outta the way." I said,
"Including the play?"'

The real punchline to the story is that, when Mostel left, seven other
Tevyes followed before *Fiddler* closed in 1972, having played 3,242
performances, overtaken *My Fair Lady* as Broadway's all-time long-
runner and been staged in more than 30 countries: the show was far bigger
than its star. Trouble is, how do you follow *Fiddler*? It's a question which
not only Stein but most of Broadway has found difficult to answer. Alan
Lerner hailed *Fiddler* as 'the triumphant finale to the glorious *Belle
époque* that began with *Oklahoma!*' – but the key word there is 'finale'.

'I disagree with Alan. People's emotions haven't changed. The problem
is, since *Fiddler*, there haven't been any musicals on the level of *My Fair
Lady* or those great shows,' says Stein, in a judgement implicit with
considerable self-criticism. 'You can't say, "My God, this wonderful show
failed on Broadway." No such show came along.'

Instead, the *belle époque* was followed by a brief Kerensky interregnum
– represented by Stephen Schwartz's *Godspell* and *Pippin* – before the
arrival of Lenin's train from Germany in the shape of Trevor Nunn's
Starlight Express from London. These three successive regimes are not
ideologically inflexible: after all, Stein, Schwartz and Nunn teamed up for
the *Baker's Wife* revival. But the show's swift closure reminds us, even as
librettists struggle to raise musical drama to the level of a straight play, of
the differences between the two forms: thanks to the dramatic credibility
imposed on the form during the *belle époque*, you can no longer glitz up a
musical with diversions, as David Merrick tried to do back in the seventies; but nor, as the '89 London production attempted, can you do a play-
sized musical. By definition, all musicals have to be large – not large in
terms of helicopters and roller skates, but large at heart – like *Show Boat*.
You can't just be like a play: here's a story; that's it. But, after *Fiddler*,
there was another problem. All those rules and principles Hammerstein
had introduced to the musical: Broadway just got too good at them; there
was nowhere else to go.

The Genius

Stephen Sondheim was a nobody until *Anyone Can Whistle*. All he'd done previously was write three solid hits, one after another: *West Side Story*, *Gypsy*, *A Funny Thing Happened on the Way to the Forum*. But *Anyone Can Whistle* (1964) was his first cult flop – nine performances and out – and inaugurated the Sondheim we know today – a genius too special for the expense-account set, the bridge-&-tunnellers and all the other schmucks who'd prefer to be vegged out at *Hello, Dolly!* 'Is Stephen Sondheim God?' asked a headline in *New York* magazine in 1994. But, if he is, he's not one of those big-time mass-market gods for Congregationalists and Baptists, but the deity of a remote tribe largely sealed off from the outside world – like those cargo culters in the South Pacific who worship the Duke of Edinburgh.

Occasionally, though, to the consternation of the cargo culters, the Congregationalists show signs of rather liking Sondheim. *Into the Woods* opened on Broadway in 1987, crept effortlessly into 1988, past 500 performances, 600, 700, nudging dangerously close to *Funny Thing*'s 964. Luckily, just when the Sondheim supplicants were figuring you might as well chuck it and trade your *Pacific Overtures* sushi kit for a *Phantom of the Opera* pop-up book, the show closed on 3 September 1989. Phew. For his next outing, Sondheim took no chances: an off-Broadway revue about Lee Harvey Oswald and other presidential assassins. Clearly, a musical about guys who've tried to stiff the Chief is going to run out of audience sooner rather than later. But, as the cherry on the cake of its commercial prospects, *Assassins* opened at the same time as the Gulf War. His unlauded contemporaries have all the big hits: Bock and Harnick (*Fiddler on the Roof*), Kander and Ebb (*Cabaret*), Charles Strouse (*Annie*), Cy Coleman (*Barnum*), Jerry Herman (*La Cage aux Folles*). But Sondheim's made it big on the scale of his flops. As he and Hal Prince lurched through the seventies, they eventually put Prince out of the producing business: the backers had all gone, their patience and bank accounts exhausted. With Sondheim and Prince, never in the field of musical theatre was so much owed by so few to so many.

He is, to quote a Sondheim title, a Broadway baby, *the* Broadway baby – schoolboy protégé to Hammerstein, young lyricist to the leading exponents of musical comedy (Jule Styne), the musical play (Richard Rodgers) and the modern through-choreographed musical (Leonard Bernstein). To these triple crowns, he is heir. Stephen Sondheim is the biggest name on Broadway, and now the only name on Broadway. To non-Broadway fans, Broadway was a parochial backwater and its musicals were all the same; no matter the subject, the treatment was the usual old formula. Sondheim has broadened their content and their form to embrace mass murder (*Sweeney Todd*) and pointillism (*Sunday in the Park with George*); he's given us plotless musicals (*Company*) and characterless musicals (*Pacific Overtures*) and musicals that go backwards (*Merrily We Roll Along*). But, in expanding Broadway's frontiers, he seems to have shrunk its population base. In the old days, Broadway made Broadway musicals that were like Broadway musicals, and everybody loved them; now Sondheim gives us kabuki musicals, and no one likes them but midtown Manhattan. Once, the shows were parochial; today, the audiences are. With Sondheim, Broadway has shrunk to its core supporters.

'Steve has all the skills of Larry Hart or Ira Gershwin,' Alan Jay Lerner once told me, 'but, unlike them, he doesn't reach out and touch.' Out there, in the rest of America, he means nothing.

'Sondheim is very New York,' said Frank Young of Houston's Theatre Under The Stars at a 1988 London theatre conference. 'A few years ago in Houston, we did *A Little Night Music* with Juliet Prowse and Hermione Gingold, and, even with those names, we couldn't sell the show. We had 300 people in a 3,000-seat theatre. You could have shot deer in there.'

Deer shooting: that's what folks do in the country. And it's hard to argue that they'd be better off putting down their rifles and listening to Bernadette Peters singing 'Art Isn't Easy'.

'He's scared to say I love you,' Sammy Cahn said to me a few years back. A lot of us are – though, if you write for the musical theatre, it's more of a problem. We're back to lyric-writing courage again and Dorothy Fields, a lyricist Sondheim admires, whose songs exude all the heady, giddy exhilaration of romance: 'Just Let Me Look At You' or 'We've Got It' or . . .

> Don't Blame Me
> For falling in love with you . . .

Ah, you say, but not all love is open-hearted, open-vowelled boy-meets-girl. Okay, then maybe a better comparison might be Frank Loesser, whom Sondheim also admires, and the fusion of pop breeziness and dramatic muscle he achieved in *Guys and Dolls*. There comes a spot in Act Two when Nathan Detriot finally has to admit he loves Miss Adelaide. No grandiloquent love duet for this couple; instead, Adelaide's hysterical, notey (tripleted) nagging . . .

> You promised me this
> You promised me that

. . . is interrupted by a broad legato protestation from the small-time crap-game promoter:

> Call a lawyer and
> Sue Me
> Sue Me
> What can you do me?
> I love you
> Give a holler and
> Hate me
> Hate me
> Go ahead, hate me
> I love you
> Alright, already, so call a policeman
> Alright, already, it's true . . .

Loesser's context makes those three little words, the tritest in popular song, fresh and convincing and in character. (I love the tempo marking on the song: 'Helplessly'.)

Three little words. In 1994, in a bizarre interview with *The New York Times*, Sondheim declared that at last he'd found love, as we'd hear in his new show, *Passion*. In *Passion*, the big love song goes like this:

> Loving you is not a choice
> It's who I am . . .

And you think: is that really an expression of love, or an intellectual defence of it?

On Broadway, *Passion*, adapted from Ettore Scola's film *Passione d' Amore*, opened with an arresting image: Clara, played by the voluptuous strawberry blonde Marin Mazzie, nude and straddling her lover. It looks like passion, but it doesn't sound like it. As much as any Brit hit mega-spectacle, the moment depends on a visual effect: the actress is naked, but the song isn't; Sondheim is always clothed, always veiled. In *Passion*, much of the evening is passed with the principals singing love letters back and forth to each other. It's emblematic of his work: not direct expression, but a considered text; not passion but a consideration of passion.

*

Merrily We Roll Along is the Sondheim musical about a composer who sells out; it's the one that goes backwards. Sometimes it seems that Sondheim, in an effort to avoid selling out, has chosen to play out his career in reverse. In the fifties, Ethel Merman in *Gypsy*; in the nineties, *Assassins* off-Broadway at Playwrights' Horizons.

Stephen Sondheim was born in 1930 to a wealthy New York dress manufacturer and his wife. But, when his parents divorced, he was moved to Bucks County, Pennsylvania and found himself in the right place at the right time. A neighbour of his mother, Oscar Hammerstein, was working on a new musical called *Oklahoma!* and it didn't take long for young Stephen to realize that he, too, was smitten by musical theatre. Although he studied composition with Milton Babbitt, he chose to apply what he learned in the commercial crap shoot of Broadway. Like Hammerstein, he's written the occasional pop song (with Jule Styne for Tony Bennett) and dabbled in films (*Stavisky, Reds, Dick Tracy*), but, like Hammerstein, he's always come back to the theatre.

He never intended to be a lyricist. In the mid-fifties, he'd written words and music for *Saturday Night*, but the show was never produced. So he made his début with *West Side Story* (1957): Sondheim's words but Bernstein's music. Everybody loves these songs – everybody, that is, except their author:

> I feel charming
> And disarming
> It's alarming how charming I feel . . .

Later, Sondheim would argue that rhyme implies education, and a sharp mind. Here's an uneducated Puerto Rican girl and she sounds like Noël Coward. But Bernstein loved the song and Sondheim could never persuade him to accept a new lyric: 'So there it is to this day embarrassing me every time it's sung.' In *A Funny Thing Happened on the Way to the Forum*, for the empty-headed romantic leads, he comes close to a merciless parody of the earlier song:

> I'm lovely
> All I am is lovely
> Lovely is the one thing I can do . . .

But not all *West Side*'s lyrics were alarmingly charming. In 1991, a musical called *Matador* passed briefly through the West End – about bull-fighting, as you might expect. The composer had done his best to put a few tourist-board Spanish touches in the music, but they were completely buried by the lyricist, who rhymed according to the cadences of English speech. On *West Side*, Sondheim knew enough to avoid that trap. Bernstein's tune for 'America' goes . . .

> Da-da-da da-da-da *da*-da
> Da-da-da da-da-da *da*-da . . .

If you were writing in colloquial English, you'd use feminine (two-syllable) rhymes:

> I'd like to go to Tor*on*to
> With the Lone Ranger and *Ton*to . . .

But Sondheim goes against the accents of the music and uses masculine (one-syllable) rhymes:

> I like the city of *San* Juan
> I know a boat you can *get* on . . .

That's what makes it sound Puerto Rican: taking his cue from that Frank Loesser novelty number, Sondheim puts the ac*cent* upon *the* wrong syl*lable* and he sings a tropical song. You marvel at how, on his first show, he knew to do that.

In rehearsal, they realized they needed a song for Tony. Lifting a speech from Arthur Laurents, Bernstein and Sondheim wrote a number that's urban, edgy and defines the character perfectly:

> Could it be? Yes, it could
> Something's Coming, something good
> If I can wait!
> Something's Coming, I don't know
> What it is
> But it is
> Gonna be great . . . !

Around the corner
Or whistling down the river
Come on, deliver
To me!

It's a brilliant distillation of youthful impatience, of the urge to be getting on to what's next: Tony – or Sondheim?

For *Gypsy*, two years later, he was supposed to be composer, but Ethel Merman, recently burned by a tyro tunesmith, demanded Jule Styne. *West Side Story* is Jerome Robbins, Arthur Laurents, Sondheim and Bernstein; *Gypsy* is Robbins, Laurents, Sondheim and Styne – a combination which makes less sense on paper. But *Gypsy* is a serious musical play disguised as a rowdy musical comedy. It certainly has the most cohesive of all show scores, written in Styne's distinctive style – what one might call literate vaudeville. The story of a driven stage mother pushing her children into showbiz was tailor-made for Styne – as a small boy, he'd done Harry Lauder impressions at the Hippodrome in London before the Great War. In *Gypsy*, he took vaudeville at its tackiest and raised it to the level of art.

He was well served by Arthur Laurents, whose tough, muscular book is superbly honed, a portrait of Mama Rose that both repels and seduces. In a genre dominated by larger-than-life ladies (Dolly, Mame), there is none like Rose. Her opening shot is that Broadway cliché, the 'I'm gonna make it' number, but, uniquely in the musical canon, Rose uses hers to put down the jerks who never will:

Some People sit on their butts
Got the dream, yeah, but not the guts
That's living for some people
For some humdrum people
I suppose . . .

That triple rhyme – 'some humdrum' – is impressive, not because it draws attention to itself but because it reinforces the architecture of the tune. Sondheim's lyrics catch the gaudiness of Styne's music, his 't' sounds spitting contempt:

Well, they can stay and *rot*!
But not Rose!

This is superb writing. 'Some People' is the exact equivalent of 'Something Coming': the character's 'I am' song. But you couldn't transfer one to the other because they're so attuned to their singers: the 't' sounds for Rose; the big, open, soaring reach-for-the-moon vowels – 'If I can *waaaaaiiiiiit*' – that tell us about Tony's dreams.

Sondheim has mixed feelings about these youthful works, and no matter how far he travels from Lenny and Jule and what he calls 'the Rodgers and Hammerstein tradition', they're always there, around the corner, whistling down the river. They never go away: *West Side* and *Gypsy* were both revived on Broadway in the eighties; on record, Bernstein did a laughable but best-selling classical gentrification job on the former with Kiri Te Kanawa and José Carreras; on TV, Bette Midler did a smash movie version of the latter for CBS. There's no better example of words set to another man's music than *Gypsy*, but what does Sondheim say about his lyrics? They're 'neat'. That's it.

He talks of these early works with a curious detachment, as if they're not really his at all. And they're not. Popular musicals belong to everyone, to every hokey am-dram ham who likes bellowing . . .

> Tonight
> Tonight
> Won't be like any night . . .

The new shows, when they came, wouldn't be like that. They would be, unmistakably, Sondheim's. Sure, you'll see your love tonight, and then what? Kids? It's the . . .

> Children you destroy together
> That make
> Perfect relationships.

And then what? Divorce?

> Will I leave you?
> Guess!

. . . which may well be the nastiest ending of any song ever. Sondheim, unmistakably.

*

He missed the sixties. He fulfilled a deathbed promise to Hammerstein to do a show with Rodgers – *Do I Hear a Waltz?* – and then laid low until 1970, when he returned to Broadway with *Company*. Musical theatre gets round to everything a little late, and Sondheim in the seventies was like a belated Broadway response to sixties rebellion. Here was the brattish nephew of Rodgers and Hammerstein, Styne and Bernstein telling Broadway that marriage is worthless (*Company*), that all middle-aged lives are failures (*Follies*), that US foreign policy sucks (*Pacific Overtures*), that we're all potential Charlie Mansons (*Sweeney Todd*). In the record biz, you can clean up with this kind of stuff. But, on Broadway, where most of your potential audience are the sort of married, middle-aged failures you're eviscerating on stage, it seems mad.

The thing is, it sort of worked – at any rate, to the extent that it earned Sondheim a popular unpopularity wholly unknown in musical theatre. From *Oklahoma!* to *Fiddler*, the Broadway musical was one of the few art forms where box-office receipts and critical admiration went hand in hand. There were, now and again, adventurous flops but no particular cachet attached to them, and, after they'd shuttered, no one bothered to assemble the cast at great expense and record an album, as Columbia Masterworks and RCA have done with Sondheim. *Anyone Can Whistle*, like *Merrily We Roll Along*, is never going to convince on stage, but that doesn't bother the buffs. It's always someone else's fault: on *Anyone*, it was Arthur Laurents' book; on *Follies*, it was James Goldman's book; on *Merrily*, it was George Furth's book; on *Pacific Overtures* and *Sweeney Todd*, it was Hal Prince's staging. Sondheim's immunity is such that, after English National Opera's production of *Pacific Overtures*, one critic, disappointed by John Weidman's book, thought it would have been better if the composer had done it himself. I didn't like the costumes in that production, but I don't think they'd have been improved by making Sondheim the designer.

So here's another irony: although the composer prides himself on embedding his score in the drama and gives no thought to take-home tunes, his fans seem happiest to hear the songs without book, staging and design, not only on the cast recording but also on innumerable recital albums by self-consciously cerebral *chanteuses* who'd explain in the seventies that, for a singer, a Sondheim song is 'like a one-act play'; by the eighties, they were saying it was a two-act play; by the nineties, three acts. But, if a Sondheim song itself is like a two-act play, who needs to see it within an actual two-act play? These songs aren't hits, but for that very reason they're all the more treasured. It's a strange experience to take a 'normal' person to a Sondheim gala, and watch the mystified looks as the first line of, say, 'There Won't Be Trumpets' is greeted with delirious applause. 'There Won't be Trumpets' was cut from *Anyone Can Whistle*. Sure, 'Maria, Maria' is okay, but to be *cut* from a Sondheim *flop* is as high praise as you can get.

In the showbiz satire *Forbidden Broadway*, Gerard Alessandrini, to the tune of Sondheim's 'Comedy Tonight', characterized his work thus:

> Something élitist
> Something defeatist
> Nothing you'd want to underwrite . . .

And then, a bearded Sondheim figure with a lop-sided smile shuffles on stage and ruefully sings 'Send In The Crowds', conceding in the middle section:

> Though I keep writing my scores
> With my usual flair
> After Act One
> No-one is there . . .

Alessandrini had Sondheim's permission to use his tunes, and why not? These are the jokes Sondheim makes about himself, wearing his commercial unviability as a badge of pride.

But making jokes about your unprofitability isn't really self-deprecating. In Britain, unlike Broadway, it's a basic entry qualification to the temple of Art. Sondheim is the first Broadway writer whom British arts institutions and critics, if not audiences, have taken to their hearts – mainly because almost all of his shows lose money, which makes him virtually an honorary Englishman. The composer's deification and the inauguration of 'the Sondheim era' (which irritates the hell out of his contemporaries) can be traced back directly to the evangelizing fervour of a small British revue, *Side by Side by Sondheim*. According to its narrator Ned Sherrin, back in 1976 you had to explain patiently who Stephen Sondheim was. How long ago that seems.

If you look at some of his most ardent champions in Britain – the National Theatre (who premièred *Sunday in the Park with George*), the English National Opera (who staged *Pacific Overtures*), BBC Radio 3 (who made him Composer of the Week) and the drama critics on the broadsheet newspapers – you might easily conclude that Sondheim makes musicals for people who don't like musicals. It always puzzles me that people who don't like Rodgers and Hammerstein or Jule Styne or Irving Berlin or Victor Herbert adore Sondheim, because all those influences pulse through his scores. He isn't a revolutionary; he sits on the throne of musical comedy as an hereditary monarch. As Michael Bennett, choreographer of Sondheim's *Company* and *Follies*, said, 'Before you can break the rules, you have to know what they are.' And Sondheim certainly does. He is a fascinating paradox: a summation of Broadway's illustrious past, and a rejection of it. Taken as a whole, his catalogue is a one-man history of American pop and theatre music. Here, from *Pacific Overtures*, is Sondheim doing an Offenbach gallop as a high-kicking French Admiral arrives to stitch up the trading concessions from the Japanese:

> *Oui, détente*
> *Oui, détente*
> *Zat's ze only zing we want . . .*

The Americans march on to Sousa, and the British sing Gilbertian patter:

> Hello, I come with letters from Her Majesty Victoria
> Who, learning how you're trading now, sang 'Hallelujah, Gloria!'
> And sent me to convey to you her positive euphoria
> As well as little gifts from Britain's various emporia . . .

And, instead of being sung by a D'Oyly Carte chorus, the instant recapitulation is growled by a traditional figure from Kabuki theatre, the Reciter:

> As well as little gifts from Britain's various emporia . . .

In *Follies*, Sondheim gives us a 'kiss' waltz, an operetta mainstay since Victor Herbert's 'Kiss Me Again':

> One more kiss before we part
> One more kiss and – farewell
> Never shall we meet again . . .

And why? Because . . .

> All things beautiful must die . . .

What? *All* things? Well, that's nineteenth-century romantic love for you.

Follies has another nod to Victor Herbert. In 1903, in the wake of the Broadway version of *The Wizard of Oz*, there was a slew of shows set in mythical, magical enchanted never-never lands. The best of these, by Victor Herbert and Glen MacDonough, was *Babes in Toyland*, with Toyland substituting for the Emerald City. In *Follies*, Sondheim turns Toyland into Loveland and, instead of babes, we have middle-aged couples – though their approach to love remains fundamentally immature:

> Bells ring, fountains splash
> Folks use kisses 'stead of cash
> In Loveland, Loveland . . .

In the twenties, instead of leading to melancholic introspection, love just made you crazy: 'You – You're Driving Me Crazy!' In an otherwise mostly contemporary score for *Company*, Sondheim suddenly reaches back to the twenties and boop-boop-be-doops his way through 'You Could Drive A Person Crazy'. In the Jazz Age, 'You're Driving Me Crazy' just meant 'I'm getting moderately excited', but Sondheim's characters are being driven *real* crazy, deranged, out of their trees. And look at his period detail:

> But worse 'n that
> A person that . . .

That's a twenties rhyme, straight out of Dorothy Fields and 'I Must Have That Man':

> I need that person much worse 'n just bad . . .

We're into the Broadway golden age now, to Cole Porter and the Gershwins and Yip Harburg. And, in 'You're Gonna Love Tomorrow', Sondheim condenses that particular Broadway quality of erudite naïveté into one couplet:

> Say toodle-oo to sorrow
> And fare thee well, *ennui* . . .

And the cavalcade rolls on. Here's Sondheim doing the Carpenters or maybe Olivia Newton-John and Cliff Richard in one of those seventies ballads full of overwrought fake climaxes and mushy melismas:

> I am
> Nothing
> You are
> Wind and water and sky
> Jodie
> Tell me, Jodie
> How I can earn your lu-u-urve . . .

But who's singing? It's John Hinckley serenading, at a distance, Jodie Foster. And how does he set about earning her lu-u-urve? He goes off and shoots President Reagan. And, for the middle-aged couples in *Follies*, sorrow and *ennui* are there what-ho-ing every miserable morning of their lives. And, in *Pacific Overtures*, the western powers are just out to rip off the Japs.

Sondheim's deployment of pastiche dates from *Anyone Can Whistle*, where his songs for the huckstering Mayoress (Angela Lansbury) all sounded like showtunes trying a bit too hard to sound like showtunes: he uses traditional musical comedy vocabulary for characters who deal in attitudes rather than emotions – almost as if they've seen so many old musicals they know that this is what they ought to be feeling at this point in the plot. The speech pathologist Wendell Johnson thought that anyone who seriously believed that . . .

> Some day he'll come along
> The Man I Love

. . . or that . . .

> Just Molly and me
> And baby makes three

. . . are all anyone needs for 'My Blue Heaven' was suffering from 'IFD Disease': I for 'Idealization (the making of impossible and ideal demands upon life)'; F for 'Frustration (at the results of the demands not being met)'; leading to D for 'Demoralization', and a retreat into schizophrenia. You *could* drive a person crazy. Sondheim is the first Broadway songwriter to endorse this point of view. In its portrait of middle-aged disillusionment, *Follies* comes close to stamping a health warning on Broadway's back catalogue: believing these songs can seriously stunt your emotional development. Stephen Sondheim knows more about Herbert and Romberg and Friml and Kern and Berlin and Gershwin and Porter and Rodgers and Hart and Hammerstein and DeSylva, Brown and Henderson and Yip Harburg and Burton Lane and Dorothy Fields than anybody else alive, and what does he tell us? That these songs are lies.

But Angela Lansbury's character isn't the only one who deals in attitudes rather than emotions. In *Follies*, 'Losing My Mind' was intended, apparently, as a George Gershwin tune (along the lines of 'But Not For Me' or 'The Man I Love') with a Dorothy Fields lyric – an appealing conceit since Gershwin and Fields never actually wrote together. Sondheim was striving for the romantic directness Miss Fields pulls off in 'The Way You Look Tonight' or 'I'm In The Mood For Love' or a dozen others. But the same affecting simplicity eludes him; the images sound forced and not entirely convincing:

The sun comes up
I think about you
The coffee cup
I think about you . . .

It's the sound of a clever man straining to be simple. 'Anyone can write clever,' Jule Styne used to say. 'The really clever thing is to write simple.' Lyric-writing courage again. At a basic level, Sondheim lacks the courage, the courage to have his characters let rip with . . .

I'm in love!
I'm in love!
I'm in love!
I'm in love!
I'm In Love With A Wonderful Guy!

Why can't they write 'em like that any more?
Because *we* aren't like that any more.
But it's not a question of love or hate or marital despair or middle-aged failure or east–west relations; it's about honest expression. In *Company*'s twitchy urban pop score there's a song called 'Another Hundred People' – about the hundreds and hundreds of people swarming off the buses and out of the subways into the city. It's a terrific image for a New York song, but, better than that, it captures the frantic desperate loneliness of city life with a directness Sondheim has rarely found since:

And they meet at parties
Through the friends of friends
Who they never know
Will you pick me up
Or do I meet you there
Or shall we let it go?

I would have liked to have heard more of *that* Sondheim.

*

For a while, Broadway seemed to have divided into two opposing cul-de-sacs: Sondheim scowling down one, while in the other was Jerry Herman, purveyor of maddeningly hummable showtunes to big ladies on staircases, in *Hello, Dolly!*, *Mame* and (overlooking gender) *La Cage aux Folles*. But whose is the ultimate 'big lady' show? The Broadway event of the eighties was the Lincoln Center gala concert of *Follies*. Back in 1971, *Follies* had been a cool dissection of nostalgia. By 1985, the cool dissection had become an exercise in nostalgia, a surrender to it: the band played 'Beautiful Girls' and, to rapturous applause, Lee Remick, Carol Burnett, Betty Comden, Elaine Stritch and the other beautiful if mature girls made their entrance. Singing the role of Roscoe was Arthur Rubin, moonlighting from his day job as vice-president of the Nederlander Organisation, the biggest theatre chain in the world. You could argue that the reason the American theatre's in the state it's in – the reason why Broadway is so nostalgic – is because of the decisions Mr Rubin makes when he stops singing and starts talking business. But it's a futile argument: Sondheim wrote 'Beautiful Girls' as a pastiche of Irving Berlin's 'A Pretty Girl Is Like A Melody', the anthem of the real *Ziegfeld Follies*. Sondheim's was supposed to be a knowing retread of an innocent original. But time blurs the distinction and now, when we gather to hear Sondheim's *Follies*, we're doing exactly as his ageing impresario says: we're glamorizing the old days, stumbling through a song or two and lying about ourselves. Not a bad definition of nostalgia. But musicals are so fixed on it we even get nostalgic about a show that's an attack on nostalgia. When Cameron Mackintosh produced *Follies* in London in 1987, the big ladies and the big staircase out-Hermaned Jerry. Privately, Sondheim called the production *Hello, Follies!*

The tunes are more complicated than Herman's, it's true. In *Passion*, 'I Read' lurches through a bar apiece of 3/2, 7/4 and 5/4, then two bars of 4/4, then back to a bar of 3/2, two bars of 7/4 this time, then a bar each of 5/4, 4/4, 5/4, 3/2, two bars of 4/4, and then 6/4 . . . For Broadway, this is complex stuff. But the very complexity, the shifting time signatures and tonality have become Sondheim's own signature: the more he avoids tunes in character for more sophisticated musical expression, the more everything he writes sounds like Sondheim. Again, another paradox: a man who describes himself not as a composer or lyricist but as a 'collaborative playwright' is returning us to the days of Hart and Porter, when, regardless of who was singing, it was the voice of the writer that came through loud and clear.

He likes the harmonic language of Ravel and Debussy, which, on Broadway, seems daring and adventurous. But how theatrical is it? George Gershwin knew Ravel, and once asked him for lessons. Ravel asked Gershwin how much money he'd made last year. When Gershwin told him, Ravel said: 'My friend, it is I who should be taking lessons from you.'

The composer and pianist Richard Rodney Bennett once said to me that, unlike Kern's and Gershwin's and Rodgers', Sondheim's songs weren't really standards: that is, there's no way to do them apart from the way they're written. And, although it had never occurred to me before, I soon realized he was right. Even the most unrespectful singers like Streisand and Sinatra, who think nothing of reworking songs as painfully slow or as ring-a-ding swingers, respectfully observe Sondheim's basic road map. In this as in much else, Sondheim is a precise negative of Broadway's Golden Age. With memories of Ellis Island not far below the surface, Broadway's first generation hymned the American dream; Sondheim, born into moneyed Manhattan, tells us it's a nightmare and, in *Assassins*, makes the great American songbook of cakewalks and Stephen Foster a soundtrack for psychopaths.

At the start of the eighties, having passed the previous decade doing savage indictments of marriage, middle age, western imperialism and industrial capitalism, he fell back on the old theme: how does an artist retain his integrity in a commercial world? The central characters are a composer and lyricist, one of whom sells out, while the other holds on to his dreams. They write a musical and audition it for a producer. He replies:

> That's great. That's swell
> The other stuff as well
> It isn't every day
> I hear a score this strong
> But fellas, if I may
> There's only one thing wrong
> There's not a tune you can hum
> There's not a tune you go bum-bum-bum-di-bum
> You need a tune you can bum-bum-bum-di-bum
> Give me a melody!
> Why can't you throw 'em a crumb?
> What's wrong with letting 'em tap their toes a bit?
> I'll let you know when Stravinsky has a hit . . .

And off he goes whistling 'Some Enchanted Evening', the sort of hummable melodee that Sondheim is accused of wilfully avoiding. The joke, though, is that the philistine producer is singing his denunciation of the songwriters' unhummable tune to the self-same unhummable tune.

But why are they unhummable? Maybe because, as *Sunday in the Park with George* led to *Into the Woods* to *Assassins* to *Passion*,

Sondheim seemed less and less interested in song form, in organizing a lyric to give it thrust and memorability. *Sunday in the Park* was another irritating, self-regarding meditation on the lot of the artist in society – in this case, the French pointillist Seurat. Sondheim wrote a pointillist score – little dabs and clusters of notes: 'Fin-ish-ing-the-hat'. But Sondheim's pointillism out lasted the show. In ending his relationship with Hal Prince and taking up with James Lapine, librettist/director of *Sunday* and *Into the Woods* and *Passion*, Sondheim has abandoned the notion of the 'concept musical' – where the subject sets the tone for the score – in favour of a sort of play set to notes. The show is the canvas, and the lyrics are dabbed on in maddening scattershot rhythmic patterns:

> Not forgetting
> The tasks unachievable
> Mountains unscalable
> If it's conceivable
> But unavailable . . .

The words run away with themselves. You can't follow the meaning, you can't always catch the consonants; all you hear are the rhymes – and the author. It's puzzling, but Sondheim sometimes seems more sensitive to the vowels and consonants Styne's and Bernstein's music demands than his own. Unlike other composer/lyricists – Berlin, Porter and Loesser – Sondheim's music and lyrics often sound oddly mismatched. The signs were there as long ago as *Follies*:

> Sweetheart, lover
> Could I recover
> Give up the joys I have known?
> Not to fetch your pills again . . .

That last line crowds too much onto too short notes. The ear can't catch 'fetchyour'. Since then, as his musical structures have become more self-admiringly elaborate, he's relied on more and more obtrusive rhymes to signpost our way around them. In a show like *Pacific Overtures*, rhyme ends up trivializing the reasoning:

> Streams are dying
> Mix a potion
> Streams are dying
> Try the ocean

Brilliant notion –
Next!

This is too neat. You can't organize complex socio-economic geopolitical issues to the convenience of over-fussy rhyme schemes. 'If a listener is made rhyme-conscious,' said Hammerstein, 'his interest may be diverted from the story of the song. If, on the other hand, you keep him waiting for a rhyme, he is more likely to listen to the meaning of the words.' 'Ol' Man River' is a powerful, memorable lyric, and there's no rhyme until the eighth and tenth lines. Hammerstein rhymes when the song requires it; Sondheim is an exercise in rhyme. In *Into the Woods*, when the mother of Jack (as in the beanstalk) tells her son to sell the family cow because . . .

We've no time to sit and dither
While her withers wither with her

. . . we're back to the pre-Hammerstein era: you're distanced from the character because all you can hear is the voice of the author. For 20 years, we've been inveigled into hailing Sondheim as a thinker on Broadway. But Broadway isn't about content, it's about form. And, when it comes to form, Sondheim has been getting sloppier show by show. 'Art Isn't Easy'? Oh, yes, it is, compared with craft.

By *Passion*, Sondheim didn't even bother listing the numbers in the programme, and you can understand why. Like opera, they no longer have titles, just perfunctory labels which you feel are for his publisher's convenience. One song is called 'Happiness', another 'Loving You'. Didn't Ken Dodd have a hit called 'Happiness'? And didn't Elvis do a song called 'Loving You'? And Minnie Riperton? These titles are so general as to be meaningless. I think of 'Good Thing Going', Sondheim's pensive ballad from *Merrily We Roll Along*, and its expert title resolution:

We had a Good Thing Going . . .
Going . . .
Gone.

And, with Sondheim, it *is* gone.

*

On 22 March 1948, Stephen Sondheim celebrated his eighteenth birthday. At the time Oscar Hammerstein was giving him a one-man masterclass in theatrical adaptation. Far away, on the other side of the world, a son was born to an English music professor and his wife. Andrew Lloyd Webber and Stephen Sondheim would share birthdays but not much else. Sondheim, born to the old disciplines of fixing and rewriting and rewriting the rewrites, has his merest trifles hailed as high art; Lloyd Webber, whose scores aspired to the inviolability of opera, is routinely despised as crowd-pleasing schlock. But, with the exception of *Sweeny Todd*, Sondheim has never initiated any of his shows. *Company, Follies* and *Pacific Overtures* started out as straight plays – until Hal Prince decided they needed bumping up with music; after *Follies* lost its entire investment, Prince, Sondheim and Hugh Wheeler cooked up *A Little Night Music* as a good old-fashioned shot at manufacturing a hit. It was the pap-peddling Lloyd Webber who found himself consumed by obsessions that, for better or worse, he had no choice but to write out: he had, in a word, passion. Sondheim was trained by Hammerstein, Lloyd Webber adored Rodgers. But both men broke faith with the peculiar amalgam of art and commerce that R&H represent. It was the British establishment who made Sondheim an artist; it was the American public who made Lloyd Webber a multi-gazillionaire – the most bizarre cultural exchange in theatrical history.

And, from somewhere at the back of the theatre, Mama Rose is goading her babies: 'Sing out, Louise!'

Sing out, Stephen.

Intermission

The Real World

The playwright David Ives sees it this way: 'It can't be an accident that the ancient Greeks contributed three basic elements to western civilisation: democracy, the theatre and the small Greek salad. . . . Is there, then, some intrinsic connection between a great, difficult popular art form and a great, difficult popular political system?' Ives thinks so. 'Consider the theatrical process. A group gets thrown together to put up a play. Over weeks of planning, weeks of rehearsal and weeks of performance, *all the people in that group have to agree.*'

It's a familiar argument: if only the world were run by the artists rather than the foaming whackos, all would be well – or better. The preferred image is Susan Sontag's *Waiting for Godot*, staged in the rubble of Sarajevo in 1993. But somehow the more potent one is David Merrick's Broadway production of *Hello, Dolly!* touring Vietnam: as the cast party got underway, the Viet Cong began shelling the city; Merrick stood on the roof, surveyed the blazing Saigon skyline and roared at his assistant, 'Isn't this sensational?' Top of the world, ma.

Who has the measure of the moment? Sontag or Merrick? The serious play sets out to address the world's affairs; the popular musical is a haphazard soundtrack to them. Which truly holds a mirror to nature?

In the Soviet Union, the relationship between state and art is formal – for example, the Moscow Writers' Congress of 1934, when the party issued its instructions on Socialist Realism. In America, it's unofficial, and the influence travels the other way. Political artists count for little; instead, the forms and conventions of mainstream entertainment are simply applied to the great offices of state. Like Bob Hope but unlike Constantin Chernenko, President Reagan felt the need for catchphrases, usually showbiz derived: 'Let's make it one for the Gipper' is a line he said in a biopic of the baseball player George Gipp; 'You ain't seen nothin' yet!' is the merest amendment of Al Jolson in *Robinson Crusoe Jr* (1916), *Sinbad* (1918) and *Big Boy* (1925) when, halfway through the show, to the frustration of his authors, he'd turn to the Winter Garden audiences and deliver an impromptu recital of 'Avalon', 'April Showers' and his other hits. Simple-minded entertainments but put over with a faith no audience could resist: that's Jolson – and Reagan, too?

But not even the Great Communicator can match the synthesis of life and art achieved by the Kennedy presidency. A few days after JFK's murder, Mrs Kennedy gave an interview to Theodore White for *Life* magazine:

'When Jack quoted something, it was usually classical. But I'm so ashamed of myself – all I keep thinking of is this line from a musical comedy. At night, before we'd go to sleep, Jack liked to play some records; and the song he loved most came at the very end of this record. The lines he loved to hear were:

> Don't let it be forgot
> That once there was a spot
> For one brief shining moment that was known as Camelot.

Once, the more I read of history the more bitter I got. For a while I thought history was something that bitter old men wrote. But then I realized history made Jack what he was. You must think of him as this little boy, sick so much of the time, reading in bed, reading history, reading the Knights of the Round Table. For Jack, history was full of heroes. And if it made him this way – if it made him see the heroes – maybe other little boys will see. Men are such a combination of good and bad. Jack had this hero idea of history, the idealistic view:

> Don't let it be forgot
> That once there was a spot
> For one brief shining moment that was known as Camelot.

There'll be great Presidents again – and the Johnsons are wonderful, they've been wonderful to me – but there'll never be another Camelot.'

Life came out on Tuesday. On Wednesday afternoon, Alan Jay Lerner, Kennedy's classmate at Harvard, was crossing the lobby of the Waldorf-Astoria, past the news stand. In headline letters above the masthead of *The Journal-American* was the quatrain of his title song. 'The tragedy of the hour, the astonishment of seeing a lyric I had written in headlines, and the shock of recognition of a relationship between the two that extended far beyond the covers of one magazine, overloaded me with confused emotions. I was so dazed that I did not even buy the newspaper.' At the time, Lerner lived on 71st Street. He started to walk home, and was at 83rd Street before he realized he'd passed his block.

In November 1963, *Camelot* was on the road. That night, it was at the Chicago Opera House, a huge barn playing to a capacity crowd of over three thousand. 'When it came to those lines,' said Lerner, 'there was a sudden wail from the audience. It was not a muffled sob; it was a loud, almost primitive cry of pain. The play stopped, and for almost five minutes everyone in the theatre – on the stage, in the wings, in the pit and in the audience – wept without restraint. *Camelot* had suddenly become the symbol of those thousand days when people the world over saw a bright new light of hope shining from the White House. God knows, I would have preferred that history had not become my collaborator.'

> Ask ev'ry person if he's heard the story
> And tell it strong and clear if he has not
> That once there was a fleeting wisp of glory
> Called Camelot . . .

The newspapers immediately dubbed those thousand days Camelot; one of the first books on the subject was called *A Fleeting Wisp of Glory*; and Kennedy's official biographer, William Manchester, chose the title, *One Brief Shining Moment*. To the further bemusement of Alan Jay Lerner, *The Oxford History of the American People* closed with the printed lyric of the song. It's not so much that the comparison is inapt – Lerner's King Arthur is a wimpy cuckold, which hardly fits Kennnedy – as that the national tragedy of a prematurely terminated presidency in the world's most powerful nation should be symbolized by a musical comedy. 'For myself,' said Lerner, 'I have never been able to see a performance of *Camelot* again.'

It's difficult to imagine any political journalist in London writing *Starlight Express: the Eighties Boom* or *Les Misérables: the Seamy Underbelly of Thatcher's Britain*. Even when events conspired to give the Iron Lady a perfect expression of scornful defiance, nobody seriously suggested that she should telegraph General Galtieri: 'Don't Cry For Me, Argentina'. At a presidential banquet in America, she attempted to mimic President Reagan's 'You ain't seen nothin' yet', but the strained over-enunciation – her inability to elide the 'g' on 'nothin'' – only emphasized how painfully foreign the Reagan razzle-dazzle was to her style of politics, and how, at core, the British, for all the mega-musicals shared the same reach-for-the-sky gigantism of Mrs Thatcher's hairdo, cannot subscribe to that fusion of showbiz and politics with a straight face. When Vince Hill sang, to the tune of 'Hello, Dolly!', 'Hello, Maggie!', the British scoffed. When President Clinton campaigned with Fleetwood Mac – 'Don't Stop / Thinking about tomorrow' – the Americans bought it. (Incidentally, we can't complain we were misled: the song distills perfectly both the vacuity and single-mindedness of the Clinton presidency.)

So, from Leslie Stuart (composer of *Florodora*) to Ivor Novello to Lloyd Webber, London has nothing to match the symmetry between Broadway and the national mood extending from the vulgar flag-waving cockiness of George M. Cohan, the Yankee Doodle Dandy, to post-Vietnam national malaise with Stephen Sondheim. For a European equivalent to America's great twentieth-century soundtrack, you have to go to Vienna. And even then, unlike the hip-hooray and ballyhoo (Al Dubin) and the roaring traffic's boom (Cole Porter), what you mainly notice about Vienna today is the silence. Walk through the big shopping streets of the city and eventually you're struck at how resistant it is to rock and pop. In every other major capital, punk and funk and rap and reggae blast from boutiques and burger joints. But not in Vienna. Here, the record stores have extensive racks of classics and opera and operetta and waltzes – and a few small bins of pop. This is a city which once had such a precise musical voice it refuses to have any other imposed upon it.

*

'The Habsburg Empire was a melting pot of various cultural streams,' says Eduard Strauss, great-great-grandson of Johann I and son of the (to date) last musician in the family, 'and Vienna was the centre of it. It is the atmosphere of Vienna that brings out music. You still feel the music in the air, so to say, of Vienna. When I go through the streets, I can well imagine that this music must have been created here.' In the Strauss biopic *The Great Waltz* (1938), there's a scene where Fernand Gravet (as Johann II) and Miliza Korjus take a carriage ride through the Vienna woods: *en route* he composes, inevitably, 'Tales Of The Vienna Woods' and every time he gets stuck there's always a hunting horn or the driver's exhortation to his nag to provide the next stage of the tune. It's a laughable scene – and yet, when you listen to Eduard Strauss, it's almost plausible: the music's out there; all the composer has to do is reel it in.

'It's a wonderful experience: we go into a dreamland and the dreams tell us about our current situation,' says Michael Kunze, German-language librettist for most of the Brit hit musicals in Europe. Inspired by the popularity of those shows, he then went on to create Vienna's first home-grown musical work in decades, *Elisabeth* (1992) – the life of Franz Joseph's Empress, murdered by an anarchist. 'The Habsburg monarchy is still alive here,' he maintains. 'If you walk around this city, if you talk to people, they talk about Elisabeth and Franz Joseph as if they were relatives who've just gone. There's a very deep relationship between this story and this city.'

Once you accept this relationship, you understand why shrunken, post-Habsburg Vienna has fallen silent. In the old days, the Austrians used to export monarchs, installing, for example, Archduke Maximilian as emperor of Mexico. So it seems entirely natural that their theatrical exports should also be scions of noble houses: *The Count of Luxembourg*, from Lehár; Princess Helene of Flausenthurn in *Waltz Dream*, from Oscar Straus (no relation); Kálmán's *Czardas Princess*; Leo Fall's *Dollar Princess* (no relation to the *Czardas Princess*). It's easy to get this crowd mixed up: in the Népszinház-Vigopera production of *A Nagymama*, the part of Countess Szeremy was played by Baroness Ödön Splenyi – or was it the other way round? Oh, well, Ruritania is in the eye of the beholder. The big Budapest hit of 1902 was Jenö Huszka's *Prince Bob*, the only Hungarian operetta set in London and the story of a son of Queen Victoria who goes out into the streets to woo a Cockney serving wench. That's Hungary's Ruritania: the United Kingdom. When a later Prince of Wales took up with a serving wench – or, anyway, an American divorcee – the Hungarians were quick to point out the plot had been lifted from a show they'd done 30 years earlier.

In Mitteleuropa, history is operetta and operetta is history: in *The Merry Widow*, Count Danilo's uniform was copied from that of the Crown Prince of Montenegro, though for the most part the show tends to highlight the quainter Balkan traditions rather than their more robust and enduring nationalist manifestations like genital severing. So, yes, in operetta, the cardboard counts are unbelievable and the plots are ridiculous. But, in this part of the world, real life is ridiculous and the characters in charge even more unbelievable. You want a King who marries a gypsy dancer? How about Carol II of Romania? Then there's King Zog of Albania, whose idea of lowering his country's national debt was to knock on the hotel rooms of American tourists and force them into playing poker with him. The Austro-Hungarian Empire expanded by marriage rather than conquest, so those outlandish operetta romances have a sort of gritty neo-documentary street cred.

But operetta deals mainly in certainties. And, as the long reign of Franz

Joseph wore on, nothing was that certain anymore. In 1889, Crown Prince Rudolph and his mistress were found dead at the hunting lodge at Mayerling – either a double suicide or something even murkier. Emmerich Kálmán later used these tragic events as the subject of a Broadway musical, *Marinka*. But, in his version, instead of being found dead at their hunting lodge, the star-crossed lovers emigrate to America and settle down on a farm in Pennsylvania. Well, you can't beat a happy ending. But this one was a particularly telling symbol of the widening gulf between operetta fantasy and reality.

Here's an operetta staple: an archduke who falls in love with a commoner. Amazingly, unlike poor old Prince Rudolph, love prevails and they live happily ever after ... for a while. On 28 June 1914, a date which reverberates on the battlefields of Europe 80 years later, operetta lost the plot once and for all: Rudolph's successor, the Archduke Franz Ferdinand, was assassinated at Sarajevo. The Balkans, so appealingly mythologized on stage, had plunged the world into war. The Habsburg Empire shrivelled away to a tiny, pointless Austrian republic; an abortive coup was described as 'bad operetta'; in Hungary, an abortive Royalist coup enlisted the help of Colonel Lehár, Franz's brother. And, for Kálmán and other European composers, that farmhouse in Pennsylvania came to represent musical theatre's own shift of gravity. Along with the Habsburgs and the Romanovs and the Kaiser, operetta also lost its throne.

*

I'm not saying I'm a Stalinist *but* ... I did get ever so slightly nostalgic for the old days when in the fall of 1989 Gennadi Gerasimov, that plausible spokesman for President Gorbachev, announced the new-look ring-a-ding-ding Warsaw Pact. 'The Brezhnev Doctrine is dead,' he declared. 'We now have the Sinatra Doctrine: you do it your way.' Back at the White House, Vice-President Quayle was encouraged by Mr Gerasimov's statement but, noting the continued presence of Soviet troops in Eastern Europe, urged him to remember the Nancy Sinatra Doctrine: 'These Boots Are Made For Walking'.

So Harold Pinter and all those other left-wing dramatists were right. There *is* an equivalence between the decadent West and the Soviet Union: they both use the same gag-writer. Jaw-jaw is better than war-war, as Churchill said, but neither can compare with haw-haw: throw away those warheads and let the PR men lob one-liners at each other. We all know, though, where the new style of bilateral communication originated.

Forty years after Zhdanov's State Committee denounced Prokofiev and Shostakovich for 'bourgeois formalism', his heirs were happy to remake the map of Eastern Europe in the image of a saloon singer from Hoboken, New Jersey. If anything represented the final capitulation of stolid, non-vernacular Marxism-Leninism, it was not what the Sinatra Doctrine meant but how it was expressed. One of Communism's last virtues was its obstinate refusal to defer to the trivial values of pop culture. True, Fidel Castro did appear as an extra in the Fred Astaire/Rita Hayworth musical *You Were Never Lovelier*, but this was some years before he took charge of Cuba. Otherwise, Communism was deadly serious. In the forties, Moscow issued a directive to their British comrades that 'the lower organs of the party must make even greater efforts to penetrate the backward parts of the proletariat'. Claud Cockburn warned that this was likely to be received as a Max Miller joke, but, Marxist theory being unfamiliar with the concept of a Max Miller joke, the Party went ahead anyway.

In their own fiefdoms, the Soviets were more forceful. In Hungary, they changed the set. 'After the war, the world of operetta changed,' says Robert Ratonyi, the great Hungarian theatre star and the only man ever to have played both Higgins and Doolittle in *My Fair Lady*, possibly on the grounds that he looks equally unsuited to both roles (he resembles a cross between the UN's Pérez de Cuéllar and the Australian cultural attaché Sir Les Patterson). 'Counts and princes were forced out. In the new socialist operetta, factory workers and collective farmers were introduced instead. In the classic operettas, Louis XIV was courting Madame de Pompadour. In the modern operettas of those days, a shop salesman was courting a mill girl. But the recipe was the same.'

The smash socialist operetta was *The State Department Store*, a hit in Hungary, though it never transferred to Broadway or the West End. I treasure, too, an old film musical of the fifties showing two young lovers embracing high above the Danube on the Buda side. They sing:

> For us this city is beautiful
> And for us the lights glitter
> Happiness awaits you here
> So love me the way I love you . . .

And then the camera cuts away to a shot of *Das Kapital*.

According to Ratonyi, 'Traditional operetta was considered a bourgeois form. The change came with *Czardas Princess*. In Budapest, I was playing the comic Count Boni and I was instructed to play him as a class enemy because a count shouldn't be likeable.' In Leningrad, on the last night of their Soviet tour, the company was invited to play for the General Sec-retary and the *nomenklatura*. Khrushchev liked it so much that he pre-sented Ratonyi and his fellow players with three gifts apiece: a camera, a refrigerator and a motorcycle. 'So traditional operetta got the green light in Hungary.'

Thus it was that, during the uprising of 1956, the regime chose to pump out non-stop operetta on the radio – presumably, to lure the people from the streets with the siren songs of escapist fantasy. In Hungarian, the word 'operetta' means 'something frivolous'. But, like a distorting mirror at a carnival, reality is there if you look carefully enough. Just as Colonel Lehár accompanied the Royalist coup, so brother Franz accompanies the '56 revolt and, briefly, *The Count of Luxembourg*, the story of a young nobleman turned struggling artist, becomes political theatre. From Magyar Radio, thanks to the carelessness of the authorities, comes a weirdly apt song cue:

> So many people! The noise! The goings-on in the street!

And then the prima donna Hanna Honthy sings:

> Confetti showers upon you
> Prince Carneval is going about with his sons
> Merry music follows them . . .

And outside the studios a mass of disaffected citizens appears . . .

> Dancing at every corner
> Streamers raining! Infernal din!

A tank rumbles down the rubble-strewn street . . .

> Hundreds of ribbons!
> Blaring trumpets!

The demonstrators shake their fists as the tank fires . . .

> A ball lands on your head
> You can but smile at this
> Fearsome masks are grinning
> With flashing eyes behind . . .

The Russian soldiers round the corner in a troop truck . . .

> So many people together in the street
> Is anything but *comme il faut* . . .

The Commie foe peer nervously from their turrets, and Lehár's chorus fills the air:

> Honour and good manners are everything
> Times will not change me
> That's how a lady stays ladylike . . .

*

In the decades after 1956, János Kádár's goulash Communism kept meat and potatoes in the shops and permitted Rice and Lloyd Webber on stage: *Evita* and *Jesus Christ Superstar* played Budapest; so did *Cats*, and *Les Misérables*. And, in penetrating the Iron Curtain, British musicals, which in London were barely credited with text at all, were imbued with the most significant subtext. In London and New York, the little urchin girl of *Les Miz* is a marketing tool, a trademark. As the cast of the satirical revue *Forbidden Broadway* sing, in a parody of the show's big ballad:

> Come see us grovel in the dirt
> Then buy a souvenir and don it
> Rich folks pay 50 bucks a shirt
> That has a starving pauper on it . . .

But, when *Les Miz* came to Gdynia in Poland, the starving pauper was a call to arms, and her tattered tricolor was replaced by the Solidarity flag.

'*Evita* had an interesting political resonance,' says Kriszta Kováts, who played the title role in Budapest in 1980. 'There was a kind of parallel between the speeches given by Evita and Peron and the speeches given by Kádár. "Don't Cry For Me, Argentina" is a very moving song and expresses so well someone making wonderful promises while we can see what's happening in reality. In Hungary, we, too, felt that, despite the promises we were given on radio and TV, nothing would become reality.'

For Hungary's frustrated musicians, these works were an inspiration – a liberation. The composer Levente Szörényi and lyricist János Bródy, a couple of sixties rockers whose songs 'reflected the political tensions in society', came up with a pop opera of their own, sprinkling a little paprika on the Rice and Lloyd Webber formula. By 1989 *King Stephen* had been seen by ten per cent of Hungary's population.

Who's King Stephen? He was made king by Pope Sylvester II and brought his country into civilized Christian Europe, turning his back on Hungary's ancient culture and the pagan leader Koppány. On-stage, it looks like a quarrel between minor members of a 1970s heavy metal band, but to Hungarians it meant 1956: Stephen the compromiser represented János Kádár; Koppány, underneath the fur hat and tunic, symbolized the leader of the uprising, Imre Nagy. As János Bródy's meditative guitar ballad put it:

> The bright has been plunged into darkness
> All it reveals is blood-stained soil
> A field shrouded in mourning
> A churchyard full of new graves . . .

'This was the most successful show of the decade,' says Bródy. 'It had an unbelievable impact. *King Stephen* roughly marks the beginning of the changes in Hungary.'

His composing partner agrees. 'We'd like to refute the notion of our piece starting anything,' says Levente Szörényi, 'but without doubt the last ten years point to it clearly. This première may have awakened the feeling of arrival in a new age.'

> Hungarians! Men and women!
> Listen to our leader Koppány!
>
> I do not ask where you were born
> Nor who your father was
> All I ask is one thing
> Shall we be captive or free?

The stadium rock blares out, the guitars whine, the torches flare, and the audience roars its approval in people-power salutes.

What keeps a culture alive? In Vienna, it died. In Budapest, it proved amazingly resilient. 'Lehár said that operetta would never die,' Robert Ratonyi recalls. 'For my part, I hope you live as long as operetta. Then you will be eternal.' Or as his bouncy TV variety show singalong proudly asserts:

> This genre has become history
> Has survived many difficult days
> Politics keep changing
> But operetta remains
> I've survived many a storm
> I'll survive this one, too . . .

And Ratonyi flashes his huge toothy smile, grabs his cane and taps his straw boater on his white hair:

Operette! Operette! Operette!
You're a capricious delight!
Operette! Operette! Operette!
One thousand moments of fun!
Operette! Operette! Operette!
You're locked in my heart!
Operette! Operette! Operette!
I'll love you all my life!

*

Far away, in the long twilight of Kremlin power, western commentators, determined to look on the bright side, began attributing some pretty
unlikely popular tastes to Soviet leaders. Yuri Andropov, to counter his
KGB hard-man's image, was widely touted as a Glenn Miller fan, but, even
if he'd ever been in good enough health to hold a press conference, I doubt
whether you'd have got very far asking him whether he preferred 'I Got A
Gal In Kalamazoo' to 'Chattanooga Choo Choo' and, if so, which
version.

It came more naturally to President Reagan, not just because of his own
background but also because in America politics is now conducted almost
exclusively through the language and imagery of popular culture – even
though, the Gipper aside, what political figure raised to office through the
dreary mechanisms of a constitutionally stable democracy can compete
with the fabulous one-offs of the entertainment world? It's a choice nicely
caught by Harold Arlen and Yip Harburg in 'God's Country', a sardonic
hymn to their native land from *Hooray for What!* (1937):

> We got no Mussolini, got no Mosley
> We got Popeye and Gypsy Rose Lee . . .

Harburg is sniping at both the Old and New Worlds, but, on balance,
most of us know which we'd prefer. If you have to have some loonytoon
figure in ridiculous uniform strutting about and making a lot of noise,
better Michael Jackson than Il Duce. But when Jacko, in the ceremonial
dress of some Never-Neverland field marshal, and his young bride, Lisa-
Marie Presley, toured Mitteleuropa, was it the triumph of American
popular culture? Or a return to older ways? Jackson wouldn't be out of
place in an operetta, nor Madonna, nor the Artist Formerly Known As
Prince. Indeed, most rock Artists these days would have been Formerly
Known As Princes if they'd been around a century ago. Before Barbra

Streisand will enter a room, whether a marble-tiled bathroom in her hotel suite or Wembley Stadium, she insists that the whole place be carpeted from wall to wall. And instead of going 'Come off it', we say, 'Right away, Miss Streisand', as we would have done for Mad King Ludwig of Bavaria.

So, the Wall crumbled, and the dissident artists in the vanguard of the struggle found themselves marginalized by glossier entertainments. Those who fought for a world safe for Václav Havel to be staged in found instead that they'd simply added another venue to the *Cats* tour. And what of musical theatre's most political dramatists? Kurt Weill went to America, never spoke German again, protested to editors when the press described him as a 'German composer', and anglicized the pronunciation of his name from 'Koort Vile' to 'Curt While'. (His friend Maxwell Anderson made a sly play on his name in the lyric to 'September Song': 'Oh, it's a *long, long while* from May to December' – the long while contrasting with the Curt While.) But Weill's partner from the *Threepenny Opera* days, Bertolt Brecht, hated America. He returned to Germany – East Germany, the GDR. And today the old fraud's highest-earning song is a reminder that even the most explicitly political art can be wrenched from its moorings. In the eighties, even before the Wall fell, 'Mack The Knife' completed its slow inexorable defection and signed up to push hamburgers on television:

> It's the great taste
> Of McDonald's
> Come on, make it . . .
> Mac tonight!

Brecht sells burgers! Now there's a metaphor – and, like all the best ones, it's accidental.

Act Two

i

The Brits

This is how they divide history: BC – Before *Cats* – and AD – Andrew Dominant. Stanley Green's exhaustive *Encyclopaedia of the Musical*, published in 1976, contains no entry for Andrew Lloyd Webber. The New York season just ended had produced *A Chorus Line* and *Chicago*, and Broadway seemed as healthy as could be expected. No one would have predicted that, within ten years, the only bankable writer in musical theatre would be an Englishman known for just one show, *Jesus Christ Superstar*, which had anyway been appallingly staged. To Broadway folk, Lloyd Webber was just one of many writers who had emerged in the peace and love era, turned out one rock musical and then disappeared. It was *Evita* that made his reputation and his next show confirmed it so triumphantly that, in 1997, in a moment of sad symbolism, it effortlessly overtook *A Chorus Line* as Broadway's all-time long-run hit. Think about it: Broadway's longest-running show – a British musical.

Like those RSC and opera directors who hit the big time with *Cats* and *Saigon* and *Sunset*, like the *Daily Mail* TV critic who made a pile from his *Les Misérables* lyrics, like the Oxford University Professor of Poetry who *still* made a pile even when his *Les Miz* lyrics were rejected, like the fellows who designed the *Phantom* and *Starlight* logos for the posters, albums, mugs, T-shirts, pop-up books, like the New York travel agents who sell London leisure breaks around the West End hits, like the Toronto impresario who built the Princess of Wales Theatre just to house *Miss Saigon*, like the German impresario who built a huge barn at a key intersection of Mitteleuropean *autobahnen* just to house *Starlight Express*, like the Hungarian impresario who cashed in on Budapest theatregoers' irritation at having to schlepp over the border to Vienna and produced a hit play called *When Are We Going to Get the Phantom?*, like the owners of all those poster sites in Tokyo, Munich, Melbourne, Gdynia, like the 40 per cent of working American theatre actors employed by Cameron Mackintosh and Andrew Lloyd Webber productions, like the publisher of this very book whose distinguished house has been enriched by T. S. Eliot's royalties for

Cats, like all of them and a lot more besides, I, too, have grown fat on British musicals. And, also like all of them, I can find no rational explanation for *Cats*.

'We were these mad people with a Shakespearean director and these boring old poems going into the worst theatre in London. All the people who were our normal sources of money, 90 per cent of them turned us down. We ended up with over 200 small investors,' says Cameron Mackintosh, noting coolly: 'The show has been averaging a 200 per cent profit since the return of capital' – that's 200 per cent per year for over 15 years.

'If you look back historically, most of the shows that have been really big international successes have been shows that people in the profession at the time have said, "Oh, well, *that'll* never work . . ." With *Cats*, after a lunch with Andrew, he took me back and played me three or four settings of T. S. Eliot's poems. And there was something about them that just sounded intriguing – sort of made my tummy start to go into knots. And I thought, "Yes, there's something here." I didn't know what that something was.'

Who does? But not many of us find it in the score. Lloyd Webber's collaborator, the late Mr Eliot, was dead, and it's a rare composer who can set formal ABAB poetry with any imagination. The music is constrained, pinched – but it's brilliantly danced. As Jule Styne once told me, 'You could throw away every song except "Memory" and it wouldn't make any difference.'

'It's an experience rather than a musical,' says Mackintosh. 'People who see the show for the first time can't quite pin down what it is. They've just had a wonderful time.'

Or as *Annie*'s composer, Charles Strouse, puts it: 'If you're paying $60, you want a lot for your money. And, whether you approve or not, *Cats* at least gives you a lot of cats.' Even then, you'd think that a show in which people crawl around the stage dressed as cats is, sooner or later, going to run out of puff. But, once you're perceived as a smash hit, there's no limit: as the posters threaten, '*Cats* – Now and Forever'.

*

At the nervous London première, the legendary Broadway showman David Merrick told Mackintosh that he'd be prepared to swap the British rights to *42nd Street* for the American rights to *Cats*. It was, ostensibly, a generous offer: *42nd Street* was a proven smash, and Merrick was prepared to give it to a tyro producer with no track record. But a wary

Mackintosh declined, and was right to do so: by the end of 1990, *42nd Street*, Broadway's biggest hit of the eighties, had earned $10 million; *Cats*' box-office receipts were . . . £510,809,266.

By the same point, *Les Miz* had taken £270,543,370 . . .

Phantom of the Opera £187,674,543 . . .

And *Miss Saigon*, which had only been running a year, £16,617,089.

In New York, Merrick had run radio commercials advertising *42nd Street* as the ideal show for people 'allergic to cats'. The trouble is not many people are allergic. T. S. Eliot's poems set to music are more profitable than the all-time motion picture champ: T. S. out-punches *ET*. In Britain, theatre is largely written about as an activity for losers – difficult, specialized, sickly, requiring protection and government subsidy and tax breaks such as the removal of VAT. For the first time since the rise of film, theatre – at least at the Mackintosh/Lloyd Webber level – is more than holding its own with newer, electronic forms. When Mackintosh and Steven Spielberg discuss movie versions of *Cats* and *Just So*, they meet as equals.

And yet, and yet . . . 'British musicals': it *still* sounds like a contradiction in terms. Then, suddenly, they were all around – the most conspicuously successful export of the Thatcher years, gargantuan, hollow, triumphalist, a soundtrack for our times and one easily despised. A British TV comedian on the lyricist of *Starlight Express*: 'If you are what you eat, then Richard Stilgoe must eat a lot of arseholes.' In 1994, Tim Rice's knighthood (following Lloyd Webber's, as Gilbert's followed Sullivan's) was met with sneering press comment about how you couldn't say 'Sir Tim Rice' with a straight face and, anyway, he hadn't had a hit since *Evita*. Oh, yeah? What about the Oscar for *Aladdin*? The songs he wrote for Broadway's *Beauty and the Beast*? The astonishing screen success and best-selling album of *The Lion King*?

But you can't blame these general detractors. After all, the folks who most loathe British musicals are those who know most about the subject. Broadway buffs look on the packed Winter Garden and Majestic like unpumped septic tanks: sure, they're at capacity, but you can't avoid the smell. One of the few men-about-Broadway who's tried to make the best of it is Martin Gottfried. In his book *Broadway Musicals* (1979), Broadway musicals were musicals written for and originally produced on Broadway; by the time of the elegantly titled sequel *More Broadway Musicals Since 1980* (1992), Broadway musicals had become *Cats*, *Les Misérables*, *Phantom of the Opera* and *Miss Saigon* – shows made elsewhere (and elsewhere wasn't even on the map in 1979) which just happen to pass through Broadway theatres en route to world domination. *No More Broadway Musicals Since 1980* would be a more accurate title. The changes in the eligibility rules recall the actress Brenda Fricker after one of those 'nights of triumph for the British film industry' in Hollywood: 'When you're drunk at the airport, you're Irish; when you win an Oscar, suddenly you're British.' In the old days, West End musicals were the incorrigible drunks at the airport; Before *Cats*, Noël Coward, Lionel Bart, Bricusse and Newley, the Rice and Lloyd Webber of *Jesus* and *Joseph* and *Evita* didn't even rate name-checks.

As that rag-bag of names suggests, the British musical isn't much of a 'tradition'. There's Gilbert and Sullivan, but their line descends, via Wodehouse, to the Americans – to the Gershwins, Rodgers, Hart and Hammerstein. The British line is a series of dots you can't connect up, little blips of activity every now and then. The best tend to defer to the Americans. Sandy Wilson scored a rare British success on Broadway in the fifties, but it was with *The Boyfriend*, a spoof of 1920s Broadway musical comedies so accurate and affectionate it could almost have been a 1920s Broadway musical comedy, albeit 30 years late.

'I've never subscribed to this idea of "The British Musical",' says Leslie Bricusse, who with Anthony Newley wrote *Stop the World – I Want to Get Off* (1960). 'When I started, there were the people writing musicals in Britain and they weren't as good as the people writing musicals in America. The man who taught me about lyric writing was Ross Parker, who's best known for "We'll Meet Again". But otherwise my heroes were American – Irving Berlin, Cole Porter – and I learned gradually not to be insular or parochial. I've never thought of songs as having national characteristics.' Maybe that's because, for most of this century, songs have had American characteristics. On *Willie Wonka*, Bricusse used the title 'Candy Man' because, he says, it's an internal rhyme and sings better than 'Sweetshop Man'. In America, in 1972, Sammy Davis Jr's single got to Number One; in Britain, the song stayed almost unknown until a recent TV commercial. I once asked Bricusse if he was going to the Frank Sinatra/Liza Minnelli/Sammy Davis Jnr. concert. 'I ought to,' he said. 'They're my family.' It would sound preposterous from most songwriters – particularly British ones. But Davis devoted half his set to Bricusse numbers, Liza flew into London especially to present him with a special Ivor Novello Award, and Sinatra recorded 'My Kind Of Girl' – an early Bricusse song submitted to a British competition but scuppered at the last moment when the Belfast jury gave all ten votes to an 'English Country Garden' type. Before *Cats*, to achieve international success, you had to Americanize yourself – whether consciously or not.

In 1989, I met Bricusse at the Cambridge Theatre, where he was preoccupied by last-minute adjustments to his book, music and lyrics for *Sherlock Holmes*, having just discovered that you can't get to Dr Watson's new residence in Surbiton from Victoria. Typical: the swanky Hollywood big shot breezes into town and immediately starts botching up the local colour. 'Not at all,' he retorted. 'I used to know you couldn't get to Surbiton from Victoria, because I was collecting train numbers at Clapham Junction when I was eight. But I haven't travelled on Southern Railways since I lived in Brighton.' When he wasn't train-spotting, young Bricusse was taking in Astaire and Kelly at the Empire, Leicester Square. For most British songwriters of that generation, growing up meant a lowering of expectations, as dreams of Hollywood were ceded to the grim reality of churning out novelty numbers for Max Bygraves. But Bricusse actually made it – from the platform at Clapham Junction to a house round the corner from Ira Gershwin.

Others had travelled this route before him – Wodehouse most famously, but also Clifford Grey, Birmingham-born lyricist of 'If You Were The Only Girl In The World', introduced by George Robey in *The Bing Boys Are Here* (1916) and the British Tommy's wartime favourite. When peace broke out, a log-jam of war-delayed Broadway imports flattened London and buried the local product. Grey went to New York and wrote two of the biggest hits of the twenties, *Sally* with Jerome Kern and *Hit the Deck* with Vincent Youmans.

Those who stayed home seemed blissfully unmindful of Broadway innovations. As late as *Robert and Elizabeth* (1964), the British still divided a show's component parts into libretto and music, as opposed to book and songs – with the woeful result that most London show scores have lyrics by playwrights rather than songwriters. For the romance between Robert Browning and Elizabeth Barrett, Ronald Millar offered the usual vague generalities and hackneyed images . . .

> The moon is as light as a feather
> When you and your love are together

. . . which reinforce the events of the previous scene rather than propel the plot forward. Later, he became chief gag-writer to Mrs Thatcher, who obviously demanded a higher standard ('The lady's not for turning', etc.). But, quite apart from content, Millar's lyrics are riddled with technical defects. No true lyricist would write . . .

> While earth contains us two

. . . because he'd know that, set to Ron Grainer's music, it would come out as . . .

> While earth contains a stew

. . . which is exactly what happens.

We're back to that old chestnut: which comes first? With the West End's biggest home-grown hit of the post-war period, *Bless the Bride*, you don't need to ask the question because you can hear the answer in the score. A. P. Herbert, stalwart of *Punch* and the House of Commons, liked to write the words first and, consequently, they fall too frequently into the same dreary ABAB pattern, alternating masculine and feminine rhymes: 'doing/done/brewing/sun', and so on. This is light verse, not song lyrics, and Vivian Ellis, like most composers constrained by a finished lyric, ended up writing predictable tumty-tumty music. When he was given his head, as on 'This Is My Lovely Day', Ellis is wonderfully lush and lyrical, and you see why many Broadway writers, including Kern, admired him. That said, it's still music, not song. The title is awkward, and the sentiment, for a love song, is not so much depressing as false:

> This Is My Lovely Day
> This is the day that I'll remember
> The day I'm dying . . .

The old double-act from German *lieder*: *liebe und tod*.

Vivian Ellis was born the same year as Jule Styne – 1905 – but, as theatre composers, they seem generations apart. Styne's *Gypsy* is the defining Broadway musical; Ellis' strictly local blockbuster is set in 1870 and could easily have been written then. *Bless the Bride* can be seen in retrospect as English operetta's parting shot, exhibiting all the nervousness of a dying form unsure how to ward off the competition. There's that quintessential symbol of fragrant Edwardiana, the garlanded swing around which the heroine flutters. But there's also a saucy bathing scene more suited to a DeSylva, Brown and Henderson Jazz Age farce, and some soft-boiled satire about Great Power politics. Next to *Annie, Get Your Gun* and *Oklahoma!*, which opened in London in the same week, it seems like a ludicrous joke.

Andrew Lloyd Webber understood. When he produced Sarah Brightman's album of songs from flop shows, he mischievously included a number from *Bless the Bride*: it's unknown in America, as are all Ivor Novello's West End hits. Lloyd Webber was inviting us, deliberately or not, to distinguish between the scale of his success and that of his predecessors.

*

Before *Cats*, the most famous British theatrical composer in America was Noël Coward. As with Anthony Newley, Coward wasn't exactly a prophet without honour in his native land, but he found both greater honours and greater profits across the Atlantic. Thank heavens, though, that his reputation doesn't depend on his musicals: one – *Bitter Sweet* (1929) – did . . . okay; the other – *Sail Away* (1961) – didn't.

'In his musicals, he was never going to catch up with Rodgers and Hammerstein,' says the satirical songwriter Tom Lehrer. '*Bitter Sweet* was apparently regarded as a landmark in its day. Now it just seems a dated operetta in the Romberg/Friml tradition. The difference is that most people couldn't recognize a photograph of Romberg or Friml – or Kern or Rodgers. Coward was a personality, and so he's come to represent that whole era in a way that nobody else does.'

This is undeniable. In *musical* theatre terms, he's not a major figure yet he seems the very personification of the 'tween-wars golden age – the clothes, the balcony, the potency of cheap music. 'Had a long think about what I really want to do,' he confided to his diary, 'a play for Gertie or me or both, short stories, a book or a musical. Wrote three lyric refrains for *Josephine*, worked at the piano. Suddenly a new and lovely tune appeared. Felt the authentic thrill. All right, the musical it shall be.'

Well, that's that settled. He might have done better to concentrate his skills. As it is, he recycles the same few tricks over and over, like rhyming (obtrusively) on the ante-penult:

> Why Must The Show Go On?
> Why not announce the closing *night* of it?
> The public seem to hate the *sight* of it . . .

It's nigh on impossible to sing this song without sounding like a Coward impersonator. In 1992, a Dinah Washington recording of 'Mad About The Boy' was revived for a Levi's commercial – and Coward fans complained because she wasn't doing the song as the Master did. He's often cited as a British Cole Porter, but Porter wrote standards: Sinatra and U2 both sing 'Night And Day', Lena Horne and the Pogues have both had a crack at 'Just One Of Those Things'; all are true to Porter, but only in their fashion. Coward's songs are so bound up with the man

169

himself – the rolled 'r's, the clipped delivery – that they defy the continual rearrangement which is the definition of a standard. In melody, harmonic support and lyric thrust, his songs simply aren't as muscular as Porter. In *The Man Who Came to Dinner*, the urbane American offered a slyly malicious parody of the Englishman's fondness for over-rhyming:

> Run, little lady
> Ere the shady
> Shafts of time
> Barb you with their winged desire
> Singe you with their sultry fire
> Softly a fluid druid meets me
> Olden and golden the dawn greets me
> Cherishing, perishing, up the stairs I climb . . .

'I know there are people who say he's a social historian,' says Tom Lehrer, 'but they're placing more weight on "Mad Dogs And Englishmen" than it can bear. Basically, what makes the song is the rhymes: "But Englishmen detest a / Siesta." He doesn't say anything except it's hot and mad dogs and Englishmen don't go inside. The rest is dressing. But plenty of people eat salad for the dressing, not for the lettuce.'

If his lyrics are perhaps over-valued, what of the music? 'Noël had to work at it,' says Peter Matz, the arranger of his Vegas shows. 'He was self-taught and could only play the piano in E flat, and you're amazed at the songs that rolled out from that – *and* he wrote plays, acted and painted. The body of songs from Rodgers and Arlen is much greater, but that's all they did.' The sign of a truly great composer is the care he puts into his comedy numbers – look at Porter's laundry lists or Bernstein's 'Gee, Officer Krupke!' and the funny songs from *On the Town*. 'Noël's songs work,' argues Matz, 'because they're such good pieces of music. What's wrong with a lot of comedy material is that musically people don't know how to structure it, so the flow that's necessary for comedy is missing. "Mad Dogs And Englishmen" is a wonderful piece of *music*.'

But Coward's particular aura derives from his style. He created his own persona and then produced a huge body of work to service it. 'He writes his plays in a flowered dressing-gown and before breakfast,' noted the critic James Agate. 'But what I want to know is what kind of work he intends to do after breakfast, when he is clothed and in his right mind.' But Coward was shrewd enough to realize that it was the flowered dressing-gown and silk cravat which defined his work more precisely than any other writer's. Decades after his death, 'very Noël Coward' can be flattering or perjorative, but at least everyone knows what it means. And occasionally, even in his most unconvincingly sentimental songs, there'll be a truly inspired touch worthy of Berlin or Porter. Let his reputation rest on one tender, literate line in 'I'll See You Again':

Though my world may go *awry* . . .

'That's lovely,' says Tom Lehrer. 'What other songwriter of the time would use a word like that?'

*

If Coward represents a specific strain of Britishness, what does Lloyd Webber stand for? American musicals celebrate America, both the city that doesn't sleep and the corn of Kansas in August. But British musicals are about cats and trains and deformed creatures who live in the Paris sewers. For all they tell us about contemporary Britain, they might as well come from outer space. In fact, one of them did: Dave Clark's *Time* (1986), with its intergalactic supreme court judge played by a giant hologram of Laurence Olivier's head with one nostril in the wrong place. But, twenty years Before *Cats*, for a few seasons, there was a distinctive native strain of contemporary London musical, written by a man who filled the stage with British types – Blitz babies from the forties, coffee-house spivs of the fifties. He blazed like a comet across the West End, and then just as spectacularly fell to earth. Yes, that's a cliché. But it always used to be the Americans who self-destructed, who couldn't cope with the price of fame. This guy gave Britain one of its own.

'I don't get a penny piece from *Oliver!*, you know,' says Lionel Bart, as we part on the pavement. So why then is he on his way to yet another rehearsal for yet another production?

'Well, it's my name on it, isn't it?'

Yes, it is – technically. But, just as *Oliver!* isn't his any more, so neither is the name. It's hard to connect the gentle, genial stage thug, a fellow who looks like he's the fourth crap shooter from the left in *Guys and Dolls*, with the mythic figure conjured by the words 'Lionel Bart'. He wrote the most successful British musical Before *Cats*, but, instead of forming a limited liability company and winning the Queen's Award for Exports, he descended bumpily through a series of limp exclamatory ejaculations – from *Oliver!* through *Blitz!* to *Twang!!*, an exclamation mark too far. By the late sixties, he'd ended up losing the rights to his most profitable work. *Lionel!* was supposed to be the story of Britain's Irving Berlin but somewhere along the way it turned into Britain's Fats Waller – an irresistible tale of artistic dissipation, of valuable copyrights squandered to sustain extravagant appetites. He was always better at show than business, the product of an era when celebrity meant partying the night away with Princess Margaret, rather than hiring Prince Edward to make the tea. He used to have the swankiest pad in town, but now he lives in a small flat above a shop in Acton, West London. It's the sort of modest accommodation to which first-time buyers might aspire after seeing Bart's charming 'Abbey Endings' commercial for the Abbey National Building Society. In the years since his fall, announcements of Bart's comeback have peppered the newspaper diaries, but so far only this – one 30-second TV spot – has come to fruition.

Meanwhile, *Oliver!* goes on and on – from Wimbledon (1960) to the West End to Broadway (1963) back to the British stage (1967) and screen (1968) and stage again (1977, 1983) back to New York (1984) and Sadler's Wells (1990) and the London Palladium (1994). It's one of the most solid and revivable musicals ever written – all the more remarkable because, in a collaborative medium which encourages specialization, the book, music and lyrics are all the work of one man. So is Frank Loesser's *The Most Happy Fella* (1956) and Meredith Willson's *The Music Man* (1957), but neither approaches the enduring success of Bart's show – a British hit in Broadway's Golden Age. Like Loesser, he'd written pop and film songs, but Loesser's apprenticeship had begun twenty years before *Guys and Dolls* and *The Most Happy Fella*. Bart, a London art school boy, had started out in a skiffle group in 1956, written some songs for its lead singer Tommy Steele, and then, in the space of a year, wrote three musicals – two for Joan Littlewood's semi-improvisatory Theatre Workshop in the East End and then *Oliver!* It's the efficiency of *Oliver!* which surprises: like Disney with Kipling's *Jungle Book*, it takes Dickens' source material and recasts it in another form, consistent in its own tone.

The secret of the show's professionalism is an elusive one. When I called to discuss the work, Bart wanted to meet in the Royal Court Hotel, which for some reason I'd assumed to be an old haunt of his from the swingin' sixties. As it turns out, he's been here only once before – one summer, when he was passing by and suddenly felt the need to duck out of a heatwave. 'It was air-conditioned, which a lot of these places aren't. But I don't suppose,' he adds, looking through the window at the grey wintry morning, 'that air-conditioning's a very big consideration at this time of year.'

I'm not really that interested in the air-conditioning, but Bart has an endearing habit of derailing the thrusting, probing questions – or at any rate re-routing them down unexpected branch lines. What, I wonder, were his major influences?

'I was very influenced,' he says in his even soft-spoken Cockney, 'by Sam Wanamaker with his tight pants, and those elastic-sided boots. Ultimately, they became Beatle boots. But I started it, in terms of making it a bit more fashionable.'

Actually, Bart's present wardrobe is pretty nineties. But, metaphorically, our entire conversation comes fully kitted out in Beatle boots and Nehru jackets. It's not just the references to John and Paul and Mick and Brian Epstein's assistant. He got so spaced out in the late sixties that the seventies and eighties seem barely to have impinged on him. Ask him about recent shows, and he pauses thoughtfully before citing Kander and Ebb's *Chicago*, which opened in 1975 but which he only caught up with at a nineties charity performance. Doesn't he feel a bit of a Rip Van Winkle?

'No,' he says, cautiously sipping his mineral water, 'because, frankly, I look at *Les Misérables* and all John Napier's other sets, and I see Sean Kenny's influence. The only thing that seems to have changed is the merchandising, and the ability to put on 30 productions of the same show around the world.'

He seems bemused by the mega-musicals, but not intimidated by them. 'The form is just a word, isn't it? Opera, operetta, melodrama . . . they're just words. We can change the words, so we can change the form. When I started, there was this thing called "living newspaper", which Ewan MacColl was doing, based on a Czechoslovakian art form. That doesn't happen much today, but it was all the go for a while. *Fings Ain't Wot They Used T'Be* . . . Somebody said it was *Guys and Dolls* with its flies undone, but what it finally was was a play with songs, not a plotted musical.'

All the same, in an age when show composers talk about recitative and *leitmotifs* and extended musical scenes, there's something to be said for songs. 'I have fancied the sung-through musical,' he says, 'but in my case it would be slightly pretentious. I'm not a composer, I just make tunes and sing them, and I sing harmonies, and some of my chord progressions are not logical, but often they work. For *Oliver!*, I did *Tom and Jerry* music. I thought in terms of people's walks. The *Oliver!* theme was really the Beadle's walk, a kind of dum-de-dum . . .':

O-li-ver! O-li-ver!

'Fagin's music was like a Jewish mother-hen clucking away. But I don't want to get high-falutin' about it. Music is important – fair enough. But just to have some kind of drab tune fitted on to even more drab dialogue seems rather pointless to me.'

Since Bolton, Wodehouse and Kern 75 years ago, musical comedy writers have felt obliged to have theories about their work. But there's something rather admirable about the way Bart just seems to do what he feels like. The lyricist Gene Lees, in the introduction to his rhyming dictionary, chastises him for the first line of 'Where Is Love?', where a one-syllable word is stretched over five notes:

> Wh-e-e-e-ere is love?

Ira Gershwin wouldn't have done it, nor Cole Porter, though Otto Harbach and Oscar Hammerstein were happy to make 'you' a seven-syllable word in *Rose-Marie*:

> When I'm calling you-oo-oo-oo-oo-oo-oo . . .

Still, it seems less odd at the end of a line. Lees reckons Bart should have tried something like 'Someone tell me where is love?', but Bart isn't exactly perturbed by the criticism. 'He should hear Johnny Mathis' cover version: at the end of it, he makes about 20 syllables out of the word. I mean, what's he going to do? Start giving Handel a hard time for the *Messiah*? Nah, I did it because it just felt okay.'

As one of the few self-contained songwriters, Bart usually produces words and music which fit together with a deceptive ease:

> Got to do my best to please her
> Just 'cause she's a
> Livin' Doll . . .

You won't find 'pleezer'/'sheezer' in any rhyming dictionary, yet it sings as naturally as (to use Bart's own model) walking. 'But, if the rhyme gets too clever, if it obtrudes on the situation, I have to write that out. Of course, not long after that we had the Beatles and a lot of the pop things which had stature, but not because they rhymed brilliantly. Noël Coward gave me a rhyming dictionary and he wrote on the front of it . . .

> Do not let this aid to rhyming
> Bitch your talent or your timing.

You can hear him saying that. But I use it only as a very last resort. I like to get behind the character. I wrote a song in *Maggie May* which is a lullaby, ostensibly being written there and then by this hooker to her sleeping lover. Around this time, Richard Rodgers wanted me to be his partner, and he looked at this lyric and said, "It *works* . . . but there are impure rhymes." I said, "That's because she's not a very good lyric writer."'

It's a neat defence, if not entirely convincing. But it also illustrates the problems faced by Bart in trying to straddle two worlds that were drifting apart. He was clearly flattered to be one of the few musical comedy boys accepted by the rockers: 'John used to say, "I hate that *ding*! cue for a song. But your stuff's not so bad. You don't see the join so much."'

But, ah, what might have been: Rodgers and Bart has a certain ring to it, even if at first sight it looks like a spelling error. 'It could be argued,' he concedes, 'that instead of being the doyen of flower power I'd have been a lot cleverer to have stayed in my *métier*, writing for the theatre and doing the odd movie score. But I was trying to be all things to all children.'

Today, he seems more aware of his limitations. 'One of the things I'm thinking about doing is a piece about contemporary London, set in front of the Festival Hall, and developing into some kind of fantasy with the homeless. But, if it involves certain music that I'm not into writing, like hip-hop or whatever, then I'll get another writer in.'

So Bart, composer/lyricist/librettist/director of *Blitz!*, didn't feel like writing his own hip-hop?

'Well, I'm not doing a lot of hip-hopping myself these days. In fact, I've got to the point now where strobe lighting really does me up. I can't handle it, I really go weird.'

Will it come to anything? Bart has several projects he's been toying with for a long time – *Quasimodo*, *La Strada* – but there are those who wonder whether he really wants to get back into a full-blown musical. He certainly has a knack of knowing which musicals *not* to do – disengaging early, for example, from both *Winnie* and *Budgie*, two West End flops of 1988. He insists, though, that he's up for it and he's got as far as lunching with Cameron Mackintosh, who's wound up owning most of Bart's rights in *Oliver!*

'Of all the people I know in this business who have had ups and downs,' says Mackintosh, 'Lionel is the least bitter man I have ever come across. He regrets it but, considering that everyone else has made millions out of his creations, he's never been sour, never been vindictive.'

The houses in London, New York, Malibu, the castle in Tangiers are gone, blown in a rash of bad business decisions and a haze of 'experiments with LSD'. Staying with Princess Margaret in Mustique, Bart staggered down for breakfast late one afternoon and found Her Royal Highness in specs poring over the accounts ledgers.

'Oy, wot you doin'?' said Bart.

'I'm doing my books,' said the Princess. 'If you'd done your books, you wouldn't be in the mess you're in, you silly bugger.' Bart's West End heirs would take her advice.

'We had too much,' says Bart. 'Sometimes – often – limitations can be your best asset.'

'His blending of recitative and dialogue and song was way ahead,' says Mackintosh. 'He ranks alongside Frank Loesser as a naturally gifted musical theatre writer. Go and see *Blitz!* and *Maggie May* and you see what an extraordinary gift he had. But his fame and his power were so great that the method of theatre he had – which was really working with a bunch of mates and throwing it together – he outgrew that. And he didn't have people who could keep him at it. He needed a really strong producer and a really strong director. I hope he finds the collaborators he needs to finish the work.'

'Cameron always said, "When you're ready, Lionel, I'll be here." Well, I am, but he's not. He said, "Look, Lionel, while you were out there doing whatever you were doing with those 12 years, I've acquired other loyalties." I'm sure if I did something new he'd change his mind,' reflects Bart, 'but I don't seem to be getting a great deal of encouragement. Cameron said, "Oh, we've got to have a script on the table." I said, "But with that formula you'd have turned down *Oliver!*" We had six songs when we went into rehearsal. I love spontaneity and I don't think things should take five years.'

*

From East End improv workshop shows to West End multinational monsters: fings are indeed not wot they used t'be. The British musicals tradition seems to be that there is no tradition in British musicals – and maybe that's its greatest advantage. Tim Rice often talks of how he and Lloyd Webber benefited from having no tradition to write in. As for the *Les Miz/Saigon* team, Boublil and Schonberg (who found success in the West End rather than their native Paris), their theatrical dreams were fired by *Jesus Christ Superstar*. Alain Boublil, then a pop writer, had sat through Broadway shows like *Promises, Promises* (book by Neil Simon, score by Bacharach and David) bored stiff by the scene–song–scene–song format. He and Schonberg were antipathetic to musicals, until they found an alternative model in *Superstar*.

Even today, they're remarkably innocent about the world they've conquered. When *Miss Saigon* opened in 1989, many critics admired the decadent, sardonic vamp of 'The American Dream' as a knowing parody of Kander and Ebb's 'New York, New York'. But Claude-Michel Schonberg said to me that, until he read the reviews, he'd never heard of John Kander: it was just a memory of the sort of razzle-dazzle New York anthems he'd heard on the radio. A while back, I had dinner with Boublil and his American collaborator on *Saigon*, Richard Maltby Jr. Over the coffees, Maltby and I drifted into musical comedy chit-chat about lyric-writing heroes like Andy Razaf ('Ain't Misbehavin'') and Dorothy Fields ('I Can't Give You Anything But Love, Baby'). 'Oh, well,' said Boublil, with disarming charm, 'now you aire tokking about zese names zat mean nussing to me, so I will say goodnight.' He didn't mean it arrogantly, but his strength is that, unlike Maltby (who promptly followed his West End success with a New York flop, *Nick and Nora*) and me and everyone else who's a sucker for the siren lullaby of Broadway, he isn't cursed by knowing which songs were cut from *Hitchy-koo of 1917*. In other words, the biggest hits of our time have been written by those who knew nothing of the world Before *Cats*.

ii

The Line

On 25 August 1980, on the eleventh curtain call of the first performance of *42nd Street*, David Merrick appeared from the wings to tumultuous applause. 'I'm sorry to have to report,' he began, and the house roared. What was there to apologize for? The show was a triumph, a magnificent backstage musical, a vindication of Broadway values, proving the truth of its most defiant and memorable line, when the director turns to his young chorine and declares that 'the two most glorious words in the English language' are 'musical comedy'. So what's to be sorry about?

'No, no,' shouted Merrick over the laughter. 'This is tragic. You don't understand. Gower Champion died this morning.'

Art and reality had merged: the choreographer/director's life and death had become a corny, melodramatic backstage musical. We all know the plot – it's in the original film of *42nd Street*: the great Broadway director Julian Marsh is warned not to do another show because the strain could kill him. In Champion's version of *42nd Street*, the title song is a lurid narrative in which the leading lady's lover dies but she dances on. The leading lady at the Winter Garden that August night was Wanda Richert; she was Champion's lover, and she had danced on. She hadn't known he was dead. Like the rest of the company, she heard it first when Merrick announced it to the audience. Immediately afterwards, he walked over to Miss Richert and embraced her. A gesture of sympathy? Or a subtle way of drawing the news media's attention to another angle on the story? With Merrick, you never can tell. He'd got himself the most memorable first night in history. As for Gower Champion, he died on the eve of his greatest success. For his fellow choreographers and dancers, it was a grim foretaste of the years ahead.

*

Shortly before *On Your Toes* opened on Broadway in 1936, the 'dance director' (as the job designation then was) requested that his billing be changed from the customary 'Dances by . . .' to the entirely unprecedented 'Choreography by . . .' In introducing this word to showbusiness vocabulary, George Balanchine signalled the start of a newly elevated status for dance in musicals, one which old-timers like Irving Berlin found not entirely convincing:

> Chaps
> Who did taps
> Aren't tapping anymore
> They're doing
> Choreography!
> Chicks
> Who did kicks
> Aren't kicking anymore
> They're doing
> Choreography!

And it didn't stop there. In 1957, with *West Side Story*, the billing changed again: 'Entire production conceived, choreographed and directed by Jerome Robbins' – a vanity despised by non-choreographing directors. 'That's like saying,' snorted George Abbott, ' "Entire part of mother played by Lizzie Flop".' The last stager to wear full imperial honours on Broadway is Tommy Tune, with *Grand Hotel* (1989) and *The Will Rogers Follies* (1991); in London, it was Joe Layton with *Ziegfeld* (1988), a pathetic postscript to the half-century of superstar choreography inaugurated by Balanchine. At its apogee, in 1979, it enabled Bob Fosse to razzle-dazzle Broadway with no book, a bunch of old songs, in fact nothing but (as its succinct title put it) *Dancin'*, and provoked that stern advocate of a writers' theatre, Alan Jay Lerner, to send Fosse a wry opening-night telegram: 'Congratulations. You finally did it. You got rid of the author.'

With the premature deaths of Fosse and Michael Bennett in 1987, the self-contained superstager – the choreographer/director – was eliminated virtually overnight. 'Well, they died, which is a sad fact,' says Hal Prince, the senior non-choreographing director. 'But I thought that pendulum would probably have to swing, because I think the predominance of dance in a musical is not necessarily a good idea. Pendulums always do swing when you see a trend take over and dance movement has gotten bloody boring.'

But then Prince has always been something of a skeptic about the dramatic potential of dance. 'If you go back to the forties, the most dated moments are the choreography. Those funeral ballets with everyone rolling around in agony on the village green – it's embarrassing as hell.'

Like everything else to do with musicals, show dance has drawn on a ragbag of different influences. There's been hoofing since George M. Cohan Yankee Doodle Dandied his way across the stage at the dawn of the century. But dramatic choreography is much more recent, and the first generation of choreographer/directors – Balanchine, Agnes de Mille, Robbins – mostly came from ballet, which gave them, initially, a sort of highbrow clout. In the decade after Laurey's dream ballet in *Oklahoma!* (1943), no show was complete without its own lyrical (and lengthy) dream sequence, a Broadway cliché which was nonetheless at its best the perfect dance tone for the Rodgers and Hammerstein musical play. The dance is integrated . . . up to a point: it's consistent with character; but you're still aware that the director's bunked off for ten minutes and the choreographer's taken over.

It was Jerome Robbins who first began to apply a consistent staging language to whole shows. *West Side Story* is a dance musical, but it's not a musical about dancers or, particularly, a musical about dances: it finds a movement tone appropriate to the Sharks and Jets, a heightened, stylized gangland bravado to match the heightened, stylized gangland language of Arthur Laurents' book. Laurents maintains that Robbins was never much good with actors and book scenes, but it's striking that his greatest achievements on Broadway are not dance shows but book musicals like *Gypsy* and *Fiddler on the Roof*. What's 'Tradition'? A book moment, a song, a dance? Even to pose the question is to recognize its redundancy: in Robbins' best work, the distinctions are meaningless; book, song and staging have blended into a whole. Yet, after *Fiddler*, Robbins abandoned Broadway and returned to ballet. And since then, excepting the Royal Ballet's Kenneth MacMillan, who dropped dead while working on the '92 revival of *Carousel*, 'serious' choreographers have had almost nothing to do with musicals. When I asked why, Glen Tetley dismissed show dancing as 'meretricious' and 'vulgar'. (I'm not sure Balanchine would have disagreed: 'He never liked musicals,' George Abbott, his director for *On Your Toes*, said. 'He did it for the money.')

'What is show dancing?' muses Tommy Tune. 'It's dancing that doesn't have to stand by itself. If you take a show dance and present it as a ballet, it's not going to hold up because, if it's doing its job, it's pushing the show ahead in some way, it's revealing something about a character or it's telling a story: when it finishes, you're not in the same place as you were before.'

When Glen Tetley talks of 'vulgar' show dancing, he's thinking of a chorus line doing a dance, he's thinking of steps. Even choreographers, it seems, have difficulty in accepting the idea that ballet principles and movement style can infuse the whole play. Cameron Mackintosh, who's never hired a choreographer/director on any of his productions, told me they were fine for shows about dance and dancers, but were less reliable otherwise.

'I think that's nonsense,' says Gwen Verdon, Broadway's premier dance star from *Damn Yankees* in 1955 through *Sweet Charity* to *Chicago*. 'The choreographers were a lot more interested in the book scenes than the book directors ever were in the numbers. When the orchestra started up, George Abbott used to go out and play golf. Yet the directors were happy to take all the credit. Even today, people don't realize what a choreographer does. In *Phantom*, in the scene with the four opera singers, there's no dancing at all. But it's still staged by Gillian Lynne, not Hal Prince. That's why, in the fifties, Bob, Jerry Robbins and Michael Kidd figured that, as they were doing so much of it anyway, why not do it all?'

*

Bob Fosse's background was vaudeville. He arrived in New York in the early fifties, at a time when show choreographers lavished their best efforts on ballet-aspiring sequences set to pseudo-balletic music. Fosse dances are the very antithesis of ballet: he went for splayed legs and knock knees instead of perfect turnouts; jagged lines of short men and long-legged women, rather than classical symmetry. Whatever you think of this as *dance*, it's a staging style that, unlike de Mille or Balanchine, takes account of the dash and splash of Broadway show music. His pre-war experiences as a boy dancer in Chicago strip joints had given him a taste for sleaze which he used throughout his career – most famously, in the film of *Cabaret* (1972). More specifically, Fosse retained a lifelong affection for the staple movement of burlesque routines, the pelvic thrust and bump. Among mostly gay choreographers, Fosse was thrustingly heterosexual, revelling in erotic exhibitionism.

Like Balanchine and Robbins, he served his apprenticeship with George Abbott. He choreographed *The Pajama Game* (1954) and *Damn Yankees*, before *New Girl in Town* (1957) broke up the partnership. 'When Bob and I did *New Girl in Town*,' says Gwen Verdon, 'we had a bordello scene which George Abbott hated so much he burnt the set. He had it chopped up out of town, taken away and burnt.' To Fosse and Verdon, it was the show's highlight; to Abbott, it was 'just plain dirty'.

'That's one reason Bob became a director,' says Miss Verdon. 'You see, that's the difference dance can make. You can say "I love you" and it might be very nice, but it's a moment and it's gone. But, if you take four minutes and do the most beautiful love dance, that really thrills an audience.'

But, even as he took to directing as well as choreographing, even as he brought fluid film techniques to theatre, Fosse stayed true to Abbott's first principle: forget Art; does it *work*? Like Abbott, Fosse kept things moving. Four minutes is right. Other choreographers indulge in repeat chorus after repeat chorus; Fosse, a supreme manipulator of audiences, kept his stagings short: leave 'em wanting more. A Fosse show is Abbott values plus strong visual style (all those white gloves and derbies), a certain cynicism and plenty of sex.

From *Damn Yankees* on, Gwen Verdon was Fosse's on-stage *alter ego*, a relationship which survived the collapse of their marriage. Indeed, she remained by his side even as he did away with all other collaborators. For *Big Deal* (1986), Fosse directed, choreographed, wrote the book and used old songs rather than a new score. But, in trying to do too much, he made *Big Deal* his first bona fide Broadway flop in 30 years.

Like Gower Champion, he pre-staged his own death – in his autobiographical movie, *All that Jazz* (1979). After open heart surgery in 1974, he'd briefly considered changing his ways, but soon resumed his hardworking, hard-playing habits. For the movie version, he characteristically gave his heart operation an unhappy ending – dying in hospital, his bodybag zipped up as Ethel Merman sings 'There's No Business Like Show Business' and the credits roll. It was typical Fosse: take the old showbiz razzle-dazzle, and give it a savage twist. When real life got around to the finale, it couldn't quite match the movie. On the day of the opening of the national tour of the *Sweet Charity* revival, Fosse collapsed on a Washington street. As always, Gwen Verdon was with him.

*

No choreographer enjoys the cachet among the rock crowd that Fosse does. Paula Abdul's hit MTV video was virtually a recreation of the Air Erotica number in *All that Jazz*; Madonna's *Girlie Tour* appropriated wholesale Fosse's poses for Liza in *Cabaret*. The videos could duplicate the images, but not the detail, not the dance. Films such as *Saturday Night*

Fever, Stayin' Alive and *Fame* were credited with popularizing dance, but in the main promoted only a bland, technique-less disco substitute: if in doubt, stick your butt out. The genre reached its nadir with Richard Attenborough's 1985 screen travesty of Bennett's stage masterpiece, *A Chorus Line*.

'That's what I call funky junk dancing,' says Gwen Verdon, whose daughter, Nicole Fosse, appeared in the movie. 'You don't have to be trained for it, you just have to wiggle. And, if you *have* been taught, it's only a problem. We're going back to the very old-fashioned dancing – animated wallpaper – where an audience is impressed just because everybody's moving the same. Like in the thirties: "Okay, bring on the girls" – and everything stops for five minutes.

'But, in the group numbers in *Oklahoma!* and *Carousel*, Agnes de Mille made the dancers part of the drama. Each one had a character. The biggest changes weren't in the solos: after all, by the time you become a star, they choreograph to your limitations. It was the group numbers that were extraordinary. When Jerry did *West Side Story*, every Shark and every Jet were individuals. When we did *Sweet Charity*, Bob gave each girl in "Big Spender" a personality. It's not just the music and lyrics, it's the staging that reveals how those girls are feeling.' You get less credit for musical comedy than you do for, say, *Pacific Overtures* but Fosse's staging is worth noting:

> Now let me get right to the point
> I don't pop my cork for ev'ry guy I see
> Hey, Big Spender . . .

But the girls are sprawled inelegantly along a single bar. The song sings of instant allure; the staging tells us they're bored stiff, going through the motions.

'You can reach a level in dance beyond words, beyond music,' says Donna McKechnie, and she should know: the shimmering sensuality of her 'Tick-Tock' dance in *Company* (1970) is beyond any *song* that Sondheim could have written at that point. The show has more traditional dance, too: one number is virtually vaudevillian, but, as staged by Michael Bennett, it packs a dramatic punch. *Company*, remember, is about Bobby's inability to find anyone to share his life.

'In "Side By Side By Side",' says Bob Avian, Bennett's longtime associate, 'we went across the stage with each couple: the husband would do the first half of the tap-break, and then the wife would do the second half. And we'd work our way across the stage through each couple until we'd get to the leading man. And he'd do his half of the tap-break, and get to the wife. And there'd be no wife there. And that's the story of the play. That was what the whole show was about and Michael did it in one four-count break.'

Fosse's ambitions were modest: 'All I ever want is to be a good show-man' – and he was, the best. But, for Bennett, dances were merely a step to a show in which *everything* danced. His last assignment was *Chess*, the stage realization of the worldwide hit album by Tim Rice and the Abba boys.

'It was just a very odd set of circumstances,' says the producer, Robert Fox. 'Michael, who I thought was a genius, wanted a "viddy-wall" with all the cameras and other equipment that involved. What he was going to do with the production was use film combined with what was happening on stage. We got the costing for this "viddy-wall" and it was £900,000. So I said to Michael, "This seems an awful lot of money." And he said, "That's the only way I can do the show. That's my vision, and, if I don't have that, I don't know how to do it. So it's either the viddy-wall and me, or no viddy-wall and no me." You're then in the position where you've employed all these actors, so you say it's Michael Bennett, the guy's got a vision, give the genius what he wants, he'll do an amazing thing with this viddy-wall.'

Two weeks later, Bennett withdrew from the show for health reasons, leaving Trevor Nunn to pick up the pieces. 'It's another guy with another vision,' says Fox, 'and he's lumbered with the viddy-wall. So you've got £900,000 of equipment that is utterly wasted.' Most of us in Fox's shoes would get pretty peeved, going into the theatre night after night and seeing a £900,000 gimmick sitting on stage doing absolutely nothing.

'Well, it did a *bit*,' he protests.

Well, yes: Robert Dougall popped up now and again and read a mock BBC news bulletin, but even so . . .

'As a producer, you're supposed to control the budget, but on a musical the budget can get out of control. If *Chess*, instead of costing £4,623,000,' says Fox, the figures clicking off his tongue so mechanically you expect his eyes to light up like a fruit machine, 'if instead of costing what it *did*, it had cost what it *should* have, about £2 million, it would have been a fantasti-cally successful show. It had a monstrous advance. You know what people are like, everyone says they've got a ten million advance. But *Chess* genuinely had £2,500,000 when it opened. It was sold out practically for a year.' Despite an eventual run of almost three years, it never made money. To Tim Rice, the London production of *Chess* was 'the most expensive workshop in history': they could change everything but the set. To watch a Trevor Nunn staging beached in a Michael Bennett concept was to be aware of the huge cultural gulf between Broadway and British musicals.

'There are certain things we do better in America,' Jerome Minskoff, producer of Fosse's last *Charity* revival, told me. 'Dancing, for example. But big English musicals can get away with so little. *Les Miz* and *Phantom* have no dancing at all. All the great musicals I ever knew had dancing in them.'

But for how much longer? A year after *Chess* opened, the reasons for Michael Bennett's withdrawal became clear. He died of Aids, far off-Broadway in Arizona. 'I'm reminded every day of how irreplaceable Michael was,' said Donna McKechnie. 'Many, many times I wonder "What would Michael do here?", and I know that, as a dancer, I'll never have that special relationship with a choreographer again.' At the time we spoke, Miss McKechnie was in London for a reworking of Cole Porter's *Can-Can*. 'I am working here with a real up-and-comer,' she insisted. 'One day, I'm sure, Kenn Oldfield will do the big dance musical, as choreographer and director.'

Well, *Can-Can* came and went, and Oldfield remains in the job which Balanchine rejected: 'dance director' – a man who arranges the dances for other fellows' musicals. There's no producer willing to bankroll a viddy-wall for him to play with, but at least he gets to do a bit of *dancing*. On some shows today, the choreographic credit, in very small print, is merely 'Movement by . . .', and you're lucky if you can get in a waving arm. That's what Lar Lubovitch settled for on Stephen Sondheim and James Lapine's *Into the Woods* (1988). As a director, Lapine likes clean stage pictures which are curiously immobile: his most famous staging, appropriately enough, was an attempt to recreate a painting in *Sunday in the Park with George* – a sort of *tableau non-vivant*. A watched kettle never boils, but, at a Lapine show, a watched stage rarely moves.

There's more going on at an Andrew Lloyd Webber evening, but not much in the way of dance. In the early eighties, he used to talk about 'the British dance revolution' and it's true that *Cats*, *Song and Dance* and *Starlight Express* gave tremendous choreographic opportunities to, respectively, Gillian Lynne, Anthony van Laast and Arlene Phillips. But *Phantom* and *Aspects* offered Miss Lynne nothing except one modest set-piece apiece – respectively, a costume ball and a circus. And, even with his danciest shows, Lloyd Webber never handed over completely to choreographers. The Second Act of *Song and Dance* had no speech, no lyrics, just dance, but the show still came under the directorial aegis of the RSC's John Caird.

'Michael Bennett once said something very amusing,' recalls Hal Prince. 'He said if you do the same thing 36 times, you can stop the show. And by that he meant that the same movement from ten or twenty dancers will finally drive an audience to a frenzy. And I saw him do it in *Follies* and then saw him do it all over again in *Chorus Line*. And, because choreographer/directors tended to think with their bodies and empha-sized text much less than movement, there was a predominant amount of dancing in their shows – because whenever you have a weakness in a show, you go to a strength to solve the weakness.'

Tommy Tune disagrees. 'As a group, we've gone for seamlessness. You don't act a scene, sing a song and go into your dance. We've sort of mixed them all up: we slide into it and we slide out of it. We call it the "guzzin-tahs": it all goes into something else. The "guzzintahs" have been fused, I think, by the director/choreographer. I don't have any division between the way a character walks on and the way he kicks his leg. It's all the same thing. There is no movement that isn't choreography in my head. The walk is terribly important – to define character and to entertain.'

As a group, though, they've gone. Bennett and Fosse and Champion and Ron Field (*Applause*) and Joe Layton (*Barnum*) and many more are dead, and the plethora of revivals and nostalgia fests has returned us to the dance hokum of Broadway's youth – the buck 'n' wings, timesteps, kicklines. Once again, chaps are tapping and chicks are kicking. They do it wittily and charmingly and inventively – especially in the Gershwin retread *Crazy for You* (1991), where Susan Stroman comes up with fresh ideas for chorus after chorus. In 'Slap That Bass', in a Busby Berkeleyesque moment, the chorus girls become bass fiddles and the guys wind up playing them.

But dances, numbers, steps: this wasn't what it was supposed to be about. We're back to directors staging book scenes and choreographers supervising the songs. Only Tune is left to argue the case for sole control: 'I'm a synthesizer,' he insists. 'I know about dance and singing and story-telling. You talk in musicals until you get to the expletive: "*Oh*, what a beautiful morning!" Then you're into song. When you can't sing any-more, then you dance. But since Michael went, I don't seem able to find somebody who does what I do, somebody I can talk with in short-cuts. I don't know any other director/choreographers.'

*

In my mind's eye, I always associate Tune with a gala performance of *Mack and Mabel* he took part in:

> If a skyful of crap
> Always lands in your lap
> Make a curtsey
> And Tap Your Troubles Away . . .

It's the sort of cheery, upbeat showtune that tap-shoes, hats, canes and Tune himself were made for. 6′6″ and a near-namesake of *Variety* slang for musical comedy ('tuner'), Broadway's last song 'n' dance man represents a lost era of tap-happy innocence. But, as the director of *Nine* (after Fellini's 8½) and *Grand Hotel*, he symbolizes the nearest New York has got to re-inventing the musical for the modern age. 'Think Berliner Ensemble,' he instructed the *Grand Hotel* company. But, as one of his chorines told him, characterizing the artless artiness of Tune's shows, 'We're the Irving Berliner Ensemble.'

The son of Mr and Mrs Tune, Tommy Tune was born off-off-off-Broadway in Wichita Falls, Texas, but then, as someone says in his 1973 show *Seesaw*, Fred Astaire came from Omaha. As a child, he never saw a stage musical. But his favourite films were always, like *Easter Parade*, about putting on shows. 'I was interested not in the story of the movie but the story of the show they were putting on. I was stagestruck before I knew the stage still existed.'

He arrived in New York in the early sixties and made his Broadway début in *Baker Street*, an unlikely Cockney hoofer behind Sherlock Holmes and Dr Watson. Already, there was a sense that the American musical was beginning to recycle itself, but, unlike now, there was at least plenty of work. 'I had a great time. You could get a show on for $350,000, so a lot of shows were happening,' says Tune. It was the heyday of the director/choreographer, when dancemen ran the show. Tune's size was as likely to be a plus as a minus, but he was a good enough dancer for his height to be overlooked. In 1965, he danced in *How Now Dow Jones*, a Wall Street musical whose stock was overvalued, but whose hit title ensured it stacked up the biggest advance of the season. 'I was forever being plucked from the chorus and given a small role. In *Dow Jones*, I ended up with a nice number. That's how the guys from Hollywood saw me and took me off to test for the *Hello, Dolly!* film. It's really a very showbizzy story. I'm this kid from Texas who came to New York with his tap-shoes.'

It seemed a natural step, the same progression from stage to screen Gene

Kelly, Tune's director on the *Dolly!* movie, had made a quarter-century earlier. As a film début, you couldn't ask for better: 20th Century-Fox, a prominent role as one of Horace Vandergelder's Yonkers feed store clerks, and a chance to stand head and shoulders above everyone else in the big production numbers. But it was *Hello, Dolly!*, goodbye, Hollywood. 'It cost $22 million,' he says, 'an enormous amount of money at that time. It was the last major musical made in Hollywood. And they'll never come back. Film musicals take longer. I don't have to be rehearsed to walk in the door, say a line and sit down in the chair. If they say, "Take it again", fine; I can just *do* it. But if you want me to *dance* in the door, jump on the table, spin around and land on a certain beat, I have to know what the music is and do it over and over until it's so natural I forget I'm dancing at all. Dances just don't happen. Maybe six weeks down the line, we'll be ready to shoot. Well, the front office doesn't want to know about that. That's why there are no film musicals.'

Tune describes himself as 'a living anachronism. I'm a song 'n' dance man, I just got here and I do it better than I've ever done it in my life. But people don't do that any more. I'm *quaint*. Musicals are *quaint*.' To a certain extent, his career has been spent keeping one step ahead of the all-singin', all-scythin' Grim Reaper. Sneaking in at the death-throes of the Hollywood musical, he then went to *The Dean Martin Show*, dancing a new number every week on TV's Number One variety programme. 'That doesn't exist any more. The TV variety show is dead.'

Then he put together an act for the top nightclub circuit. 'Very nice act, all Gershwin, Cole Porter, Irving Berlin. I played across America for one year. I go to do it again, but sorry, the Venetian Room in San Francisco's just closed, the Pump Room in Chicago's closed. I keep getting in on the end of everything, but at least I'm there before it goes completely.'

Michael Bennett brought him back to musicals for *Seesaw*, casting him as a choreographer and letting him create his own numbers. The finale – 'Wait!' cries Tune after a mere 15 choruses. 'We gotta have a bigger finish!' – is one of those high-stepping hymns to Broadway optimism. Today, we recognize it as one of the last 11 o'clock numbers which sound as if its authors meant it. Once again, Tune had got there just in time:

> It's Not Where You Start, It's Where You Finish
> And you're gonna finish on top!

By now, even the superstar stagers seemed to be running up against dance's limitations: Bennett's shows were about dancers (*Ballroom*), Fosse's were about thugs or shyster lawyers or purpose-gals but were invariably staged as vaudevilles (*Chicago*). To many, the vocabulary of show dance is too narrow. 'So what?' says Tune. 'Old plus old equals new. You can't create a dance without the flatball change. It's in everything. It's a wonderful mode of linkage, so how are you gonna do without it? It's like cutting off an arm, it's part of you. But the end is: what is the character expressing?'

To its detractors, most dancers seem to be expressing dancing. Sure, Tune has his big numbers – the 'Famous Feet' salute to Astaire et al in *A Day in Hollywood, a Night in the Ukraine* or the cowgirls dancing with blow-up dolls in *Best Little Whorehouse in Texas*. But, as far as the meat of the drama is concerned, his ambition often exceeds his reach. With both *Grand Hotel* and *The Will Rogers Follies*, what made Tune a shoo-in for the Tonys year after year was an ability, as sole surviving director/choreographer, to get a crudely workable handle on the properties. *Grand Hotel* had been written by Luther Davis, Bob Wright and Chet Forrest in the fifties, not long after their big hit *Kismet*. Back then, it had closed on the road; one of its songs dates back even further, to the twenties. Tune's concept was to direct it as a sort of silent movie for the TV age. 'In America,' he says, 'our attention span has gone from the 47-second soundbite to the 11-second soundbite. They had Gregory Peck on a programme the other day and he was reduced to one sentence: "And here at the opening we have Gregory Peck." "Well, I think it's just wonderful." "Thank you very much, Mr Peck." In America, we don't watch television, we watch *what else* is on television. So I tried to do this show as if I had a remote control.'

He tore up Luther Davis' script and reassembled it in tiny fragments. The critics loved it, but the writers had mixed feelings. 'Well,' Robert Wright told me, 'it's Tommy's *vision* of our show.' Wright and Forrest prefer to see their well-aired differences with Tune as part of the general trend towards 'director power'. 'Back in the twenties,' Wright recalled, 'George Pierce Baker said, "Remember this. A director's theatre is a theatre in decline." As marvellous as it may be, someone has still got to sit down with a pencil and paper and write something.'

Professor Baker taught, among others, George Abbott and Eugene O'Neill and Philip Barry, which is good enough for me. But he didn't know the half of it. If a director's theatre is a theatre in decline, in what sort of shape is a director's theatre with only one director left? In *The New York Times*, the ads for *Grand Hotel* showed an award-festooned Tommy Tune standing astride the musical's logo. He wasn't in it, he didn't write it, but it was *his* show; he was the bankable name.

But how bankable is Broadway's most bankable director *really*? *Grand Hotel* was a tasteful bore, and a strictly local hit: it had the best notices you've ever seen in London, and belly flopped. The design he insisted on for *The Will Rogers Follies* meant that you couldn't see it from the side seats, which meant that those seats couldn't be sold, which meant that, although the show ran for years, the producers and investors never made any money. On the road tour, the show's star attraction, the dog act, got left in a van on the street; the van caught fire and the poor mutts burnt to death. 'Pity it wasn't Tune in there,' one investor said to me.

His shows don't entertain like Fosse's, nor do they have the dramatic weight of Robbins'. More and more, you're aware that he's inherited by default. And he does practically everything these days: *Grand Hotel*, *Will Rogers*, *Bye, Bye, Birdie*, *Tommy Tune Tonite*, *Grease*, *Busker Alley*, a short-lived sequel to *The Best Little Whorehouse in Texas*, which was tacky even by his standards.

'I don't want to work with anything but the best,' he says, 'but the idea that I "busy myself with lesser works" makes me real angry. And anger is not where I reside.'

Wherever Tommy Tune resides, by the time he moves on, the neighbourhood looks like a graveyard. The man who got to Hollywood, to Dean Martin, to the Pump Room just in time picked perfect timing to get to the director/choreographer business.

*

Even if the reduced state of dance on Broadway is only a temporary lull, the styles, the traditions, the big numbers may all die in the meantime. When Jerome Robbins put together a grand retrospective of his best work from *Fiddler*, *Gypsy* et al, he had to reconstruct the dances from the memories of the original performers, those that were still around. 'The dances that were filmed will survive,' says Gwen Verdon. 'Thank God they filmed *West Side Story*. And there's some more material on badly shot video. But the rest, I think, will just disappear. When we revived *Sweet Charity* in 1986, I was the only one who remembered everything. They just start the music and off I go like Pavlov's dog. But I won't be around to do that forever.'

And, even if we remember the steps, will we remember what they're for? In 1996, for the first time in over a decade, Broadway saw a new dance musical: *Bring in 'da Noise/Bring in 'da Funk*. Directed by George C. Wolfe, with choreography by Savion Glover and rap poetry by Reg E.

Gaines, *Bring in 'da Noise* is a 'celebration' of black rhythms from tap to hip-hop. 'Celebration' is a soft option for theatre: it excuses you from making drama. So, as Glover dances, we hear his recorded voiceover say, 'It's raw, it's rhythms, it's us, it's ours.' Although there are satirical squibs aimed at black caricatures from Bill 'Bojangles' Robinson to General Colin Powell, Glover is right: it's raw, it's rhythms, it's noise, it's funk – but it's not drama; it's dance about dance.

Still, Glover is New York's newest dance star, and, shortly before *Bring in 'da Noise*'s Broadway opening, he flew to Hollywood at Quincy Jones' invitation to participate in the Oscars ceremony. Gene Kelly had died a few weeks earlier, and, as his most famous number was heard, Glover was seen in silhouette rat-a-tat-tatting his way across the stage. But why do we love Gene Kelly doing 'Singin' In The Rain'? Because the number is a joyous expression of his mood at that moment in the story:

> What a glorious feeling!
> (*Splash*!
>> *Splash*!)
> I'm happy again!

Glover's dance, by contrast, was not a joyous expression of character and situation. It was just taps, just mechanics, just the clicketty-clacketty-click of his shoes. It's a choreographic equivalent of rap: the triumph of the backing track.

But what remains now of Robbins' and Fosse's and Bennett's ambitions for show dance? 'I think there are still people who don't appreciate the range of dance,' says Donna McKechnie, 'but there are also plenty of young dancers who were fired by seeing *Chorus Line* when they were young. That's still an inspiration to people, because that show was the purest metaphor, and Michael edited it like a movie: it was very simple. There was just a line on the stage, we were all in leotards. It wasn't big or flashy, but it ran for 15 years.'

Miss McKechnie is right. *A Chorus Line* is no more or less than what it says: a line of gypsies in leggings auditioning for the chance to be one of the faceless phalanx behind the star at a Broadway musical. It was Michael Bennett's Valentine to the massed ranks which he, unlike most dancers, had managed to escape, and its subject and form gave it a special resonance denied to other long-runners like *Hello, Dolly!*, *Life with Father*, *My Fair Lady*. In its way, the show was the gypsy's revenge: forget Ethel Merman, Mary Martin, Gwen Verdon; the longest-running show in Broadway history had no headliners, only the chorus.

In other backstage musicals, they'd have gone out as youngsters and come back as stars. But, unlike the crazed director of *42nd Street*, the sentimentally dictatorial father-confessor in *A Chorus Line* offers his auditioning dancers nothing but a job: the play makes us accept the chorus as characters in their own right; they deserve the leading roles more than the heroes of all those other schlocko backstage yarns, but all they get to do is serve unnoticed in one of those mechanical kicklines. And, as the plot goes, so does the cast: in 15 years on Broadway, from 1975 to 1990, *Chorus Line* never had a star and never made one. On the 3,389th performance, when the show became the all-time long-runner, 332 of its graduates crowded onto the stage of the Shubert Theatre to form the most gloriously swollen chorus ever seen on Broadway. But the biographies in the expanded *Playbill* demonstrated as well as anything in the play the vicissitudes of a life in show dance: some *Chorus Line*rs had moved on to *Cats* and *Cage Aux Folles*, some were running dance schools, one was 'compiling a "gypsy cookbook"', another was 'teaching computer programming'. Still, that's showbusiness – where hope springs eternal. As Marvin Hamlisch and Edward Kleban put it, 'Kiss today goodbye / And point me t'ward tomorrow.'

That awkward concertina-ed 'toward' causes a raised eyebrow or two among more fastidious writers. Nor is the general thrust and the title of the number, 'What I Did For Love', anything new. But Broadway musicals still like hit songs, and the rest of *Chorus Line*'s score is either too tied to the book or too peppered with 'shits' and 'craps' to get much airplay. 'That song was a real cheat,' Hamlisch admitted. 'I said, "Listen, guys, we have nothing to play on variety shows. You can't put 'Tits And Ass' on television." So I wrote "What I Did For Love" as a song you could pull out and do on Mike Douglas. Joe Papp said he wanted to cut it, because it felt stuck in. He was right – and I was.'

But it still felt stuck in. After *Chorus Line*'s first night off-Broadway, at Joseph Papp's Public Theatre, Bette Midler came up to one of the authors, James Kirkwood. 'She said to me, "It's such a pity. You almost had a hit. But that awful song – what was it? something about what they did for love? – that threw it right down the toilet. Oh, well." She was trying to be sympathetic.'

It's an old theme: better to have loved and lost than never, etc. In the show, though, 'What I Did For Love' is applied not to some sweetheart but to the theatre itself, to the dance line which will always be every gypsy's first love. Hamlisch got his hit, recorded by dozens of singers. But, in the intervening years, something even rarer happened. The song may be cliché, but, as *Chorus Line* swelled to assume a unique place in the affections of the vast supporting cast of American showbusiness, the dancers believed it enough to make it work. The cast's own memoir of the show is titled *What We Did for Love*. Seeing the Broadway production not long before its close, I found myself, despite my better judgement, with a lump in my throat. Written for opportunistic commercial reasons, the song had come true and real.

In that respect, as in many others, *A Chorus Line* is a typical musical but to the *n*th degree: those dancers might really believe they did it for love, but they need a couple of pro songwriters to articulate it. Touted as an exception, the show still proves several rules. Most musicals are adaptations, but *Chorus Line* is famous as the only show to be improvised on to Broadway – from Michael Bennett's first midnight pop-therapy rap sessions with 22 dancers in a studio owned by Buddhists. These gypsies' experiences formed the basis of the play's characters, and one of them, Nicholas Dante, became a co-author. But he was harnessed to James Kirkwood, who never heard the tapes of Bennett's sessions until he'd finished his first draft. And even though Kirkwood, like Hamlisch and Kleban, had never written a musical before, he was an experienced playwright and novelist. In any case, when the going got rough, Bennett, like many directors, called on the ever reliable Neil Simon to punch up the script with zippy one-liners.

The dancers were mostly reluctant to acknowledge the show was *written* at all. To them, Bennett was the superstager who hadn't forgotten his roots, who'd proved that a choreographer and his dancers could create the ultimate musical – no sets, no costumes, no stars, just them. But things were never that innocent. 'It's not *show*business, it's show*business*,' snapped Bennett in rehearsal. That said, he was also able to embrace his producer at that landmark record-breaking performance and sob, with utter sincerity, 'I love you, Joseph Papp.' More than most, Bennett, the choreographer of *Follies* and *Company*, personified the contradictory mix of sentimental camaraderie and rampant egomania which makes up the Broadway theatre. *A Chorus Line* is heartfelt, but it's also manipulative. Nothing wrong with that: audiences at musicals *like* to be manipulated, just as playgoers enjoy boasting of how they *work* during serious drama. It's the difference between a morning jog and a massage, and Bennett was Broadway's master masseur. His characters' lives were catchpenny, but the dances made them unique.

'I saw *Damn Yankees* with Gwen Verdon,' he said, recalling his first trip to New York as an eleven-year-old. 'There it all was, everything I wanted.'

He worked an echo of that moment into the show: 'I'm going to be the next Gwen Verdon,' says one girl. When *Chorus Line* opened in 1975, Miss Verdon was starring in Bob Fosse's *Chicago*, another showbiz fable but almost an inversion of Bennett's: the story of a murderess who cashes in on her fame and goes into vaudeville; at the end, she throws flowers to the audience as if to say, 'Screw you, suckers. You bought it, too.' *Chicago* did boffo biz until Verdon left and then spluttered to a close. Both plays use showbusiness as a metaphor for the American dream, but *Chicago*'s cynicism eventually exhausted its audience; in *Chorus Line*, as much as *42nd Street*, underneath the tough veneer beat hearts of gold. But look at today's fifteen-minute tabloid grotesques: Amy Fisher, the Long Island Lolita who parlayed her story into TV movies for all three US networks; Tonya Harding, the ice queen from hell who, even before the cops began questioning her, was already negotiating book deals; Lorena Bobbitt, the penis-severing manicurist who, like Demi Moore and Goldie Hawn, went on to pose for *Vanity Fair* . . . As it happens, I first heard about the Bobbitt case from Gwen Verdon. 'Watch what the media do with this,' she said. 'It'll be just like *Chicago*.' *A Chorus Line* is the apotheosis of America's most enduring myth, but which show tells us more about the world we live in? In the misguided 1985 film of *Chorus Line*, Richard Attenborough and his orchestrator Ralph Burns tried to bring out the darker edge of the high-kicking hats-and-canes finale, to show how soulless and robotic a perfectly blended dance machine can be – that there's no identity, no individuality. But, as you leave the theatre, all you're doing is tapping your feet and clicking your fingers. Whatever the lyric ambivalence of 'One Singular Sensation!', in the end the performance seduces the drama away from itself – the oldest musical trick of all.

Bennett hoped it would create a greater audience for dance, but the failure of his next show, *Ballroom*, suggested that *Chorus Line* had simply put young American yearning in its most universally appealing form. Only when the real-life tragedies of its creators began to outpace anything on stage did the play's (by now) period charm start to feel uncomfortable and self-deluding. 'We were all young when we wrote it,' James Kirkwood told me in 1988. 'We used to talk about doing *Chorus Line II*, looking at what those dancers were doing ten years later. Well, of course, ten years later they were still doing *Chorus Line*. And now we'll never do *Chorus Line II* because Michael Bennett died of Aids and Ed Kleban of cancer. And you start thinking, "Is this a countdown? Will we all go during the run?" Now, at our anniversary celebrations, it's like *Phantom of the Shubert Theatre*.'

At next year's anniversary, there was one less: Kirkwood, too, had died of Aids. A year later, his co-writer Nick Dante succumbed to the virus. And cast member after cast member after cast member . . . *A Chorus Line* had indeed become a symbol of American show dance but in a way its creators could never have foreseen.

The Fags

'Print what you like,' says William Finn when we meet. 'I always sound like a jerk in interviews anyway.' He can't quarrel with the basic facts: William Finn is a fortysomething composer/lyricist, ancient by the standards of tennis players but positively precocious in the Broadway theatre, where the leading practitioners are over 60, if not actually dead. A big, shambling fellow, much given to hysterical laughter, Finn always wanted to be famous by the time he was 30, and he was. 'But,' he says forlornly, 'I've become a little obscured since then.' On jury duty in New York a few years back, Finn was congratulated on his hit musical by both the prosecuting and defence lawyers and the court stenographer. Unfortunately, all of them had mistaken him for the composer of *La Cage aux Folles*. 'Can you believe it?' he moans. 'I had to say, "No, that's a different homo show".'

Finn's homo show was *March of the Falsettos* (1981), which was preceded by *In Trousers* and succeeded by *Falsettoland*, which were combined into *Falsettos*, which eventually landed on Broadway and earned Finn the distinction of having written the Main Stem's first 'out' musical. Anything less like Jerry Herman's opulent transvestite frolic is hard to imagine. The *Falsetto* trilogy features a character called Marvin, who leaves his wife for another man. At the time, I earnestly enquired whether it was pleading for greater tolerance. Finn fell around laughing. 'Are you nuts?' he said.

Er, not entirely. Audiences at musicals are reluctant to be told things they don't want to hear, and, traditionally, writers with a conscience have opted for what now seems like quaintly dated liberal moralizing. Think of *South Pacific* and Hammerstein's angry lyric 'You've Got To Be Carefully Taught' – to hate and fear folks who are different. It's a classic plea for greater tolerance which, in a classic commercial theatre compromise, the characters are never obliged to test: the US airman gets killed in action and his Polynesian girlfriend is left alone. Finn's world, in contrast, is presented on a take-it-or-leave-it basis, a tone set by the title of the opening number for *March of the Falsettos*: 'Four Jews In A Room Bitching'. His characters just *are* – and what they are is gay.

Of course, there have always been gays in the theatre. In *On Your Toes* (1936), Larry Hart wrote:

> Each poor man has a wife he must stick to
> Men of fashion can be cocky
> To be caught in flagrante delictu
> Is too good for the average mockey

. . . which was taken, apparently, as a commendation of homosexuality, one of those things which are 'Too Good For The Average Man'. Then there was Cole Porter, who with Monty Woolley used to go cruising the docks for rough trade. One thinks of the brilliant lyrical compression of 'Find Me A Primitive Man':

> I don't mean the kind that belongs to a club
> But the kind that has a club that belongs to him.

Although he was the kind that belongs to a club, the latter half of this couplet sums up Porter's own taste in men. But Porter was the exception. The evidence for Hart's sexuality is inconclusive, and any guy of 4'10" winds up making do, regardless of gender. 'Because of his size, the opposite sex was denied him,' said Alan Jay Lerner, 'so he was forced to find relief in the only other sex left.' Even then, he doesn't seem to have found that much relief. He lived with his mother and various passing aunts and it was left to his friend, the infamous Doc Bender, to procure for Hart what brief companionship he enjoyed. According to one alleged lover, he was deeply closeted, literally: after sex, he'd get up and go and cower in the closet for the rest of the night. Mabel Mercer famously called him the saddest man she ever knew. You can hear it in the songs:

> Falling in love with love
> Is falling for make believe . . .

But Hart, who never in his life had a girlfriend or boyfriend, could also skewer precisely the assumptions of intimacy. 'One of my favourite songs,' Mort Shuman, the adaptor of *Jacques Brel Is Alive and Well and Living in Paris*, once told me, 'is "It Never Entered My Mind". When Hart wrote . . .

> You have what I lack myself
> Now I even have to scratch my back myself

. . . I thought, "Yeah. I've always had this little place on my back I can't quite reach", and I thought about the times I've asked a lover to scratch it for me. That's brilliant writing.'

Brilliant, but strictly observational. Hart was lonely, Porter enjoyed a marriage of convenience, Lerner was a serial monogamist and Kern, Rodgers, Ira Gershwin lived the eternal boy/girl romances they preached in their songs. Homosexuals were sufficiently rare in the theatre that, around his Broadway début in 1913, George Abbott had no idea such men existed. When a colleague snuck up and kissed him on the back of the neck, Abbott turned round, slugged the guy and put him in hospital.

Seventy-five years later, in the film *Good Morning, Vietnam*, Robin Williams is teaching English to a class of Saigon schoolchildren and makes reference to someone who comes from Queens – as in the borough of New York City.

'What are Queens?' asks one of the kids.

Williams replies: 'Tall, skinny men who like showtunes.'

This joke is becoming ubiquitous. In 1994, on the CBS sitcom *The Nanny*, two children are playing chess, when one asks the butler: 'What do you do with queens?'

He says: 'Stand them round a piano and play selections from *Gypsy*.'

In another CBS TV show, *Northern Exposure*, the town bigshot is shocked to be taken by a newly arrived gay couple for one of them simply on the basis that his record collection consists of Judy Garland, Ethel Merman, Gwen Verdon and Carol Channing.

When did it happen? When did a form mocked as insipid, bland 'family entertainment' come to be associated with homosexuality? There are no statistics for these things, but, on the basis of my own unscientific research, I would say that, of the longest-running shows of the 1940s, some two-thirds had a homosexual contribution in the writing/staging/producing department. By the 1960s, the proportion of long-runners with a major homosexual contribution was up to about 90 per cent. Certainly, it's hard to take issue with Leonard Bernstein, who once told a friend: 'To be a successful composer of musicals, you either have to be Jewish or gay. And I'm both.'

He was both with a vengeance. Towards the end of his life, when he'd attempt to cajole everyone into a singalong of 'Ev'rybody Out Of The Closet', it seemed as if Lenny was determined to come out on everybody's behalf.

*

Once upon a time, Broadway was the only place you could go for any kind of sex in songs. They wouldn't play Porter's 'Love For Sale' on the radio, but you could hear it in the theatre:

> Who will buy?
> Who would like to sample my supply?
> Who's prepared to pay the price
> For a trip to paradise
> Love For Sale . . .

It's said that Porter, who considered it his favourite song, wrote it about a rent boy. At any rate, for *The New Yorkers* (1930), it was felt that it would be more acceptable if sung by 'a coloured girl', Elisabeth Welch. I'm told 'I've Got You Under My Skin' was also popular with homosexuals in the 1930s. But, gay or straight, sex was rarely far from Porter's mind, and, although the title said 'Let's Do It (Let's fall in love)', the lyric made clear that he had more transitory encounters in mind:

> Moths in your rugs do it
> What's the use of moth balls?

You didn't get that on radio or at the movies: it was all still 'The bells are ringing/For Me And My Gal . . .' Broadway songs hinted at less formal unions:

> I'll sing to him
> Each spring to him
> And worship the trousers that cling to him
> Bewitched, Bothered And Bewildered am I . . .

But rock 'n' roll outpaced showtunes. Who wants left-field sidles up to sex when Mick Jagger's singing 'Let's Spend The Night Together'? Heterosexuals no longer needed the coded sexuality of Broadway songs. But, for homosexuals, the sly, coded sexuality became even more appealing – because the vast majority of gays were themselves still leading sly, coded lives. And now that heterosexuals were no longer convinced by musical comedy love stories, it was even better: musicals, just as Larry Hart said, were 'Too Good For The Average Man'. Instead of insipid backporch spooning, musicals gave you songs like 'You Can't Get A Man With A Gun' – a big favourite today with the New York City Gay Men's Chorus.

The gay movement owes much to one towering homosexual icon: Judy

Garland. Her most famous film role provided a discreet password in a less tolerant world: 'Are you a friend of Dorothy?' A wake held to mark her death sparked the Stonewall riot and a long march out of the shadows. American homosexuals adopted Garland's suffering as an emblem of their own. But Broadway gave them a full range of supporting players: larger-than-life ladies spilling out tales of love gone wrong. Musicals don't have to be camp, but they exist in a heightened reality – lavishly dressed, lavishly emotional – and that exaggeration seems to appeal to the gay consciousness.

Then again, with one or two exceptions such as *The King and I* and *The Music Man*, there are hardly any good strong, straight male roles in musicals. It's all either Principal Boys – Mary Martin as Peter Pan and Nellie Forbush, two of the great trouser roles – or Pantomime Dames: Carol Channing as Lorelei Lee and Dolly Levi, or Angela Lansbury as Mame, or Ethel Merman as the hostess with the mostes'. We still joke about Broadway being boy-meets-girl but, in fact, hardly any musicals are concerned with conventional heterosexual romance. These women aren't young; they're middle-aged and matronly, and they usually have a nephew or a weedy milksop in tow. You can do your own pop psychology, but, to invert the old cry of 'My mother made me a homosexual', homo-sexuals have made some of the greatest mothers ever created in American drama. There's a cartoon quality about Broadway leading ladies which makes them the nearest thing to a female drag queen. For gays, pop music offered no similar thrills. Even the gay dance scene borrows extensively from Broadway – through either disco divas like Grace Jones doing 'La Vie En Rose' or the Pet Shop Boys teaming up with Liza Minnelli to do a thrashing Eurodisco version of 'Losing My Mind'. By comparison, the earth-bound blokiness of rock was exposed for all to see in 1992 when Wembley Stadium staged its all-star salute to Freddie Mercury, the late lead singer of Queen. One by one, leathery old rockers ambled on to do cover versions of Freddie's hits, with all the life drained out of them. Finally, Liza Minnelli entered to sing 'We Are The Champions' and blew the roof off. And you realized that poor old Freddie had been in the wrong business all along. Like Liza, he dressed in basic black. Like Liza, he was a Broadway baby. He should have graduated to being one of Jerry Her-man's big ladies on the staircase in *Mame* or *Dolly*. Frankly, his legs were better than most of Jerry's girls.

But when were musicals going to come out? In the sixties, *The Boys in the Band* led a few other Broadway straight plays out of the closet. But, in musicals, apart from a gay choreographer played by Tommy Tune in

Seesaw (1973) and a bit of drag-queen psychotherapy in *A Chorus Line*, nothing. The Broadway musical encompassed everything except the one subject its creators were specially expert in. There are respectable precedents for this: musical comedy has never subscribed to the dictum that you should write of what you know; Rodgers and Hammerstein were urban Jews, but, instead of writing about that, they wrote about Oklahoma and Maine and Siam. Besides, if the entire genre has a gay sensibility, who needs a show specifically addressing the subject?

And then, in 1984, a big mainstream Broadway musical edged out ever so slightly. *La Cage aux Folles* was based on a French film about a homosexual couple who run a transvestite nightclub and the farcical consequences of their son's impending marriage. The boy and the girl got to kiss. The boy even got to grope his future mother-in-law's breast. But, for the two principals, not so much as a peck on the cheek. 'That was deliberate,' says the director Arthur Laurents. 'I knew it was very important that there shouldn't be so much as a kiss between those two guys or half the audience would have walked out.' On both Broadway and in London, they cast heterosexual actors who were eager in the programme notes to thank their wives and kids. It was a typical Broadway compromise. The show became just another warm-hearted, conventional Jerry Herman musical, only this time, as if recognizing that Dolly and Mame and the other caricature broads had been drag queens all along, the big lady on the staircase was a guy in a frock:

> It's my world
> That I want to have a little pride in
> My world
> And it's not a place I have to hide in
> Life's not worth a damn
> Till you can say
> Hey, world
> I Am What I Am.

From Jerry Herman, this was powerful stuff. Most of his big-lady-on-staircase numbers are saying nothing more than hello, Dolly or Mame or Mabel. Herman made this one a proud affirmation of self.

Laurents' balancing act seemed to work. *La Cage aux Folles* became the biggest new American musical of the day. But the following year Liberace and Rock Hudson died, and introduced a new word to the majority of theatregoers: Aids. In 1986, the London production flopped at the Palladium. Aids, they said, had reduced the appeal of the show. 'Well, I'm not sure,' says Herman, sadly. 'The Palladium wasn't really the ideal theatre.' But it happened back in America, too: the road companies of *La Cage* just faded away. Laurents and Herman and librettist Harvey Fierstein had done their best to ensure that nothing about their homosexual principals offended musical theatre's middle-aged, middle-class, conservative audience. And, in the end, the audience rejected the show anyway. Fags weren't funny any more; fags meant disease and death. One minute *La Cage aux Folles* was the biggest homegrown hit of the day; the next it was gone.

I wonder if Herman wishes he'd written more songs like 'I Am What I Am' and let the show go down fighting. There was another big, full-throated number in the show, with a lyric of deceptive simplicity:

> The Best Of Times is now
> What's left of summer but a faded rose?
> The Best Of Times is now
> As for tomorrow, well, who knows?
> Who knows?
> Who knows?
> So hold this moment fast
> And live and love as hard as you know how
> And make this moment last
> Because The Best Of Times is now
> Is now
> Is now
> Now!
> Not some forgotten yesterday
> Now!
> Tomorrow is too far away . . .

The last time I heard the song sung live was when I wandered into a bar in Greenwich Village packed with drama queens gathered round the piano and determined to hold the moment fast because, for many of them and their emaciated, cadaverous friends, tomorrow was too far away. When Jerry Herman wrote it for the flamboyant transvestites in *La Cage*, could he have had any idea of the catastrophe about to engulf Broadway's workforce? Or was he, in the best tradition of musical comedy songwriting, just enlarging and universalizing the moment? Either way, how strange that Herman, composer of the most determinedly old-fashioned music on Broadway, should have provided the most comforting song for this most modern of scourges.

In William Finn's homo show, a quartet of high male voices sings:

> Who is man enough to march to
> The March Of The Falsettos?

On Broadway, not many were. Aids posthumously outed musical comedy. Week after week, the obituary columns of *Variety* confirmed that this most mainstream and conventional form was written, staged and performed by homosexuals. In Tommy Tune's cabaret act, there's a rather mawkish moment when the star lists all the people that 'I miss': on and on the names roll, all but five or six of them dead from Aids. I find it hard to watch *A Chorus Line* these days: its innocence seems self-deceiving; its portrait of show dancers' lives included everything yet missed the one thing that transformed the dance world out of all recognition. Musical theatre's failure to encompass the one issue of explicit concern to it makes you ponder both the range of the musical and its maturity.

*

One of the minor pleasures of *Show Boat* are the play-within-the-play scenes, of rough-hewn Mississippi audiences engrossed in the hokey old melodramas that chugged their way across the continent for most of the last century. Next week, *East Lynne*? If only. Hammerstein's affectionate show-within-the-boat spoofs remind you of a lush era when Ol' Man The'ter, he jes' kept rollin' along, week after week, story after story: not just teary tales of distant exotics like Lady Isabel Mount Severn and Sir Francis Levison, but the vast panorama of nineteenth-century life – in 1879, there were 49 companies of *Uncle Tom's Cabin* alone, and hundreds of lesser dramas of railroads and land claims, sheriffs and preachers, hoboes and drummers. Now, at the 1994 revival of *Show Boat*, Broadway audiences pay 70 bucks a pop to go to the Gershwin Theatre and watch a spectacular high-tech re-creation of hammy Victorian mellers. As an image of theatrical withdrawal, it's hard to beat.

But it's not merely a matter of production activity. Where have all the plots and characters, where has all the *life* gone? In the late summer of 1994, still convalescing from that spring's Broadway revival, I went to see *Damn Yankees* at the Weathervane Theatre, which sits on the edge of the woods a few miles out from Whitefield, New Hampshire, and is New England's northernmost barn theatre. I was feeling in need of something innocent and summer-stocky, and there'd been a jolly magazine article by a local teacher who'd successfully auditioned for the company. Of course, it wasn't like that at all. Most of the players were struggling professionals from out-of-state and the evening began with the director urging us to drop some money in the Broadway Cares / Equity Fights Aids collection bins and wear a red ribbon. Well, I gave a couple of bucks, and so did a few other folks, but I didn't see anybody take a red ribbon. Aside from the fact that it wouldn't stand out against plaid, I can't think of anything sillier or more irrelevant or more blithely un-'aware' than wearing an 'Aids Awareness' ribbon in Coos County, a sprawling wilderness where the White Mountains fall away and the headwaters of the Connecticut dribble out to the Quebec plain. You could throw a giant chicken cook-out and have wild unprotected sex with everyone of either gender in the whole county and never contract HIV. Aids, we were told, 'is an epidemic that affects us all', but in Coos County, statistically, you're more at risk from a logging accident or from hitting a moose. ('Brake For Moose – It Could Save Your Life,' warn the road signs. 'Collisions This Year: 211.') There are no plays about logging or moose collisions or rural unemployment. At intermission, as we milled outside that barn in the cool evening air of the north woods, I looked at the company and I looked at the locals: which group would you say was isolated, insular, parochial . . .?

At the theatre these days, the most striking images are invariably off-stage. Several First Act curtains later, I was at the Arena Stage in Washington for Terrence McNally's *A Perfect Ganesh*, a play about two women from Stamford, Connecticut, one of whose son has been queer-bashed to death and both of whom are touring India. This intermission we were again outside, this time in the theatre's parking lot, with a sprinkling of diplomatic plates and the handicapped space occupied by a limo. Everyone was standing around making polite social chit-chat apparently deaf to the DC police roaring past, sirens screaming: fresh from White-field, NH, I seemed to be the only one who noticed.

At the Theatre Communications Group National Conference that year, Edgar Rosenblum of Connecticut's Long Wharf insisted that theatre is as essential to life as any public service: 'The fire department is *not* more important than art,' he said. 'If you will save people, what will you save them for?' But, viewed from the parking lot at the Arena Stage, the theatre is a refuge from life. Conversely, in Whitefield, after dropping your money in the Aids bucket and heading back to your Cape or trailer, life is a refuge from theatre.

In the new *Damn Yankees* there's a line that symbolizes the dreary obsessions of the theatrical dead-end we're complacently painting ourselves into. It comes during a scene in which the Devil and Lola are wandering through Limbo and gleefully chuckling at the great lovers of history – Romeo and Juliet, Tristan and Isolde, J. Edgar Hoover and Clyde Tolson. It's not the cheapness of the shot (even the 1993 'Gay Edgar Hoover' biography couldn't find any real proof of a physical relationship); it's not the expensiveness of the shot (why pay Broadway prices for a topical gag your morning disc-jockey or late-night talk-show host will give you for free?); it's the technical unsoundness of it: *Damn Yankees* is set in the fifties, when Hoover and Tolson were very much alive. So the joke has to be shoehorned in: 'They're not even dead,' points out Lola. 'I know,' chuckles the Devil gleefully, 'but I just can't wait.' It gets a laugh, but it's a cheap laugh, at the expense of the play: half the score has Joe (the star baseball player) yearning for the wife he's left behind, but the director Jack O'Brien couldn't care less about this relationship. In rehearsal in 1955, Stephen Douglass (the original Joe) asked at one point what his motivation for a particular scene was. 'Your salary,' said Mister Abbott, famously. I hope the new Joe was on a good salary, because O'Brien sure didn't give him any other reason.

At the San Diego try-out, I suggested to Mister Abbott he get the Hoover gag removed. But it made it to New York, and even to the Weathervane's barn in New Hampshire, where, the biogs told us, one of the cast had just come from rehearsals in New York for *J. Edgar Hoover – the Musical*. What's the betting the title's as good as it gets? Just as it is for all the other fifties schlock which so preoccupies Greenwich Village: *Space Bitch, Chorus Girls on Mars, What Would Esther Williams Do in a Situation Like This?* and *I Could Go on Lip-synching*, to name a handful plucked randomly from one month in 1988. Across New York, fifties chickens are coming out to roost. In Victor Garber's bitchily malicious reading, the Hoover/Tolson joke is delivered with all the withering scorn gays reserve for the chronically closeted. Round the block at Tony Kushner's *Angels in America*, Roy Cohn attempts a defence: he's not homosexual, he says, because a homosexual is, by definition, powerless; he's a heterosexual who happens to fuck men.

In the closeted theatre of the fifties, it was the other way round: some of America's greatest stage creations were homosexuals who happened to fuck women: Tennessee Williams wrote boy-meets-girl because he couldn't write boy-meets-boy, and his views on marriage should be seen in that light. But how long ago it seems: in New York in the nineties, the nearest thing to a homegrown hit musical is *Kiss of the Spider Woman*, and the nearest thing to a homegrown straight play (if you'll forgive the term) is *Angels in America*. In three decades, we've gone from Williams' constrained masterpieces to indulgent self-celebrations like *Hysterical Blindness and Other Southern Tragedies that Have Plagued My Life Thus Far*, a revue by a thespian gay about growing up a gay thespian. You can look on this as tremendous progress, or as proof that American theatre is simply shrivelling to its core audience. *Hysterical Blindness* is a silly campy title for Leslie Jordan's show, but, if you're looking for a diagnosis of modern American drama, it's spot on, neatly encapsulating both the paranoia and self-absorption of the contemporary stage.

*

I remember once standing transfixed by the banality of one farewell message on an Aids memorial quilt: 'Ready for my close-up now, Mr De Mille.' The thought that all this man, facing death, could find to sum up his life was a hand-me-down drag-queen cliché was almost unbearably sad. When so many of those consumed by Aids see themselves in theatrical terms, dramatists have trouble returning the compliment. Early Aids plays liked to take an inventory: the glands, the sweats, the lesions. More recently, authors have turned to a sort of *deus ex machina*: in Kushner's *Angels in America*, Aids prompts a heavenly visitation; in McNally's *A Perfect Ganesh*, it's the Indian deity Ganesha. Both men seem to be struggling to ennoble and dignify the disease. *Angels in America*, a 'gay fantasia', is fun because it's epic. But Aids is epic *and* banal – and the latter is too awkward for writers to confront, especially when they're concerned to be well-intentioned.

So, in *A Perfect Ganesh*, mother and son pass the evening duelling in song cues: 'So sue me – that's from *Guys and Dolls*.' 'Shut up and dance – that's from *Gypsy*.' It's not that the Indian hotel manager says 'another bloody re-run' when the word should be 'repeat' or that he sings 'Here she comes – Miss America!' when he'd never have heard the Miss America theme because India has a booming film and TV industry and music business of its own. Anybody can nitpick about words and phrases here and there; it's what they, cumulatively, signify: in recent shows, McNally gives the impression that he doesn't know anyone outside the theatre, that he can't conceive of characters except in showbiz terms. Oddly enough, this is the chief characteristic of the gay prisoner in McNally's *Kiss of the Spider Woman*, a man who sees his life in movie fantasies. He's in gaol, and it helps him get through it. What's McNally's excuse? In his next play *Love! Valour! Compassion!* the biggest laugh came when a musical theatre buff says he's had nightmares about a revival of *The King and I* starring Tommy Tune and Elaine Stritch – a divine intervention to be sure, but again the sound of a theatre talking to itself. McNally's play is about eight gays weekending at a farmhouse in Dutchess County, New York, and what's depressing is not that they're all gays, but that they're all showfolk: they are the kind of people you meet if you work in the theatre; you're grateful that he's raised his horizons sufficiently to locate the play up the other end of the Taconic State Parkway. If musicals have found it difficult to produce a metaphor for Aids, then Aids is in danger of becoming a metaphor for New York theatre: shrunken, emaciated, unable to see beyond the window sill. On my way to Whitefield, the waitress in Bethlehem, NH, told me she wasn't one for the theatre but that, when she's sick, she likes to get out the videos of *Gigi* and *My Fair Lady*. She and McNally's 'compassionate Washington-area première' aren't so very far apart: it's theatre as a sentimental retreat from life – Lerner when you're low.

Aids has glamourized death to a degree unseen in the arts for a hundred years, but not until 1996, in a small off-off-Broadway space called the New York Theatre Workshop, were its nineteenth-century antecedents acknowledged in explicit formal terms. With hindsight, Jonathan Larson's *Rent* was inevitable: as its long march through the arts has continued, Aids has been romantically exalted to the point where its political and metaphorical burdens can no longer be borne by the dreary naturalism of the (so to speak) 'straight' play. So Larson turned to Puccini: for, like the tubercular heroines of the last century, the person-living-with-Aids, in defiance of his enfeebled physical condition, must be shown on stage to soar and sing with ravishing beauty. Unintentionally or otherwise, he even offers the inverted word order beloved of opera librettists:

> How can you connect in an age
> Where strangers, landlords, lovers
> Your own blood cells betray?

Rent is *La Bohème* translated to the nineties and into rock opera, and moved to Manhattan's East Village and a junkie equivalent of *Cats*' junkyard set: aside from HIV-riddled transvestite sculptors, there are video artists and lesbian performance artists, all of whom, even the few who don't actually carry the virus, are 'living in the shadow of Aids'. But, where Puccini's Mimi was delicate and passive, Larson's Mimi is a tougher cookie, an HIV-positive heroin addict and S&M dancer. (For those readers who don't frequent downtown bondage bars, I should explain that

S&M stands for Sondheim & Madonna, at least in terms of the character's choreographico-musical provenance.) As in the original, Mimi's tiny hand is frozen, though in this instance it's because she needs a fix.

But, increasingly in New York theatre, what happens onstage seems merely the play-within-the-play in some broader drama happening all around. *Rent* is a rock opera about dying young, and, a few days before its opening, its young composer/lyricist/librettist was found dead in his apartment, achieving a darkly exquisite synthesis of life and art. Because his show has an HIV-positive songwriter among its characters, it was assumed that Larson was yet another conscript of Aids. In fact, it was a freak aortic aneurysm. Even more unlikely, Larson seems to have been straight – and thus the first hit musical 'about' Aids was the work of a (professionally) closeted heterosexual.

I find it hard to tell from *Rent* how promising Larson was. Puccini, regardless of whether he was writing *La Bohème* or *Madam Butterfly*, wrote like Puccini. Larson writes a bit like rock, a bit like soul, a bit like Sondheim, a bit like this, that and the other from one number to the next, struggling, as pop theatre composers have struggled for years, to use the stunted musical vocabulary of the rock era to serve the needs of drama. His world view though remains consistent – not least in its vehement objection to Brooks Brothers, or even J. C. Penney. *Rent* raises a toast . . .

> To riding your bike midday
> Past the three-piece suits . . .

As cocking snooks go, it's not entirely satisfactory. *Rent* reminds me of one of those eighty-year-old Japs they find in the jungles of Borneo who doesn't know the war is over. These guys don't know the war's over, and that they won. So on and on the song proceeds, determined to shock us with a Porteresque laundry list of downtown pleasures, culminating in:

> To sodomy
> It's between God and me
> To S&M
> La Vie Bohème . . .

Well, maybe not *that* Porteresque. Porter's catalogue songs are worldly, at least in the sense that a good proportion of the world puts in an appearance:

> You're a rose!
> You're Inferno's Dante!

You're the nose
On the great Durante!

By contrast, Larson's lyrics suffer from tunnel vision:

To Sontag
To Sondheim
To anything taboo . . .

Taboo? Sontag and Sondheim? These are surely the prevailing orthodox-
ies. Indeed, in the whole play, Larson doesn't produce a single original
thought – on sex, Aids, poverty, American capitalism. Apart from sodomy, he's in favour of junkies, drag queens, dykes and not paying rent, but
not, on the whole, America:

You're living in America
Leave your conscience at the tone . . .

The dextrous word play for which he's been praised strikes me as technically suspect: 'curry vindaloo/Maya Angelou', like 'sodomy/God and
me', is not a dazzling three-syllable rhyme but a weak one-syllable identity
('-loo/-lou', '-my/me'). As for plot, drama, character, they fly by in broad
brush strokes, buried under the sound and fury of the score. And, in
this staging, the obtrusive lip microphones, emphasizing that these are
performers not characters, seem designed to pre-empt any discussion of
the show's deficiencies as drama.

But all that's irrelevant. The milieu, the subject matter, the upbeat view
of Aids combined with the young author's death were enough to rouse
The New York Times to a cheerleading campaign unseen since *Sunday in
the Park with George* opened in 1985. Back then, the drama critic of the
Times hailed the show as a breakthrough – such a breakthrough that it
could not be contained by a single review. Week after week, some further
significance in the work was discovered and discussed in the paper's arts
pages; every Sunday was a *Sunday in the Times with George*; it broke all
records as Broadway's longest-running review. The effect was to keep a
steady stream of traffic heading to the box-office – not enough for the
show to recoup its investment but enough to let it stagger on for a year and
catch the eye of the Pulitzer jury, which gave it the prize for 1985. I'm told
that at a *Times* editorial meeting shortly afterwards there was consternation that the paper hadn't won a single Pulitzer that year. Someone said:
'But we did. For Drama.'

Well, the *Times* won another Pulitzer Prize in Drama, with the first
musical to take the award since *Sunday*. Students of the constantly

accelerating trajectory of contemporary celebrity will note that they pulled this one off in a fifth of the time: the *Times* had to work *Sunday* for almost a year; they stitched up the Pulitzer for *Rent* in little more than a month, a month filled with background features on its deceased author's childhood friends and think-pieces pondering from every conceivable angle its ground-breaking qualities. Those of us who thought *Rent* The Rock Opera had a pretty simple-minded narrative have to concede that it's a model of subtle dramatic development compared to *Rent* The Legend: the late Jonathan Larson was catapulted by the Pulitzer jury from Mildly Promising Contender for a Most Promising Newcomer Award to the same hallowed pantheon as Eugene O'Neill, Thornton Wilder and Frank Loesser without having to undergo anything as tiresome as a career. The price of fame is low *Rent*.

Larson was 35, a couple of years younger than George Gershwin at the time *his* career ended. But Gershwin left us a catalogue of songs and concert works and *Porgy and Bess* and the very first Pulitzer-winning musical, *Of Thee I Sing*. Larson was merely young and promising, adjectives which now apply to any musical theatre writer still living. Would he have proved a major theatrical talent had he not been felled by that freak aneurysm? I don't think so. Not many musicals are the creation of a lone individual in book, lyrics and music, and, when they are, it's usually because – as with Meredith Willson and *The Music Man* – that's the only subject the guy knows how to write. *Rent* feels as if Larson poured everything he had into it: it was his world, the only world he knew.

At the New York Theatre Workshop, down in the East Village, if you'd entered by the wrong door, you could easily have mistaken the auditorium for the set and the audience for the cast – both were groups of rather self-conscious downtown bohemians. I was reminded of the 1984 British miners' strike, when a group of miners' wives formed a 'theatre collective' and began staging plays about miners' wives to groups of miners' wives. *Rent* winning the Pulitzer is like a football team winning the championship on the strength of having done a few workouts in front of its own cheerleaders. It's the first blockbuster hit show to do away with the need for an audience.

In April, it transferred to Broadway and the Nederlander Theatre, a tatty house that has been further tattied to give it a convincingly bohemian air: an East Village theme-park to counter Disney's *Beauty and the Beast* theme-park up the road at the Palace. In the first few days, Billy Joel and David Bowie and Ralph Fiennes came to pay their respects. And then, blinking and bewildered, looking lost in that huge Broadway barn, the cast settled down to the daunting task of winning over the bridge-&-tunnel crowd and the out-of-towners and doing for Aids what *Hair* did for the Vietnam War: that's to say, the audience had a great time and then went out and voted for Nixon. Old-time musicals wanted to make us feel good; the new school wants to make us feel good about feeling bad. And, just to make sure, *Rent*'s amateur-hour director keeps bringing the cast downstage to sing anthemically into our faces, as if daring us not to be moved.

Well, I was moved, but not because of the transvestite sculptor or the lesbian performance artist. In Puccini's bohemia, the artiness is merely the specific characteristic of universal characters. Likewise, *42nd Street*'s myths are central to America's idea of itself: 'You're going out there a youngster, but you've got to come back a star!' But there's nothing mythic or emblematic or enlarging about the characters of *Rent: La Bohème* is about everyone, *Rent* is about its participants. I was moved by its inability to move us, by its inability to speak to the world beyond. The ravages of Aids in the theatre have obscured a larger death, of theatrical culture and its metaphorical power.

*

La Cage aux Folles was a last fling for the good-time Broadway musical with a new score. In its place came the Brit hits: 'square' musicals, as one of Broadway's leading figures told me, and rare musicals, too – musicals with no gay sensibility whatsoever. Far from being 'Too Good For The Average Man', these shows are good only for the average man and his matronly blue-rinsed consort. Would the virus of British musicals have run so rampant through the theatrical body politic if Broadway's energy and morale hadn't been so collectively sapped by a real-life plague whose conscripts, like the chorus on a Ziegfeldian stairway to paradise, are without number? Today, the best shows in town – the nearest to the zest and professionalism of the Golden Age – are Aids benefits and memorial services. George S. Kaufman famously called Broadway 'the fabulous invalid'; by the eighties, the image had become literal. I asked a producer whether Jonathan Larson would be too far out for Broadway.

'Oh, no,' he said. 'Now he's dead, he'll fit right in.'

We are all minorities: Indian hotel clerks, New Hampshire loggers, HIV-positive showtune quoters. A theatre that loses interest in all but a few select minorities is doomed. After the 1994 Tony telecast, Frank Rich

iv

The Rock

In 1989, the Barbican in London celebrated the twentieth birthday of *Jesus Christ Superstar* with some special concert performances. A more or less conventional orchestra shuffled on stage, we applauded the leader and the conductor, Anthony Bowles (the original MD), and he raised his baton. At this point, the whine of an electric guitar was heard from stage left and an informally coutured axeman entered, grinding the musical's opening theme on his Stratocaster as he made his way to the platform. It was a neat trick: the symbolism of this outsider intruding on traditional theatre forces recreated exactly the impact of rock on Broadway in the late sixties.

Broadway was the last hold-out against rock and its 'revolution'. According to *Rolling Stone*'s Robert Palmer, 'It was mid-fifties rock 'n' roll that blew away, in one mighty, concentrated blast, the accumulated racial and social proprieties of the centuries.' Gosh. *Billboard* magazine would agree: its 'Hot 100' chart reference books all use 9 July 1955, when Bill Haley's 'Rock Around The Clock' hit Number One, as Year Zero of 'the rock era'. It's nonsense and it's easily demolished. Listen to the makers: Elvis admired Dean Martin and Eddie Fisher; Chuck Berry told me he wanted to sing like Nat 'King' Cole. Look at the label of 'Rock Around The Clock': one of its authors was born in the nineteenth century; Mitchell Parish, lyricist of 'Stardust' and 'Sweet Lorraine', once described it to me as 'a good conventional Tin Pan Alley song'. And on Broadway, in 1948, long before Year Zero and Bill Haley and Elvis, the score to *As the Girls Go* by old timers Jimmy ('Sunny Side Of The Street') McHugh and Harold ('Time On My Hands') Adamson included a number called 'Rock! Rock! Rock!' with the tempo marking 'Groovy'.

Step back a little further: the Original Dixieland Jazz Band recorded for RCA, and so did Elvis; Tony Bennett recorded for Columbia, and so did Bob Dylan, and Michael Jackson: they throw out the babies but the bathwater remains the same. The corporate continuity tells its own story about the rock 'n' roll 'revolution': it's revolution Romanian-style, where the ruthless manipulative Ceauşescu figure – Mitch Miller – gets toppled and replaced by a more popular frontman, but behind the scenes all the same people are in charge. It's the most outrageous confidence trick in popular culture: rampant commercialism masquerading as permanent revolution. But who can doubt its success?

Sometimes even rock critics wise up. On a British TV documentary, Sean O'Hagen deplored the fact that Mick Jagger nowadays just swanks about with members of the aristocracy: 'The Stones,' he bemoaned, 'are now about as dangerous as Perry Como.' This is a routine slur, despite the fact that Como has made a couple of decent albums in the last two decades, which is more than you can say for the Stones, and that his shimmering, eerie recording of 'Toyland' has kept the song potent and current: it doesn't sound like a chart smash, but it doesn't sound like it was written for a 1903 Victor Herbert operetta either. But poor old Perry has no known position on the Vietnam War; he has no known position on Marianne Faithfull, or at least not one involving a Mars Bar. All he does is sing, and for this he's reviled.

On Broadway, this re-ordering of priorities was disastrous. Before the rock hegemony, the theatre song sat at the apex of popular music; the most famous songwriters were show writers. Tin Pan Alleymen longed to cross the tracks – as Berlin had done, and Gershwin, Styne, Loesser and even Bob Merrill (from 'How Much Is That Doggie In The Window?' and 'Where Will The Baby's Dimple Be?' and 'She Wears Red Feathers' to the lyrics for *Funny Girl*). But rock 'n' roll's bogus revolution painted Broadway into a corner it never quite got out of: musicals stood aloof from rock and became, by definition, staid, conservative, middle-aged – something your parents go see on their wedding anniversary. The new generation – the Paul Simons and Carole Kings – were lost to the theatre. The exceptions which proved the rule were Burt Bacharach and Hal David: they wrote one show score, for *Promises, Promises* (1968), and never came back. For 40 years, Broadway values have been locked in a struggle against rock and have lost on every front. At first, only the singles chart succumbed; next fell the album chart (whose biggest sellers had hitherto been Broadway cast recordings); and, in the late sixties, after a final flourish with *My Fair Lady* and *The Sound of Music*, the film musical faded away. (Bob Fosse's *Cabaret* movie is not, strictly, a musical: he shrewdly eliminated all the 'book numbers' – sung by Cliff's landlady and her suitor in their lodging house and grocery store and so on – and kept only the 'real' songs, performed in the Kit Kat Klub; Fosse understood that young moviegoers no longer accepted the musical's defining convention – that a guy could walk down the street and burst into song with full orchestral accompaniment.)

This ratchet effect isolated Broadway from the wider culture. If Broadway's music was now officially damned as nostalgic and old-fashioned, how could its shows be anything but nostalgic and old-fashioned? If your music is primarily associated with the past, how can you use it to comment on the present? Before rock, we had contemporary musicals: *No, No, Nanette, Anything Goes, Pal Joey, On the Town, Call Me Madam, Damn Yankees* . . . After rock, musicals started to live in the past. Sometimes, they were new old musicals, like Jerry Herman's *Hello, Dolly!* (turn of the century) and *Mame* ('tween the wars); sometimes, they were just plain old, like the retooled *42nd Street* (Warren and Dubin songs from the thirties) and *Crazy for You* (Gershwin songs from the thirties).

To those who believe popular music should be raw, soulful, earthy, passionate and the authentic expression of mainly black folk artists rather than all-white bourgeois exploiters, then obviously effete little midtown showtunes will be everything they despise. It's pointless to argue that the finest achievements in pop culture are a coalescence of art, which is incidental, and craft, which is crucial. To George Gershwin, *Porgy and Bess* was an obsession, and he had no choice but to write it out. To his brother Ira, it was a professional lyricist's latest assignment. Pop music today has its smattering of fitful artists but a conspicuous lack of craftsmen – those who provide the rules, set the standards, ensure there are minimum entry requirements. It's instinctive. When Jimmy Van Heusen and Johnny Mercer wrote 'I Thought About You' . . .

> I peeped through the crack
> And looked at the track
> The one going back to you

. . . they didn't sit around figuring, 'Hey, this is a train song, so we need lots of monosyllables with plenty of 'k' rhymes to bounce staccato off the notes and thereby emphasize the clicketty-clack rhythm': that came naturally. Is it better than Schubert? That's up to you. But at least it's efficient. Confronted with 'Fuck Tha Police' by Niggaz With Attitude . . .

> Searchin' my car, lookin' for the product
> Thinkin' every nigger is sellin' narcotics

. . . Mercer would barely have registered the content, but he would have raised an amused eyebrow at the attempted rhyme of 'product' and 'narcotics' and, more than that, would have been astounded at how the words are not, in any way, *musical* words shaped to the notes or intervals. Well, who'll go to bat for the rappers? But even rock's supreme artist, leaving aside his wilful obscurantism, is wholly indifferent to words as sounds – words as *music*. Bob Dylan might be a great prophet, he might be America's true political opposition, he might be a handsomely bound Ivy League-approved poet, he might even have 'the rude beauty of a southern field hand musing in melody on his porch' (Robert Shelton in *The New York Times*), but he is not, on the whole, any sort of songwriter.

*

But who wants to be Mister Squaresville? When rock did edge into off-Broadway houses and then the Main Stem itself, legit critics smiled indulgently in the manner of elderly white Anglican clerics at a black revivalist meeting. *Salvation* is 'naughty, of course', wrote *The New York Times*' Clive Barnes, who back in the sixties hailed New Dawns with the frequency of an insomniac cockerel, 'but its naughtiness has the impertinence of youth rather than the slime of age.' Don't remember *Salvation*? Ah, how soon the slime of age encrusts. When you scrape it off, one show can still be dimly glimpsed, as much a product of its time as *The Earl and the Girl* or *Four Jills and a Jeep* – and, if anything, even sillier. *Hair* introduced Broadway's tired businessmen and matinee ladies to free love, free drugs and free verse, and passionately opposed the Vietnam War, the dull conformity of work and – less explicitly – the structural integrity and solid craftsmanship of the American musical. At the première in 1968, faced with 'the dawning of the Age of Aquarius', Richard Rodgers opted for an early night: he walked out after Act One, which ended (for reasons as unclear as the lighting) with the entire cast in the nude.

Hair was the first Broadway show to have a song named after anal intercourse – 'Sodomy' – and, in an even more radical breakthrough, the first to have a song named after a British provincial town – 'Manchester, England'. As you'll have gathered, titles weren't the authors' strong point: a number about anal intercourse in northern England would almost certainly have been called 'Manchester Sodomy'. *Hair* was slapdash and self-indulgent but it had dandy timing. It played the Biltmore for nearly five years; at one time, there were seven other companies on the American road; and, in an era when showtunes and the Hit Parade had parted company, the Fifth Dimension took 'Let The Sun Shine In' to Number One.

Within a few years, the impertinence of youth had settled into two forms of expression: rock musicals were either camp cults – *The Rocky Horror Show*, *Little Shop of Horrors* – or pop pageants like *Time*. Faced with a form that refused to recognize any of the requirements of drama, admirers simply trumpeted the defects as virtues: 'Now the authors of the dowdy book,' wrote Barnes after *Hair* was restyled for Broadway, 'have done a very brave thing. They have in effect done away with it altogether.' Well, I never. Why didn't Rodgers and Hammerstein think of that? There's the solution to the perennial problem of musicals. Book trouble? Throw the thing out. For rock musicals, it seems to be the only option.

There's a moment in Dave Clark's *Time* (1986) which defines the genre. In this show, the planet is up before the intergalactic court for having committed crimes of war and hatred and so on, and Cliff Richard, counsel for the defence, is pleading in mitigation that earth has produced one force for good – rock 'n' roll – and that, because of this, we shouldn't be consigned to oblivion. Rock's sense of its own worth is indestructible: personally, if rock 'n' roll really was the planet's only redeeming virtue, I'd press the nuclear button today. Anyway, Lord Melchisidec, the judge in the case, goes around talking, as members of the judiciary are wont, with a chilly, sneering, circumlocutory pedantry. Until suddenly, he bursts (and for once that's the word) into song as a manically funky hipster: '*Heeeeeeeey! I said heeeeeeeey!*,' he begins, abandoning his punctilious enunciation in favour of the strangulated melismas beloved of fake soul music. Previously, the trick had been to provide a singing voice consistent with the character and his speaking voice. The judge's actions make about as much sense as the nuns in *The Sound of Music* launching into 'I'm Just A Girl Who Cain't Say No'. Dave Clark claimed that *Time* heralded (what else?) a new dawn for the musical. Wrong. It was a glimpse of nuclear winter.

Bob Carlton's *Return to the Forbidden Planet* (1989) takes this schizophrenia of book and score to its logical conclusion. The plot is a sci-fi *Tempest*, the dialogue modified Shakespeare, the score a ragbag of sixties pop. 'But soft,' says Captain Tempest, 'what light in yonder airlock breaks?' It is Miranda, complete with ponytail, bobbysox and pointed bra cups. Cue for a song? 'I . . . love the colourful clothes she wears,' sings the Cap, picking 'Good Vibrations'. The rock 'n' roll is played straight, and the Shakespeare just passes the time between, mocking the very idea of dramatic integration. The nearest we get is when a meteor storm is sighted on the radar and the Captain gasps: 'Goodness! Gracious! Great balls of fire!' Inevitably, *Forbidden Planet* became London's latest 'cult hit', which is to say that all the usual considerations of drama are completely abandoned.

*

According to Stephen Sondheim, 'Pop music is swell for rock concerts. Whether they are rock concerts called *Hair* or *Jesus Christ Superstar* or rock concerts called rock concerts doesn't matter. But when it comes to telling a story through character, then I think it's useless. Since so much of pop music depends on electronic amplification, the minute the people start to speak, after they have just screamed at you through a microphone, you're going to have an anti-climax. That's why, when they try to make rock versions of stories like *Georgy Girl*, it can't work out.'

'It's the same percussive beat,' Jule Styne said to me, 'whether the girl and the feller are going out, getting drunk and having a good time, or whether she's leaving him and ruining his life. Happiness or sadness, it's all the same. That's not dramatic. I like rock because of its freshness – like when the Charleston came along. But it doesn't belong in the theatre.'

Styne showed a sense of proportion: rock *is* about as fresh as the Charleston – and try using that for the soliloquy in *Carousel*.

Buddy (1989), a phenomenal smash biotuner in the West End, illustrates the problem. Rock 'n' roll is a revolution of attitude rather than content. If you didn't know the tunes, you'd assume Buddy Holly's soupy lyrics decorated some backporch spooners from the turn of the century:

> Stars appear and the shadows are fallin'
> I can hear my honey callin' . . .

Or:

> You give me all your lovin'
> And your turtle-dovin' . . .

Or:

> When Cupid shot his dart
> He shot it at your heart . . .

That's an advance on Dorothy Fields or Johnny Mercer or Oscar Hammerstein? Not only are these songs impossible to use dramatically, they're also too vague to use as incidental music, to underline or punctuate aspects of Buddy Holly's life, or even, more generally, the 1950s. 'I wrote it for you,' he assures his gal before the ballads. Yes, but how can you tell?

There are, it should be said, pop records with interesting words. But ever since Bob Dylan and the invention of the gatefold sleeve, rock lyrics are something you strain to catch – is that an oblique, allusive image? or did you just mishear? – and then check on the album cover later. Alan Jay Lerner used to bemoan to me that someone like Paul Simon never wrote for the theatre. Actually, he contributed a quatrain to *Mass*, as a present for Leonard Bernstein. But, in any case, would a musical drama suit Simon's elliptical style? Originally, Oscar Hammerstein wrote:

The corn is as high as a cow-pony's eye . . .

He changed the image to 'elephant' not just because the corn was, technically, higher than a cow-pony but also because, on Rodgers' notes, the word was difficult to understand. When you're sitting in a theatre, you get one chance to grab those lyrics as they're flying through the air at you. Paul Simon once took me through his song 'Hearts And Bones':

One and one-half wandering Jews . . .

He explained to me that it was one and one-half because the song was about him, and he's Jewish, and his then wife Carrie Fisher, who's the daughter of Eddie Fisher, who's also Jewish, and Debbie Reynolds, who's not; hence, one and a half. So far, we'd spent about ten minutes deconstructing just five words, but I felt on top of them and was ready to move on. Then Simon said, 'But it's also a reference to the flower.'
'Pardon?'
'There's a flower called Wandering Jew.'
'There's a flower?'
'Yes.'
'Ah.' And you realize that, had Simon followed Lerner's advice and started writing musicals, we'd have had to get to the theatre at 10.30 in the morning to read up on the textual footnotes.
Back in the days of the spirit of '68, in an episode of the British sitcom *Please, Sir!*, Joan Sanderson's steely spinster schoolmarm tried to get with it by singing a song from *Hair*. She mangled the lyric and, as it turned out, came up with an accurate prophesy: 'This is the ageing of the dawn of Aquarius . . .' We are all rockers now: the hippy draft-dodgers are middle-aged theatregoers; there's a baby boomer in the White House and, thanks to his $76,000 cut and blow-dry on the runway at Los Angeles, he even briefly restored hair as a political issue. But, if the Age of Aquarius ever dawned, it was all over by lunch-time. The 1977 *Hair*

revival ran a month, the '79 film was stillborn, and Broadway retreated to *Sugar Babies* and *La Cage aux Folles*. The first 'American Tribal Love Rock Musical' was also the last and, even with a monopoly in its field, survived mainly, like Jerry Lewis movies, on revivals in Europe. As with President Clinton's joints, you can smoke it but you can never inhale: in Britain and America, it doesn't quite convince. Galt MacDermot, the American theatre's first rock composer, had a moderately successful sequel to *Hair* with a rock version of *The Two Gentlemen of Verona*, but by then audiences were beginning to wonder whether, like his cast, the Emperor had no clothes. Muddled and undisciplined, MacDermot seemed to have no idea which of his songs were any good, and his half-rock, half-theatre musical mutant failed to satisfy fans of either. It was left to the British to develop a more efficient fusion of musical theatre and the Top Forty: *Hair* proved to be the dawning of the Age of Lloyd Webber.

*

'The new generation of American writers have not found a new musical voice that speaks to large numbers of the audience,' says Cameron Mackintosh. 'In Europe, Andrew and Tim were influenced by pop music, Claud-Michel and Alain were influenced by pop music. They've created this wonderful hybrid.'

Jule Styne once complained to me about 'that junky rock thing' in *Phantom of the Opera*, by which he meant the title song. But, just as only on Broadway could Stephen Sondheim be considered a serious composer, so only on Broadway could Andrew Lloyd Webber be considered a rocker. What he *doesn't* sound like is Broadway – and maybe, in an era when show music seemed frozen and set, that was enough. Youthful works like *Jesus* and *Joseph* had a pop larkiness. The fashion for biblical musicals soon faded, but the more sinister trend which Rice and Lloyd Webber helped establish – big subjects told in a through-sung rock idiom – survived for another two decades. *Pace* Stephen Sondheim, *Jesus Christ Superstar* is not bloated and pretentious and has the great merit of Tim Rice's irrepressible cheek. As Herod, a biblical hipster, taunts Christ:

> Prove to me that you're no fool
> Walk across my swimming pool . . .

Like Noël Coward's, Rice's wit often makes you more aware of the lyricist than the character. In later works like *Blondel*, this has sometimes led him astray, but, on *Superstar*, it was a means by which Rice could bring imagery, colour, style and, most important, a point of view to the text. Lacking Rice's droll playfulness, most lyricists tackling biblical or historically remote or cosmic themes get swamped by the enormity of their subject, and drown in a sea of well-meaning, earnest vacuities. Unlike *Hair* (chaotic) or *Time* (pompous), *Superstar* makes some kind of sense.

Lloyd Webber, too, deploys genuine rock elements as astutely as they've ever been used in drama, confining rock's unrelenting hysterical drive mainly to the songs for Judas, who's pretty driven and hysterical himself. He uses it again as Pontius Pilate counts out the 39 lashes, an insistent accompaniment which reinforces the Roman's sense of his own degradation. For Mary Magdalene, though, he opts for the gently jazzy 'Everything's Alright'. *Superstar* is that rare thing: a rock musical which tries to use rock to differentiate character, an ambitious undertaking in which Lloyd Webber succeeds more effectively than in later scores.

He was never very credible as a rocker. There's a story of him arranging a session to record a rock version of one of his songs and rushing out of the control room with a last-minute exhortation to the boys: 'Okay, chaps, remember: I want maximum aggression.' In *Cats*, *Starlight* and then *Phantom*, Lloyd Webber has progressively but shrewdly diluted the more raucous elements of rock in a gloopy pop / Broadway melange. He still has Number One records, but he now exists in the same relationship to contemporary trends – to hip-hop-house-ambient-techno-garage-industrial-bungalow – as operetta did 80 years ago: 'Ah! Sweet Mystery Of Life' from *Naughty Marietta* was a pop hit without being, as 'Alexander's Ragtime Band' was, in the prevailing pop idiom. Eventually, Broadway fused the two styles, and for some 40 years pop and show songs operated to broadly the same techniques.

I doubt whether a similar rapprochement is possible today. But who cares? Who loses? In 1981, Joe Dolce's 'Shaddap You Face' and Aneka's 'Japanese Boy' and Bucks Fizz's 'Making Your Mind Up' and Adam and the Ants' 'Prince Charming' all got to Number One; 'Memory' didn't. But which do you reckon is the highest-earning song fourteen years later? And 1981 was a boom time for pop music. Name this week's Number One record. Go on, without looking it up. There, in a nutshell, is pop's problem. In 1955, you wouldn't have had to look up 'Rock Around The Clock', nor in 1942 'White Christmas'. Whether you think popular music is less musical than it used to be is a matter of opinion, but it's certainly less popular.

*

Remember Kern and Hammerstein using 'After The Ball' in *Show Boat* to pinpoint precisely the era: the 1890s. What's the soundtrack for the 1990s? Hardly any of us will have consciously absorbed this week's Number One, most radio stations won't play it and record sales are so fractured only a few thousand people need to buy it to get it in the charts. Marshall McLuhan got it almost exactly wrong: we had more of a 'global village' 80 years ago when, still before radio and with records barely out of wax cylinders, Irving Berlin stepped ashore at Southampton and was asked by a British immigration officer whether he was the celebrated composer of 'Alexander's Ragtime Band'. Today, the world that beckons to us is a global tower block where we all do our own thing and nobody knows their neighbours: you can tune to 24-hour country classics, but I'll stick with the gangsta rap station. We may not be coming to the end of history, but we are coming to the end of *popular* pop culture. It may sound odd, at a time when the serious newspapers are full of rock and pop pages, when Russian spokesmen speak of the Sinatra Doctrine and Elvis-impersonator President Clinton blows his sax on TV talk shows; but, when politicians cite you and cultural commentators start culturally commentating on you, it's a sure sign the game's up. Nobody wrote profiles of Charles K. Harris, and he couldn't have cared less: in the 'After The Ball' days, popular culture was less cultural. He made a fortune in the heyday of sheet music, when every home had a piano. You went to see *A Trip to Chinatown*; you bought a copy of 'After The Ball' afterwards: that's synergy.

Today, Thorn-EMI and Warner-Chappell control between them a quarter of the global music market. Those famous hyphens symbolize the complex corporate miscegenations of the eighties: henceforth, we were told, the same company would invent the technology, record the album, publish the songs, film the video of the making of the album, place the title track as the theme to a big movie, license the book and the plastic doll and the Burger King movie-meal tie-in. In the mid-eighties, in the wake of Michael Jackson's *Thriller*, the all-time best-selling album, critics fretted about a world where every radio station in every city was pumping out the same bland multinational coffee-table rock. Instead, pop music is hopelessly fragmented and the Los Angeles Police Department photographs of Jacko's genitalia are likely to sell more copies than his next record.

Meanwhile, who are the truly global celebrities? Mickey Mouse and Sonic the Hedgehog. The people's favourites are mostly non-people now, much as the leathery old rock crowd bemoans this: what's the difference between Sonic the Hedgehog and the corporate headquarters of any major record company? One's got pricks on the outside, the other's . . . Ah, but from the corporations' point of view, it all makes perfect sense. Sonic's never going to cancel his world tour; no embittered catamite can finger Pluto or Goofy. Whom would you invest in? Slowly but inexorably, the rock megastar is on the run. In Britain, Our Price Records has dropped the last word from its name, not wishing to alienate fans of Super Mario, Sonic and the other computer-game boys. Super Mario has even annexed one of rock music's most hallowed traditions: just like Elvis, Bowie and Madonna, he made a terrible movie.

Michael Crichton, the *Jurassic Park* / *Rising Sun* man, would probably find a Japanese conspiracy in this. After all the claims of rock music, this is the way it ends, not with a bang but with the blip-blip-blip of the kids' computer games. We see the future and we despair: after we've raised a generation which spends its first twenty years in virtual reality, we may be pining for the good old days of glue-sniffing and crack addiction. Parents will be sighing, 'When we were their age, we just sat around listening to Phil Collins. Whatever happened to the days when we *didn't* make our own entertainment?'

'Rock Around The Clock' *is* a dividing line of sorts, but not the one we think. The half-century before Bill Haley was the best that American popular music has ever known, years which saw the rise of jazz, country, blues, good commercial film music, fine pop songs of which a few could reasonably claim to be the only true art songs in the English language . . . and an indigenous musical theatre. Everything since then has just been a mining and re-mining of seams opened up in the century's early years, until now the ground is exhausted. You don't have to buy all those 'raw' and 'earthy' clichés to recognize that popular art is better when you just get on with it, and that intellectual respectability would seem on the evidence to be far more harmful than any of the hedges and compromises demanded by the cloth ears of commerce. Jazz 'purists' resent Louis Armstrong for ending his career growling through 'Hello, Dolly!' and 'What A Wonderful World', but it still beats ersatz fusion tone-poems. George Gershwin made a pile of dough hosting a radio show sponsored by a laxative and used the money to write *Porgy and Bess*; today, Stephen Sondheim is told continually he's a genius, writes two shows a decade, and has seen his chosen form dwindle from American popular culture's central thruway into a forgotten little back road. Now, rock music's headed the same way. The last pop icon, Madonna, is a metaphor for the industry: she has her feminist significance pondered by college courses, she poses nude with assorted genders and species, and her record sales go into free fall. She's so desperate now she's even recycling musical comedy. Ever since 'Material Girl' with its *Gentlemen Prefer Blondes* costumes and choreography, there's been a hermetic separation between the act and the music. The stagings are pure showbiz; the songs have been reduced to aural wallpaper. If her musical arranger was half as droll as her choreographer, she might still have a recording career.

In September 1993, she opened her world tour of *The Girlie Show* on stage at Wembley Stadium but framed by an artificial proscenium arch, with velvet drapes, just like the small-time Chicago burlesque of Bob Fosse's boyhood, as seen in *All that Jazz*. Next, she's Liza Minnelli in *Cabaret*: black boots, shorts, vest, bare arms, hair tightly cropped, eyes cast upward in a forlorn search for little-girl-lost vulnerability. Then it's twirling umbrellas for a sort of synthesized 'Singin' In The Rain', and *King and I* Orientalisms, and the 'Ascot Gavotte' from *My Fair Lady*. Give her 15 minutes and an entire twentieth-century vaudeville comes parading by. For *In Bed with Madonna*, she dismissed Kevin Costner and his epithet for her show – 'neat'. Yet maybe Kevin got her better than we knew. The materially minded girl leafs through pop's back catalogue and goes, 'Hey, why not? That'd be neat.' As pop culture degenerates to a succession of unfelt poses, Madonna is simultaneously a fabulous conflation of all that's gone before and a denial of any kind of future.

And every night, from the stage at the Gershwin Theatre, in the lowest-tech medium of all, a solo singer is taunting us:

> After The Ball is over
> After the break of morn
> After the dancers' leaving
> After the stars are gone . . .

The dancers are leaving, the stars are gone. A few years ago, after I'd interviewed him for a TV special, Paul Simon wondered gloomily over lunch whether, after a century of commercial pop music, there was any-where left to go. Every 30 years, he explained, the corporate guys flagged a little and had to go pilfering from some or other vernacular tradition: in the twenties, jazz; in the fifties, rhythm 'n' blues; in the eighties, world music – West African rhythms, Latin American salsa. 'The trouble now,' said Simon, 'is that they've nowhere left to steal from.'

In the nineteenth century, white folks latched on to Negro songs, smeared their faces with burnt cork, and made a killing in minstrel shows. At the turn of the century, while black ragtime composers starved, white Tin Pan Alley hacks stuck 'rag' in the titles of their novelty songs and sold millions. In the fifties, r 'n' b numbers such as 'Roll With Me, Henry' were bowdlerized into 'Dance With Me, Henry' by white singers who then cleaned up on the Hit Parade. For more than one hundred years from the Christy Minstrels to Pat Boone, whitey has been seizing any half-decent black musical ideas and doing weedy but lucrative cover versions. If I were a person of colour and casually switched on *Oprah* and the rest, I'd reckon white folks were now doing the biggest cover version of all: appropriating my sense of oppression. Today, we are all victims: 50 per cent of American women are date raped, 80 per cent of lesbian parents are denied day-care facilities, 100 per cent of celebrities are abused as children or are abusers of children or are undecided pending the outcome of their next memory-recovery session. This is the minstrel show of the alienation business, metaphorically smudging on the black-face for an easy-listening arrangement of the real thing. These days (to quote Ellington), we all got it bad, and that ain't good, especially when most of the oppressed are about as convincing as Pat Boone singing Fats Domino. The song is ended, but the malady lingers on; all is pose and attitude. Can white men sing the blues? No, but black men have forgotten how, too. Black or white, though, anyone can buy a metaphorical bus ticket to the ghetto. The long-term problem of rap, metal and grunge is that – unlike Jolson, Crosby, Sinatra, Presley, the Beatles – they're strictly for losers.

'At school,' says Cameron Mackintosh, 'when everyone else had moved on to the Beatles, I still liked Cliff Richard. And I think that's stood me in good stead in the theatre.' In other words, musicals can't be on the so-called cutting edge because, by the time you've got your grunge musical up on stage, grunge will be out and splurge will be in. How many pop trends have come and gone while *Cats* has been playing the New London Theatre? Besides, in today's music business, you're famous for everything but the music: Kurt Cobain, who went a-grungin' to his grave, is famous for being dead. He became a household name without ever having produced a household song, a model example of contemporary short-cut celebrity. Charles K. Harris and his contemporaries took tabloid news stories of human interest and turned them into hit songs. A century on, we've reversed the process: the guys with the hit songs turn themselves into tabloid news stories, and 'Hit Parade' now means a bunch of gangsta rappers getting together and showing off their gunshot wounds. In 1994, while on bail for a sexual assault charge, Tupac Shakur was pumped full of bullets and narrowly avoided being reduced to One-pac Shakur; one year and five minutes after Tupac's shooting, his comrade-in-rap Randy Walker, producer of 'Strictly 4 My N.I.G.G.A.Z.', was shot dead; a few months later, Tupac himself was killed in a drive-by shooting; Ol' Dirty Bastard had his liver blown away by gun-totin' dirtier bastards; Slick Rick took pre-emptive action and, consequently, had to record his latest album while doing time for attempted murder; and Snoop Doggy Dogg's murder trial collapsed on technical grounds. This is the weird odyssey pop music has taken since the mid-fifties – from 'How Much Is That Doggy In The Window?' to 'How long is that Doggy in the gaolhouse?'

Rap is the logical consequence of promoting social over musical content: the reduction of the tune to a banal stationary backing track, the debasement of lyric-writing to a formless pneumatic laundry list of half-baked hoodlum exhibitionism. Forget all those bogus generalizations about 'energy' and 'drive'; *musically*, Ice Cube's 'The Nigga Ya Love To Hate' isn't a patch on 'Honeysuckle Rose', never mind 'All The Things You Are'. If Ice Cube wasn't rappin' about terminating an unwanted pregnancy by booting his woman in the belly, none of us would be the slightest bit interested. And even then, we're not *that* interested. This is one 'authentic black experience' that doesn't travel beyond the ghetto.

*

Meanwhile, multinational corporate rock continues its own lop-sided tango. To sign Paul McCartney, Columbia gave him not only $20 million but the entire Frank Loesser publishing catalogue. Since then, McCartney's new albums have lost money for Columbia while Loesser's old songs have earned a fortune for McCartney: in 1995, as Jerry Zaks' revival of *Guys and Dolls* closed on Broadway, a new production with Matthew Broderick of *How to Succeed in Business without Really Trying* moved in. When Bono, at the 1994 Grammies, pledged to continue 'fucking up the mainstream', he didn't seem to appreciate: he *is* the mainstream, and it's as fucked up as you can get. So a few surviving grizzled old rockers totter round ever bigger stadiums with bigger lasers and bigger sound systems and the phoney rebellion seems even more fatuous. In Britain in the early nineties, there was much media debate about whether stand-up comedy is the new rock 'n' roll. But try this: rock 'n' roll is the new golf – it's something middle-aged square guys do at weekends in ridiculous clothes.

Rock battered Broadway for four decades, depriving the theatre of an entire generation of writers. But the worst is over. Oh, sure, pop singles, which have been in ever steeper decline for 15 years, can still throw up a monster smash: in 1992, 'I Will Always Love You' by Whitney Houston became one of the top ten all-time best-sellers. But here indeed is an emblem of the times: for one thing, it's an old song, written by Dolly Parton in the seventies; secondly, it's a country song – country music is now America's biggest seller, perhaps because country is still about songs and titles and lyric imagery, as opposed to videos and backing tracks and haircut imagery; thirdly, it needed a big movie – *The Bodyguard* – to make it a hit. This is pop music in the nineties, propped up by the back catalogue and exposure in other media. So, in 1991, Bryan Adams' '(Everything I Do) I Do It For You' finally broke the record of the longest-running Number One – Slim Whitman's 1955 recording of the title song from *Rose-Marie*. But Adams' single isn't so very different from Slim's: one's a song a show, the other's a song from a film, Kevin Costner's *Robin Hood*. Exactly a century earlier, Reginald De Koven's *Robin Hood* gave the Broadway theatre its first lasting hit with 'Oh, Promise Me'.

Pop has taken a century to come full circle. Today, pop music is like show music: it needs a situation. If you're a mainstream pop artist with a big ballad, you need a movie; if you're a good-looking boy group like Take That, you need a video; if you're a techno scratch programmer, you need a sweaty warehouse with a crowd that's off its collective face on E. In their way, they're all situational songs – just like Loesser's in *Guys and Dolls*. If that's the competition, show music can more than hold its own. And which outlet offers you the best chance of matching Loesser for longevity?

'Today, sure, a song's a big hit,' said Jule Styne, 'but only for a few weeks. I said to my son, "Play me that Billy Joel song I like." He said, "Wait'll you hear the new one." The *new* one? The old one's only been around two months. So what happens? Songs that were big five years ago you don't even hear anymore. But I still hear Berlin, I still hear Gershwin. That's forever.'

V

The Jokes

By one of those weird coincidences, *Sunset Boulevard*'s London opening was also a closing. In July 1993, as *Sunset* rose at the Adelphi, the sun set on *City of Angels*, its folding announced at the Prince of Wales, just another West End casualty on the boulevard of broken dreams. Same time, same place – Hollywood fortysomething years ago; same sorta subject – a screenwriter and his conscience; same references – wisecracks about Cecil B. De Mille.

But, instead of *Sunset*'s £4 million advance, *City of Angels* was facing a £2 million loss, and its flummoxed producers were trying to figure how, with everything so right, everything went wrong. They'd woken up three months earlier to virtually unanimous raves: 'A musical comedy made in heaven!' and so on. Remember that old Broadway saying when some much-derided schlock runs and runs? Nobody likes it but the public. With *City of Angels*, it seems, *everybody* liked it but the public.

In New York, the problem is supposedly one all-powerful critic – the Butcher of Broadway. In London, the critics don't butcher enough. They loved Tommy Tune's tasteful, professional but uninvolving *Grand Hotel*; they especially loved Pam Gems' incoherent rehash of *The Blue Angel*; and, in both cases, shortly after opening, I remember seeing knots of paying customers standing outside at the interval, examining the rapturous quotes and wondering why they weren't getting it. Perhaps because they spend so much of their time seeing Ibsen and Shakespeare, London critics seem to like musicals which aspire to the condition of a play. They adored *City of Angels*, but mostly because of its sharp, knowing machine-gun script and the direction of the spoken bits. Those reviews should have rattled the producers: in London, if you want to see actors walking around on the stage saying clever things to each other, you go to a straight play. In *Cats* and *Phantom*, nobody says anything worth listening to and, if you don't know a word of English, you can still follow everything that's going on (like so much in Britain's decaying capital, the West End depends on tourists). Indeed, a knowledge of the English language can be a positive disadvantage.

It's unfair. I liked *City of Angels* because I like Cy Coleman's music. I love 'Hey, Big Spender' and all the other songs he wrote back in the days when 'musical comedy' was a going concern and show scores were smart and sassy and satirical and New Yorky. The British were always hopeless at that kind of musical and, whether by accident or design, they hit upon something they could do better than Broadway. In doing so they upped the ante: a new Lloyd Webber or Cameron Mackintosh musical isn't just a night at the theatre, it's an *event*. Significantly, at *City of Angels* it was the £30 seats which proved hard to sell. For that price, you want *Miss Saigon*. It's not the same going back home and saying you saw a show where there were some pretty funny fellows and some nice songs.

*

'Musical comedy's difficult,' admits Cy Coleman. 'When I was doing movies, I used to say, "Why don't I ever get a good melodrama?" Comedies are very hard, you never get the credit you should. But, in a good melodrama, you hold one note, change four chords and you're up for an Academy Award.' Serious art is supposed to be about serious subjects, and in the eighties even musicals succumbed. The through-composed West End pop-opera Coleman regards as 'a *Reader's Digest* version of opera. It seems to give people the feeling of culture.'

It gives them the *feeling* as opposed to the culture?

He snorts his distinctive, sneezy-wheezy laughing-gas laugh: 'A-hur-hur-hur. That's what I said.'

When I mention this to Cameron Mackintosh, he snaps, 'What does Cy Coleman know about culture?'

In *Miss Saigon*, there's an 11 o'clock number for the Eurasian fixer: 'The American Dream'. When Bill Brohn handed in his first orchestration for the song, Mackintosh told him to try again. He wanted something more sardonic and sinister; it was 'too Cy Coleman' – by which he meant big, brassy, swingy, jazzy. Coleman no longer looks quite the way he did back when he posed for the cover of his album *If My Friends Could See Me Now* as if he were doing a cigarette ad for *Esquire*, or when he played piano every week on *Playboy* magazine's TV show, but there's still a whiff of the supperclub about him: the minute he walks in the joint, you can see he's a man of distinction, a real big spender; he comes on like Mister Hip. But there's more to it than that. In the best Broadway tradition, Coleman is funny but literate: he knows *something* about culture. 'The Rhythm Of Life', the druggy preacher's anthem from *Sweet Charity*, is a sort of Broadway fugue; *On the Twentieth Century* (1978) is a comic opera – Rossini on the railroad. At seven, he played Carnegie Hall and seemed destined to be a concert pianist. His favourite composer wasn't Berlin but Beethoven. Then jazz intervened and, while still at high school, Coleman was asked to play for the publisher Jack Robbins. 'He pronounced me the new Gershwin, because everyone who walked in that day and was young was the new Gershwin. Then he told me to write three piano preludes like Gershwin. So I wrote the fourth, fifth and sixth preludes of Gershwin. A-hur-hur-hur.'

Forty years on, the preludes were released on a CD of concert works by Broadway composers. 'They said, "Have you written any classical pieces?" And I said, "Yes, I've got these three Gershwin-like preludes . . ."'

Before the preludes, there was a fiendishly difficult sonata which Coleman claims to have misplaced.

'Surely you can play it from memory?'

'Sit down and order dinner,' he says, and turns to the keyboard.

The question is whether his theatrical judgements are as sound as his musical ones. He was offered a lifetime contract at Universal – 'I could have a big house in Beverly Hills and not go to previews' – but he chose to stay in New York. There's a story of Coleman inviting various distinguished Broadway luminaries to a private screening and telling them, 'This *has* to be our next show.' Then he put on a bawdy British trouser-dropping *Carry On* film. Ten minutes in, Hal Prince stood up and insisted Coleman switch it off.

Carrying on through the eighties, he wrote *Home Again, Home Again*, which never made it to Broadway, and a show set in alimony gaol which unfortunately did. Anyone can churn out a *Bernadette* or *Which Witch*, but it takes real professionals to embarrass themselves that badly in full view on the Main Stem. For an active composer, a glorious past is no compensation: as one Coleman song bluntly puts it, 'It's Not Where You Start, It's Where You Finish'.

'These aren't the Rodgers and Hart days,' he says, recalling an era when writers could do four shows a season and, hits or flops, you were shot of them after three months. He began working with Larry Gelbart on *City of Angels* in 1982; it opened on Broadway over seven years later. 'Years ago we used to have records of our stuff on the radio before the show opened,' Cy sighs. Not any more – though Coleman sometimes seems to be leading a one-man campaign to reverse the trend. In the months before *The Will*

Rogers Follies, he was doing the big song – a loping western ballad, 'Never Met a Man I Didn't Like' – at benefit performances all over town. Just before opening, he sang it at the Eye, Ear and Throat Hospital.

'You should have seen him,' said his lyricist Adolph Green. 'There wasn't a dry eye, ear and throat in the house.'

Musical theatre is a solemn business these days. But Coleman and Green still manage to give the impression they have a good time. These are funny guys. They wouldn't want to write *Cats* or *Phantom*.

*

Wit was Broadway's first major contribution to musical theatre, bringing a much needed sense of proportion to a form permanently teetering on the brink of ridiculousness. Instead of the woolly generalities of Mitteleuropa, punctuated by the token non-comic comic song, Broadway gave us a unique form of literate slang – specific, quirky allusions couched in a rich, urban vernacular set to the rhythms of the day. From Kern and Wodehouse on, Broadway songs were among the smartest and funniest writing of the day.

And now? The age of the technomusical spectacle diminished music and lyrics in general and wit in particular and sent our leading composer, fleeing the roller-skating monster he created, scurrying to the lush uplands of operetta. *Phantom* obviously isn't hurting from its woolly lyrics: it's in the West End, on Broadway and all points north, south, east, west. Perhaps the very irrelevance of its and *Cats*' lyrics is the reason for those shows' universal appeal; perhaps wit is more local. Certainly, it's hard to imagine all those big town wiseacres of Broadway's heyday meaning much in, say, Gdynia, Poland, where *Les Miz* did boffo biz. Don Black, *Sunset*'s lyricist, is a musical comedy man at heart but these days finds himself instead writing through-sung musicals with Lloyd Webber. 'Because there isn't a book with dialogue,' he concedes, 'a lot of the time you're just singing information.' So, instead of gags, we get a tremulous, overwrought, head-on supply of plot exposition. Ho, ho, ho, who's got the last laugh now?

More than anything else, wit demands a mastery of form. Old-time Alleymen, confined to 32 bars in AABA, used to refer to less constrained songs like 'Begin The Beguine' as 'tapeworms'. Today, tapeworms are the norm, and form of any kind is unfashionable. Well, fair enough. If writers want their ballads to sound like track five on a duff Mariah Carey album, that's their affair. Good lyricists, though, use structure as a shorthand.

Betty Comden and Adolph Green, working on *Wonderful Town* (1953), were instructed by Rosalind Russell to write her a number that went: 'Da-da, da-da, da-da, *joke*! Da-da, da-da, da-da, *joke*!' In its way, this is as good advice as any, distilling as it does the requirements of structure and momentum. Indeed, all it needs is something about placing your title as a cushion, and it could define most of the classic Broadway catalogue songs:

> He was shy and awful modest 'cause he was so high bred
> When the wind blew up my bloomers would his face get red
> He undressed with all the lights off until we was wed
> He Had Refinement . . .

Da-da, da-da, *joke*, title.

I happen to be quite fond of Dorothy Fields' lyric (from *A Tree Grows in Brooklyn*) because it endows its singer with a rather touching pathos. But, as the rise of the musical play continued at the expense of traditional musical comedy, funny songs became harder to place. Rhyme, as Stephen Sondheim has pointed out, denotes a certain sophistication. So, if you're writing for unsophisticated characters, you have to find other ways of being funny. Coleman and Fields pulled it off in the 'Soliloquy' from *Sweet Charity* (1966), setting Charity's banal recollections of a pedestrian relationship to a gently shimmering bossa nova:

> In no time at all
> I find we're very much in love
> And I'm blushing
> Like a sentimental slob
> And he's kissing me and hugging me
> And all the time he's bugging me
> To go out and try to find myself
> A better paying job . . .

The contrast between the tackiness of the relationship and its sophisticated musical setting makes it funny and sympathetic.

I'm surprised more shows haven't tried this, but, in a world which prides itself on matching words and music, a *mis*match is still sufficiently novel to have considerable comic mileage. In the film *It's Always Fair Weather*, Comden and Green wrote a lyric for an army reunion where, as often happens, the best of pals discover they no longer have anything to say to each other. As they sit wishing they weren't there, the restaurant's discreet little palm court ensemble strikes up 'The Blue Danube', to which tune the old comrades muse to themselves:

This thing is a frost
I'd like to get lost
Old pals are the bunk
This guy's a cheap punk
And that one's a heel
And I'm a schlemiel
Can these be the guys
I once thought
I could never live without?

To match these sentiments to Strauss's waltz is a genuine comedic inspiration. For a similar situation in *Wonderful Town*, they and Leonard Bernstein came up with 'Conversation Piece', about what Green calls 'the deafening sound of silence'. It's set at a dinner party, at which each fruitless attempt to get the conversation going . . .

'I was reading *Moby Dick* the other day.' (*Pause.*) 'It's about this whale.'

. . . is followed by a massive musical deflation. It's not even songwriting – just dialogue and music in separate compartments – but it is a fresh dramatic resolution to a familiar situation. And it's not, like so much show humour, just wisecracks. Bernstein makes it *musically* funny. As he pointed out to me, because the content is pure musical comedy, people overlook the fact that his treatment of the situation is as intelligent and inventive as in any high-falutin' opera.

As a rule, the sign of a really great composer is the trouble he takes over his comic songs. Everyone assumes that a funny number is a lyricist's moment and the composer just ticks over until we're back to the big ballads. Not true. Invariably praised for their slick rhymes, Porter's best laundry lists work because of their music:

If old *hymns* you like
If bare *limbs* you like
If Mae *West* you like
Or me un*dressed* you like . . .

You don't notice the device because the words and music are so indivisible, but in this song – the release of 'Anything Goes' – Porter keeps the 'you likes' set on repeated notes but then, on the emphasized rhyme words, the melody changes, stepping up the scale chromatically. That's what gives the song forward propulsion; that's why it seems to be getting *funnier*.

Bernstein was equally scrupulous over the comic stuff. But these days, the very term 'musical comedy' has come to sound old-fashioned. We don't think of Comden and Green or Neil Simon or Larry Gelbart; we think of *No, No, Nanette* and all its camp send-ups. After the integrated musical play, the concept musical and the through-sung pop opera, does musical comedy have anything to teach today's writers? I think so. Even tragedy needs wit. 'I wanted "Gee, Officer Krupke" in *West Side Story*,' says Arthur Laurents. 'I felt we needed a comic moment for the dramatic tension: in my opinion that makes it stronger. And I was very clever: I sold it to them on sheer gall. I said it's like the porters' scene in Shakespeare, and it was a high-toned enough argument to get it through. But it only works in a tense dramatic situation; that's the only thing that justifies it. They shifted its position in the movie, and it doesn't work. But it works on stage because kids particularly would kid around when they're in danger of real trouble. And dramatically it's tiresome when you're in a sober, serious situation and you have sober, serious dialogue and music. The audience is way ahead. But writers think if someone comes out with this enormous kvetch it makes it important. It doesn't. It lacks wit, it lacks attitude, it's all so obvious.'

'Lenny was really a bit out of his medium,' says Sid Ramin, *West Side*'s orchestrator. 'He felt very strange trying to write a vaudeville piece, but of course it's so much more than a vaudeville piece. He was so proud of the bass notes in "Krupke": nobody but a fine comical composer like Lenny could write something like that. But he was so grateful for things like a little orchestral brass peck that you would put in after a lyric that would never occur to him. And, when he would hear that little nothing fill that, God, you don't even think about, he would say, "Wow! Listen to that!" ':

> The trouble is he's lazy! (*Peck!*)
> The trouble is he drinks! (*Peck!*)
> The trouble is he's crazy! (*Peck!*)
> The trouble is he stinks! (*Peck!*)

And to end the song? Bernstein uses the oldest of vaudevillian sign-offs . . .

> Shave and a haircut
> Two bits!

. . . with new lyrics:

> Gee, Officer Krupke
> Krup you!

It's not just a funny idea; the rightness of the delinquents' response makes the tragedy of *West Side Story* more real.

*

In musicals, wit depends on a combination of talents. Cy Coleman's problem these days is that, Betty Comden and Adolph Green aside, the lyricists aren't always up to the composer. On *City of Angels*, David Zippel is a clever fellow if you can follow him. But lines like 'your fertile lies don't fertilize' seem designed to be read on paper, and even then they're hard to figure. One of the reasons we love Coleman's early hits is because his first songwriting partner, Carolyn Leigh, planted fat, simple words that bounce off the notes:

> Hey, Look Me Over!
> Lend me an ear
> Fresh out of clover
> Mortgaged up to here . . .

The lyrics are the weakness in *City of Angels*. It never quite throws off the impression that it's a funny play with a great incidental score, as opposed to a story told in songs. 'I thought wouldn't it be nice to write a *real* jazz score,' says Coleman. 'Not *showbusiness* jazz, but one with the real tempos and instrumental riffs. So I went to Larry Gelbart and said I wanted to do a jazz musical with a private eye. Then he called me up and said he wasn't having any fun. So he concocted the two stories – the Hollywood scriptwriter and the movie he's writing – which was wonderful, because it gave me not only my jazz score but also a movie score, another place to go musically.' The play about a film, based partially on Gelbart's own experiences in Hollywood (he's the writer of *M*A*S*H* and *Tootsie*), is a hoot, but it doesn't seem to require songs. The music, in turn, doesn't seem to need the play. At a songwriters' get-together, Marilyn Bergman, lyricist of 'The Way We Were', came up to Coleman and said, 'I've just seen *City of Angels*. Who was that *trombonist?*'

Coleman said: 'Marilyn, did you like the *show?*'

He got Tonys for *City of Angels* and *Will Rogers*, and now he's up to his neck in *The Life*, on which he and Ira Gassman have been working since the seventies. 'It's about people who are living in the bowels of New York,' he says. 'It's not musical comedy, it's a *passionate* piece.' The word is that it's Coleman's *Porgy and Bess*. There must be many who hope that the last surviving musical comedy composer won't turn his back on the genre for long, but, in a world where operetta earnestness, self-pity and solemnity are in dreadful abundance, who can blame him? There are still plenty of jokes out there – in movies, in sitcoms, in stand-up – but the theatre doesn't seem to know how to musicalize them.

' "You're The Top/You're the Coliseum"?' Paul Simon, a funny fellow in a downbeat sorta way, once said to me. 'We don't define wit that way any more.'

*

In July 1993, *City of Angels* got a second set of great notices from the London press. A few weeks earlier, almost in passing, Andrew Lloyd Webber had commented that he'd enjoyed the show but he couldn't remember a single tune from it – and he was a musician. The critics begged to differ. The reviews of *Sunset Boulevard*, almost to a man, compared it unfavourably with *City of Angels*. So the producers decided to cancel their closing notices and struggle on for a few more months. It made no difference: the show ended its run well into the red. Broadway humour, it seems, no longer travels.

There are exceptions. Boom or bust, in London and New York, there's usually room among the mega-spectacles for one smash musical comedy every half-decade. In the early eighties, it was *42nd Street*; in the late eighties, *Me and My Girl*; in the early nineties, *Crazy for You*. But all three use songs more than 50 years old. It appears we love Gershwin so much we don't need any new 'musical comedy' scores. The form which best expresses the hip-hooray and ballyhoo of Broadway is dead as dead can be. *Sunset Boulevard*'s plot – the story of a silent-screen star washed up by all the new talking pictures – could almost be a metaphor for how the traditional American musical was left behind by London's high-tech operettas. A musical comedy made in heaven? *All* musical comedy's in heaven.

The last two of these quinquennial smashes were directed by a soft-spoken Englishman, Mike Ockrent. Most of the Brit hit stagers – Trevor Nunn, Nick Hytner – are not known as yuck merchants, but Ockrent is, so he seemed the right guy to consult about what, in an age of joke-free shows, remains of musical comedy. In 1991, he published a novel called *Running Down Broadway* about the musical theatre critic of *The Independent*, which I then was, and the director of a big Broadway musical, which Ockrent was about to become. Life imitates art, eh? As a study of an arts writer on *The Independent* in the late eighties, it's uncannily accurate: the musical theatre critic is a total loser, a bedsit deadbeat, a sexual inadequate with suicidal tendencies – though Ockrent denies that it's based on me on the not altogether reassuring grounds that '*un*like you, he lives in Willesden'. Notwithstanding the vividness with which he brings Willesden to life, as a portrait of Broadway, the novel is slightly twee – you can sort of tell it was written by an Englishman whose introduction to this world was backstage movies: for example, producers still scream 'You schmuck!' at their directors as opposed to 'You cocksucker!' Yet here he is: the toast of New York, the slick superstager of *Crazy for You*, the show with which the British subsidized directorate (the Nunns and Cairds and Hytners) moved on from pop operetta and annexed musical comedy, too.

Admittedly, the Americans don't see it that way. In Shubert Alley, *Crazy for You* was the show that brought the Gershwins back to Broadway and, according to *The New York Times*, heralded the exhilarating triumphant re-birth of the American musical. 'Frank Rich's piece was basically, "Thank God, it isn't British",' remembers Ockrent. 'But he does another review the next day on W Q X R . . .'

'You mean W Q X R?'

'Is it? If it's not called Melody Radio or BBC 2, it's a mystery to me. But he did mention then, almost apologetically, that I was British.'

Ockrent has had hits before – *Passion Play*, *Educating Rita* – but today he finds himself as the unlikely successor to George Abbott and Gower Champion: the king of musical comedy – a shrunken rump of a realm, to be sure, but what's left of it is his; he's the first call a producer makes if the property's got a joke or two in – whether it's Dickens (*A Christmas Carol*) or Tom Hanks (*Big*). It was his re-tread of *Me and My Girl* that first brought him to the attention of the Americans. In the 1930s, it had been a strictly local hit that, like most British musicals of the period, never travelled. Half a century later, Ockrent and Stephen Fry exhumed the piece. At the West End press call, the director overheard a photographer say, 'I don't give this six weeks.' Ockrent bet him a cheeseburger it would run at least seven; it did: seven years – though he's still owed the burger. 'We just did it because we thought it would be fun as a Christmas show at the Leicester Haymarket . . .' But it played Broadway, Tokyo, is still touring Britain, and made Ockrent the obvious choice when the producer Roger Horchow decided he wanted to revive another thirties property, the Gershwins' *Girl Crazy*.

In their original forms, these musicals were harmless bits of nonsense for the tired businessman audience. Today, they come riddled with subtext. I mention to Ockrent that, a few years ago, when I'd described *Me and My Girl* as a musical comedy about a Cockney who inherits an earldom, he'd pointed out that, in fact, he'd taken a neo-Brechtian line on the material.

'That's right,' he says.

'Er, just remind me: what exactly was the neo-Brechtian line again?' Like most of the audience, I found the Brechtian line less easy to remember than the line about 'Apéritif?' 'No, thanks, I've brought my own.'

'Well, it's all sorts of notions about class and British imperialism . . .' He recalls how he'd been very taken by some prince interviewed by Robert Lacey on a TV series about European aristocracy and how he'd wanted to raise the subject of ancestor worship, which is what gave the prince an advantage over a fellow like himself who could only trace his family one and a half generations back to somewhere in Mitteleuropa, and how he carefully selected the ancestors of the Cockney earl to represent different stages in imperial history since the twelfth century . . . 'And out of that sprang the number "Men Of Hareford", where the ancestors come out of their paintings and start tapping . . .'

'But it's the tapping you remember . . .'

'Yes, but I think it was Hal . . .'

(Ockrent is one of the few Britons who can plausibly first-name drop Hal Prince.)

'. . . or maybe it was Steve . . .'

(And Stephen Sondheim.)

'. . . who said that, whenever you're working on a musical that appears to be light and fluffy, it's crucial to have a really important thought that underpins the thing. It's not just Fred meets Sally, Sally loses Fred, then they get together. That isn't enough today. That's the big difference between what we're doing in the nineties and the way it used to be. We've all come out of university . . .'

'So it's just to salve your conscience?'

'Well, the people working on it have to get some satisfaction. And, in the end, it isn't satisfying to whip up a soufflé if you haven't cooked the venison just before it.'

In the old non-red meat days of 1930, *Girl Crazy* was about a Jewish cabbie who goes west and becomes a mayor, or maybe it was a Jewish mayor who goes west and becomes a cabbie, or a mayor cabbie who becomes Jewish. Venison-wise, what's *Crazy for You* about?

'Well, the venison is about cultural renewal. The soufflé is "Let's put on a show, let's do up the theatre and everybody lives happily ever after." But the meat of it is that this is a town, Deadrock, that has died; the culture is dead; everybody's asleep, nobody does anything. Then in comes this guy with enormous energy who wants to be a dancer, who wants to have rhythm and he enthuses this town with a whole new life: he gives them rhythm, he gives them their culture back.'

'In other words, it's a metaphor for the state of American showbiz?'

Ockrent looks at me scornfully: I'd mistaken his haunch of venison for a soggy quarter-pounder. 'It's a metaphor for the state the world is in. Look at us here: we're cutting back on our grants and our subsidies, we never believe culture is important, we never support it, and, if you don't have a culture, you have no life . . .'

'So this glossy sappy-happy song 'n' dance bonanza is, in fact, an argument for increased state subsidy of the arts?'

'Absolutely. Philip Hedley would be very happy with it.' (Perhaps a less thunderous name-drop this: Hedley is the Artistic Director of the Theatre Royal, Stratford, in London's East End.)

As it happens, *Crazy for You* is the first of Ockrent's hits not to originate in the subsidized theatre, while his productions for commercial managements have proved pretty uncommercial: *Look! Look!* was a short-lived play about the audience that never found one of its own; *Follies* (1987) was a textbook definition of a *succès d'estime* – a success that runs out of steam. '*Follies* said a lot about marriage and hopes dashed, and that's an important topic. But if it's something called *Follies* at the Shaftesbury, you expect to see a traditional follies. If it had been called *Middle-aged Spread* . . .'

'You'd expect Ray Cooney?'

'Okay, *Middle-aged Dread*. But the point is you'd know not to take Gran'ma for an undemanding night out.'

He doesn't accept the easy précis of his career, as a division between splashy hits and more ambitious but less lucrative works. There are, he reckons, just as many important intellectual threads running through *Crazy for You*. Moreover, his approach to this show is no different from his early productions at the Traverse in Edinburgh, when he was heavily influenced by Peter Stein of Berlin's Schaubühne Theatre and worried, in his dramaturge C. P. Taylor's phrase, about 'the paucity of modern philosophy'.

Today, there's no paucity of philosophy about Ockrent. Indeed, whenever you enquire about a specific lyric or even a throwaway joke, he inevitably expands it into a discussion on geopolitical socio-economic trends post-Thatcher. In his novel, *The Independent*'s musical theatre loser schmucko plans his suicide while listening to Streisand sing

Sondheim: 'Jesus, I love musicals!' he moans. Ockrent loves 'em too, but, a physicist by training, he needs to know why.

'I do love Broadway, it's consummately professional, it's enthusiastic. When you cast the chorus in London, you say "We'd love you to be in the show" and they nod quietly and go "Uh-huh". "We're going to start rehearsals on September 21st." "Uh-huh." "So we'll see you then." "Okay." And off they go: all very cool, very English. You do the same thing in America and they go, "Wow! Yo!" There's no pretending that it doesn't mean much. On *Crazy for You* in London, we've been working on the accents and I've been trying to explain that it's more than the accents: it's the way sentences are structured, even the body language is different, you come *forward* to talk. We hate display, we believe children should be seen and not heard – and where's it got us? It's got us in the worst recession, we're a third-rate power . . .'

Like the fourteenth chorus of an Ockrent First Act finale, the sheer exuberance is infectious. Musical comedy as a metaphor for *everything*? I'll settle for that. 'So what you're saying,' I ask, 'is that Britain wouldn't be such a depraved hellhole if we all went around as if we were auditioning for a musical comedy on Broadway?'

But even Ockrent knows when to stop. 'Er, no, Mark. I wouldn't say that. I wouldn't agree with that at all.'

vi

The Star

If you want to analyse the most significant theatrical trends, look at the *Broadway Celebrity Cookbook*. The first thing you notice about the *Broadway Celebrity Cookbook* is that there are no Broadway celebrities in it, excepting Gwen Verdon and Angela Lansbury who, to my great regret, are now inactive in the theatre. The rest are not so much celebrities as reasonably competent actors – the kind who make a nice living in *Cats* and *Les Miz* without provoking more than one in a thousand theatregoers to consult the cast list. If you want to see the American theatre's *real* stars, you have to pay 500 bucks and head over to Lincoln Center for a one-off charity gala with some glittering personage of yesteryear who's no longer willing to risk her legend being dented by the whims of the *New York Times* drama critic. Or you can catch Debbie Reynolds or Ann Miller cleaning up on the road in a dwindling number of proven successes. In 1994, Carol Channing returned to *Hello, Dolly!* for a thirtieth anniversary revival. But when did Dolly ever go away? In our collective memory, she seems to have been touting the thing from town to town for decades – inspiring one despairing LA graffiti artist to amend an evangelical billboard – 'JESUS, SAVE US FROM HELL' – to 'JESUS, SAVE US FROM HELLO DOLLY REVIVALS '.

Having lost the stellar names it's made and unable to generate enough product to create any new ones, Broadway now has to bus in stars from other firmaments: Brooke Shields took over in *Grease*, Jerry Lewis signed for *Damn Yankees*, Donald Trump's girlfriend Marla Maples turned up in *The Will Rogers Follies*. At her audition, she didn't sing or dance but she did do cartwheels across the stage. 'If you want to see actors acting,' one producer told me, 'there's a hundred shows. But, if you want to see Marla Maples doing cartwheels, we're the only game in town.' But why stop there? Why not Jerry Lewis and Marla Maples in *A Streetcar Named Desire*? Or Jerry Lewis and Dean Martin? What's the diff? For many of these stars, a revival is simply an easy sleepwalk. We hear a lot about how actors agonize over motivation, performing Buddhist meditation exercises before curtain-up, etc, but no such burdens weighed heavily on Rudolf Nureyev cleaning up on the 1989 US tour of *The King and I*. He passed much of the evening in his dressing room 'phoning pals back in Europe and apologizing for having to cut the conversation short but he had to go on stage and sing 'Shall We Dance?' One night, he forgot to hang up the receiver and, when he realized he was paying for the call, he spent the rest of the scene miming agitated telephone movements over Mrs Anna's shoulder to the stagehands in the wings. I expect the audience briefly roused itself and collectively mused: 'I don't remember *that* from the movie.'

Every so often, having played every available theatre on the road, one of these flea-bitten old mutts wanders into New York; we sit there dazed as the tatty scenery wobbles in front of our eyes, but come away marvelling at the indestructibility of these shows. What, after all, can you do with Rodgers and Hammerstein or Lerner and Loewe? Richard Rodgers said it all during the try-out of *South Pacific*, breaking up a late-night production meeting where everyone was wondering whether they should trim this or tinker with that. 'Fellers,' he declared, 'this show is perfect. Let's go to bed.'

Four decades later, the producer of *South Pacific*'s London revival took much the same view. 'I had a bit of a problem at first,' said Ronald S. Lee, 'because the director had this "concept". I mean, who needs concepts with Rodgers and Hammerstein?'

Hmm. That's easy to say if you've got Mary Martin and Ezio Pinza or even, as a successful American tour had, Robert Goulet. In the *Dolly* days, there seemed to be an endless procession of *grandes dames* descending that famous staircase: Carol Channing, Ginger Rogers, Martha Raye, Betty Grable, Pearl Bailey . . . But, by the star-less eighties, the line of leading ladies was spluttering to a halt. 'Look at *Woman of the Year*,' James Kirkwood told me, citing Kander and Ebb's hit of 1981. 'They started with Lauren Bacall, then got Raquel Welch and Debbie Reynolds. But who's left after that? Annette Funicello?' (Miss Funicello, you'll recall, is a graduate of *The Mickey Mouse Club* and Frankie Avalon's co-star in *Beach Blanket Bingo*.) Unable to find anyone to succeed Debbie Reynolds – or, more accurately, anyone to succeed her who means anything at the box office – *Woman of the Year* folded.

At the time we spoke, Kirkwood was working on a diary of the year and a half he spent on his play *Legends*. On the book's jacket, he intended to have a picture of himself in a straitjacket with Mary Martin and Carol Channing dancing on his head. 'The producer fell out with Carol, so I said, "Whatever you do, don't fall out with Mary." So then he fell out with Mary. They both hated him. When Mary left, we had Ann Miller lined up, but Carol said she wanted Julie Andrews, so then she said she'd leave, so then we had nobody. Stars!' snorted Kirkwood. 'That's why it's a relief to have a show like *Chorus Line* where you just need good, talented youngsters. In fact, I think that's one of the reasons it's now in its fourteenth year. The show is bigger than whoever's in it.' In fact, since *Chorus Line*, the biggest hits have bypassed stars entirely: *42nd Street, Cats, Starlight Express, Les Misérables, Miss Saigon* . . . Even *Phantom of the Opera*: Michael Crawford's performance was a bonus but, around the world, the show plays to capacity without him.

But what about the shows writers wrote when we still had stars? The ever dwindling talent pool available to the theatre makes most of Broadway's back catalogue unfeasible, *Sweet Bird of Youth* as much as *Sweet Charity*. Musicals, in particular, are about larger-than-life characters: Charity, Dolly, Mame, Rose, Nellie Forbush, Annie Oakley . . . How can you have larger-than-life characters with smaller-than-life actresses? In the old days, the staging was ordinary but the acting wasn't; in our time, the staging is extraordinary but too often the acting isn't. We have dispensed with representationalism in the sets, only to transfer it to the acting.

And now, Ronald Lee notwithstanding, even Rodgers and Hammerstein need concepts. In 1992, Cameron Mackintosh inaugurated a series of classic musicals at London's National Theatre. The first was *Carousel*, which soon transferred to the West End and thence to Broadway – a case of coals to Newcastle, or even clams to New England. But the truth is that, in New York, the Rodgers and Hammerstein office, which is as protective of its catalogue as the D'Oyly Carte was of Gilbert and Sullivan, would have been unlikely to allow such a production to originate in their own backyard. Rather than 'revival', Mackintosh and his director Nicholas Hytner prefer the word 're-examination': their *Carousel* has a re-orchestrated score, replaces the Agnes de Mille choreography with new dances by Kenneth MacMillan and opts for bold, spare designs rather than the usual old-fashioned literal sets and frontcloths; instead of a jolly Rodgers singalong, Hytner focuses on Hammerstein's ceaseless questioning about how American communities function.

It doesn't all work. In the more overwrought moments, I occasionally found myself pining for the Chislehurst Amateur Operatic Society, who'd have rattled through the thing in half the time. And I disagreed with

Hytner over his decision to cast a black actor as stolid, respectable Mister Snow, not because he's black (although, as a resident of northern New England, I know they're thin on the ground up there) but because his entrance, greeted with a huge laugh, is a musical *comedy* moment in a musical *play*; the performance is at odds with the tone of the piece.

But who'd have ever thought we'd be having these kinds of arguments over R&H revivals? This is something new to musicals: not star performances, but star productions. I've yet to meet anyone moved by the leading man's 'Soliloquy' or the central romance, but they've plenty to say about the set and the staging and the themes. Hytner cut his teeth on opera and classic plays and then directed *Miss Saigon*, which gave him a rare opportunity to work with writers who aren't dead. He once described to me arriving one morning and explaining that he'd had some wonderful directorial notion that would involve the authors amending only one small section. The composer, Claude-Michel Schonberg, gave him a polite look which he broadly interpreted as 'Fuck off and do what we wrote.' So, for *Carousel*, it was back to dead guys.

Thanks to the RSC and the National, most of Britain's hot-shot directors make their names with very old plays: we don't talk about a 'revival' of *A Midsummer Night's Dream*; we marvel at the brilliant concept of staging it in Ceauşescu's Romania. In America, in contrast, a director can't build a reputation on the classics: hardly any theatres do 'em. And 're-examinations' of old musicals tend to get de-railed along the way.

In 1983, Peter Sellars, the opera director, was signed to mount a new version of the Gershwins' *Funny Face*, presumably because the producers had mixed him up with the other Peter Sellers. He decided to strip away the inane musical comedy froth to reveal the brooding, neo-Brechtian savage indictment of the Depression underneath. Needless to say, he was removed during rehearsals. Tommy Tune took over and the finished show, instead of a dark Expressionist exploration of the failure of capitalism, was two and a half hours of tap-dancing. That's 're-examination' New York style: a slick but heartless entertainment, in whose grim footsteps Jerry Zaks' *Guys and Dolls* and Jack O'Brien's *Damn Yankees* have willingly followed.

In Britain, though, the idea of 'radical re-appraisal' is central to the theatrical culture. We now see that philosophy applied not just to *Carousel* but to more recent musicals, like Declan Donellan's production of *Sweeney Todd* or Sam Mendes' *Assassins* – both strikingly different from the New York originals. British theatre is a directors' club and it's easy to forget that sometimes the writer is inconveniently living. A less successful

Sondheim revival inserted a number from the film version, despite the objections of the composer.

'But this is my vision of the piece!' the director said.

'Um, well, I wrote it,' Sondheim is supposed to have replied.

In the eighties, the British were seen as expert manufacturers of their own grotesque spectacles. In the nineties, as *Carousel* opened in New York, Main Stem showfolk were confronted with an unpalatable truth: never mind *Cats* or *Phantom*, the West End had begun annexing Broadway's back catalogue. For the last of the superstar stagers, it was a challenge he couldn't resist. In Toronto, far away from Broadway's merciless gaze, he began 're-examining' the original American musical.

*

It's easy to go astray with *Show Boat*. The laughable RSC/Opera North production of 1990 restored all the cuts made in 1927, turned a coherent two-act musical into a sprawling three-act mish-mash and ruined one of the great stage masterpieces for a generation of London theatregoers. So what would Harold Prince do with it? After its Canadian try-out, the new *Show Boat* berthed at the Gershwin Theatre in New York in the fall of '94.

All musicals are balancing acts, but with this one the first call comes on the very first word:

> *Niggers* all work on the Mississippi
> *Niggers* all work while the white folks play . . .

As we know, in 1927 it provoked an audible gasp. It is not nice, but not-niceness is such a rare quality in musicals that, for that reason alone, it merits preservation. This isn't the lumbering didacticism of Sondheim in his 'Children Will Listen' mode; it just *is*: dramatic truth presented on a take it or leave it basis. Needless to say, in a culture which can't be bothered to distinguish between dramatic indictment and personal endorsement, Oscar Hammerstein's original lyric has long since been whitewashed out: by the 1936 movie, it was not 'niggers' but 'darkies'; by the '46 Broadway revival, 'Coloured folk work on the Mississippi'; in the Jerome Kern biopic *Till the Clouds Roll By*, 'Here we all work'; and in the 1966 revival, weary of euphemistically sidestepping the matter, they just junked the opening black chorus completely. In 1988, when EMI produced a lavish recording of the 'original' *Show Boat*, the conductor John McGlinn found himself turned down by many black performers who objected to the word 'nigger'; the opening ended up being sung by a chorus of whey-faced effete Englishmen – not an option in the theatre. Yet the continuing controversy only confirms Hammerstein's original judgement: we'd rather bleach the past than face it; 'nigger' is uncomfortable because it's the right word in the right place.

So how does the dean of Broadway directors approach this little difficulty? Well, he comes up with an ingenious solution: he buries the line. Prince's *Show Boat* has a curtain (made up of sepia rotogravure enlargements of the kind usually found on the wallpaper of the more ambitious American steak house) and, when the curtain rises, there is, as in 1927, an audible gasp. This time, though, we're gasping at the set: Eugene Lee, using a combination of physical scenery, film projections and computer technology, has created a 3-D Mississippi River in perfect perspective, and, along the far bank, the *Cotton Blossom* comes serenely gliding. Having paid 75 bucks, we applaud gratefully – all over the first words of Kern and Hammerstein's chorus. For the record, the downtrodden barge-toters and bail-lifters in the foreground sing 'Coloured folk work . . .' But who cares? They could sing 'Physically challenged Latino pre-op transsexuals work on the Mississippi' and we'd still be cheering the set: the song and the distinctly unsweaty stevedores are mere decoration.

It sets a worrying tone: is this going to be the first *Show Boat* where you can't see the show for the boat? The boat and the river are important: they hold the story together as it pours across the decades. But how do you convey that? Prince and Lee give us a *tableau vivant* straight out of the *Ziegfeld Follies* and a triple-decker steamboat shunted on and off (amid plenty of scenery rumbling from the wings): indeed, the director has interpolated 'I Have The Room Above Her' from the second movie version for no discernible reason other than it gives him a chance to show all three storeys of his boat – Gaylord's room, Magnolia's room,and the rooftop where they meet. He's like a malicious department-store elevator: he stops at every storey, yet manages to miss the one story you're interested in – Gaylord's and Magnolia's ill-starred romance. 'Hal likes to direct scenery,' Prince's mentor George Abbott was wont to chuckle, and, in this number, you see what he means: the song is not remotely convincing as an expression of the riverboat gambler's emotions at this point in the drama; it is there purely as a pretext for a staging gimmick.

Somewhere around this scene in Act One, Prince's *Show Boat* stops being simply careless and sets itself up in active opposition to the qualities that make the show worth reviving in the first place. It's a staging that would have impressed Florenz Ziegfeld, the original producer: he devoted his life to *tableaux vivants*, leggy showgirls, stairways to paradise, and every other known form of visual distraction. Yet his longest-running hit and most lasting legacy is a show that sells on its book and score: you'll remember how Kern wrapped up the boat and the water – four notes for the *Cotton Blossom*, simply inverted to represent Ol' Man River. It's not that Prince and Lee's big boat and Kern and Hammerstein's big score are incompatible; it's that the former all too often swamps the latter. The show now lists from one side to the other, unable to agree on a coherent staging vocabulary. The stage pictures are cluttered, with too many elements jostling for attention. Late in Act One, during a hitch in one of the plays-within-the-play, Cap'n Andy has to get up and hold the fort. Poor John McMartin got the worst notices of his career for this vaudevillian knocka-bout. But why blame him? Unlike Nicholas Hytner in *Miss Saigon*, Prince never manages to shrink that huge Gershwin stage to human size. McMartin has about as much chance as me doing card tricks at Yankee Stadium.

Take the dance arrangements, witty variations of tempo and orchestra-tion reminiscent of Susan Stroman's earlier work on *Crazy for You*. But, in *Crazy*, Miss Stroman's choreographic turns grew organically from the songs and plot point, as natural expressions of character and emotion – delightful, romantic, fantastic, but still *true*. Here, they seem grafted on to the play: they look like contractually stipulated choreographer's moments (this is a recurring problem with Prince shows: see *Phantom*'s 'Masquer-ade' scene). So, for example, toward the end, when Parthy and her grand-daughter launch into a duet, it turns into a wild Charleston on the levee. Except that Elaine Stritch isn't up to a Charleston these days, so she's forced to bail out of the number after the vocal. Thus, a song which is supposed to be about her relationship with her granddaughter becomes just another anonymous chorus cavalcade. Star solo, dance break – with neither rhyme nor reason to connect the two. Hammerstein is the man who made sense of musicals; at times, Prince's revival seems determined to undo his life's work.

That's what's so weird: the more Prince 'modernizes' the thing, the more old-fashioned it looks – not just in the dis-integrated dance, but also in the secondary romance; Frank and Ellie seem far more like conven-tional musical comedy juveniles than they did in 1927, but only because Prince isn't interested in them. In Toronto, several black community spokespersons denounced this production as racist. They're right: the black characters are the only ones treated with dignity and respect; the whites are reduced to musical comedy stereotypes.

Prince has also abandoned the Second Act opener – newlyweds Gay and

Nola take in the 1893 Chicago World's Fair – because he thinks it 'irrelevant' and just a 'popular convention'. Okay, let's take a look: the original scene includes 'In Dahomey', an exotic Zulu number performed, naturally, by exotic Zulus who live round the corner and have never been east of Chicago. *Show Boat* is social history and musical history: when Nola gets her big break, it's with a lousy 'coon song' she learned in the kitchen with the Negro domestics; whitey happily takes his cultural lead from the black man, even as he insists on the Negro's obvious inferiority. 'In Dahomey', one could argue, is a counterweight to 'Ol' Man River', an Act Two opener to balance the stevedores of the Act One opener. One could argue it for another ten pages, but it's only a three-minute song: the point is there are perfectly cogent intellectual underpinnings for Kern and Hammerstein's curtain-raiser. What's the justification for Prince's rewrite? 'In Dahomey', the World's Fair and Gay and Nola have gone. Instead, Nola gives birth to a daughter, and Parthy serenades the baby with 'Why Do I Love You?'

But hang on: 'Why Do I Love You?', in its whole identity, is a boy / girl song. It's the 'happy interlude' beloved of motion pictures, a brief assertion of bliss whose very innocence foretells upheavals to come. It's fast, it's capering, it's an exhilarating dizzy whirl in the illogic of love:

> Why Do I Love You?
> Why do you love me?
> Why should there be two
> Happy as we?

Gay and Nola assume the answers to their questions. But, as events prove, nothing can be assumed. Take it away from them and you unbalance the play: the chief problem with this production is that you never feel, with the principal romance, that there's anything real at stake. But take it away and give it to Elaine Stritch as a lullaby to a baby, and you're just rubbing the authors' noses in it. Even slowed down as ponderously as here, this tune can never be a lullaby. Besides, the lyric just won't support it. A gran'ma wouldn't sing to a newborn babe:

> Can you see
> The why or wherefore
> I should be
> The one you care for?

It just ain't true. Then, in the final stretch, to shoehorn the damn song into place, Prince has to rewrite Hammerstein:

> You're a lucky boy
> I am lucky, too
> All our dreams of joy
> Seem to come true . . .

'Boy' / 'joy', 'too' / 'true': that's the rhyme scheme. Elaine Stritch sings:

> You're a lucky girl
> I am lucky, too
> All our dreams of joy . . .

Does 'girl' rhyme with 'joy'? Even if you're not a lyric-writer, you can tell something's not quite right here: the words don't correspond to the rhythmic stresses of the tune. How come nobody – not his producer, Garth Drabinsky, not the orchestrator, Bill Brohn, not the 70-plus cast, not the Rodgers and Hammerstein office – said to Prince, 'Hey, man, you can't dump on the writers like that?'

What do you gain from giving 'Why Do I Love You?' to Elaine Stritch? Nothing. But Miss Stritch, though not a star as we used to understand the term, is the biggest name in the cast, and, as Abe Burrows liked to say, a character who doesn't sing in a musical isn't really in the show. So, having cast Miss Stritch in the part, Prince has to find her a song. Hence the new Second Act opener: star-pandering, and nothing more. If ever a 'popular convention' was dated and 'irrelevant', it's this. It's one thing to pander to Ethel Merman or Gwen Verdon: they did the work and sold the show. But to reorient *Show Boat* so that a non-singing character can get a solo returns us to the theatrical dark ages – to the world Kern and Hammerstein set out to alter forever.

Does Prince's lyric-trampling matter? After all, on paper the song looks trite and simple-minded. Hammerstein, though, was a more restrained rhymester than Hart and Ira Gershwin. He over-rhymes on 'Why Do I Love You?' because the mood of the song is impossibly optimistic: the rhymes signal that the sentiment is too pat. Conversely, when he's got something big to say, he puts the rhyming dictionary back in his drawer ('Ol' Man River'). It's not just about altering 'lucky boy' to 'lucky girl' because the gender of the object of affection has been amended: I think Kern and Hammerstein are entitled to have their intentions respected. When Julie – ravaged by booze and disillusionment and fierce stubborn loyalty – sings 'Bill', she says:

> His form and face
> His manly grace

Are not the kind that you
Would find in a statue . . .

'That you' / 'statue'. Lonette McKee sings 'that *you* / Would find in a
*statu*e' – such a perverse and stilted accenting that you have to assume
she's been instructed to blow the rhyme. I don't mind, in principle, Prince
reconstructing *Show Boat*, but I do object to him lazily ignoring the
authors' own standards of discipline. This is what's so unnerving about
his first major revival. A distinguished British opera director once told me
he could only see shows like *Phantom of the Opera* in places like Vienna
where the foreign language acted as a huge condom, protecting him from
Lloyd Webber contamination. But you don't need to understand the
language: Prince's staging is so bold and clear, there's nothing to be gained
from listening to the vapid operetta generalities of the English text.

American admirers of this director have always regarded *Phantom* as
an aberration, but in some respects it's the ultimate Prince show, the piece
in which he finally triumphed over the English language and proved the
redundancy of words. *Show Boat*, alas, is not *Phantom*: you *need* the text.
This revival is alarming because it suggests that America's most distinguished director can no longer hear the words. Before *Show Boat*, we had
star vehicles; after *Show Boat*, we had shows; now, even the greatest show
is no more than a star vehicle for the director.

*

And what of the real stars? Those men and women who aren't merely
players? All gone, one by one. For a faint echo of what musicals used to be
about, you had to be at the Lunt-Fontanne Theatre on Broadway on 28
January 1996. Speaking personally, this was the first time I'd ever seen
anyone attend their own memorial service. And, by the final curtain (and
how sweetly archaic these legit terms now sound), she seemed to have
interred an entire theatrical culture in the vault with her.

28 January was Super Bowl Sunday, a day when even the effetest
musical comedy ninny gets hit on by cab drivers and news vendors and
waitresses and is expected to have an opinion on Dallas over Pittsburgh.
America's schedule is reorganized to defer to this great TV ritual; the streets
are eerily empty and, as you slink along to the Lunt-Fontanne, their silence
is accusatory. Whatever small amount of press attention the last performance of *Hello, Dolly!* might normally have merited, its inept choice of
closing date had cruelly squandered. The Super Bowl is mass culture, one
of that select group of annual rituals that binds the nation together; the

250

theatre, on the other hand, is elite, sophisticated, exclusive. No matter that the Super Bowl is a promoters' gimmick cooked up in the late sixties; that whatever 'sport' might once have been involved is now entirely subservient to the needs of television; that the teams are steely business franchises for whom the home-town label is good only until another municipality pitches them a more favourable tax deal; that the players earn so many gazillion dollars a year they'll never have to encounter anyone as lowly as *you* ever again; that the only seats worth having are reserved for a corporate nomenklatura and that Joe Schmoe with his Bud and his pizza slumped in front of the TV has as much chance of getting to the moon as to the Super Bowl. No matter, too, that theatre sends its shows out to nowheresville towns that will never see an NFL team, much less the Super Bowl; that its leading players play eight games a week not for millions but for a few thousand, and spend their lives in hotels and dressing-rooms a football star wouldn't hang his spare jockstrap in. No matter, none of it: the Super Bowl is mass culture; theatre is elite, exclusive.

Super Bowl XXX, *Hello, Dolly!* 32. That's not the final score, but their ages. In 1964, *Hello, Dolly!* was still out there, still part of mass culture. It became the longest-running and highest-grossing Broadway show ever; the title song was a Number One record. But, 32 years later, by the time the Super Bowl refuseniks gathered in the Lunt-Fontanne for the final performance, *Hello, Dolly!* seemed as shrivelled and shrunken as its leading lady. I've never been a fan of either the show or the star and, when this revival came back to Broadway the previous November, I passed. I'd caught it on the road and found it heavy going, a self-regarding evening in which the audience is intimidated into continuous ovations. Carol Channing is supposedly an indestructible old trouper who's never missed a performance, but it seems to me her act trades with cool calculation on at least its potential destructibility. Once upon a time a star had to get re-elected every night, to prove her stardom right there and then before our eyes. Now the only ones left are like those Presidents-for-Life in ramshackle banana republics. Once, we were roused to our feet because they were dazzling, wonderful, brilliant; now, they command standing ovations merely for standing. Watch Miss Channing as she descends that famous staircase in the title number: we applaud with relief, as we do when an old nag successfully negotiates a tricky course at a point-to-point. It's not showbusiness but showjumping – and even then, the show steadfastly refuses to jump.

Still, this production got great notices in New York, for drama critics are a sentimental crowd. Producers are always complaining about reviewers 'butchering' their shows and irresponsibly endangering the future of legitimate theatre. In practice, both groups show considerable unanimity. Both the producers and the critics were on the side of, say, *Swinging on a Star*, a tired, third-rate revue. Unfortunately, the public proved more resistant. It was the same with Miss Channing's 'triumphant' comeback. You don't need graphs and demographics when, before your very eyes, a six-year Broadway blockbuster withers away to a sickly three-month revival.

At the Lunt-Fontanne, those who'd seen Carol Channing first time round declared that nothing about her performance had changed. I can well believe it. Trouble is, everything else in the world has changed utterly, leaving Miss Channing like some freakish mutation beached on the sands of time. She is 75 now, and, like any cartoonist's caricature, the signature features have overpowered everything else: the wig, the eyelashes, the rouge, the silly maddening squeaky voice from the big cartoon mouth are exactly the same, and from halfway down the orchestra it's hard to see what, if anything, is connecting them up. All stars reflect their audiences: across three decades, as a huge mainstream hit dwindled into a camp cult, Carol Channing wound up as her own female impersonator.

She is efficient. She does Dolly's schtick, all the bits of business (to use a couple of other quaintly greasepainted terms), brilliantly. But what's a crowd-pleaser without the crowds? That last afternoon, virtually every number stopped the show, impregnable in its defiance:

> Before The Parade Passes By
> I'm gonna go and taste Saturday's high life!

But it's a Sunday matinee – and the parade *has* passed by, in every sense.

Miss Channing appeared bewildered by what had happened. She has no home, she lives in hotels, she's spent three decades touring either in *Dolly* or her only other hit, *Gentlemen Prefer Blondes*. She never made the transition to movies or TV: Marilyn Monroe swiped her first role, and Barbra Streisand her second. And, though she may regret the injustice, she must surely know that, away from greasepaint and footlights, in the duller electronic forms, she is merely a grotesque. The same season, Julie Andrews and Carol Burnett also returned to Broadway to be hailed as glorious theatre stars, but we know (and their box office receipts prove it) that their star power derives mainly from their work elsewhere. Miss Channing was the last pure theatre star, and in a cruelly competitive season it was an illusion impossible to sustain.

At the curtain call, she promised she'd be back later this year – on tour, not Broadway. And, as we filed out, the walk-out music added a final taunt:

> Dolly'll never go away!
> Dolly'll never go away!
> Dolly'll never go away . . .

But she has gone away, and she'll never be back.

The Flops

It couldn't have happened to a nicer show. The British composer had been an admirer of Martin Luther King since his schooldays; he went to Detroit to study gospel music; he spent months of Sundays in the Ebenezer Baptist Church; he took a non-violence philosophy course in Atlanta; against the claims of a rival version by an actor from the Birmingham soap opera *Crossroads*, he secured the support of King's widow; equally impressive for someone who's never written a musical before, he pulled off a deal with Decca for a pre-production recording of the score.

And then the peace and harmony began to unravel.

It's 7 April 1990 at the Piccadilly Theatre in London. Up on stage, Timothy O'Brien's design concept is a road: the literal road on which the civil rights movement marched, but also the metaphorical road of their lives. It is surprisingly smooth, at least compared to the pot-holed, contraflowed tailbacked highway the show itself has taken *en route* to tonight's first preview. To date, *King – The Musical* has lost three librettists, two directors, one lyricist and the support of Mrs King and the King Center. At stake for the producers is £3,500,000 plus whatever they blew on *A Little Night Music*, an unsuccessful transfer they moved into the Piccadilly as a stopgap in order not to lose the theatre during what's proving to be one of the longest booking tailbacks in West End history. Fellow managers, eyeing the body count, confidently predict *King* won't hold the Piccadilly for long: 'They'll be out by – oh, mid-June,' I was told by one producer in need of a home for his own musical.

This sort of stuff is meat and potatoes to your average Broadway composer: they expect it and they *enjoy* it; what's a musical without bloodshed? But at the eye of this storm is a composer as unlike the New York piranhas as you could imagine. Meek, mild-mannered Richard Blackford looks like a high-school piano teacher, youngish but prematurely greyed. If you were told he was in showbiz, you'd assume from his sweater that he'd once been an extra on *The Andy Williams Christmas Show*. Yet here he is, a composer of four decently obscure operas, steering a backstage melodrama which lurches across Baz Bamigboye's *Daily Mail* gossip column every other day.

He glides serenely through the theatre, apparently oblivious to the carnage. If a flustered look occasionally furrows his brow, it's only because he's trying to remember which of the many hands who've worked on *King* for a day did what: 'That's one of *Maya Angelou*'s lyrics . . . Then in Act One there's a lyric by – er – *Alistair Beaton* . . . A lot of what we see is *Graham Vick*'s, although he doesn't want to be credited with it . . . and a lot of what's in the book is *Richard Nelson*'s, although I *think* he's also chosen not to be credited . . .' Pathetic. He *should* be dismissing his ex-collaborators as useless motherfuckers the show's well rid of, but instead, with scrupulous, almost painful decency, he's fussing about getting their present billing status right. Only when he recounts Alistair Beaton's contention that *King*'s traumas put it right up there with the most notorious Broadway bloodbaths and then beams with pride, do you begin to suspect that lurking within this wimpy highbrow might be a Jule Styne in embryo.

Beaton, just elevated from 'additional lyrics' to equal billing, reckons appearances are deceptive. 'Richard is incredibly warm and gentle, but, when we met, he didn't strike me as the sort of person who could see a major musical through all the Scyllas and Charybdises. But you remember when Gorbachev came to power and everyone said, "What a charming man" and then Gromyko said "Yes, but he has teeth of steel . . ." Well, Richard has got teeth of steel. He had moral and political motivations for doing this show, and he tries to stick to those. But when the show is threatened he can fight very hard indeed. Even then, though, he's a model of good behaviour. I'm a much more bad-tempered bastard.'

On his last first night, Beaton stood on the Palladium balcony waving to the crowds like King Zog of Albania: the show in question was *Ziegfeld*, which shortly after opening lost its star and director, while most of Beaton's and Ned Sherrin's book was dumped or rewritten by distinguished men of letters like Tommy Steele. The show then had a second first night, to which Beaton wasn't invited, though he did 'phone me afterwards to check whether he was still mentioned in the programme. 'I suppose you could say I'm the biter rather than the bitten this time. But, tempting as it would be to see it as some sort of historical revenge on the world, there is a difference. Throughout all the travails of *King*, I've never stopped thinking that it was worth fighting for, whereas frankly *Ziegfeld* was a misconceived frivolity from the beginning, and Ned and I were fighting a deep feeling of contempt for the audience from other forces, who thought they didn't need a story, just give them lots of costumes and glitter and the coach parties will be happy. *King* is a show based upon respect for the audience.'

But, after *Ziegfeld*, why get involved with another musical in trouble? 'The subject interested me, so I agreed to meet Richard and Graham Vick, who was that week's director. And I thought the music was *great*! I mean it. Really.' His own appeal to *King*'s producers may have been for more practical reasons. Following Maya Angelou's decision to make herself unavailable for rehearsal, Beaton was one of the few lyricists in town who can work at speed.

After three months of frenzied writing to accommodate the patchwork amendments of passing book-authors, the score now divides 50/50 between his and Angelou's words. But you won't hear that on the record, which, having been made some time ago, features mostly Angelou lyrics and only three of Beaton's. Decca are a bit peeved about missing the hot new numbers written since, but they're unlikely to countenance a re-recording. After all, they've done that once already, when Jack Briley, screenwriter of *Gandhi* and Blackford's first lyricist, pulled out: the cast then had to be re-assembled to sing Angelou's rewrites.

Since her own retreat, Miss Angelou has taken some severe potshots at the show from across the ocean. But, while she was undoubtedly the best known of *King*'s writers, was she any good as a lyricist? There's a long pause before Beaton replies: 'She's written some beautiful ballads.' Blackford regrets her 'unavailability' but insists that 'in the crucial rehearsal period, you can't write lyrics by fax and 'phone. If we get it right, we'll have the best of both worlds.' As evidence, he offers first a song by Beaton:

> When Martin was a nobody
> They treated him like dirt
> Now he brings the coloured vote
> Just watch the white man flirt . . .

Then one by Angelou:

> Equal rights and civil rights
> That's supposed to be the plan
> But who can blame me if I say
> I want some in my hand?

Or maybe 'in my han''. The dodginess of that rhyme aptly conveys the difference between the professional technician and the Pulitzer Prize-winning poet. Others involved cite the same problems which led to James

Fenton's removal from *Les Misérables*: poets write lyrics which look dandy on the page but don't always serve the needs of book and staging or sit on the music terribly well.

But then, whoever writes the lyrics has to suffer comparisons with the man's own words. Blackford *has* set 'I have a dream' but, eager to avoid the accusations of predictability and opportunism that attend biotuners, he's used it contrapuntally as part of a complex musical scene which owes more to the lay-out of an opera score than Broadway.

'I have a dream,' said King, 'that one day my four little children will be judged not by the colour of their skin but by the quality of their character.' Off-stage, Blackford, a white Briton, deploys the speech as a defence against Angelou's and the King Center's complaints about the lack of black Americans on the creative team: 'At the time the estate withdrew their support, Coretta King had not read Richard Nelson's book. It's right that there should be input from black Americans. Whether the book *has* to be written by a black man, I would dispute.' Nonetheless, Lonnie Elder, a black playwright settling for the semi-detached credit of 'Book overseen by . . .', has replaced Richard Nelson, a white playwright who replaced Ron Milner (black), who replaced Jack Briley (white); meanwhile, in the director's seat, Clarke Peters (US, black) has taken over from Graham Vick (UK, white), who took over when Götz Friedrich (Federal Republic of Germany, Aryan), creator of the Royal Opera's tube-tunnel *Ring* cycle, withdrew because of ill health – psychosomatic, some say, and it hasn't prevented him from continuing with opera commitments. Peters has never staged a musical, and there were rumours that John (*Les Miz*) Caird and Terry (*Carrie*) Hands were 'hovering in the background' – where, presumably, their RSC regulation black garb blends into the shadows and makes it harder for them to be picked off by snipers. But Caird and Hands, secure in their bunker at the Barbican, are at pains to point out that it was no more than half-an-hour of informal advice to the producers at the RSC offices.

'It's been distressing,' admits Beaton, 'to see arguments between blacks and whites. Martin Luther King dreamed of a time when people would not be judged by their colour, and that ideal has not always informed the spirit we were working in. But I think we're through that now.' As we cross the stage, Blackford's hailed by his producer, Hans Flury, from Switzerland (presumably another tensely negotiated ethnic compromise): 'Good news from Atlanta!' The King Center can live with the new book and are back on board. It's sad that a man who believed in universal brotherhood should be the cause of so much factional in-fighting, but

Americans have long known what a potential hornet's nest King's legacy is. Showbusiness, though, operates to its own morality, and one result of the traumas has been that an insignificant box-office advance has begun to swell – proving either that there's no such thing as bad publicity or that there's some truth to stories of customers prefacing their purchases with, 'This is the Elvis musical, right?'

It wasn't enough, though. Three months later, that rival producer was right: *King* was out by June.

*

Stoll Moss are London's biggest theatre owners. Their late president, Louis Benjamin, once showed me the graphs for West End ticket sales and pointed out the clutched straws by which each dip in receipts is rationalized – 'Libyan crisis', 'Royal Wedding', 'Weather v. bad', 'Weather v. good'.

'We've got an awful lot of excuses,' he said. 'But it's all rubbish. It's like the old excuse when takings were down at the Finsbury Empire: "Polo at Hurlingham". I took £300,000 at the Palladium last week. D'you think I care what the bloody weather was like?'

Commercial theatre – as it's laughably called – is one of the great mysteries. You make money or you make excuses. In 1991, it was Saddam Hussein who, despite his onerous duties brutalizing Kuwait and launching rocket attacks on Israel, apparently found time to close *Children of Eden* and *Matador*. This is only an extreme example of the peculiar internalization of the landscape which attends anyone working on a new musical. 'The show dominates every aspect of your life,' Betty Comden once said. 'If someone says, "They've just launched a nuclear strike on us", you think, "Gee, will that hurt us at the box office?" '

As I mentioned, in April 1995, I happened to be in Oklahoma City for the try-out of a new musical about Jack Kennedy. A couple of days before opening, a huge bomb reduced the Federal Building to rubble, killed over 150 people and plunged the state into round-the-clock bereavement solidarity. 'My God, this is terrible!' I cried to the producer, assuming he'd have friends dead or injured in the blast. 'How are you holding up?'

'Well, we're at capacity tonight,' he said, 'and business for the weekend looks pretty good.'

But, whatever evidence Oklahoma might offer to the contrary, in London, it seems, the swirling currents of international politics and domestic terrorism have no other purpose but to close down West End musicals. It's never the fault of the book or the score or the subject.

*

Four years after *King*, and, speaking of swirling currents, the West End is still hung up on biotuners. The life of Robert Maxwell as a musical? There don't, at first glance, appear to be many points of contact between the bloated tycoon who fell off his yacht and the lyric stage – although, interestingly, there is a composer called Robert Maxwell. His biggest hit was the song 'Ebb Tide', whose text would seem tailor-made for the grand finale: 'First the tide rushes in . . .'

Anyway, the producer of *Maxwell the Musical*, Evan Steadman, decided to go for a different tack and use recycled G&S favourites. All proceeded smoothly until the eve of previews in February 1994, when *Maxwell* suddenly seemed strangely reminiscent of, well, Max. Max is Max Bialystock, the fictional impresario in the film *The Producers* who, to defraud his investors, cooked up a musical so bad it would close on opening night. *Maxwell the Musical* has gone one better than Bialystock's comparatively tasteful *Springtime for Hitler*: thanks to the Attorney-General, it closed *before* its opening night – indeed, before its first preview.

At the time, my suspicious mind immediately began trying to figure out what Bialystocky Maxwellian scam Evan Steadman was operating. These are deep waters, as Holmes would say. But, unfortunately for conspiracy theories, Steadman was his own investor: the show's cost, £1.1 million, was borne by him alone. He was just another naïve whacko obsessed by a dud musical until the High Court intervened. The Court granted an injunction on the grounds that his show might prejudice the forthcoming trials of Maxwell's sons: presumably, it's one thing for your father to be a ruthless granny-beggaring crook but, if it were to get about that he was the leading character in a musical, your reputation would *really* suffer. The Von Trapp progeny, now running a ski lodge in Vermont, would endorse that line, reckoning that, having been given 16 going on 17, they should be out on parole by now. Still, one thing we can say with certainty is that, rather than taking four million at the box-office (or even, in the Maxwell tradition, four million *from* the box-office), *Maxwell the Musical* would have belly-flopped.

Just look at it: produced not by an old legit hand but by a former Maxwell business associate, with a score composed (involuntarily) by the late Sir Arthur Sullivan with lyrics by Colin Bostock-Smith, a versatile TV gag writer who's supplied material for everyone from Clive James and Terry Wogan to, well, now I come to think of it, me and Sandi Toksvig. Whatever Colin's comedic gifts, whatever Sir Arthur's musical talents, whatever Steadman's Maxwell Business Communications chairmanship expertise, the whole (and Maxwell's one hell of a whole) is weirder than the sum of its parts.

Other than Cameron Mackintosh's and Andrew Lloyd Webber's, all British musicals are weird.

Which Witch: Take the Norwegian who scored *nul points* in the Eurovision Song Contest, add a director whose only experience with songs was on a long-ago TV series (Dennis Potter's *Pennies from Heaven*), and just for good measure throw in a lyricist best known as one half of camp cabaret act, Kit and the Widow.

Leonardo: Written by a sixties pop act known for one hit ('Concrete And Clay'), paid for by the government of Nauru in the South Pacific from their guano profits – a not inappropriate investor.

Bernadette: Written by two schoolteachers, staged by the director of *The Black and White Minstrel Show* and *Morecambe and Wise*, designed by a guy who chose to set the thing in a grotto resembling (as a leading producer put it) 'a giant coiled turd'.

Matador: Composed by the guy who wrote Gary Glitter's pop hits, with a book by a fringe playwright who'd never done a musical, directed by an opera guy who'd never done a musical, with flamenco choreography by a Spanish guy who'd never done a musical, a star from an American TV cop show who'd never done a musical, and the bulls represented by men in black polo-necks waving sticks.

Metropolis: Written by the American composer of 'You Light up My Life' (a big hit in the late seventies for Pat Boone's daughter) yoked, in an unlikely union, to a radical British fringe playwright and *Time Out* contributor, and translated from the original gibberish: as the diabolical mastermind bent on world domination sings,

> I must search day and night
> Find for her features right.

But, in *Metropolis*, there were hardly any features right. No wonder extensive excavations into the cellars of the Piccadilly Theatre were required: here was a show which plumbed new depths with fabulous unprecedented consistency, maintained over almost three hours. The problem with Fritz Lang's 1920s expressionist masterpiece / boring old silent film (delete according to taste) is that its apocalyptic nightmare is so dated: from H. G. Wells to George Orwell, all predictive fiction says more about the age in which it was written. We all know that, rather than (as Lang had it) reducing us to mindless automatons operating machines all day long, the beckoning future now offers quite the opposite: self-reliant computers whirring away, while the masses are sedated by lesbian movies on the PornoSat video monitor. The only mindless automatons will be the ones grinding out British techno-musicals.

American musicals, even the flops, are by Kander and Ebb, Stephen Sondheim, Hal Prince, Neil Simon. British musicals are a series of creative blind dates kinkier than anything dreamt up by the most depraved back-bench MP. Anything goes: a couple of years ago, there were rumours of *Edward and Mrs Simpson – The Musical* with Tom Jones in the title role. 'Which one?' you're probably wondering. All these shows soon realized they'd bought themselves a one-way ticket on the oblivion express. I expect, if you were to talk to the government of Nauru or the thousands of devout Catholics who contributed their savings to *Bernadette*, that, with the benefit of hindsight, they'd quite like to have been closed down prematurely by the High Court. Perhaps, fresh from his *Maxwell* triumph, the Attorney-General Sir Nicholas Lyell, should have set himself up as a latter-day Lord Chamberlain, protecting London theatregoers from affronts to public decency and protecting would-be musical impresarios from themselves.

But still the dance goes on . . . And every few months another British musical prepares to sink quite as easily as Robert Maxwell. 'What went wrong with *Peg*,' recalls its director Ian Judge, 'was that the producer was a millionaire and we all got presents every day at rehearsal. All the chaps got baskets of fruit and all the ladies got bouquets, we had a first night party on the Orient Express, there was money for days – but no book. The whole reason for the show was that it had to open on his mother's 80th birthday. When we said "But we have to rewrite the book and do it somewhere else before we come into London", he would say, "No, no, she'll be very upset." Anyway, the old bat didn't come, and we went down the toilet.'

The Depilators

As Andrew Lloyd Webber pointed out to me, in real terms the biggest advance ever was for Irving Berlin's *Mr President*. And, if you're saying, 'Mister *Who?*', well, you can probably figure out what happened to it. An advance isn't much more than a *promise* to purchase – so, even though by 12 July 1993, *Sunset Boulevard* had cost £3 million and stacked up an advance of £4 million, that doesn't mean you're a pre-sold hit. For most of us at the Adelphi that Monday evening at seven – backers, critics, schmoozers, minor celebrities, genuine celebrities – there's still a tingle about a big West End first night that seems the very essence of theatre. The subsidized boys at the Barbican and across the river make much of 'the right to fail', but, in reality, good or bad, most of their shows just complete their allotted slots in those incomprehensible repertory timetables, safely protected by the corporate umbrella of the RSC or NT logo – and these days, even more perversely, if anything smells like a hit they put it in the 28-seat studio space so no one can get it: boffo smash or colossal floperoo, who can tell? If you want to exercise the right to fail, do a musical.

So, at *Sunset Boulevard*, the buzz was one of anticipation: are we in on the ground floor of the next mega-hit? Is that first big theme in the overture going to be Lloyd Webber's next 'Memory', the tune that haunts our elevator rides for the next 15 years? Is this the hot ticket far-flung cousins from New Zealand will pester us for when they come over here – even though, by then, the same damn production with the same damn poster will be playing Toronto, Tokyo, Budapest, even Wellington? Musicals are mad, but even those who quibbled about the feminine rhymes in Act Two, Scene Three knew, at the first night of *Phantom* and *Miss Saigon*, that we were witnessing the launch of a hit.

And the other shows? 'If it's a real disaster, I think you wait till the opening night,' says Bill Kenwright, producer of *Blood Brothers* but also a lot else he'd prefer to forget. 'But, I promise you, you do know on the opening night.'

'A few times I have sniffed it during the technicals and the first previews,' says Cameron Mackintosh. 'And I get that awful knot in my stomach knowing that, whatever I do, the iceberg's cut too big a hole in the hull.' You'll forgive him the seafaring analogy: after *Cats*, *Les Miz*, *Phantom* and *Miss Saigon*, he produced *Moby Dick*, which, despite the Mackintosh office's confident assertion that the show 'was keeping its head above water', sank with all hands.

'So I retreat to the bar,' continues Mackintosh, 'and pray that it will be a mega-disaster so I can pull it off straight away. The worst thing to have in the theatre is a near success.'

'Theatre,' sighs Robert Fox, producer of *Chess* and *Anything Goes*, 'is everybody's second business. Whoever you meet, they say, "Why don't you find another *Miss Saigon*? Why didn't you think of *Cats*?" They've always got the answer. It's so obvious from the outside: if *they* can do it, why can't *we*?'

The German producer of *Starlight Express* thought he could do it, and, as Mackintosh had done with *Les Miz*, he persuaded the Royal Shakespeare Company to go along for the ride. So, in 1988, I went to Stratford to see an early preview of the RSC's *Carrie*. 'Well, it's not *that* bad. It's fixable,' an American producer said to me afterwards. 'But the first thing you'd have to do is sack the director.' I pointed out to him that as the man in question, Terry Hands, was also the Artistic Director of the RSC this was about the one thing you could absolutely guarantee would *not* happen. 'Oh, yeah,' he said. 'I'd forgotten they've got that weird system here.'

In Britain, regardless of its deficiencies when it comes to *Carrie*, the 'weird system' of director-driven subsidized theatre is seen as the norm – or, anyway, the ideal. So, in the serious newspapers, even when West End commercial drama is under discussion, the producer is rarely mentioned, whether by oversight or the vague feeling that somehow it's distasteful. Their moment comes only when disaster strikes, as it did in 1990 for Harold Fielding. *Someone Like You* had everything wrong with it, from its colourless title and Civil War setting to its unlikely writing team of Fay Weldon, Petula Clark and Dee Shipman. Its folding was not unexpected but its suddenness, as brutal as Broadway, was: no euphemistic closing notices ('Must end in three weeks prior to national tour!'), just padlocks on the theatre doors front and back, equally surprising to both cast and audience. Fielding had overstretched himself after his epic flop *Ziegfeld*; his company had gone bust, and the liquidators had moved in. His obsession with Ziegfeld was always something of a vanity: Britain's greatest showman salutes America's greatest showman. Now the parallels were even closer: Fielding had followed his predecessor into bankruptcy. The stars, authors, stagers emerged unscathed; the buck, or rather lack of them, stopped with Fielding.

*

When *Ziegfeld* opened in 1988, most of us discussed it in terms of 'Ned Sherrin's and Alistair Beaton's new show' or 'Joe Layton's production', even though the only person who genuinely merited that proprietorial apostrophe was Fielding. Critics are, perhaps unsurprisingly, reluctant to admit to the notion of a producer's theatre. Until relatively recently, *Plays and Players*, which prides itself on being a journal of theatrical record, didn't even include the name of the producer among its exhaustive production credits (down to 'fight sequence consultant'). At British awards ceremonies, unlike the Broadway Tonys, only the authors get to collect the Best Play and Best Musical trophies; the producers are kept firmly offstage, as if they're not deemed to be part of the 'creative team'. It's a common misconception: the producer is the guy who relieves the artistic types of the need to worry about anything as vulgar as money, and then, having fulfilled his sordid but sadly necessary function, keeps out of the way.

In other words, any guy can be a producer as long as he can lay his mitts on the folding stuff. Alfred Bloomingdale, of the famous department store, thought this was the case and decided to mount his own musical, *Allah Be Praised*! 'What do you think?' he asked Cy Howard after the Boston try-out. 'Al,' said Howard, 'close the show and keep the store open nights.' If only EPI Products had been given similar advice. EPI Products are three sisters called Krok – Arlene, Sharon and Loren – who make the revolutionary Epilady Hair Removal Device, as well as EpiSmile, EpiPed and EpiSsentia Skin Care. In 1989, they decided to produce a Broadway musical, *Meet Me in St Louis*.

The original 1946 film is often mocked as a Vincente Minnelli chocolate box, but it was gritty *cinéma-verité* compared with the Kroks' version. Vast quantities of Epilady, EpiSmile, EpiPed and EpiSsentia had been applied to the book and score and staging to ensure they had the most scrupulously depilated musical ever seen. The effect on the audience was the equivalent of an EpiDural. The result was an EpiCflop. It was never entirely clear why the hair-removers went into showbusiness, but, as the failure of *Meet Me in St Louis* underlined, it's far harder to revolutionize the American theatre than American follicle-tweaking habits.

It's easier to spot who can't cut it than to assess accurately those who can. But wipe out every Michael Codron production from the record books, and you'd be depriving British theatre of much Beckett, Pinter, Stoppard, Frayn and a lot more. Remove Kermit Bloomgarden and there's no *Death of a Salesman*, *The Crucible*, *A View from the Bridge*. Maybe Arthur Miller's plays would still have got on, but whether they'd have done so in stageable shape or whether they'd have found an audience is another matter.

Today, Miller blames his failures of recent years on the commercial values of the American theatre: London still has plays, he says; New York only has 'shows'. But the sad truth is that none of the plays he's written since is as good as the ones he wrote during his partnership with Bloomgarden. Coincidence? I don't think so. In the heyday of the Broadway theatre, it was accepted that the most important relationship was that between the author and his producer.

If you follow that line, you can produce a parallel history of theatre often more revealing than the theories preferred by scholars. We usually trace the development of musicals as a progress from star vehicle ('Al Jolson in *Sinbad*') through author power ('Lerner and Loewe's *My Fair Lady*') to the era of the superstager ('Michael Bennett's *Chorus Line*'). But where does that leave, say, David Merrick? His catalogue contains what could be read as examples of all three: Carol Channing in *Hello Dolly!*, Bacharach and David's *Promises, Promises*, Gower Champion's *42nd Street*. Yet, above all else, they're essentially Merrick musicals.

Similarly, Britain might be guilty of overstating Andrew Lloyd Webber's composer clout. Why are *Starlight Express* (which didn't recoup on Broadway) and *Aspects of Love* (likewise) not hits on the same mega-scale as *Cats* and *Phantom*? Perhaps because the latter pair, unlike the former, were produced by Cameron Mackintosh, who's also responsible for *Les Miz* and *Miss Saigon*. The Mackintosh empire is the sort of commercial operation Broadway's supposed to be about, yet never has been: the same handful of posters advertising the same handful of shows on every railway platform in the world.

For American showfolk, the posters are painful, especially the upstart Brit's splendid isolation above the title: 'Cameron Mackintosh presents *Miss Saigon*.' In New York today, the list of producers required to finance one Broadway show is as long as a football team, though far less cohesive. First, it was multiple producers, then corporate producers – the record companies, the movie people, and pretty soon you're reaching for the Epilady. Because Mackintosh's four long-runners are all sell-out hits, many champions of the subsidized theatre, who you'd have thought would have more pressing demands on their time, like to deride the impresario and his *confrères* as mere crowd-pleasers. It's true the theatre has always had cynical managers like Abe Erlanger, producer of *Rebecca of Sunnybrook Farm* and *Pollyanna,* who (according to P. G. Wodehouse) never accepted a play unless it first met with the approval of a 12 year-old boy who accompanied him to every audition and whom Erlanger claimed had exactly the intelligence of the average American theatregoer. Yet most great producers are the opposite: they have an almost touching naïveté about them. *They* like a show, so perhaps other people will. At the end of *Ziegfeld*'s second first night, after a muted ovation, Fielding stood at the back of the stalls, a small man who didn't come much past thigh height next to his leggy showgirls, looking at the audience with that odd expression he always has, a mixture of eagerness, enquiry and puzzlement, as if to say, 'I did this for you; what don't you like about it?'

The *second* first night. *Ziegfeld* was Fielding's show: his idea, his kind of subject, told in his lavish, opulent style. The rest of 'em were just hired hands, as he demonstrated within weeks of its shaky opening by replacing the director/choreographer, the librettists and the star, Len Cariou – Broadway's leading leading man, star of *Applause, A Little Night Music* and *Sweeney Todd* but dismissed by Fielding with the appalling slur, 'He's really a Shakespearean actor.' He kept cutting the book scenes, insisting that 'my audience' didn't want or need that sort of thing; he brought in Tommy Steele, Wendy Toye and others to perform emergency surgery; he replaced Cariou with Topol, an Israeli unable to master the American accent and who therefore wore a pop-up yellow rose in his buttonhole which popped up when he was speaking as Ziegfeld and collapsed when he was speaking as Topol the narrator. Fielding changed everything except the frocks, which he was stuck with, and then invited the critics back for the world première, take two. It didn't save the show but it ensured that *Ziegfeld* went down the way it had started – as a Fielding folly.

He said he'd be back, but don't hold your breath. As Ziegfeld went, so did his British contemporary, the pre-eminent West End producer of the thirties:

> You're The Top!
> You're a brontosaurus
> You're The Top!
> You're a Cochran chorus . . .

Today, C. B. Cochran's name is still synonymous with pre-war musicals and revue, but it was his misfortune to outlive that era into a more dramatically demanding theatre and see the Cochran chorus wind up as extinct as the brontosaurus. He dismissed the notion of a musicalized *Pygmalion* as 'frightful', he picked old-fashioned subjects of which fewer and fewer ever took the stage and, when he died in 1951, the man who'd made millions left the footling sum of £22,921 10s 6d. 'Any fool can save money,' he once said. 'It takes a wise man to know how to spend it.' But producers are like crap-shooters: they can never quit when they're on a roll. Jed Harris, the maverick boy wonder so loathed that he was the direct inspiration for both Disney's Big Bad Wolf and Olivier's Richard III, had at the age of 28 four of the biggest hits on Broadway and later produced *The Front Page* and *Our Town*. But, by the time of his death in 1979, he was reduced to dire poverty.

*

Almost all producing careers end in failure. Showfolk lionize the likes of David Merrick and marvel at his exploits – how, when Shubert Alley wiseacres were predicting the demise of *42nd Street* after seven years, Merrick pushed curtain-up back to 8.15pm, adopted the slogan 'Broadway's *Latest* Hit!' and picked up enough trade turned away from the sell-out *Phantom* across the street to restore the show to profit. For the next year, the producer's leering face beckoned from atop Times Square: 'David Merrick,' pledged the poster, 'is holding the curtain for you!' It looked like Igor ushering you in to Castle Frankenstein. By then, for most people, Merrick was a figure from beyond the grave. 'Well, I don't really like to criticize him,' Joseph Stein said to me. 'I mean, I'm not sure if he's really alive still . . .' The sentence tailed away, as it occurred to Stein that even death might not deflect Merrick from the ruthlessness with which he settles even the most trivial score. By the late eighties, a stroke had removed him from public life. But the legend endured. When the stroke struck, Merrick was in the process of divorcing his wife. Suddenly, he was at her mercy. After the initial hospital treatment, she had him moved to the Rusk Rehabilitation Center at First Avenue and 34th Street. Unable to speak, unable to walk, but determined to recover control of his affairs, Merrick bided his time and then, briefly left unattended, sprang himself from the hospital: he drove his wheelchair down the corridor and out onto First Avenue, steered himself six blocks in savage beating rain, ducked into a Korean noodle factory on Second and, soaked and exhausted, scribbled on a piece of paper the name of Mort Mitosky, a friend and lawyer.

Showmen, we call them. And, in the end, the man becomes the show, the only one left. Not long before his death in 1975, P. G. Wodehouse, reading in the paper about a couple of Broadway stinkers that had closed in weeks losing hundreds of thousands of dollars, added a thankful PS to his usual Christmas greeting to Ira Gershwin: 'Ira, we are well out of this.' Back in the twenties, Plum and Ira and George and Guy Bolton had teamed up for *Oh, Kay!*, a quintessential piece of musical comedy fluff about some fellow living out at a mythical Long Island resort called Beachampton who falls in love with a doll who's posing as a cook in his house so she can keep an eye on the hooch which her brother, a bootlegging earl, has smuggled into the country from his yacht . . . You get the idea. The whole thing was cooked up in ten minutes, and the show's production schedule was unaffected even by Ira's appendectomy. While he was recovering, his friend Howard Dietz was co-opted as emergency lyricist and casually ad-libbed some potential song titles, including that of the big ballad, 'Someone To Watch Over Me'. The show recouped its investment in three months, ran a further four and a half at the Imperial, and then cleaned up on tour for a couple of years.

That was 1926. In eloquent contrast, the 1990 revival was in development for longer than the original's entire run, and its official number of 'previews' would have constituted half a respectable Broadway engagement in the old days. I say 'official number' because, for a few weeks, most of the previews were private showings for David Merrick. Throughout October, Merrick's display ads and *The New York Times* theatre listings announced 'Today's performances times'. But every evening the staff at the Richard Rodgers Theatre turned away any customers who showed up. Inside, the cast played eight shows a week on full salary to an empty house – empty, that is, except for Merrick in a throne-sized wing chair specially placed in the centre aisle.

Finally, Merrick was satisfied, and *Oh, Kay!* began previews proper, its opening postponed till November. The reviews, when they arrived, were surprisingly generous: critics are sentimental about the last showman. But Frank Rich in *The New York Times* was scathing. Within days, Merrick acted. The Monday after the first night, I arrived in Manhattan from the wilds of northern New England and was surprised to find that, everywhere I went, folks kept trying to swipe my copy of the *Times*. 'Where d'you buy that?' they'd demand to know.

'Up north,' I'd say.

'You've got the national edition? Here, lemme see.'

Inside the arts section was a huge heart-shaped ad containing two negative quotes from Friday's paper, one from Rich's devastating pan, the other from Alex Witchel's likeably trashy stage gossip column: 'Things are not as OK at David Merrick's *Oh, Kay!* as at least one cast member would like.' (This was a reference to Mark Kenneth Smalz, on whose behalf Equity was taking Merrick to arbitration for denying the actor his curtain call, one of those wrangles which seemed set to run longer than the show and in the end probably cost as much.) Underneath these non-endorsements, the producer signed off: 'At last, people are holding hands in the theatre again! . . . To Frank and Alex – all my love, David Merrick.'

Merrick's good-humoured Valentine had revealed that Rich and Miss Witchel were dating: the magisterial demolitions of his show had been made by a pair of canoodling lovebirds. When Rich saw the ad in the first edition, he demanded it be pulled, and the *Times* agreed: they don't mind their writers being hated and feared, but they won't let you snigger at them. The story was picked up by other media – which was Merrick's objective all along. Faced with Rich's review of *Oh, Kay!*, most producers would have closed the show immediately. But Merrick thought he had a crowd-pleaser and that, if he could get enough of the crowd to gamble on a ticket, he'd pull through. The publicity stunts had worked before: this is the man who scoured the phone book, found namesakes of critics like Howard Taubman and Walter Kerr, bussed them in to see *Subways Are for Sleeping* and then plastered their quotes all over the press advertisements.

The difference is that, back in 1961, the gimmick lit up the box office. In 1990, Merrick's 'heart' attack did nothing for *Oh, Kay!* Merrick was supposed to epitomise the demonic savagery of commercial theatre, but there was something almost quaintly innocent about both the show and the off-stage behaviour. All around him, the Brit blockbusters loomed, towering anonymous cash-cows which raked in the loot without any need for 'look at me!' personality producer's gimmicks. When Merrick's in charge, there's no knowing which way he'll jump. In the sixties, he closed *Breakfast at Tiffany's*, the pioneer super-flop, before it opened, issuing a public apology to New York theatregoers for insulting them by ever peddling such sub-standard fare. But, with *Oh, Kay!*, he couldn't let go. The show closed on 5 January 1991 after just two months – but Merrick insisted it was just a 'winter hiatus'. He re-opened it in April, at a new theatre, the Lunt-Fontanne: it barely lasted the week.

We're so awed by Merrick's Machiavellian scheming that, at first, we assumed the closure was part of some master plan. There was talk that

Merrick, with another divorce in mind, was deliberately trying to haemorrhage as much dough as possible on the show. But producer's cynicism isn't that sophisticated. If you ask theatre professionals who was the best Dolly of all, they'll say Bibi Osterwald, an understudy for Betty Grable and most of her predecessors (Martha Raye, Ginger Rogers) who finally got a shot at the role herself. Unfortunately, she did nothing at the box office. So Merrick, with no white gals left, brought in Pearl Bailey and an all-black cast. There's no reason why *Hello, Dolly!* should be all-black – it's not a black show, it has no black sensibility – but the novelty paid off. It's a measure of Broadway's deterioration over the next 20 years that, for *Oh, Kay!*, Merrick *started* with an all-black cast: again, it's not a black show, it has no black sensibility – but the gimmicks you'd once resort to to stave off long-run fatigue were now needed up front. The time and energy he expended on retooling this piece of Jazz Age candy-floss for the nineties would have struck Wodehouse, Bolton and the Gershwins as ridiculous. It symbolized contemporary Broadway: talented men waste years trying to fake what used to come naturally. The youthful naïveté and energy of *Oh, Kay!* is irresistible, a reminder of the virtues of musical comedy in the days when nobody took it seriously. But, if you try to invent 'youthful energy', you end up with an inanely grinning Barbie doll: you can move her into an appealing pose, but the minute you turn your back she falls down. Merrick used all the techniques, all the flim-flam he'd lavished on *42nd Street*, but *Oh, Kay!* was different in one crucial respect: there was no show.

*

Merrick was the last of the line, a final defiant follicle resisting the tide of Epilady. Broadway has passed into the hands of the four-wallers – the theatre owners, the Shuberts, the Nederlanders and Jujamcyn – and hordes of co-co-co-co-co-co-co-producers, none of whom is big enough to start a show on his own. Whatever you think of his shows, the repository of Broadway values is Cameron Mackintosh: a lone producer whose most important relationship is with his writers. Of Boublil and Schonberg, his authors on *Les Miz, Saigon* and *Martin Guerre*, he says, 'We never go ahead with anything unless all three of us agree.' And you can see it on stage: he produces the shows those guys write; he's not engaged in some ramshackle razzle-dazzle sleight-of-hand operation.

'Cameron is really much more of an old-fashioned producer,' says Andrew Lloyd Webber, 'in that he has strong creative views. Sometimes

I don't share them but he has strong views on practically everything.'

True. But he never loses sight of the show he started out to produce. To follow *Grand Hotel*'s try-out in 1989, with the authors banned from the theatre and Peter Stone brought in to beef up the book and Maury Yeston to provide extra songs, is to glimpse a ceremonial re-enactment of some ancient folk ritual whose original purpose has been lost in the mists of time. Can you imagine, a month before *Martin Guerre* opened, Mackintosh banning Boublil and Schonberg from the theatre and calling in Lloyd Webber? Most of the fellows on Broadway these days are playing at being producer: they sack the assistant choreographer because it's the sort of thing a producer does.

He's relaxed, as he can afford to be. In August 1990, Actors' Equity announced that Jonathan Pryce would not be permitted to re-create his role in the Broadway production of *Miss Saigon* because, as a Eurasian role, it should be played by an Asian-American (I hope I've got the hyphen right); the casting of Pryce was racist. Instead of spending his time buried away stitching up some squalid compromise, Mackintosh spent most of the following day at Sadler's Wells with a dozen young students, watching presentations of the shows they'd been working on with Stephen Sondheim, first holder of Oxford University's Cameron Mackintosh Chair in Contemporary Theatre. Making small talk during an intermission, I asked whether he'd caught the Sondheim version of Aristophanes' *The Frogs* playing in West London.

'Certainly not,' he said. 'It's a racist production. The Frogs aren't played by real Frenchmen.'

'You've got $26 million,' Colleen Dewhurst, Equity's President, told Mackintosh. 'What do you care who plays the part?' There speaks one of America's most distinguished actresses: hey, acting; what's the big deal? But he did care. Because, in the end, the freedom to produce is the only artistic freedom that matters.

*

'People think it's pretty easy to be an impresario,' said Harold Fielding. 'Believe me, it ain't. It ain't easy at all.'

Ziegfeld's relaunch was a bizarre occasion for regular first nighters – we deadbeats on the aisle plus the usual minor celebrities – forced for once to sit next to, God forbid, members of the despised coach parties whose champion Fielding had been since *Charlie Girl* 30 years ago. The show failed not because he tried to give 'em what they wanted but because he tried to give 'em what *he* wanted. Producers succeed when their taste happens to coincide with the public's; when the popular mood changes, few manage to adapt. All they can do is hope to stay in business until the public swings back to them, as happened to Merrick, after a decade of flops, with *42nd Street*. But, for all of them, for Merrick and Fielding and one day Mackintosh, too, the final curtain falls prematurely. Fielding's shows were schlock, but they were the sort of schlock he liked, as near as any musicals get to being the personal expression of one man's taste. Producing a musical, says Michael (*Metropolis*) White, is like trying to control a runaway horse. Today, we have runaway horses designed by committee – vast agglomerations above the title, the shifting interests of money-raisers, theatre owners, provincial tour bookers. I picture Harold Fielding, old and stooped, dwarfed by the silly beads and feathers of his chorines, and I think of what our theatre has lost.

ix

The Maximalist

'Andrew Lloyd Webber's music is everywhere,' sniffed Malcolm Williamson, Master of the Queen's Musick, in 1992, 'but then so is Aids.' He subsequently apologized – at least to people with Aids. On the whole, Aids gets a better press. As a spelling, 'Musick' pretty well sums up the feelings not just of critics but also of Broadway insiders, all those Kern/Gershwin/Rodgers/Bernstein/Loesser/Styne/Sondheim fans who've watched aghast as he's inherited by default. 'Why,' Lloyd Webber once asked Alan Jay Lerner, 'do people take an instant dislike to me?' 'It saves time,' said Lerner.

Well, that's the way Alan told it. Back in the days when he was writing *My Fair Lady* and *Gigi*, that sort of tart wit would have been in the script. But by 1986, when Lloyd Webber briefly turned to Lerner for help with *Phantom of the Opera*, musicals had become earnest and overwrought and portentous, and the only snappy gags were told backstage – usually at the composer's expense. In his presence, they're more tactful. 'I asked a famous conductor about minimalism,' Lloyd Webber once told me, 'and he said, "I'm sorry, Andrew. There's no point explaining minimalism to you. You're a maximalist."'

Maximum volume, maximum technology, maximum hype, maximum money . . . By 1993, *Cats'* net profits in North America alone topped $100 million, and its take-home tune, 'Memory' (with Trevor Nunn's lyric based on T. S. Eliot), was even more ubiquitous than Williamson could have imagined: there's a clock tower in San Diego that plays it; and, in the trial of football hero and alleged double murderer O. J. Simpson, what was it the microphones picked up when the defendant finally broke his long silence? O. J. was humming and softly singing to himself . . .

> Midnight
> Not a sound from the pavement . . .

It reminds him of his children, he said. Bloody hell, you can't even turn on the O. J. trial to get away from Lloyd Webber.

Memories are made of this. Charles Hart, lyricist of *Aspects of Love*, once suggested a song title to Lloyd Webber: 'You Can't Live On Memories'.

Lloyd Webber looked up and said: 'Trevor Nunn does.'

I was told a while back that Lloyd Webber had earned more not only than poor Malcolm Williamson but all other British composers in history put together. It may or may not be true, and heaven knows how you'd compute such a statistic, but it sounds so plausible as to be almost unremarkable. And, as the shows have swollen, the critical dismissals have grown ever terser: Ken Bloom's *Musical Theatre Companion* devotes the same three words to *Evita* and *Cats* – 'sound and fury'; *The New Yorker*'s listings section wearily maintained week after week that *Starlight Express* was 'a bore on roller-skates'.

Roller-skates, cat costumes, crashing chandeliers: when you think of Lloyd Webber, it's not always the music that springs to mind – no matter how hard he tries. 'Did you see that piece in *Variety*?' he sighed at the time of *Aspects of Love* (1989). ' "You Can't Out-hype Andrew." What do they mean? We haven't advertised anywhere. It's *Miss Saigon* clogging up the bus sides.' But, by *Aspects*, it was, as Cameron Mackintosh puts it, 'the hype hyping the hype'. *Aspects* recouped before it opened, but with Lloyd Webber you take that for granted. A substantial proportion of the London and New York theatre communities depends for its living on his shows, and the pressure all around is for everything to get bigger and more expensive. Fifteen years ago, Dewynter's, the artwork designers, was a one-man operation; today, mainly because of Lloyd Webber's commissions, they occupy two floors of prime office space high atop Leicester Square. Naturally, for *Aspects*, they'd come up with a glamorous front-of-house design, and Lloyd Webber was obliged to explain that the show's needs were more modest. This, he said, was a five-character romance, eschewing deafening synthesized sound for a 14-piece line-up, the core of which is a string quartet. 'Intimate, intimate, it's got to be intimate,' he impressed on me at dinner not long before opening.

'Yeah, intimate,' echoed his lyricist Don Black.

The thing about Lloyd Webber is that he talks a lot of bunk which, at the time, is apparently heartfelt, but which he'll cheerfully contradict a few weeks later. By the opening of *Sunset Boulevard* (1993), the maximalist was back in town. Norma Desmond may have been ready for her close-up now, Mr De Mille, but, in John Napier's huge stairway-to-paradise recreation of her Hollywood mansion, she was a tiny stick figure lost in the scenery. The Lloyd Webber line now is that people don't want small musicals, they want big shows; the big shows are the ones that fill theatres around the world.

And so Lloyd Webber's company does a deal in Germany whereby a huge new theatre is built to house *Sunset* and any future Lloyd Webber properties. And the critics fret because, according to the inverted snobbery that goes with the job, in drama small is beautiful. I've done a bit of this myself. When *Phantom of the Opera* opened in October 1986, I ranted impotently about how the composer should resume his partnership with Don Black, lyricist of *Tell Me on a Sunday* (1980), and, instead of cats and trains, apply his talents to more naturalistic subjects. Since then, he's written *Aspects* and *Sunset*, both people shows, both with Black. It would be flattering to think he'd done so at my suggestion, but it's obvious to anyone that Lloyd Webber' success in the backwater of British musicals is so unprecedented that he can only pace himself, reaching his own conclusions about where he – and, therefore, musical theatre – ought to be heading. For good or ill, *Cats*, *Starlight*, *Phantom* and *Aspects* are works *he* originated, dominated in every department by his personality.

'That's why, since *The Odessa File*, I haven't composed for the cinema,' he says. 'I can't write for somebody else's projects.'

*

He is vulnerable now – a classic example of imperial overstretch. Watching tired businessmen fidget through *Aspects of Love* in 1989, one of his collaborators said to me: 'With *Starlight Express*, Andrew showed he was critic-proof. With *Aspects*, he's out to show he's audience-proof.' With *Sunset Boulevard*, he had to demonstrate he's lawyer-proof. There was a discreet pay-off and a carefully worded back-of-the-book credit to original lyricist Amy Powers (dumped before the London opening); a million bucks to Patti LuPone (dumped for Broadway); and even more to Faye Dunaway (dumped for Los Angeles). If, as in the Billy Wilder film, the lifeless body of the author is found floating face down in the swimming pool, there's now an endless procession of leading ladies descending that fabulous *Sunset* staircase: 'Ready for my out-of-court settlement now, Mr De Mille.'

But the casting is only the symptom, not the cause, of *Sunset*'s difficulties. In what happened between the Sydmonton try-out and the New York opening, all the struggles between old Broadway and England's bloated musical maximalist come into peculiarly sharp focus. From the start, the story of the young screenwriter ensnared by a forgotten star of silent pictures was odd territory for Lloyd Webber. Unlike most American writers, he's never been very interested by showbizzy backstage fables, preferring to concentrate on all the 'God, what an awful idea for a musical!' ideas. Lloyd Webber is routinely derided as a cynical purveyor of commercial schlock to the bridge' n' tunnel crowd, but okay, if you did want to manufacture a hit, what would you pick? *42nd Street* or a bunch of twee T. S. Eliot poems staged as a Eurodisco pop video? *City of Angels* or Thomas the Tank Engine on roller skates? Hey, why didn't I think of *that*? At least, Lloyd Webber's got rich from all the surefire money-losers. To look at recent Broadway offerings – *The Will Rogers Follies, Dreamgirls, Barnum, They're Playing Our Song, Chorus Line* – you'd be forgiven for thinking that, to American dramatists, there's no business *but* show business. Even *Sunday in the Park with George* is only *The Jolson Story* in pointillist drag.

Yet here we are on *Sunset Boulevard*: Lloyd Webber yoked to a proven hit title. 'It's not the subject, it's the treatment,' he likes to say. So what have he and his co-authors, Don ('Born Free') Black and Christopher (*Les Liaisons Dangereuses*) Hampton, done to it? Well, as Billy Wilder enjoyed saying in the run-up to the 1993 West End première, 'The boys hit on a great idea: they didn't change a thing.'

In musical theatre, I'm not sure that's a compliment. For one thing, if you turn a talking picture about a silent screen star into a stage musical about a silent screen star, you're bound to lose a few ironies – especially as Wilder cast a genuine silent star in the role and then gave her, a woman who despises what words have done to movies, all the best words in the movie: 'I *am* big. It's the pictures that got small', etc. At the Minskoff, *Sunset Boulevard* is bigger than ever, but the pictures have got real small. The authors have kept the subject cinematic yet are denied the cinematic effects it needs. Where Wilder gave us Gloria Swanson in mesmeric close-ups, Trevor Nunn's staging and John Napier's gilt-dripping Gothic monster set frequently push Norma Desmond upstage, making her smaller than life.

And who needs a small Norma Desmond? In 1950, Billy Wilder could have cast, say, Joan Crawford, and the film would have worked nicely enough. But, with Swanson, you're already halfway there: you don't have to persuade the audience that she's a faded star from a lost era, because she *is*. The self-disgust William Holden's hack on the make feels as he succumbs to Swanson's grotesque cartoon of a woman is easily communicated: it's still weird just to see the two of them in the same frame. There was none of that with Patti LuPone in London. Casting Swanson, you get Norma Desmond fully formed – and true: a necessary corrective to Wilder's cynicism. Casting Miss LuPone, you just get someone who does musicals.

If you're searching for the Gloria Swanson figure in the new *Sunset*, look no further than Lloyd Webber himself – and not just because he's prone to weird hand movements and mad stares. Here is a man who, as much as any silent screen goddess, believes that gestures, images and music are a more sophisticated form of storytelling than mere talk. The only show he's ever composed in which people *talk* was *Jeeves* (1974, written with Alan Ayckbourn); it was also his only certifiable failure. 'I'm fond of *Jeeves*,' he later said to me, 'but I did learn that, frankly, the book musical, in the sense of dialogue interrupting the musical line, is not for me. Whether you like it or not, this *is* opera.'

It's an assertion that doesn't cut much ice with the highbrow crowd, but Lloyd Webber can claim the mantle of Verdi and Puccini more plausibly than, say, Philip Glass, if only in scale and form – and priorities. 'We are collaborative animals,' he concedes. 'I do, however, like to control what's done with my scores. The composer must dictate the evening because you are, in the end, the dramatist. It's marvellous if you've got a director like Trevor Nunn to argue with at a later stage, but Trevor has changed practically nothing; he's accepted completely the idea of a musical structure you don't tamper with.'

In a milieu where Gershwin, Weill, Bernstein and Sondheim have had their scores shredded by the whims of try-out audiences in New Haven, the paramountcy of the composer is a revolutionary concept. 'We've moved on. You can't say, "We're in trouble, Andrew, so back to the flat, come up with a big Act II belter, and whack it in." ' Freed from the crazy merry-go-round of rewrites, Lloyd Webber is the first major show composer since Weill with time to orchestrate his own scores. 'We are,' he emphasizes again, his eyes gleaming demonically, 'back into opera.'

What could Broadway do? Too late to reach for the garlic and crucifix and expel him from the sacred precincts of musical comedy. Even his beloved Richard Rodgers, he feels, never quite fulfilled his potential because he never attempted a 'sung-through' piece, an astonishing statement to those who can't imagine how the tension of the auction scene in *Oklahoma!*, where Curly and Jud bid for Laurey's picnic hamper, would be improved by being musicalized. And I suspect that Lloyd Webber only hit upon the form because his first collaborator, Tim Rice, was more interested in having hit records than in writing dialogue scenes.

But, for better or worse, this is the revolution Lloyd Webber has wrought: musicals are now 'sung through'. 'They call these Lloyd Webber things "through-composed",' Arthur Laurents told me. 'They're not through-composed – they're sung . . . *incessantly*. But that's not the same thing.' Kurt Weill used to say that American audiences didn't want 'Would you like a cup of coffee?' set to music. In other words, in a musical, you have to justify the music. In *Aspects of Love*, no-one sings 'Would you like a cup of coffee?' but they come pretty close:

> *Shall I make* [*pause*] some coffee?
> One cup of fresh coffee . . .

Later:

> Will croissants and fresh coffee do?

And:

> An espresso? Or cappuccino?

Later still:

> Get our guest an armagnac . . .

Not to mention:

> A glass of house white for me . . .

And:

> Another armagnac . . .

Aspects merits a place in theatrical history if only as the first show where more drinks are ordered in the libretto than at intermission. No *musical* distinction is made between conversational trivialities and big character soliloquies: banal chit-chat and key moments of emotional stress are carried by the same melodic phrase, effectively according them the same weight. The precise tension of a musical – the raising of the stakes, as dialogue turns to underscored speech, then to verse, then to chorus – has simply been abolished. Every time I've seen *Aspects*, the audience has responded most to the handful of spoken lines, laughing at . . .

> Do you dance with women of your *own* age?

. . . hushed at . . .

> Don't be too long, Alex.

I don't think these lines are meant to be that significant. It's just that they provide a respite from an otherwise unrelenting, swamping score.

'It does get a bit uncomfortable at times,' says Don Black, 'when you're singing information. Of course, audiences have gotten used to it, so I've had to get used to it. And if for 20 minutes it's all "My name is this and your name is that", all very nice and pleasant, and then suddenly a tune comes out that's got a title and could obviously work out of context, it's like the sun coming up, it's a wonderful goose-bumpy moment.'

Aspects has 'Anything But Lonely', 'Seeing Is Believing' and the ubiquitous 'Love Changes Everything': all that's different, Black seems to be saying, is that we now lead into them with sung rather than spoken passages. But it goes beyond that. When everything's sung, the relationship between music and lyrics loosens. In a conventional musical, the lyricist's job is not the same as the book writer's: he can't merely set dialogue to music or be descriptive or soliloquize; he has to find a lyric idea that vindicates the move into song. Whether you think Jule Styne is a better composer than Verdi is up to you; but it's not difficult to argue that, in the relationship between the elements and in the fusion of music and lyrics, the American musical is formally more sophisticated, more discriminating, than opera. On BBC Radio's *Start the Week*, Lloyd Webber's remarks about book shows and dialogue were underlined by an indulgent chortle from the host (and screenwriter of *Jesus Christ Superstar*) Melvyn Bragg: 'Cue for a song, you mean?'

But, in shows like *Phantom* and *Aspects*, it's not only the song cues that have disappeared, but also the songs. Lloyd Webber is fond of 'Some Enchanted Evening', but, in a Lloyd Webber show, 'Some Enchanted Evening' would be reprised 15 minutes later as 'May I use the bathroom?'

Which begs the question: if he's Rodgers, who's Hammerstein? Tim Rice developed a dramatic, narrative style all his own. But, although 'I Don't Know How To Love Him' and certain others are superbly crafted, he is not essentially a colloquial lyric-writer. He avoids the rhythms of everyday speech and writes dense, allusive, often deliberately inelegant lyrics. But he also deflected the pomposity of the music: he was Eric Morecambe to Lloyd Webber's Ernie Wise. Don Black, who's honed his craft not only in the theatre (his first show was a musical about premature ejaculation, which, predictably enough, came off very quickly) but also the less exalted workshops of film (*Diamonds Are Forever*), pop (hits for Michael Jackson) and TV (the song themes for *Howard's Way* and *EastEnders*), has come nearest to imposing on Lloyd Webber the indivisibility of words and music which the Broadway boys aimed for. *Tell Me on a Sunday* is filled with potential hit titles –

'Come Back With The Same Look In Your Eyes', 'Take That Look Off Your Face' – whose phrases fall approximately as they would be spoken: songs, not tunes.

'Andrew,' Charles Hart once said to me, 'changes lyricists the way other men change their underpants' – a vivid image which accurately distils the relationship. Even more unusually, Lloyd Webber likes to change underpants in mid-stream. Whether working with Richard Stilgoe (*Starlight* and part of *Phantom*) or Hart (who took over on *Phantom* and started *Aspects*) or Black (who was brought in on *Aspects* and survived till *Sunset*), Lloyd Webber prepares the groundwork himself: 'I'm quite incapable of writing the words, but I lay out what I believe the libretto ought to be. That's one of my strongest assets.'

'When you work with Jule Styne or Charles Strouse,' says Black of his Broadway partners, 'they'll say, "Wait'll you hear this song", and you'll come up with a title and they'll say, "Hey, that'd be great for Frank! Or Barbra!"' – that's Sinatra and Streisand. 'They're thinking of that little moment, *their* moment. Andrew is very concerned about the set designer, arrangements, everything that makes up the evening. He's the only one I know who doesn't talk in terms of just tunes.'

Okay, not just tunes, but, granted that, the music's always in charge. 'We're now dealing with a huge public demand for through-written music,' Lloyd Webber claims. But it may just be that simple-minded extravaganzas like *Cats* or *Starlight Express* or the broad emotional brush strokes of *Phantom* made dialogue irrelevant: what's to talk about? *Aspects*, a sexual carousel of no particular consequence, presents the opposite problem: what's to sing about?

*

And now there's *Sunset*. And for the first time in 20 years, we have a Lloyd Webber show in which people walk around talking – not just the odd line, but whole scenes, no underscoring, no music at all and even, occasionally, a real live cue for a song. Gracious, it could almost be a Broadway show. With *Sunset*, Lloyd Webber has turned his back on the through-composed form he virtually invented, the style in which he's cast every one of his hits since *Joseph and the Amazing Technicolor Dreamcoat*. In other words, a musical about a woman left behind by changing fashions has become itself a return to old-fashioned values. It's as if Billy Wilder had said to Swanson: 'You're right. Let's do this as a silent movie.'

If you wanted to find a genuine stage translation for *Sunset Boulevard*, for a talking picture about a silent film star, how about this? An ageing musical comedy star, her career obliterated by the new school of through-composed elephantine pop operas. You could stick Carol Channing in it, or Mitzi Gaynor, or Ann Miller: bizarre creatures beached by time and taste, lacquered and bewigged, fantastic and outlandish. Here, surely, are the contemporary equivalents to Swanson: in *Sugar Babies*, Ann Miller, under her concrete coiffure, in basque and fishnets, rat-a-tat-tatting with cane and tap shoes, aroused a similar combination of awe and pity.

I'm not being whimsical. The casting difficulties of *Sunset* can be traced back to Lloyd Webber's first rule: it's not the subject, it's the treatment. The Broadway musical, burdened by its glorious tradition, crumbled away because everyone got too expert: nominally new shows, like *La Cage aux Folles*, opened looking like revivals. Whereas, even if you were going to adapt those T. S. Eliot poems, would you do it like that? (Up in heaven, Eliot must sometimes look down at his 1983 Tony Award for Best Book and Score and marvel: 'You mean, I wrote that thing?') When *Cats* celebrated 5,000 performances at the Winter Garden, David Letterman observed on the CBS *Late Show* that it marked the 5,000th occasion that a guy had turned to his wife and said: 'What the hell is this?' The problem with *Sunset* is that it's not a 'What the hell is this?' production. *Cats* and *Starlight* are freak shows, assaults on your sanity; *Sunset Boulevard*, which is about a freak, is an incredibly rational adaptation. It operates, almost, to Rodgers and Hammerstein rules.

Since *Cats*, Lloyd Webber's scores have been presented to his lyricists as a *fait accompli*: all the words can hope to do is cling on for a few bars before the juggernaut shrugs them off and rolls on. In *Aspects*, for example, there is a relaxed, bisexual sculptress lounging about in pedal-pushers. Suddenly, when she sings, she turns into Jeanette MacDonald chasing big open-vowelled top notes. This is not a plausible singing voice for the character. In *Sunset*, though, Lloyd Webber has, for the first time, managed to distinguish character in music. So Joe Gillis (Alan Campbell) and his pals at Paramount sing in a breezy pop vernacular. It's not just that all the best lines from the movie have been left in, but that Don Black's lyrics have imbibed their spirit. Mimicking Cecil B. De Mille, one of his extras sings of Paramount's latest Biblical epic:

> Every girl in my chorus line
> Is a genuine Philistine . . .

It's a droll aside, but it takes the same pleasure in word-play that the old-school lyricists did. This is, in itself, a novelty from Lloyd Webber, but what's also new is his understanding that these sentiments, these people need to be differentiated musically: they sing in breezy 6 / 4 shuffles, jittery 5 / 8s, exuberant mambos. Conversely, for Norma, he's written a silent film score: she sounds, musically, like a creature from another world, conjured by clean, spare, almost translucent 4 / 4 ballads, whose eerie strings and woodwinds hover like the soundtrack to a trance. The orchestrations are elusive, ambiguous – a surprisingly psychological score from a composer we've come to associate with lush operetta certainties. But it's not just music, with Black and Hampton playing Giacosa and Illica to Britain's Puccini wannabe: with this score, we're back, at last, to *song* ideas.

There are, of course, the ludicrous miscalculations beloved of Trevor Nunn and John Napier, including a supposedly filmic car chase in which the actors frantically spinning steering wheels in toytown automobiles *do* remind you of a film chase, but unfortunately only Kermit the Frog trying to shake off Miss Piggy in *The Muppet Movie*. Inevitably, when Norma returns to Paramount, Nunn and Napier can't resist out-De Milling Cecil in their sets and costumes. But they barely register. Instead, your eye is drawn always to the principals and their story. In the best scene, there is one of those rare occasions when character, song and dramatic impulse are perfectly in tune. Norma returns to the sound stage and, as a Paramount old-timer slowly turns the spot on her, she blinks and, briefly restored to the limelight, comes alive again:

> I don't know why I'm frightened
> I know my way around here . . .

On next year's Johnny Mathis album, 'As If We Never Said Goodbye' will be just another love song. But, in context, it sums up the real romance at the heart of the show, and, from a composer reviled for empty gigantism, it's an episode of fierce intimacy.

*

Why then, for all that and the biggest advance in American theatre history, is there the sense that *Sunset* isn't *quite* a *bona fide* hit? One reason is simply that Lloyd Webber now knows too much. Offered *Cats*, Hal Prince assumed it was a sophisticated British political metaphor which he, as an American, hadn't picked up: 'Is one of these cats Disraeli? Gladstone?'

'Hal,' said Lloyd Webber, '*Cats* is about *cats*.'

The naïveté of the piece, horrifying to Broadway pros, is understandable. Where Sondheim began as Hammerstein's pupil and then served as lyricist to Bernstein, Styne and Rodgers, Lloyd Webber has had to find his way alone. Since the break with Tim Rice (who initiated *Evita*), he seems to be retracing musical theatre's history, adapting the forms to his own style. *Cats* and *Starlight* are the equivalents of the Kiralfy Brothers spectacles of the 1880s; *Phantom* is a turn-of-the-century operetta; *Sunset Boulevard* is a gauche attempt at an American musical play – and, like so many Broadway musical adaptations, that's what it looks like: an adaptation. Like earlier Wilder adaptations – the Neil Simon/Bacharach and David version of *The Apartment*, Jule Styne's *Some Like It Hot* – it never transforms itself into anything in its own right. Lloyd Webber is right: it's not the subject, but the treatment. And this treatment never quite vindicates the choice of subject. You watch it; it's fine, it's professional – but you don't see the need for it.

Rattled by the initial reception in London, Black and Lloyd Webber went back to work and musicalised great chunks of the dialogue, in an attempt to Lloyd Webberize the piece. Everyone else, meanwhile, fell back on what Broadway always does: quick, we're in trouble; find a star. This, too, is new for Lloyd Webber. With *Cats*, *Starlight*, even *Phantom*, who cares who's in the cast?

In Hollywood a while back, I happened to be at a dinner with *Magnum* hunk Tom Selleck and his wife, who told me they'd met when Tom came to see *Cats* and was so impressed by one of the prancing pussies (I forget whether she was playing Grizabella or Skimbleshanks or merely a supporting feline) that he arranged to see her afterwards. Celebrities have been romancing chorus girls since the *Florodora* sextet all married American millionaires at the turn of the century, but Selleck must be the first theatregoer even to *notice* anyone in *Cats*, never mind make a reliable stab at what sex they are (in London, most of us would be wary of emulating Tom for fear we'd wind up dating Brian Blessed). He's the exception that proves the rule, for the genius of *Cats* is this: how would you know someone in it was acting badly?

True, Glenn Close helps. First, she *is* a film star, but, second, one whose close-set crater eyes and angular off-centre features seem to belong to an earlier generation of Hollywood women; third, her most famous role is in *Fatal Attraction*, so we, unlike poor Joe Gillis, know it is unwise to get mixed up with her: all theatre, but especially musical theatre, is an exercise in shorthand. Miss Close has also worked hard: although her speaking voice is flat and modern (Betty Buckley, who replaced Patti LuPone in the West End, conveys a better sense of social isolation), her physical perform-ance misses nothing, whether maternally cradling her dead chimp, scut-tling chimp-like up the stairs herself or stroking Joe's neck from behind as if she's Salome and he's already on the platter. These are memorable stage images, even if they do have the effect of leaving the non-Norma scenes a little empty. Miss Close is mistress of the house in a way her predecessor never was, but much of the impact is due to smoother co-ordination: the vast set, the glitter and shadows, the columns and pediments, which buried Patti LuPone, now seem to be choreographed to the leading lady's movements.

So the headless chickens on Broadway run around pronouncing it just a star vehicle. The public have got the message, too. As I left, the woman next to me turned sourly to her husband and said: 'Well, it's nothing with-out her.' But look at Glenn Close's last show: *Death and the Maiden*, with Mike Nichols, and a Tony Award for Best Actress. It did no business; it was nothing *with* her. Glenn Close is a star in this role, *because* of this role.

*

It's always something else: it's Glenn Close or Michael Crawford or the chandelier. '*You* say that *Phantom* is only spectacle,' Lloyd Webber once said to me, 'but that's just not true. In three years, it sold three million double-sets around the world, four Top Ten singles. That's nothing to do with production values, because no way have all those people seen the production.'

He's right. Today, Lloyd Webber is the only composer to enjoy Hit Parade success with showtunes. 'The Perfect Year', with Don Black's wonderful New Year's Eve lyric, was a hit for Dina Carroll, though embellished by a lot of phonily soulful ululations – Lloyd Webber is happy to re-cast his songs for *Top of the Pops*. But, with 'Love Changes Every-thing', he stuck to his guns. 'On the record, it went down originally, and I said, "Sorry, I've got to let Michael Ball's voice go up to B flat." The company said, "No radio station's going to play that. How do you get into the next record?" Well, it got to Number Two, and what did it was Michael on television actually being able to hit, full frontal, *live* that B flat.'

Some of us find that sort of thing rather corny, but Lloyd Webber's willingness to have his music conversationally warbled Henry Higgins-style disappeared – along with Roger Moore – during rehearsals for *Aspects*.

There are always precedents. Yes, Lloyd Webber is the first composer to have five shows running simultaneously in the West End. But Otto Harbach, lyricist of 'Smoke Gets In Your Eyes', had five productions running together on Broadway. Remember Harry B. Smith? The most prolific librettist in theatre history, with 300 shows and 6,000 songs, none of which is known to day except 'The Sheik of Araby', usually heard as an instrumental without Smith's lyric. Remember New York's first superstar composer, Reginald De Koven? He wrote the America operetta smash of the nineteenth century, *Robin Hood*; today, most reference books don't even mention him. All theatre exists in the present tense.

If a writer's lucky, just once in his lifetime he coincides with the perfect subject. For Alan Jay Lerner, it was *My Fair Lady*. It would have horrified him, but, underneath the limousine liberalism, I don't think he was so far from the urbane, charming misogyny of Henry Higgins. He once said to me that, after *Fair Lady*, whenever he sat down to write for male characters, they tended to come out sounding like Rex Harrison. *Gigi* and *Lolita, My Love* (1971) are both variations of the same theme: older, worldlier men finding young unformed girls and moulding them. There was something of this in Lerner's own life. He was a serial monogamist, married eight times, and, though at the end he found real happiness with Liz Robertson, there's no doubt that, in one of his final lyrics, there's more than a touch of autobiography:

> I've seen how lovely loving starts
> And slowly turns to martial arts
> I've Been Married
> I've tossed and turned and couldn't sleep
> From counting minks instead of sheep
> I've Been Married . . .

When you've been through seven alimony agreements, you get a little jaded: women are frivolous creatures to be bejewelled and begowned – not so very different from Henry Higgins' assessment. With *Pygmalion*, Lerner and the milieu and the characters were made for each other.

Lloyd Webber, to date, had been married thrice: Lerner's tally is one Broadway record which even Andrew might have difficulty breaking. But, at the first night of *Phantom*, more than a few in the audience were shocked at the barely submerged sub-text of autobiography. Lloyd Webber had always had to endure cruel remarks about his looks in the British press, though, in fairness, he's just a bit of a goofball who hung on to his seventies wardrobe a little too long (it took his third wife,

Madeleine, to get his hair under control). Still, he must have found more than a few personal resonances in the story of a disfigured composer hiding away from the world whose music can express itself only through the voice of a beautiful singer, and who hopes to win her love with his melody. The role was played by his second wife, Sarah Brightman. Whether or not it was his music that attracted her to him, it's certainly true that it was she who inspired his greatest score.

Greatest score? Yes, because this story and these characters were perfectly matched to his broad, sweeping, soaring melodies. *Aspects* needed someone more cynical, *Sunset* someone more psychological; but *Phantom* was made for him: Lloyd Webber made the show sing, full-throated and open-vowelled. I hope one day Stephen Sondheim also finds his 'Music Of The Night'.

Around the time of *Aspects*, he liked to point out that he was only the same age – 41 – as Sondheim was at the time of *Company* in 1970, when he was known principally as the lyricist of *West Side Story* and *Gypsy*; the great innovations lay ahead. Lloyd Webber treads cautiously when discussing Sondheim – at a mere mention of the name, he shifts awkwardly as if someone's twisting a pineapple up his bottom – and it must rankle that, while the latter's been deified, he's been pilloried as a purveyor of mindless pap. 'You're wrong,' he insists. 'I can show you with Rodgers and Hammerstein. They had all that, too, you forget. I'm not saying that defensively. I remember the review of *Evita* that said I always did grim shows in RSC black boxes.' He shakes his head in disbelief. 'Then overnight I became Mister Glitz.'

So, with Sondheim retreated to the wilder shores off-off-Broadway for fringe revues like *Assassins*, the commercial musical theatre's hopes rest, as they have done for a decade, on Lloyd Webber. 'It's not my fault everybody copied *Starlight*,' he moans. 'But that's why it was important that the musical got back to the values of the score. Some of my things are good, some not so good. In any case, it's now really urgent that we see some other writers coming on.'

Nobody discusses it much, but neither *Starlight* nor *Aspects* recouped its investment on Broadway. The hype goes on, but the automatic mega-hit machine hasn't been firing on all cylinders. Lloyd Webber's never seemed bothered. 'I've just started to find a voice I'm really proud of, and who knows? I'll probably have three or four turkeys in a row. But so what? I was a schmuck at school because I liked *The Sound of Music*. Musical theatre is the only thing that's ever made me tick. Whatever happens, success or failure, I'll still be there.'

The Future

In the summer of 1990, Cameron Mackintosh cancelled *Miss Saigon* on Broadway. He had London's latest hit all ready to go. He had a terrific central performance from Jonathan Pryce. But Actors' Equity, an exceptionally powerful union in a mostly non-unionized society, were insisting that Pryce's role had to be played by an Asian-American. Mackintosh, whose various North American companies of *Cats*, *Les Misérables* and *Phantom of the Opera* made him easily the biggest employer of American actors, stood firm, taking advertisements in American newspapers explaining to advance bookers that he'd be returning their money. All $26 million of it.

$26 million: the largest advance ticket sale in Broadway history. As the implications of *Saigon*'s cancellation sank in, a flurry of giddy excitement ran through the somnolent New York theatre community like a nymphomaniac rabbit. Suddenly, Mackintosh's rivals were faced with the prospect of one of their own shows inheriting that massive $26 million. Which hit in waiting would it go to? *Ziegfeld Presents Will Rogers* (as it was then called)? *Annie II* (as it was then called)? Or maybe *Oh, Kay!*, the all-black hot Harlem version of an old musical by that distinguished black Harlem novelist P. G. Wodehouse? After a few days of giddy elation, grim stoicism set in with the realization that, while some of that $26 million would have been picked up by other shows, most would have gone nowhere near the theatre. Had *Miss Saigon* not opened, many of the customers would simply have put their refunds towards a week in Florida or sheetrocking the garage or enlisting the kids in a drug rehab programme.

After its mid-eighties blues and its late-eighties blues and its early-nineties blues, Broadway has reduced its expectations, 'repositioning its product' (as the marketing men say) some way below the British blockbusters. Its hits are, in the main, purely for local consumption, an inversion of the rule which operates in most other areas of entertainment, where, for example, America has Bob Hope, but Britain has Russ Abbot. Even when the box office receipts of a Broadway show do go through the roof, it's only to find they have a marginally better view of *Miss Saigon* or *Sunset Boulevard* climbing into the stratosphere, a difference of scale which Mackintosh emphasized by announcing a new top ticket price for *Saigon* of $100 – $40 higher than his competitors. Instead of deterring the traffic, it only increased the feeling that this wasn't merely a night at the theatre but a fabulous must-see phenomenon.

And yet, for all the ballyhoo, the overwhelming sense when *Miss Saigon* finally opened in New York was of an era drawing to a close. Mackintosh himself had announced that he would not be embarking on any new musicals. In that case, I asked him, what about *Just So*, which subsequently opened under his auspices at a London fringe theatre? 'I've stuck to what I said,' he insisted 'That's not "new". I've been developing the show with the writers for five years.' Leaving the Mackintosh office a couple of weeks later, I bumped into Andrew Lloyd Webber. Ah-ha, I thought. Doubtless these twin pillars of the British musical were meeting to plan a brand new monster smasheroo. But apparently not. Just a routine meeting to discuss *Phantom* in Reykjavik – or was it *Cats* in Dubrovnik?

Which is part of the problem. To its critics, the modern musical is the nearest anybody's got to fooling all of the people all of the time, but, even so, it's no get-rich-quick scheme. It requires years of work before the opening – and after. Even if he never produces another new show, Mackintosh will still be kept busy supervising the international reduplications of *Cats, Les Miz, Phantom* and *Miss Saigon*. Detractors who regard these shows as the artistic equivalent of junk food are correct in at least one respect. Ensuring the precise global reproduction of Big Mac and the other existing delicacies is such a complex operation that it now takes years for McDonald's to introduce as slight a variation to its menu as a Sausage and Egg McMuffin.

Around the same time as Mackintosh, Lloyd Webber, with a new wife with horsey interests, also toyed with the idea of abandoning musical theatre. But, with his film version of *Phantom* stalled, he returned to a project he'd first attempted a decade earlier, the musicalization of Billy Wilder's *Sunset Boulevard*. (First time round, Norma Desmond made her final descent of that fabulous Hollywood staircase to what subsequently became the tune for 'Memory'.) Eventually, after supervising a classic revivals programme at the National and a new production of *Oliver!*, Mackintosh also relented, to produce Boublil and Schonberg's *Martin Guerre*. But from *Aspects of Love* to *Sunset Boulevard* proved the longest gap between Lloyd Webber shows since his career began – so long that *Aspects* had already closed by the time *Sunset* opened. And, for Boublil and Schonberg, from *Miss Saigon* to *Martin Guerre* was even longer: six years. The Lloyd Webber/Mackintosh era has been one of bigger but fewer hits.

Ever since the dawn of the industrial revolution, British entrepreneurialism in whatever field is always atrophied by respectability. I remember, in the summer of 1994, attending David Frost's summer party and sharing a joke (as they say) with Tim Rice and the rock star and Live Aid energiser Bob Geldof. Lloyd Webber approached: 'Sir Timothy!' he cried, with mock formality.

'Sir Andrew!' responded Rice, with an elaborate Gilbert-and-Sullivan bow.

'Do you realise,' St Bob Geldof, KBE, said to me, 'you're the only one of us without a fokking knighthood, you useless fokker?'

Well, yes. But I wonder if this isn't part of the process by which instinctive populism gets seduced into bland corporate complacency. Don Black recalls, during the writing of *Aspects*, Lloyd Webber suggesting it might be useful to do a workshop performance in front of a small, invited audience – David Frost, the Earl of Gowrie, Mrs Thatcher, the cabinet minister John Gummer, etc., etc.

'I get it,' said Black. 'You want to find out what Joe Public thinks.'

Quite accidentally, Lloyd Webber has been an anticipator of shifting audience tastes for two decades. But it may be that, as happened to his hero Richard Rodgers after *The King and I*, he's got predictable. Will the new school of British 'pop opera' ever again see quite such a blessed conjunction of author and subject as *Phantom*? 'That's unfair,' says one of Lloyd Webber's investors. 'It doesn't have to be *Phantom*. For all you or anybody else says about *Aspects of Love*, everyone's done very nicely out of it.' True – in London, where *Aspects* made a profit of around 30 per cent. But, in New York, it ran out of audience and lost its investment. For the first time since *Jeeves* in 1975, *Aspects* revealed the composer's mortality. Unlike his other West End long-runners – the unholy trinity of unstoppable behemoths, *Cats*, *Starlight Express* and *Phantom* – *Aspects* was just another musical. No composer is infallible and Lloyd Webber is too shrewd to have fallen for all the guff about his 'unprecedented' success. But the incredible worldwide success of *Cats* and *Phantom* has aroused expectations of 'the British musical' that its tiny group of practitioners can hardly be expected to satisfy. After the almost total redefinition of the musical as a huge broad-brush spectacle, it's hard to adjust to a world where Lloyd Webber shows just 'do very nicely'. After all, the Mackintosh/Lloyd Webber camps are just about the only guys who can get their shows on, and they can manage only two per decade. For everyone else attempting a new musical, they now figure on eight years from page to stage.

What's so sad is that a decade and a half after *Cats* the same two men are still the only game in town for musicals. To judge from the number of other successful creators of West End hits, Lloyd Webber and Mackintosh have the shortest coat-tails in history. You can count on two fingers the smash British musicals without either of these guys' names on the marquee: that slick thirties retread, *Me and My Girl* and a Willy Russell play punctuated by duff songs, *Blood Brothers*. Otherwise, the so-called British musical revolution is chiefly characterized by its spectacular kamikaze casualties: *Time, Mutiny, Ziegfeld, Winnie, Metropolis, King, Bernadette, Matador, Which Witch, Children of Eden* . . .

*

So by the summer of '96 there was a lot riding on *Martin Guerre*, and no end to the gossip: there were rumours of problems with the director, Declan Donellan, who'd never staged a new musical; the orchestrator, Bill Brohn, had quit; the wise and worldly lyricist, Herbert Kretzmer, had been replaced by a callow youth. And then Cameron Mackintosh postponed, again, the show's opening – this time to July, to allow space for a 'work-shop' period. To the casual observer, such entertaining carnage could only lead to disaster. But it's important to remember: *C'est magnifique, mais ce n'est pas la guerre, c'est seulement Martin Guerre.*

For one thing, most of the participants had been in this situation before. Seven years earlier, Brohn was brought in on *Miss Saigon* when Mackintosh decided to dump the original orchestrations at a cost of £185,000. Kretzmer was called in to write *Les Misérables* only because Mackintosh fired poet-turned-lyricist James Fenton, whose words looked great on paper but were mostly unsingable. 'Fired' (his word) by Mackintosh, Fenton settled for just under one per cent of the gross, which means that to date he's made about £10 million. You'd have to give an awful lot of poetry readings to make that kind of dough, but that's the thing about a hit musical: there's plenty of money for everyone, even the guys who screwed up. As for delaying the première, well, as noted earlier, tell it to the Kiralfy brothers.

Martin Guerre, the story of a French soldier who returns from the war years after everyone thought he was dead, is based on a famous Toulouse court case of 1560. Since then, it's inspired innumerable lawyers, poets, historians and dramatists, beginning with the first tell-all behind-the-scenes account by Judge Jean de Coras. Montaigne used the case to discuss the uncertainty of evidence, Leibniz to debate the very meaning of identity. In our own time, the story has inspired the movie *Le Retour de Martin Guerre*, with Gérard Depardieu, and a Hollywood imitation thereof, *Sommersby*, starring Jodie Foster and Richard Gere. Neither motion picture took a third of the time the stage version took. 'People keep saying to me,' said Herbert Kretzmer, '"I hear you're working on *The Return of Marvin Gaye*".' That might well have been easier.

Almost alone in today's musical theatre, Mackintosh believes that the most important relationship on a show is between the authors and the producer, and he works with Boublil and Schonberg until they and he are fully satisfied. If you've ever seen the old MGM film *The Band Wagon*, you'll know how easily a pretentious British director (in this case, played by Jack Buchanan) can ruin a perfectly good musical. Mackintosh has used innumerable pretentious British directors – Trevor Nunn, Nicholas Hytner – but he's never let them run away with the show. Were the difficulties on *Martin Guerre* an assertion of his faith in the primacy of the authors or a sign of fundamental difficulties?

A few months before, strolling through South Kensington, I'd bumped into Alain Boublil and we went for a coffee. 'How's it going?' I asked. 'Well, eet is vairy interesting,' he said, Gallicly. 'Eef it works, it weel be because . . .' – and he proceeded to explain. But I was struck by a qualification I'd never heard him use about *Les Miz* or *Saigon*: '*If* it works . . .'

As the show marched nearer to its rendezvous with destiny, the early word seeping out from run-throughs was, according to some, that it was the best British musical ever and, according to others, that there was far too much dancing in it. As previews began, there were wild but persistent rumours that the show drew heavily on the sixteenth-century French equivalent of tap-shoes: clogs.

The man in charge of the clogs was Bob Avian, who danced in *West Side Story* and *Funny Girl* and *Hello, Dolly!*; worked on the prototype Sondheim concept musicals, *Company* and *Follies*; and helped make *A Chorus Line* the longest-running Broadway show of all time. And then one day, at his hunting lodge in Connecticut, Avian sat down with a script Cameron Mackintosh had sent him for a new musical called *Miss Saigon*: 'I read it and I go, "Wait a minute! Where are the showgirls? Where are the tap numbers?" My friends ask me what the big choreographic opportunities were and I tell them: the reunification of fucking Vietnam and an attack on American materialism.'

He has a point. Whatever else *Les Miz* and *Phantom* are famous for, it's not dancing. But the Broadway community in which Avian spent some 30 years has gone, and, as a rare survivor of the *ancien régime*, he's made his peace with the Brit-hit revolutionaries. Of the nineties megamusicals, some are produced by Mackintosh, some are written by Lloyd Webber, some are directed by Trevor Nunn – but *all* are choreographed by Avian: *Miss Saigon, Sunset Boulevard*, and now *Martin Guerre*.

A week before opening, among all the other debris at the Prince Edward Theatre, there's not a clog to be seen. The stalls bar is piled high with scenery, including a huge set of cart wheels; the rehearsal pianist and copyist are poring over last-minute tweaks to the score; and Avian and I are looking for a corner to talk in. 'Try downstairs, by the poster of *Rio Rita*,' suggests Cameron Mackintosh, mischievously. 'That was one of your early shows, wasn't it, Bob?'

Actually, no. *Rio Rita* – the one about an eponymous heroine wooed by an unsavoury Mexican who is secretly the masked bandit known only as the Kinkajou – was a New York hit in 1927. There were more shows then and less riding on any individual one, but, picking your way through the jumble at the Prince Edward, you're struck by how little things have changed: if you score a hit, you can market it more efficiently, with T-shirts and web-sites and theme-parks, and you can ship it to more places, in Eastern Europe and Latin America; but *making* a hit . . . that's no more scientific for *Martin Guerre* than it was for *Rio Rita*.

So, even as Mackintosh takes high-toned directors from the classic and opera and turns them into big musicals men, he's canny enough to protect himself by installing Avian alongside. It's a perfect arrangement: Avian has tons of showbiz savvy and, in contrast to most choreographers, no desire to direct. But, unlike so many Americans working in the British theatre, he isn't one of those snobbish anglophiles. At his place in Connecticut a few years back, the only evidence of British culture I could find was pinned up in the kitchen: Parkinson's portrait of the Queen, the Queen Mother and Princess Margaret in matching velvet cloaks. 'I love it,' said Avian. 'They're like the McGuire Sisters playing Vegas.' In a way, that's how he works on *Martin Guerre*: you're looking at a bunch of actors in period dress behaving very solemnly, but Avian applies the same showbiz principles he would to the McGuire Sisters.

'Bob, can you take a look at this?' says Mackintosh, and we troop into the stalls to check a new transition. There are three peasant hovel-like structures on the stage, which revolve, and, as they do, two characters emerge and sing a couple of lines of recitative. Avian pronounces himself happy.

Wonderful, but what's it got to do with dancing? We're talking inches away from that set of cart wheels, on which presumably some French peasants – maybe Martin himself – arrive or depart. Once upon a time, you used to get cartwheels in show dance; now, you get cart wheels. What, I wonder, would Michael Bennett have made of his old pal's new work. 'He would not have accepted these shows. He didn't do anything he didn't understand – like sixteenth-century France. He wouldn't have even read the script. He was a kid from Buffalo, he didn't finish high school – although he won his Pulitzer Prize.'

Maybe Bennett had the right idea. When *Martin Guerre* eventually opened in July 1996, it couldn't have been further from the kind of theatre Avian and Bennett grew up in: the latest British mega-musical had spent several million pounds apparently in order to argue the merits of Protestantism versus Catholicism.

In that original 1560 court case, Bertrande de Rols had claimed that the man she'd been living with in the Pyrenean village of Artigat for the last three years was not her husband Martin Guerre, but an imposter. The real Martin had abandoned her 12 years earlier, and then a man resembling him had returned. Now she had discovered that the man she took to be her spouse was really one Arnaud du Thil from a Gascon village 40 miles away. The judge took a dim view of all this and was about to rule against Bertrande when Martin Guerre *lui-même* suddenly showed up, having been away soldiering in Spain. The court sent Bertrande back to Artigat with Martin, and sentenced Arnaud to burn at the stake.

Both screen versions suggest the woman's complicity in the imposture: in it she sees, according to one of the authors of the French film, 'a momentary sense of possibility in the tight world of the sixteenth-century village'. This is an intriguing subject for a musical, but not for the kind of musical Boublil and Schonberg write. In both *Les Miz* and *Saigon*, they pinpointed small human dramas against the great canvas of history. Schonberg writes big, declarative, somewhat overwrought ballads ideal for, say, the scene in *Miss Saigon* when the Vietnamese girl begs the father of her child, a US marine, and his new wife to take the little boy with them back to America. It's easy to mock this sort of thing, but every night, in London and New York and around the world, you can hear audiences a-weepin' and a-wailin'. Besides, in *Saigon*, Boublil and Schonberg offered a modestly hopeful formal advance: they proved you could apply the through-sung form to a naturalistic, contemporary subject. They didn't get any credit from the Broadway whingers: 'Oh, sure, *Madam Butterfly* set in the Vietnam War. Anyone could do that.' But the point is, nobody did. And, while we're weighing the merits of Puccini retreads, *Madam Butterfly* relocated to Vietnam raises the stakes; *La Bohème* relocated to Greenwich Village (as in *Rent*) diminishes them: it's the triumph of New York theatre parochialism.

But *Martin Guerre* isn't that kind of story and what's wound up on stage suggests that, having embraced Puccini, Victor Hugo, Eva Perón and T. S. Eliot, the London mega-musical has finally run up against the limits of the form. Most critics wrote of the piece as an 'operetta of our time', but operetta deals in certainties – and the story of *Martin Guerre* is a more complex, psychological drama. The key scene is the return of the false Martin and Bertrande's reaction. Even the Hollywood version understands that: you're never sure what's going on inside Jodie Foster's mind, what accommodations she's reaching within herself. In a musical version, it calls for music and movement – something faltering and ethereal like the old *Merry Widow* waltz. Instead, she says that she knows he's not the real Martin and next thing you know they're singing:

> And All I Know
> Is that all I want to be
> Is to be close to you . . .
> I love you so
> And the love of you
> Is all I'll ever know . . .

It's a curious fact that, in obliterating the distinction between dialogue and song, between speech and soliloquy, the through-composed musical is paradoxically the most literal of forms. Everyone spends a lot of time singing exposition at each other . . .

> PIERRE: Protestants could soon be spreading all about.
> MME DE ROLS: Well, my dear Pierre
> That can never be . . .

. . . and, when they're not relaying information, the lyrics tend to be static and head-on. All the ambiguities of the story have been sacrificed, because that's not how Boublil and Schonberg write. So, because they've picked a subject their style can't accommodate, their collaborators have tried to nudge the show closer to their previous work. To match the human tapestry of *Les Miz*, the village of Artigat has been promoted to the foreground, which means we have to sit through a tiresome parade of cardboard cutouts – bawdy peasants, old crones and village idiots. As an equivalent to the dramatic backdrop of *Miss Saigon*, the story has been shunted forward a few years so it can be set against the religious wars:

> A God who was born in a stable
> A pauper who gave his life to save us . . .

The only acceptable God to modern entertainment values, it seems, is a compassionate, inclusive non-judgmental type who believes in generous welfare provision. But, even with a topical spin, it's unlikely that differences between Catholics and Protestants in sixteenth-century France could ever have had the same emotional tug for a modern audience as the Vietnam War.

When I met Mackintosh a few weeks after *Martin Guerre* opened, to decidedly cool reviews and highly wobbly word-of-mouth, he was disarmingly honest. 'A woman giving up her baby,' he said, harking back to *Saigon*. 'That's primal. We don't have anything primal in this story.' Broadway musicals were the work of a small select group of people, which is why, eventually, they all began to sound and look the same. In London, Mackintosh developed a knack of teaming Boublil and Schonberg and Lloyd Webber with quirky, unlikely collaborators – often, in fact, fellows who didn't much like musicals. But everything that worked on the earlier shows failed to click on this one. The unknown Charles Hart was a gamble that paid off on *Phantom*. But Edward Hardy, a neophyte lyricist whose youthful workshop songs hinted at real talent, flounders here in off-the-peg peasant ribaldry – 'Needs a proper man to provide a proper poke' – and not a single strong song idea. Declan Donellan is the respected founder of the Cheek By Jowl company and has directed Shakespeare and Ostrovsky and Ibsen – all of whom are director-proof. Here, he's been given a co-adaptor's credit, but, unlike Nunn, Caird and Hytner, his storytelling has failed him: at the end, audience members were muttering to themselves whether it was Bertrande or Martin who'd converted to Protestantism. His long-time partner, the designer Nick Ormerod, has eschewed both the big theatrical gestures of *Miss Saigon* (the helicopter, the Ho-Chi-Minh statue) and the clean stage images of *Les Miz* and dumped the whole thing on a drab set with nothing but three endlessly revolving post-and-beam lifeguard stands to look at. Only Bob Avian with his clogs has succeeded in finding any kind of distinctive vocabulary for the piece. But that and Schonberg's music aren't enough: we've become used to thinking of British musicals as fabulous freaks – 'sports', as the orchid growers say – but, in the same way that *They're Playing Our Song* is a generic

Broadway musical, *Martin Guerre* looks awfully like a generic British musical.

We shouldn't be surprised: matching Boublil and Schonberg with the *Martin Guerre* material and then tossing in the director and designer of the Cheek By Jowl company is every bit as weird a combination as on *The Black Crook*. But sitting in the stalls a week after opening you could feel the audience willing it to be better: they wanted to feel that same lump in the throat, that same exhilaration as on *Saigon* and *Les Miz*. Luckily for them – or, anyway, subsequent patrons – Mackintosh is a fighter. Despite being lumbered with the wrong director, the wrong designer and the wrong lyricist, he went back to work immediately after opening. He had 40 per cent of the show re-written completely – new scenes, new lyrics, new music. 'My God,' gasped Avian, looking at the revised script. 'You've done all this in six weeks?' Can he make the show another *Les Misérables*? No. Can he make it better? Yes. Is it in the theatre's interest that he turns the show around? Absolutely. For who else is there? For the first time since *Cats*, here was a big Cameron Mackintosh show that seemed unlikely ever to come to New York, or at least not in anything remotely resembling its present shape. That should have been Broadway's opportunity – except that there's no one left to seize it.

*

If 'British musical' still sounds vaguely oxymoronic, 'Broadway musical' is nothing more than a real-estate designation. In New York, the 'theatre community' – producers, stagers, writers – is mostly dead or fled; the only muscle left is in bricks and mortar, the guys who through historical accident find themselves owning huge hangars in mid-town Manhattan and need something to put in them. A Mackintosh musical is a dream booking: it'll tie up the theatre till the next century. So, as in that most unlikely Broadway Brit hit of the eighties, *Me and My Girl* – the one where the crumbling old family discovers the only heir to the earldom is some Cockney sparrer from Lambeth – they've decided to make the best of it.

Well, as they say in New England, you can put your dog in the stable but it don't make him a horse. What's left of 'Broadway' in *Les Miz* or *Starlight Express*? Broadway is a glorious 70-year tradition proceeding smoothly through the birth of distinctively American musical comedy with Bolton, Wodehouse and Kern, the structural advance of the Rodgers and Hammerstein musical play, the rise of integrated choreography with Agnes de Mille and Jerome Robbins . . . But what's any of that to do with a lush 'through-composed' operetta like *Phantom* or a dance-free 'chamber opera' like *Aspects of Love*? America's various musical theatre masterclasses once brimmed with confidence: these are the rules, these are the boys who invented them, this is why they work. Now there's only the forlorn recognition that sometimes you can know too much for your own good, that that glorious tradition – Kern, Porter, Loesser, Styne – is a crippling burden you can't crawl out from under. Faced with the mega-spectacles from London, Broadway buffs either gave up or ignored them, hoping they'd go away and we could all get back to proper musicals. Those who tried to come to terms with the new masters took refuge in an oft-quoted Lloyd Webber line: 'A show doesn't open until it opens on Broadway.'

I suspect he was being either polite or sentimental. A few years back, Cameron Mackintosh joked to New York's biggest theatre owners, the Shuberts, that Broadway was now merely the first stop on the American tour – which, on balance, is probably the correct assessment. Had Equity not backed down in their dispute with Mackintosh, the Main Stem big shots would have been faced with a grim precedent: for the first time this century, a major musical hit would have been denied to New York audiences; to see *Miss Saigon*, they'd have had to fly to London or even Toronto, where Honest Ed Mirvish was prepared to custom-build a theatre for the show and where, in any case, the weekly profits would be bigger than in the big town. Even after they caved in, the lingering impression was still of an industry now so parochial and unimaginative it simply couldn't comprehend the global scale on which Mackintosh operates. Broadway's *supposed* to be ruthlessly commercial, but it's only so in the nickels-and-dimes sense of a second-hand car dealer. Look at *42nd Street*: a showbiz fable set in Broadway's backyard, adapted from a half-century old movie with a score pillaged from the catalogue of two dead guys. Or take *Grand Hotel*: its success in 1989 was hailed as the new dawn of the Broadway musical, yet it's merely Tommy Tune's super-slick retread of a show that folded on the road in the fifties, written by the *Kismet* team of Luther Davis, Robert Wright and George Forrest, all now octogenarians. These are the cocky young punks taking the American theatre into the twenty-first century. Broadway smashes are now old movie musicals, like *42nd Street*, or back-catalogue tune-ups, like the 'new' Gershwin show *Crazy for You*. I like these musicals, and in the gangsta rap era there's plenty of great show and pop tunes that are worth reviving. But, in broader theatrical terms, there is, literally, no future in these shows: it's like a ventriloquist sticking his hand up a corpse. If you break down the components, New York still has better lyricists, librettists, orchestrators, choreographers and directors, but the sum of the parts is invariably greater than the whole. Even the few new hits they were able to muster during the eighties seemed to be born middle-aged – like Jerry Herman's *La Cage aux Folles*, yet another of his brassy broads on staircases.

It's hard to find a connection between *La Cage* and *Les Miz*, and it's difficult to know whether it's worth the effort searching. Musical theatre has more expectations than rules, and its history unfolds like a drunk staggering through a maze. Most of it wouldn't make any difference if it all happened the other way around. I've had mesmerizing conversations about the Baltimore try-out for *The Whirl of Society*, when Fanny Brice, whose husband, of course, was the author of 'If You'll Be My Lolly, I'll Be Your Pop' and 'Sasha, The Passion of the Pasha', and Willie Weston, the Dutch comic playing Baron von Shine, were joined in the cast by Gaby Delys, the legendary French star celebrated for her 'Oo, naughty boy!' catchphrase and romance with Manuel II of Portugal . . . Baron von Shine, Manuel II of Portugal? Which one's real? Which one's fictional? And which, if either, was the Passion of the Pasha? The more you know about musicals, the more you wonder whether you need to know anything.

*

And what of the British Revolution? In April 1990, at the end of the season of *Miss Saigon* and *Aspects*, the Society of West End Theatre assembled to bestow Olivier Awards on the year's finest dramatic presentations. After sating its appetite for grown-up drama by handing out straight-play honours to David Hare's *Racing Demon*, Michael Bogdanov's staging of *The Wars of the Roses*, Fiona Shaw's electrifying *Electra* and other rigorous, gruelling, challenging, etc., the committee then left its collective marbles with the hat-check girl and gave the Best Musical award not, as expected to *Miss Saigon*, but to that schlock curiosity, Bob Carlton's *Return to the Forbidden Planet* – the 'cult hit' which relocates *The Tempest* in outer space and punctuates it with sixties pop.

Best Musical? On the very night of the awards ceremony, *Aspects of Love*, unloved and unnominated by the Oliviers, was opening on Broadway. Now I stand second to none in the buckets of ordure I've dumped on

Lloyd Webber over the years, but I think he was hard done by. SWET itself also felt a little sheepish about leaving him with profits-without-honour and chose to end the ceremony by clumsily underlining the eccentricity of its deliberations: Jane Asher offered *Aspects* best wishes for a successful New York opening and the band played 'Love Changes Everything'. This was the only native composition heard in the entire evening.

Otherwise, at the apogee of the British Musical Revolution, the nominees included a score by two Frenchmen and an American (*Miss Saigon*) and one by another American (*The Baker's Wife*, a revival of which had already closed). However, the real foreigners are not the Frogs and Yanks, but the diverse hands responsible for the 'scores' of the remaining two nominations, *Buddy* and *Forbidden Planet*. The former was cobbled together from Buddy Holly's pop hits, the latter from a more general scouring of geriatric jukeboxes, from Jerry Lee Lewis to the Beach Boys. These are the illegal immigrants of theatre music, the equivalents of those Nicaraguan babysitters whose cheapness and availability was so appealing to President Clinton's Justice Department nominees. The difference is, when word of the illegal babysitter got out, the Justice nomination was withdrawn. At the Oliviers, the nomination went through – and won. And so, 50 per cent of the music performed at what was meant to be a celebration of London theatre in 1990 came from the Hit Parades of 30 years ago.

Not that a skilled author can't give an artificially created score some dramatic propulsion and characterization. Richard Maltby Jr did with the Fats Waller catalogue in *Ain't Misbehavin'*. But there's no attempt at dramatic function in autofloccinaucinihilipilifications like *Buddy* and *Forbidden Planet*. Such limited charm as *Buddy* possesses derives from its almost childlike innocence in presenting itself as no more or less than a rock'n'roll revival concert. And, for this, it's nominated over Andrew Lloyd Webber, Don Black and Charles Hart – who, for better or worse, are the only future the British musical has as a living form.

One idiotic award is not in itself of great consequence, and SWET felt foolish enough afterwards to adjust the categories the following year. But it is a revealing indicator of the prevailing cultural environment. Perhaps because the plays and musicals communities are more separate in London than in New York, the Olivier committee seemed unaware that musicals are supposed to have writers. Or perhaps, surveying the most successful British theatre works since 1980 (*Cats* and co.), the British theatre establishment would *rather* musicals didn't have writers. Stern and exacting when it comes to straight plays, they're apparently deter-mined to keep musicals as mindless nights out. 'I don't think musicals can ever be art,' Fiona Shaw, that electrifying Electra, tells me. 'I like them as entertainments, but there's a ceiling on the form that stops it going beyond that.'

And I think of 'Ol' Man River', and wonder where Miss Shaw's ceiling is.

*

Her old bosses at the Royal Shakespeare Company had a crack at raising the ceiling in 1988, with Terry Hands' production of *Carrie*. The original schlock-horror novel's power derived from the destruction of that most reassuring symbol of American small town continuity, the high school senior prom, and Stephen King has updated the story in successive editions to reinforce his point: Carrie is not some bizarre misfit from another time and place but a direct threat to us and our cosy, familiar world. She experiences her first period during school showers and, ridi-culed and abused, is pelted with tampons by her classmates. Everything thereafter is a consequence of this humiliation.

But Terry Hands saw this slight story of an adolescent girl seeking peer group acceptance as a Greek tragedy. To this end, he staged the show not in a recognizable high school but on a bare monochrome set enclosed by sterile, all white, high-tech walls: *The Black and White Menstrual Show*. Hands neutered the drama: his production was, in every sense, bloodless. *Carrie* the musical should have been *Grease*, not Greece.

Carrie symbolized the ongoing struggle in the musical, between its natural tendencies to mindless nostalgiafest on the one hand, and the push towards a semi-operatic twilight zone on the other. Theatre, these days, is so peripheral to cultural life that, for the most part, it's no longer a form but only a venue: a chance to see things you know you liked in other media – whether the collected correspondence of *Vita and Virginia* or the ham-fisted *Tribute to the Blues Brothers* – live on stage. On Broadway, the most significant development of the nineties has been the emergence of Disney as legit producer with *Beauty and the Beast*. The audience goes into the Palace Theatre for no other reason than to see the movie repro-duced as exactly as possible. It's worked so well that Disney is now planning to do the same all over the world with the rest of its catalogue: legitimate theatre as merchandizing.

London responds, meanwhile, with *Forbidden Planet*, and *Copa-cabana* (after the Barry Manilow hit single), and *Buddy*, and *Patsy Cline*, the story of another American singer who never lived long enough to redeem her frequent-flyer miles but who, otherwise, was even duller than Buddy Holly. At one time, show songs used to break into the pop charts. Now, the pop charts have broken into the shows. Mort Shuman had the failure of his 1988 musical *Budgie* at the Cambridge compounded by the success at the same theatre of *Forbidden Planet*: there, to shrieks of delight, his first hit, 'Why Must I Be A Teenager In Love?', was sung on a cardboard space rocket by Miranda after a row with her dad, Prospero. The most recent song by Charles Strouse, the distinguished composer of *Annie*, to be heard on a West End stage is 'Born Too Late', a piece of juvenilia he wrote for the Poni-Tails in 1958 and cheerfully resurrected for the West End compilation *The Fabulous Singlettes*. The creators of all these productions understand that, whereas contemporary pop is hopelessly fragmented and conventional showtunes are now meaningless to many, for those under 55 American popular songs of this period are the nearest thing to a common cultural vocabulary. But what will we do in 20, 30 years when there are no pre-sold hit catalogues to buy into?

At the other end of the spectrum, the tragedy of musical theatre is that its greatest talents seem to wish oblivion on the form. After the extraordinary achievement of *West Side Story*, Leonard Bernstein just stopped. Later, he wrote *Mass*, with its ersatz rock elements; *1600 Pennsylvania Avenue*, of which it would be politer to say nothing; *A Quiet Place*, an atrocious opera in which he turned his back on the principles which underpinned his finest stage work; and he spent the last years of his life tinkering with *Candide*, a Voltaire operetta whose characters include a woman with only one buttock – but, then, the whole show is half-assed.

'We all wanted to do something again after *West Side*,' says Arthur Laurents, 'and Lenny was hipped on it being important. He kept saying, "It's gotta be important." And it just seemed such a truism but I said to him, "If it's good, it'll be important." He was too carried away with that because of his classical peers saying to him, "You are going into the gutter when you write that Broadway stuff." He was a victim of classical snobbism, and he went out of his way to complicate his talent. Years later, Lenny and I started to work on a piece called *Alarums and Excursions*. I had given him a three or four page treatment, and he was excited about it. And then he began writing it and that's where the opera thing came up. He was making it into an opera and I did not want to write an opera. I don't like opera very much, because the language is twisted to fit the music and

I'm a playwright. I don't like this repetition of words that one has in opera to make it fit the notes. Ten times they say . . .

Go, go, don't stay, go, please don't stay, go

. . . and I've gone by then.'

It's the old debate, argued by Blitzstein, Weill, Gershwin, Berlin, Kern and Lehár, too. According to Stephen Sondheim, 'In any realistic terms the musical is hilarious.' Granted that some people will never swallow a fellow bursting into song in the middle of a busy office or a packed courtroom, the book show comes closest to having its cake and eating it, of maintaining the real world and yet bringing musical drama to it. *Street Scene* (1947), revived in 1989 at Scottish Opera, is a convincing marriage between the naturalism of a play and the musicality of opera. In Elmer Rice's book, the inconsequential colloquial exchanges of the New York tenement house slide unobtrusively into long musical passages of operatic passion: Kurt Weill's music (despite Langston Hughes' disappointing lyrics) seeps into the book until it engulfs it; then, emotionally drained, the score recedes and conversation resumes. 'The singing takes over whenever the emotion of the spoken word reaches a point where the music can speak with greater effect,' said Weill at the time.

John Mauceri, Scottish Opera's music director, has a cute line about *Street Scene* being the only opera whose heroine is a housewife. But, as *Street Scene* has Broadway dialogue scenes, the conclusion we ought to draw is that the operatic form is no good for housewives. The two big pop operas, *Phantom* and *Les Miz*, are both set in the nineteenth century – the sort of shows, to quote Lee Shubert's brute dismissal of costume drama, where people write letters with feathers. These stories and characters are from the mists of history; they suit a form from the mists of history. But what of other stories? stories from our time?

Aaron Copland, a 'serious' composer, once said he was thinking of writing a musical like one of Irving Berlin's – as if this was something he could knock off on a wet weekend. He never got round to his musical, but Alan Ayckbourn did, so did Anthony Burgess and Fay Weldon. Terry Hands, when artistic director of the Royal Shakespeare Company, proclaimed his show *Carrie* as the first serious 'music-drama' since *West Side Story*; the choreographer of another mega-flop *Bernadette* hailed *his* show as the most ambitious dance musical since *West Side Story*; Elton John regularly talks about writing a musical which will be the most important breakthrough since (all together now) *West Side Story*. Musicals seem to attract have-a-go nutters, all blissfully ignorant, all latching onto the last musical they dimly recall having seen on TV on a Sunday afternoon. Simon Gray, who is apparently a distinguished British playwright, wrote a droll newspaper piece about how he'd been invited to do a musical with Betty Comden and Adolph Green but that he'd never heard of them. They've written songs like 'The Party's Over', films like *Singin' in the Rain*, and their shows stretch from *On the Town* to the 1991 Tony winner, *The Will Rogers Follies*. So who's Simon Gray?

But somewhere between Gray's self-defeating highbrow snobbery and the over-refined expertise of the old pros on Central Park West lies the demented amateurism of the British musical. I've wrassled bears on the frozen tundra; defended my gold stake in the Rio Grande against gangs of predatory, inbred mountain men; taken out three units of Soviet artillery with my bare hands as an undercover CIA agent in Afghanistan; but being a judge on the Vivian Ellis Prize for new musicals in 1990 was my toughest assignment yet. There was a contemporary musical about an accountant:

> Two years ago my dad was convicted of fraud
> A crime he did not commit
> He claims he was set up, someone getting even
> With two years inside he was hit . . .

Then there was 'Once In A Lifetime', the big ballad from yet another version of *Cyrano de Bergerac*:

> Look at me and say
> Love will find a way
> Give me just one day . . .

As Tim Rice pointed out, there have been a zillion songs called 'Once In A Lifetime': it's the sound of somebody content to write up the first idea that occurred. Dissenting from Rice's and Don Black's and Andrew Lloyd Webber's and Cameron Mackintosh's cool reaction to the entries, someone in the audience observed that such masterpieces as Stravinsky's *Rite of Spring* and Debussy's *L'Après-midi d'un Faune* had also been dismissed at first hearing. We may not know it for years to come, he reckoned, but the workshop had been 'a hotbed of hugely significant work'.

Well, as they say on Broadway, don't faune us, we'll faune you. My experience of hot beds is not as extensive as I would wish, but I figure you'd have a steamier night with a hibernating sloth than with the Vivian Ellis Prize entrants. Alastair Beaton, co-writer of *King* and *Ziegfeld* and therefore relishing the chance to see some musicals which were even worse than his, told me that his favourite lyric from the Vivian Ellis ran:

My life has been marred by normality.

Sadly, musical theatre itself is in perpetual danger of being marred by normality, by scores which are tasteful but lifeless, roadshow Rodgers or roadshow Sondheim or roadshow Lloyd Webber, whatever the fashion of the moment is. I think of young Andrew: the schmuck at school who liked *The Sound of Music*. As Don Black and Tim Rice have both said, normal people don't write musicals. And normality is no way to make a musical. Bring on the perverts.

Exit Music

The Survivor

In 1993, while Broadway celebrated its centenary, George Abbott was at his home upstate rewriting his 1955 hit *Damn Yankees* for a major revival. So, I enquired, what's the new script like? He was non-committal, then added modestly, 'But it's better than what most 106-year-old writers are doing.'

When you're 106, standing ovations at showbiz get-togethers are automatic. 'I'd like to think you're applauding me for my distinguished career in theatre,' he'd say, 'but I know it's just because I'm so goddamned old.' Abbott has always been goddamned old, though, older even than his oldest collaborators, Irving Berlin, Rodgers and Hart and Hammerstein; older than Eugene O'Neill, who was in the year below him in Professor Baker's famous playwriting course. 'Always remember,' says Hal Prince, 'George was too old for World War One.'

But on Broadway these days the only people who aren't dead are incredibly old, and it seemed eerily fitting that the oldest of the lot endured even as everything around him crumbled, including the theatre Broadway named in his honour, the George Abbott – now a parking lot. At an Abbott centenary symposium, the moderator solemnly announced: 'The George Abbott Theatre is no longer standing.' 'No, but he still is,' shouted someone in the audience – which is what counts. Broadway is too inclined to sentimentalize and memorialize the good old days; Abbott preferred to live in the present. Come hit or flop, his reaction the morning after opening night was always the same: 'What's next?'

On the bits of Broadway that aren't yet parking lots, is anything real any more? Take this alleged centenary: there's a playhouse on Broadway marked on a city map of 1735; Niblo's Garden was built at Broadway and Prince Street in 1828; Lester Wallack made his Broadway début at a Broadway theatre called the Broadway Theatre in 1847. But, like a faded starlet, Broadway insists on lying about its age. If we take this typical bit of trashy marketing opportunism at face value, Abbott was older than Broadway and, if only because so little else has survived, came to be seen as its embodiment: he made his acting début at the Hudson in 1913 in a play called *The Misleading Lady*; he was still playing 82 seasons later a few hundred yards away in the grey concrete precincts of the Marriott Marquis; and his first hit as a playwright was titled, with a neatness historians can only marvel at, simply *Broadway* – a wonderful Jazz Age melodrama full of gangsters and showgirls that seems in its vernacular rowdiness the very essence of New York theatre.

But sometimes the exception proves the rule. The personification of Broadway was very unBroadway: he wasn't Jewish or homosexual or East Coast or gushily theatrical; he didn't live in the past and he didn't bullshit; he dressed formally and his nickname was an anti-nickname – Mister Abbott. Many of his protégés were variously Jewish homosexual East Coast gushy nostalgic bullshitters, but, even then, they didn't seem *that* Broadway at first glance. To pluck a creative team at random, Jerome Robbins, Leonard Bernstein, Betty Comden and Adolph Green are revered today as Broadway bluechips. But, in 1944, who'd have thought that a ballet choreographer, a symphony conductor and a couple of Greenwich Village satirists had a Main Stem musical in them? Mister Abbott did, and I don't think any other Broadway director (were there any other Broadway directors in 1944?) could have maintained the balancing act needed to pull off *On the Town*.

> New York, New York!
> A helluva town!

'I always thought that was the best New York song,' Mister Abbott tells me half-a-century later. 'But the new one's better – the one the little girl sings . . .' He's thinking of another trio of Abbott protégés, Liza Minnelli and Kander and Ebb:

> Start spreading the news
> I'm leaving today
> I want to be a part of it
> New York, New York!

The songs and the myths have got stronger, even as the town's declined. Born in 1887, Mister Abbott arrived in New York via the Lackawanna Railroad and a ferry cross the Hudson. After *The Misleading Lady*, he got a part in *The Queen's Enemies* (1916) and then *Lightnin'* (1918). It's a play about a boozy teller of tall tales who owns a hotel on the California/Nevada border: there's a line drawn across the lobby so that guests coming to procure a divorce don't find themselves in the wrong state.

Winchell Smith and Frank Bacon wrote it, but it needed work, so Smith asked Abbott for help. It was the first play he ever fixed and he did it so well it became the longest-running show in Broadway history until overtaken by *Abie's Irish Rose* seven years later. By his thirties, Mister Abbott was the leading writer / director / producer of farce and melodrama; at the age of 43, he co-wrote the Oscar-winning *All Quiet on the Western Front*, one of the first masterpieces in the infant talking picture industry; at the age of 48, he turned to musical comedy. Beginning with *Jumbo* in 1935, he staged 26 musicals in 27 years, 22 of which were hits – a record unlikely to be broken; in that period, there were only two weeks when he wasn't represented on Broadway by one, two or three productions. He directed and co-wrote Rodgers and Hart's best shows (*On Your Toes, The Boys from Syracuse, Pal Joey*), then *On the Town, Call Me Madam, The Pajama Game, A Funny Thing Happened on the Way to the Forum* – and in between he still found time for a couple of straight plays per season. At 72, he won a Pulitzer Prize for *Fiorello!*; at 75, he had three hits running simultaneously on Broadway; at 96, he became the oldest director ever to stage a Broadway hit, with his revival of *On Your Toes*; at 98, he took the show to London and became the oldest director to stage a West End hit; at 102, he became the oldest director to stage an off-Broadway flop; at 106 he was back on Broadway with the new *Damn Yankees* . . . He worked with David Belasco, author of the original *Madam Butterfly*; he was still working in the age of *Miss Saigon*. Or to put it in non-theatrical terms: most Americans know where they were when President Kennedy was asassinated; he could remember where he was when President McKinley was assassinated back in 1901.

As befits a man with that perspective, a man who saw Communism come and go, Mister Abbott was not, in any sense, a political dramatist. But, in the mid-fifties, he was asked to stage a rally for Adlai Stevenson – an odd choice considering it was Abbott's 1950 hit *Call Me Madam* which gave Stevenson's opponent his campaign song, 'I like Ike'. Nevertheless, he said yes and went down to Madison Square Garden only to find that the Democrats invariably turned up late for rehearsal, which he hated, and, worse, hadn't learned their lines. He withdrew from the rally.

It's tempting to see this as some sort of political metaphor. At any rate, it embodies Mister Abbott's approach to his art: he was a practical man of the theatre, open-minded about content because he understood that what counts is how efficiently you serve it. He made sense of comedy and musicals, establishing rules we still work to today, and he was lucky enough to practise his craft when there was still enough of it around to practise on. In that crowded 1927–28 season of 264 new plays and musicals, he had four of them, including his landmark weepie, *Coquette*. A month later, *Show Boat* opened, and the night after that Edna Ferber and George Kaufman's *The Royal Family*, and a couple of weeks later Eugene O'Neill's *Strange Interlude*. *Show Boat* and *Strange Interlude* alone justify the other 262. Today, a season's worth of openings barely scrapes into double figures. But it's a delusion to think you can slice off the lower levels of the pyramid without affecting the heights the top brick can reach. Abbott worked with great artists, professional craftsmen and inferior hacks, and he did his best by all of them.

*

He refined his skills on farce, on *Room Service* and *Three Men on a Horse* and *Boy Meets Girl*. Farce is the most logically demanding form of theatre, the most disciplined, and Abbott applied those disciplines when he moved into musicals. He had no theories about theatre, but, when it came to specifics, he was full of good advice: 'I always find that the most successful comedy songs come from a line in the book. If you're looking for an idea for a comic song, find the line in the play that gets the biggest laugh and make it into a song. Reprise the line as a song.' There's one answer to Second Act problems, and when Jule Styne, Comden and Green were in Boston with *Bells Are Ringing* (1956) that advice saved the show.

'Judy Holliday says that she won't open in New York if she does not have an 11 o'clock song,' Styne remembered. 'She had a comedy scene but she wanted an 11 o'clock song. Comden and Green worked all day. Nothing. She liked nothing. So I stayed home from the theatre one night, and then it came to me: what is the thing they laugh the most at in the play of *Bells Are Ringing*? It's when she says, "I worked at the Bonjour Tristesse Brassiere Company." The Françoise Sagan book was Number One at that time. So I sat down and I wrote:

> I'm going back
> Where I can be me
> At the Bonjour Tristesse Brassiere Compan*ee* . . .

Wow! You should have heard that in the theatre. Just like Abbott said it would be. She did it with imitations of Jolson and all the other things. And it worked – thanks to George.'

This is play-making on the hoof, but you can do it only if you've dissected the structures of drama. The younger generation gave it fancier names – the 'integrated musical', the 'concept musical' – but Abbott was the first to understand the ways in which you could bind book and score together, and the first to appreciate the need for stylistic cohesion.

'More directors, writers, composers, lyricists and performers have come out of the Abbott atelier than from any other single figure in the history of the American theatre,' says Hal Prince, who came to work for Abbott half a century ago and, in the 1995 'phone book, was still listed as sharing an office in Rockefeller Center with him. 'It's not because he's lived to 106, but because he's so secure about himself that he's not begrudging in his generosity and encouragement.' He served as 'apprentices' sorcerer' to talents as disparate as George Balanchine, the first Broadway choreographer to be billed as such; and Nora Ephron, whose letters from college he turned into a hit play in 1963; and Styne and Bernstein, Comden and Green, Robbins and Fosse and Prince, Frank Loesser and Garson Kanin, Gwen Verdon and John O'Hara, Gene Kelly and Stanley Donen, Sammy Cahn and Morton Gould, Carol Burnett and Natalia Makarova, Shirley MacLaine and Liza Minnelli, Adler and Ross, Bock and Harnick, Kander and Ebb; and Stephen Sondheim's first show as composer . . . His family tree extends through his own work to *Born Yesterday* and *Guys and Dolls* and *Fiddler on the Roof* and *Evita* and *Sweeney Todd*. Nine decades after Mister Abbott had his first play produced, it's difficult to find a Broadway musical which hasn't been written or staged by an Abbott graduate – hit or flop, *Phantom* or *Cyrano*, *Kiss of the Spider Woman* or *The Red Shoes*, *Passion* or *The Will Rogers Follies*.

But just as representative of 'the Abbott touch' is Clifford Goldsmith. Who? Clifford Goldsmith, born 1900, Aurora, NY, died 1971; high school nutritionist. Goldsmith had one good idea for a get-me-to-the-junior-prom farce, he wrote it up, Abbott fixed it, produced it and staged it, and *What a Life* became one of the most successful plays of the day, and then a long-running radio series. Goldsmith never had another hit; presumably he went back to the high-school nutrition business, whatever that is. But, like Philip Dunning (*Broadway*), Maurine Dallas Watkins (*Chicago*) and Ann Preston Bridgers (*Coquette*) and a dozen other one-hit footnotes to theatrical history, he had his moment – thanks to Abbott.

'When I started,' he told me, 'the typical musical just stuck a song in with a cue like "Isn't it a nice day?" and then they'd have a song about the nice day.' Mister Abbott introduced logic to the form – not for fancy notions about art, but just because he prided himself on doing a professional job. Prior to taking over the star role in *Wonderful Town*, Carol Channing asked: 'Who *is* Ruth Sherwood?' 'Ruth Sherwood is whoever plays her,' he answered. He cast actors because they were right as people: he didn't want them *acting*. 'I did a film with Woody Allen,' says Gwen Verdon, 'and he kept saying, "Don't act. Just say the words." And I thought that was very strange because Mister Abbott 40 years before had said the same thing: "Don't act. Just say the words." '

*

Of today's hits, he said to me, 'I love the way the English have taken the thing over and spent all that money on it. It wasn't that we didn't have the money, we didn't have the *thought*. The English were backward, we thought they knew nothing about musicals. Now we're eating out of their hand.'

He looked more like a puritan New England farmer than a Broadway director, a severe authority figure with piercing eyes, who in rehearsal always wore a necktie and never removed his jacket. After a gruelling technical rehearsal of *Wonderful Town* in 1953, Rosalind Russell marvelled at his energy: 'Isn't Mister Abbott amazing? You know he's sixty-six!' He was still amazing at a hundred, raising himself up and clambering out of a stalled elevator at the Algonquin Hotel, walking downstairs and then across town in 97-degree temperatures. At 107, he walked a little unsteadily and needed support, and preferred to write in an easy chair with a butcher's board across the arms. Otherwise, he was much the same as ever, still chasing another hit. He had little time for the notion of the 'undeserved flop'. Once, I mentioned to him how much I'd enjoyed *Frankie*, his update of the Frankenstein story relocated to the Catskills, which he co-wrote with a young Lloyd Webberish composer and directed off-Broadway at the age of 102. 'That's what I call wasted time,' he snapped, and returned to what he considered more fruitful areas of conversation. At 102, a guy can't afford wasted time – especially in an arena where new musicals now take almost a decade to reach the stage. Abbott's successors transformed popular theatre into art – and forgot to take the audience with them: the heirs to Abbott and Rodgers gathered all their expertise, all their technique, and lavished it on *Passion* and *The Petrified Prince*. The theatre needs hits: it was because Abbott had given Prince three in a row that the young producer could afford to take a chance on *West Side Story*; Abbott's production of *A Funny Thing Happened on the Way to the Forum* gave Sondheim the financial cushion to indulge himself with *Pacific Overtures* and *Assassins*. Hard-core Sondheim groupies tend to look on *Forum* as an aberration: good grief, it ran three years and made piles of money; best not to mention it. But Sondheim himself in his more generous moments points out that *Forum* is, if you give it a moment's thought, one of his most formally experimental works. For one thing, it's the only musical farce that's ever worked. Farce is difficult to musicalize because there's too much plot to fit any songs in, and, if you try to use songs in the traditional Rodgers and Hammerstein sense, it all gets too relentless. *Forum* uses the songs as a respite: instead of, as in a musical play, advancing the situation or illuminating character, they bring the play juddering to a halt; they're a chance to stand still and catch your breath. Mister Abbott took a one-set no-romance anti-musical and made it seem such an obvious, natural hit that its innovations were completely overlooked.

You find this throughout his career. He delivered hits, but *On Your Toes* (1936), only his second musical, was the first Broadway show with a dramatically integrated ballet; *The Boys from Syracuse* (1938) was the first Shakespearean musical; *Pal Joey* (1940) was the first with an anti-hero; *On the Town* (1944) was the first with a symphonic score; *Look, Ma, I'm Dancin'* (1948) was the first dance musical; even *Wonderful Town* (1953) has a musicalized dinner party scene far more radical than anything Bernstein wrote when he moved into opera proper with works like *A Quiet Place* . . . Abbott never indulged innovation: it's not its own justification. But would Rodgers have gone on to do *Oklahoma!* and *Carousel* if Abbott hadn't shown him, in their five shows together, that musicals could have their own dramatic integrity?

*

At a 100th birthday seminar, an earnest drama student asked him, 'Mister Abbott, when did the theatre first become tainted by commercialism?' '1601,' he replied, 'when Shakespeare said to Burbage, "Now let's get this show to a bigger theatre."' Abbott was as confident cutting Shakespeare as Comden and Green, and here *is* a funny thing: as the years go by, *Kiss Me, Kate* and *West Side Story* seem more and more products of their era, and no great threat to the originals; but, in transforming *The Comedy of Errors* into *The Boys from Syracuse*,

Abbott streamlined the structure, loosened up the comedy, and ended up improving on Shakespeare. Ever since, the most successful versions of *The Comedy* have always given the impression that they'd much rather be doing the musical; Shakespeare directors have devoted most of their energies to finding substitutes for Rodgers and Hart, drafting in everyone from Sir Arthur Sullivan (London, 1952) to the calypso balladeer Cy Young (Bristol, 1960); the best production of recent years – Trevor Nunn's for the RSC – threw in the towel and decided what the hell, let's do a musical.

A couple of seasons ago, Dame Judi Dench staged *The Boys from Syracuse* at the Open Air Theatre in Regent's Park and this is what she did: as the three ladies are doing 'Sing For Your Supper', she brought on a man dressed as a giant chicken; unable to stage the song, she decided instead that the song needed help. The trouble with the contemporary theatre is that its stagers are all giant chickens: rather than convince you of the material, they panic, and distract you from the material with irrelevant flim flam. Abbott never did. In New Haven with *Call Me Madam*, he suggested that Irving Berlin write another contrapuntal number, like one he remembered from 40 years earlier, 'Play A Simple Melody'. Berlin came back with '(You're Not Sick) You're Just In Love'. Abbott and Robbins were so confident of the song that they told Berlin it would be sung unstaged: no lights, no dancing, nothing to get in the way. It stopped the show. Conversely, struggling with a campy romp called *Out of this World*, he junked Cole Porter's 'From This Moment On'. In 1994, I asked him how he could possibly have done such a thing. 'I'd do it again tomorrow,' he growled. 'It slowed the show.' He was the first director to bring dramatic considerations to musical structure: it had to be the right song in the right place.

It made a difference that he was a writer/director in a writer's theatre. Before Abbott, directors were traffic cops: they looked after the star and moved people on and off. Today, directors are the only stars left: the '94 *Show Boat* stars Hal Prince; in 1927, who knew or cared who directed it? (Zeke Colvan.) Abbott knew that, in a theatre where the directors are the stars, you soon run out of anything to direct. In 1994, at the Public Theatre, Prince devoted a year of work, almost 30 actors and three-quarters of a million dollars to *The Petrified Prince* and ran up against the limits of his power. In the end, the property matters: there *is* a difference between Kern and Hammerstein or Sondheim, on the one hand, and Michael John LaChiusa, on the other, and the slickest stager in the world can't hide it:

Feel
If you can feel
Then you can speak
Shout
Rise . . .

It isn't worth Prince's trouble.

Fashions change, but, years after they went their separate ways, Prince respected Abbott enough always to arrange a private full-dress performance of his shows before his mentor. So Abbott would sit fifth-row centre, and the cast would play *Cabaret* – in three acts. 'Put it in two acts,' said the old play doctor afterwards. Prince did, and you marvel today at how, structurally, it could ever have been otherwise: the First Act finale, where the waiters sing their sweetly beguiling 'Tomorrow Belongs To Me' and then you see for the first time their swastikas, seems so obviously the First Act finale you can't believe it took Abbott to point it out. In the sixty years after *Jumbo*, there were a few he missed. '*West Side Story* was one of my great mistakes,' he said. 'I was offered it, but I thought it was silly. They talked like a lot of kids and sounded to me nothing like tough guys. When I saw it, I loved it.' He was generous enough to realize that his pupils were graduating. Impressed by a Hal Prince staging moment in *Phantom*, he leaned over to his wife Joy and said, 'Well, that's something he didn't learn from me.'

'He doesn't think in terms of what is now called the concept,' Prince told me, 'but he thinks about the arc. He knows the trajectory of a show, which is why he's had so few disasters in a lifetime in the theatre. He was the master of American farce comedy but there is never a dishonest moment on the stage. Characters are always consistent with their character. He never slams a door for the sake of slamming a door, he slams it for a reason. His shows are honest, peppy, energetic – *really* energetic, and that's another thing I learned from him. There's so much phoney energy in the theatre: people think that by running around in circles like a crazed tiger, you're displaying energy, and, in fact, you're not. You can have energy in the stillest place in the world, and he knew that.' Even as he organized and disciplined comedy and musicals, Abbott never confused tempo with speed. Today, that mistake has become routine. Jerry Zaks' heartless burlesques of *Guys and Dolls* and *Anything Goes* are full of 'phoney energy', and, even as the director's heaped with honours, you wonder: if these weren't revivals, if we didn't already love them, would Zaks' stagings persuade us of their merits?

From its concoction of fake centenaries to its obsession with revivals, we know that Broadway wishes it could turn the clock back. But all it can do is fake it. Abbott took the most stylized and artificial forms of theatre – farce and musicals – and filled them with recognizable Americans in street clothes. Perhaps it's more difficult than it sounds, at least to judge by the grim cartoons of Zaks and co. Or perhaps all the 'lively arts' eventually devour themselves: like pop music and TV, Broadway has acquired too much of a back catalogue to be anything other than self-referential and post-modern. Abbott liked to quote the one about holding a mirror up to nature; today, shows are about shows, not nature.

*

I liked the way he wasn't consumed by theatre. Almost to the end, after auditions (which he invented, by the way: before, actors were interviewed in the producer's office and then rehearsed unpaid) he'd take his leading ladies dancing at Roseland. 'We were doing a mambo and I missed a count,' says Gwen Verdon, 'so he sat me down and hired a hostess. For a moment, I thought I'd lost the show.' He played tennis well into his eighties, when the last of his old partners died. Then he took up golf. For his 106th birthday, his wife had a new swimming pool put in so he could do his laps every morning. On the first day, Mister Abbott, who'd been swimming for over a century but was a little out of practise, climbed in and sank like a stone. As he was fished out, he said: 'Damn thing doesn't work. Send it back.'

He grew up in Wyoming; he worked as a cowboy, and one of his early acting roles was as a cowboy; to Hal Prince and others, he looked like Gary Cooper. Certainly, he shared both Cooper's famous economy of language and his integrity. It was fascinating to watch him in San Diego, in the theatre night after night, those bright piercing eyes fixing the stage, anxious to whip *Damn Yankees* into shape for Broadway. At dinner before the opening, he filled the glass of his friend, the dancer Natalia Makarova. 'How's the wine?' he asked. 'So-so,' she said. A few moments later, she enquired how the show was. 'Same as the wine,' he said.

So-so? How so?

In *Damn Yankees*, Mister Abbott wrote what's possibly the most irresistible song cue in musical comedy, a locker-room pep talk from the coach:

'Now listen to me. This game of baseball is only one-half skill. The other half is something else. Something bigger.'

(*Ding!*)

> You gotta have Heart!
> All you really need is Heart!
> When the odds are saying you'll never win
> That's when the grin should start . . .

Substitute 'theatre' for 'baseball' and there's the recipe which kept Abbott on Broadway for eight decades. In an age when our stage offers either the slick but unfelt or the honest but incompetent, we could all learn from the Abbott model: skill plus heart – or, as he'd put it, peppy but not phoney; or, if you like, efficient but true. If either half gets out of kilter, you're in trouble. Mister Abbott's is a cue for all songs.

It goes without saying that by the time the new *Damn Yankees* had been 'revised' by the director Jack O'Brien, those lines had gone missing. O'Brien's *Damn Yankees* didn't have heart: it was a camp turn for Victor Garber as the Devil, plus some chorus numbers. O'Brien got away with it (as other revivals have done) because of the strength of the material and our residual affection for it. It opened on Broadway in March 1994 and afterwards, as usual, Mister Abbott told friends, 'I'm available.' After all, even off-duty, the most reliable of show fixers couldn't resist rewrites. A couple of years earlier, golfing with his wife Joy, he suddenly dropped his clubs and collapsed; the colour drained from his cheeks, his eyes closed and his breathing slowed. 'I'll go get help, darling,' said Joy. 'Just lay there.'

'"*Lie* there"!' Mister Abbott corrected her and then passed out.

He died at his home in Miami Beach on 31 January 1995, aged 107 and a half. The day before, he'd been working on a new production of *The Pajama Game*, dictating rewrites. Mister Abbott's was an American life, and a life in the theatre, from ranches and brothels to Tonys and Pulitzers. And, to the end, the old play doctor was still trying to work out how to fix the show.

Would that we could.

END

Acknowledgements

Almost everything I know about musicals comes from other people, from writers, stagers, producers and performers who've been good enough to share their accumulated wisdom with me. It came as a shock to realize, when writing this book, how many of them have since died. Indeed, during the final revision of the text, one more passed on: Irving Caesar, lyricist of *No, No, Nanette* and the epitome of Tin Pan Alley in a rowdier, more artless age. I first met him when he was a comparative whippersnapper in his late 80s, and he took me through the genesis of his greatest hits: ' "Swanee"? Wrote it in ten minutes.' ' "Tea For Two"? Wrote it in seven minutes.' Then he'd sing them to you – a small, white-haired man in bow tie and candy-striped blazer, bellowing away unaccompanied except for the puffs of his cigar and the squeaks of his fully reclining Barcalounger. A couple of years later, he told me, ' "Swanee"? Wrote it in six minutes.' ' "Tea For Two"? Wrote it in four minutes.' I was alarmed. At this rate of anecdotal attrition, he'd soon have taken less time to write them than it took to sing them – and what would happen then? When he told me he wrote 'Swanee' in two minutes, I somehow knew it would be the last time I saw him. He died just before Christmas 1996, aged 101½.

He never cared much for rock and its ancillary activities: a couple of years back, he told me he'd written an anti-drug song called 'Who Needs Marijuana, Baby, When All I Wanna Marry Is You?' 'Don't tell me,' I said. 'You wrote it in three minutes?' I like to think of him up there on his celestial Barcalounger bugging the hell out of dead rock stars with it.

Caesar's great line was 'Remember, kid, no one knows nothing' – which is probably true. Nonetheless, I'm grateful for all he and his confrères have let me in on.

I would also like to thank Helen Sprott, who, during her time at Faber and Faber, commissioned this book, and also Belinda Matthews and Matthew Evans, who saw it through to completion. I'd also like to thank Tom Sutcliffe of the *Independent*, who was the first person in the United Kingdom to ask me to write about musicals, and who gave me a fancy title, too: when the Immigration Officer at Heathrow asked me the purpose of my visit, I replied that I was here to take up a position as Musical Theatre Correspondent of the London *Independent*. 'That's a job?' he said. Thanks to Tom, it was.

Above all, I'm grateful as always to my assistant Moni Haworth.

Mark Steyn
Québec
December 1996

For permission to reprint lyrics in this book the publishers gratefully acknowledge the following:

Artisjus: 'The genre has become history' and 'Operette! Operette! Operette!' (Robert Ratonyi); 'The bright has been plunged into darkness' and 'Hungarians! Men and women!' (János Bródy).

BMG Music Publishers: 'He bumped off his uncle' (from *Hamlet*) (Frank Loesser).

Bocu Music: 'I must search day and night' (from *Metropolis*) (unattributed), by permission of Bocu Music.

Campbell Connelly & Co. Ltd: 'Don't Blame Me' (words and music by Jimmy McHugh, Dorothy Fields), © 1933 MGM Corporation, USA. Rights assigned Robbins Music Corp., USA Campbell Connelly & Co. Ltd., 8/9 Frith Street, London w1v 5tz. Used by permission. All Rights Reserved; 'Big Spender' and 'Charity's Soliloquy' (music: Cy Coleman; words: Dorothy Fields), © 1965 by Dorothy Fields and Cy Coleman. Rights assigned to Notable Music Co. Inc., in co-publication with Lida Enterprises Inc., USA Campbell Connelly & Co. Ltd., 8/9 Frith Street, w1v 5tz. Used by permission. All Rights Reserved.

Carlin Music: 'As Time Goes By' (Herman Hupfeld); 'If You Could See Her' (from *Cabaret*) (John Kander and Fred Ebb); 'Tradition' (from *Fiddler on the Roof*) (Sheldon Harnick and Jerry Bock); 'One More Kiss', 'You're Gonna Love Tomorrow', 'Could I Leave You' and 'Losing My Mind' (from *Follies*) (Stephen Sondheim); 'You Could Drive A Person Crazy' and 'Another Hundred People' (from *Company*) (Stephen Sondheim), by permission of Carlin Music.

Essex Music Group: 'Where Is Love?' (Lionel Bart).

Faber Music Ltd: 'Memory' (from *Cats*) (Trevor Nunn's lyric based on T. S. Eliot), by permission of Faber and Faber Ltd.

Famous Music: 'Upon the island from . . .' (from 'Sing A Tropical Song') (Frank Loesser/Jimmy McHugh), © 1942 and 1944 by Paramount Music Corporation, copyright renewed 1969 and 1971 by Paramount Music Corporation, by permission of Famous Music Corporation.

Frank Music Corporation: 'Take Back Your Mink' and 'You promised me this' (from *Guys and Dolls*) (Frank Loesser), by permission of Frank Music Corporation.

Glocken Verlag Ltd: *The Merry Widow* (English lyrics by Christopher Hassall), ©

1958 Glocken Verlag Ltd. For the British Commonwealth of Nations, its Protectorates, Dependencies, Eire and all the United States of America Glocken Verlag Ltd. For all other countries, published by Ludwig Doblinger (Bernard Herzmansky), reproduced by permission of the copyright owners; *The Count of Luxemburg* by Franz Lehár (original lyrics copyright Glocken Verlag). Translation reproduced by permission of the copyright owner of the original.

Hargitay Verlag AG: 'Equal rights and civil rights' (from *King – The Musical*) (Maya Angelou).

International Music Publications Ltd: 'Say that ev'rything is still alright', 'Sweet as can be', 'God Bless America', 'What'll I Do', 'I'll be loving you', 'There's No Business', 'I can't recall who said it' and 'Chaps' (all Irving Berlin). **International Music Publications Ltd (and EMI Music Publishing):** 'You gotta have Heart' (from *Damn Yankees*) (George Abbott, with Richard Adler and Jerry Ross) and 'He collapsed' (from *A Tree Grows in Brooklyn*) (George Abbott, with Betty Smith); 'Something elitist', 'Though I keep writing my scores' and 'Come see us grovel in the dirt' (from *Forbidden Broadway*) (Gerard Allesandrini); 'Livin' Doll' (Lionel Bart); 'My Blue Heaven' (Walter Donaldson); 'I'm In The Mood For Love' and 'Grab your coat and get your hat' (Dorothy Fields); 'You can't hear a sound' and 'When the children are asleep' (from *Carousel*) and 'I'm in love!' (from *South Pacific*) (Oscar Hammerstein II); 'I'll be your nincompoop', 'I could show my prowess' (from *Wizard of Oz*) and 'We got no Mussolini' (from *Hoorah for What!*) (all Yip Harburg); 'How can you connect in an age', 'To riding your bike midday', 'To Sontag' and 'You're living in America' (Jonathan Larson); 'Hey, Look Me Over' (Carolyn Leigh); 'Maybe the Sun' and 'What a day this has been' (from *Brigadoon*) (Alan Jay Lerner); 'It's a happy feeling . . .' (Mitchell Parish); 'Oh, What A Beautiful Mornin'', 'You've got to be taught', 'Do you hear a waltz?', 'Her long, yeller hair', 'The furtive sigh', 'Don't want nuthin'' and 'The corn is as high as a cow-pony's eye' (all from *Oklahoma!*) (Rodgers and Hammerstein); 'We'll have Manhattan', 'Our future babies' and 'I'll sing to him' (from *Pal Joey*) (Rodgers and Lorenz Hart); 'Time' (from *Do I Hear a Waltz?*) (Stephen Sondheim). **International Music Publications Ltd (and Stratford Music Ltd):** 'They've burst your pretty balloon' and 'I'm going back' (from *Bells Are Ringing*) (Betty Comden and Adolph Green). **International Music Publications Ltd (and Warner Chappell Music):** 'Hey There' (from *The Pajama Game*) (Adler and Ross); 'When I get my name in lights' (Peter Allen); 'The trouble is he's lazy' (from *West Side Story*) (Leonard Bernstein); 'Picture you' (from *No, No, Nanette*) (Irving Caesar); 'Kiss me once, then kiss me twice' (Sammy Cahn); 'I try hard to stay controlled' and 'New York, New York!' (from *On the Town*), and 'This thing is a frost' (from *It's Always Fair Weather*) (all Comden and Green); 'Why Must The Show Go On?', 'Though my world may go awry' and 'Do not let this aid to rhyming' (Noel Coward); 'A ghost and a prince meet' (from *Hamlet*) (Howard Dietz); 'Noisy boys long and lean' (from *The Rink*) (Frederick Ebb); 'Hello! Ma Baby' (Ida Emerson and Jo Howard); 'It's Not Where You Start' (from *Seesaw*) and 'He was shy and awful modest' (from *A Tree Grows in Brooklyn*) (Dorothy Fields); 'The march of the falsettos' (William Finn); 'My bonds and shares' (from *Crazy for You*) and 'A title' (quotation) (Ira Gershwin); 'Funny Face' and 'The man I love' (George and Ira Gershwin); 'Sir Paul was frail' (from *Camelot*), 'It never entered my mind' and 'If my heart gets in your hair' (from *Pal Joey*), 'Each poor man has a wife' (from *On Your Toes*) and 'You have what I lack myself' (all Lorenz Hart); 'This Is My Lovely Day' (from *Bless the Bride*) (A. P. Herbert); 'Before The Parade Passes By' and 'Dolly'll never go away' (from *Hello, Dolly!*) (Jerry Herman); 'I have often walked down this street' and 'Tonight, old man, you did it' (from *My Fair Lady*), 'Don't let it be forgot' and 'Ask ev'ry person' (from *Camelot*), 'I've seen how lovely loving starts' (all Alan Jay Lerner); 'The moon is as light as a feather' (from *Robert and Elizabeth*) (Ronald Millar); 'Fools Rush In' (Johnny Mercer) and 'I Thought About You' (Johnny Mercer, with Jimmy Van Heusen), all lyrics by Cole Porter; 'Bewitched' (Rodgers and Hart); 'My fatherland, it is for thee' and 'Though I say not' (from *Merry Widow*) (Adrian Ross); 'You'll be swell' and (with Arthur Laurents) 'Some People sit on their butts' (from *Gypsy*), 'Loving you is not a choice' (from *Passion*), 'Streams are dying' (from *Pacific Overture*), 'We've no time to sit and dither' (from *Into the Woods*), 'We had a Good Thing Going', 'I saw My Fair Lady' and 'That's great. That's swell' (from *Merrily We Roll Along*), 'Attend the Tale of Sweeney Todd' (from *Sweeney Todd*) (all Stephen Sondheim); 'There are good stones' (from *Gypsy*) (Jule Styne); 'Just dig that scenery floatin' by' (from the film, *High Society*) (unattributed); 'Searchin' my Car' (from 'Fuck Tha Police') (Niggaz With Attitude).

London Management Ltd: 'When Martin was a nobody' (from *King – The Musical*) (Alistair Beaton), by permission of London Management.

Music Sales Ltd: 'The Way You Look Tonight' (Dorothy Fields); 'Niggers all work . . .', 'Come On And Pet Me', 'Who', 'Only Make Believe', 'The game o-of just supposi-ing', 'Don't look up an' don't look down', 'Why Do I Love You?' and 'When I'm calling you' (all Oscar Hammerstein); 'After The Ball is over' (Charles Harris); 'You're here And I'm Here', 'And when I told them' and 'All The Things You Are' (all Jerome Kern); 'Can you see', 'You're a lucky boy', 'His form and face' and 'Feel' (all Hal Prince); 'And I cert'nly am goin' to tell them' (Herbert Reynolds); 'If a pair of blue eyes . . .' and 'Thro' the forest wild and free' (Harry B. Smith); 'I feel charming', 'Could it be?', 'Tonight, Tonight', 'I like the city of San Juan' and 'Children you destroy together' (from *West Side Story*) (all Stephen Sondheim); 'I've always liked the sort of song', 'When it's Nesting Time In Flatbush', 'But I'm pining', 'They learn to eat spaghetti', 'Take me where you hear all those saxophones moaning', 'Why pick on some poor little thing', 'For all the punch that march of Mendelssohn's has', 'What bad luck! It's . . .', 'Let's Build A Little Bungalow In Quogue', 'Down at the gate', 'It's quite a humble train, you know', 'I wish that I had lived there', 'Crying never yet got anybody anywhere', 'He can't play golf or tennis or polo', 'A motor car he cannot steer' and 'It's a land of flowers' (all P. G. Wodehouse); 'Shall I make (pause) some coffee?' (unattributed).

Oliver Promotions Ltd: 'Got to do my best to please her' (from *Oliver*) (Lionel Bart), by permission of Oliver Promotions Ltd.

Peermusic (UK) Ltd: 'Oh Boy' (Norman West/Bill Tilghman/Sonny West) and 'That'll Be The Day' (Buddy Holly/Norman Petty/Jerry Allison) (from *Buddy*), © 1957 MPL Comms Inc, USA, Peermusic (UK) Ltd, 8–14 Verulam Street, London, used by permission.

The Really Useful Group Ltd: 'All I Ask Of You' (from *Phantom of the Opera*) (music: Andrew Lloyd Webber; lyrics: Charles Hart; additional lyrics: Richard Stilgoe), © 1986 The Really Useful Group Ltd, London. All Rights Reserved. International Copyright Secured; 'This Time Next Year' (from *Sunset Boulevard*) (music: Andrew Lloyd Webber; lyrics: Don Black and Christopher Hampton), © 1993 The Really Useful Group Ltd, London. All Rights Reserved. International Copyright Secured; 'As If We Never Said Goodbye' (from *Sunset Boulevard*) (music: Andrew Lloyd Webber; lyrics: Don Black and Christopher Hampton with contributions by Amy Powers), © 1993 The Really Useful Group Ltd., London. All Rights Reserved. International Copyright Secured; 'King Herod's Song' (from *Jesus Christ Superstar*) (music: Andrew Lloyd Webber; lyrics: Tim Rice), © 1968 and 1970 The Really Useful Group Ltd., London. All Rights Reserved. International Copyright Secured.

Paul Simon Music: 'Hearts and Bones' (Paul Simon).

Every effort has been made to obtain permission from all the copyright holders of material included in this edition, but in some cases this has not proved possible. The publishers therefore wish to thank all those copyright holders who are included without acknowledgement. Faber and Faber Ltd apologizes for any errors or omissions in the above list and would be grateful to be notified of any corrections that should be incorporated in the next edition.

Bibliography

Abbott, George: *Mister Abbott* (Random House, New York, 1963).

Abbott, George and Richard Bissell: *The Pajama Game* (Random House, New York, 1954).

Abbott, George and Betty Smith: *A Tree Grows in Brooklyn* (Harper, New York, 1951).

Barrett, Mary Ellin: *Irving Berlin: A Daughter's Memoir* (Simon and Schuster, New York, 1994).

Bentley, Eric: *The Playwright as Thinker* (Reynal and Hitchcock, New York, 1946).

Bolton, Guy and P. G. Wodehouse: *Bring on the Girls* (Simon and Schuster, New York, 1953).

Bordman, Gerald: *American Musical Theatre: A Chronicle* (Oxford University Press, New York, 1979).

Brahms, Caryl and Ned Sherrin: *Song by Song* (Ross Anderson, Bolton, 1984).

Burton, Humphrey: *Leonard Bernstein* (Faber and Faber, London, 1994).

Citron, Stephen: *The Musical from the Inside Out* (Hodder and Stoughton, London, 1991).

Donaldson, Frances: *P. G. Wodehouse* (Knopf, New York, 1982).

Fields, Herbert: *A Connecticut Yankee* (Tams-Witmark, New York, 1927).

Gershwin, Ira: *The Complete Lyrics* (Pavilion, London, 1994).

Gershwin, Ira: *Lyrics on Several Occasions* (Knopf, New York, 1959).

Gottfried, Martin: *Broadway Musicals* (Abrams, New York, 1979).

Gottfried, Martin: *More Broadway Musicals since 1980* (Abrams, New York, 1991).

Green, Stanley: *Encyclopaedia of the Musical* (Dodd, Mead, New York, 1976).

Hammerstein, Oscar, II: *Lyrics* (Simon and Schuster, New York, 1949).

Hammerstein, Oscar, II: *Oklahoma!* (Random House, New York, 1943).

Hart, Lorenz: *The Complete Lyrics* (Knopf, New York, 1986).

Idelsohn, A. Z.: *Thesaurus of Hebrew–Oriental Melodies* (Breitkopf, Berlin, 1914–1932).

Kissell, Howard: *The Abominable Showman* (Applause, New York, 1993).

Lerner, Alan Jay: *The Musical Theatre: A Celebration* (Collins, London, 1986).

Lerner, Alan Jay: *The Street Where I Live* (Hodder and Stoughton, London, 1978).

Mordden, Ethan: *Rodgers & Hammerstein* (Abrams, New York, 1992).

Morley, Sheridan: *Spread a Little Happiness* (Thames and Hudson, London, 1987).

Porter, Cole: *The Complete Lyrics* (Knopf, New York, 1983).

Rodgers, Richard: *Musical Stages* (Random House, New York, 1975).

Rosenberg, Deena: *Fascinating Rhythm* (Lime Tree, London, 1992).

Stein, Joseph: *Fiddler on the Roof* (Pocket Books, New York, 1965).

Walsh, Michael: *Andrew Lloyd Webber: His Life and Works* (Abrams, New York, 1989).

Wilder, Alec: *American Popular Song* (Oxford University Press, New York, 1972).

Wodehouse, P. G.: *Author! Author!* (Simon and Schuster, New York, 1954).

Wodehouse, P. G.: *Performing Flea* (Jenkins, London, 1953).

Wodehouse, P. G. and Guy Bolton: *Bring on the Girls!* (Simon and Schuster, New York, 1953).

Zadan, Craig: *Sondheim & Co* (Harper and Row, New York, 1986).

Index